**Lords of the Earth** The Entwined Destiny of Wildlife and Humanity

The Natives were Africa in flesh and blood. The tall extinct volcano of Longonot that rises above the Rift Valley, the broad Mimosa trees along the rivers, the Elephant and the Giraffe, were not more truly Africa than the Natives were—small figures in an immense scenery. All were different expressions of one idea, variations upon the same theme.

**Isak Dinesen, *Out of Africa* (1937)**

# Lords of the Earth

## The Entwined Destiny of Wildlife and Humanity

Cyril Christo, Marie Wilkinson, and Lysander Christo

## Foreword

I can never forget the first elephant I saw. It was when I went to Tanzania (then Tanganyika) for the first time in 1967. I don't remember all the details now, only that I was being driven by the Park warden around the rim of the crater. Suddenly the car stopped and there, just off the road and feeding quietly on the lush vegetation, was a small group of elephants, three or four females and some youngsters. I could not count exactly, as there were others further among the trees. We got out of the car and walked closer, and I stood in wonder and in awe. For some 20 minutes we watched them, and then the whole group, the largest matriarch bringing up the rear, slowly wandered into the thick forest.

I have met many other elephants since then. When I was camping with Hugo van Lawick, my first husband, on the floor of the crater some years later, we spent many hours watching the elephants that frequented the forested areas. And later, in the Ruaha National Park, I became even more closely connected to individual elephants, such as the one the rangers named Rafiki (meaning "friend" in Swahili) with her twin calves. And Rashidi, the oldest elephant I have ever seen. So ancient that his ears drooped, and the skin of his legs had sagged and was bunched around his ankles.

And then there was the time Iain Douglas Hamilton introduced me to his very favorite female, Virgo, in Lake Manyara National Park. As I followed him towards her, he told me to reach out, and she extended her trunk and blew gently on my fingers. What a magical moment.

Of course, most of my animal observations in Africa were of the chimpanzees of Gombe National Park, the species most like us in their biology and behavior. Chimpanzee brains are structured amazingly like our own, so it is hardly surprising that they are also highly intelligent. Like us, they have distinct personalities, minds capable of problem-solving, and emotions such as contentment and sadness, anger and despair. And, of course, they feel pain.

In fact, it was the in-depth understanding of chimpanzees that forced scientists to admit that there was no sharp line dividing us from them. That we were not, after all, the only thinking, feeling beings, unique and set apart from the rest. That the difference between us and other animals was of degree, not of kind, and that we were part of the amazing animal kingdom on Planet Earth.

Elephants are equally intelligent—and their memories are extraordinary. I can never forget the excitement, the joy of two individuals who had been cruelly parted for over 30 years, and who were reunited when the younger was brought to join the elder one at a sanctuary. It brought tears to the eyes of all who witnessed that moving reunion.

When I look back on my own times spent with elephants it is with a mixture of joy—and infinite sorrow. For the world I knew when I first arrived in Africa has changed. Forests have been razed and the human populations have increased, moving farther and farther into the shrinking habitats of wildlife. Trophy hunters pay money to shoot the bull elephants with the biggest tusks—the very individuals who should be responsible for the genetic strength of future elephant populations. So that they can proudly mount the heads on their walls. And now, with the ever-increasing price of ivory, there is terrible, devastating poaching.

True, more and more people are becoming involved with stopping the poaching on the ground in Africa. But increasingly, their lives are in danger. Rangers, trying bravely to protect the elephants in their parks, are too often shot in the course of duty. And those trying to implicate and deliver to justice those associated with the illegal trafficking, the illegal export of ivory to other countries, are sometimes involved in "unfortunate" lethal "accidents." The future of these iconic and wonderful animals is at stake, and those fighting to save them need all the help they can get.

That is why *Lords of the Earth* is so important. It is a truly magnificent collection of Cyril Christo's and Marie Wilkinson's haunting black-and-white photographs not only of African elephants, but of Africa's indigenous peoples too. Along with the text by Cyril and Marie, it is a profound study of these highly intelligent and social animals and the humans who have learned to live with them and revere them.

I hope this book will inspire others to join the fight on behalf of the elephants and the brave and dedicated people who are risking their lives to stop the killing and to bring the traffickers to justice.

**Jane Goodall**

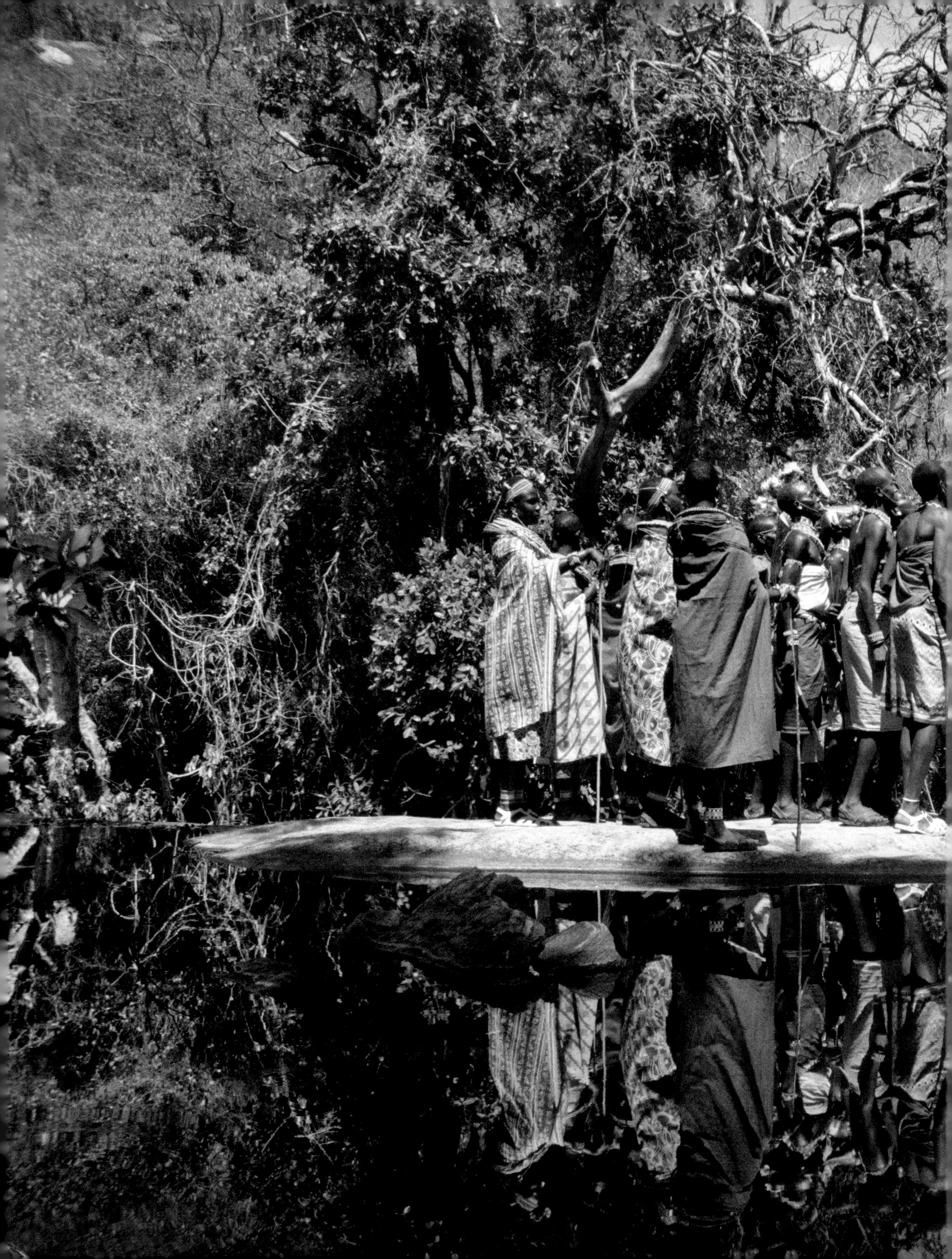

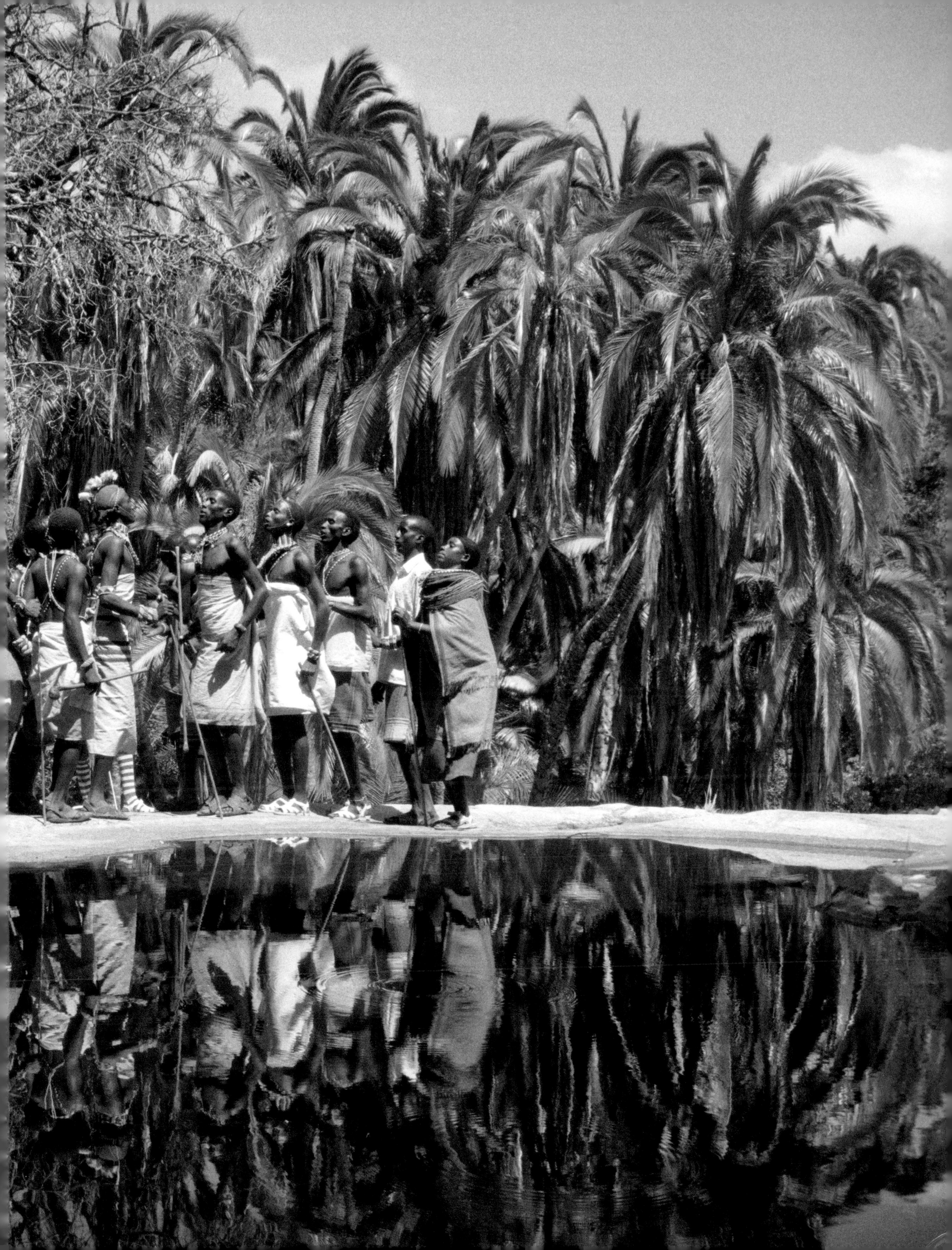

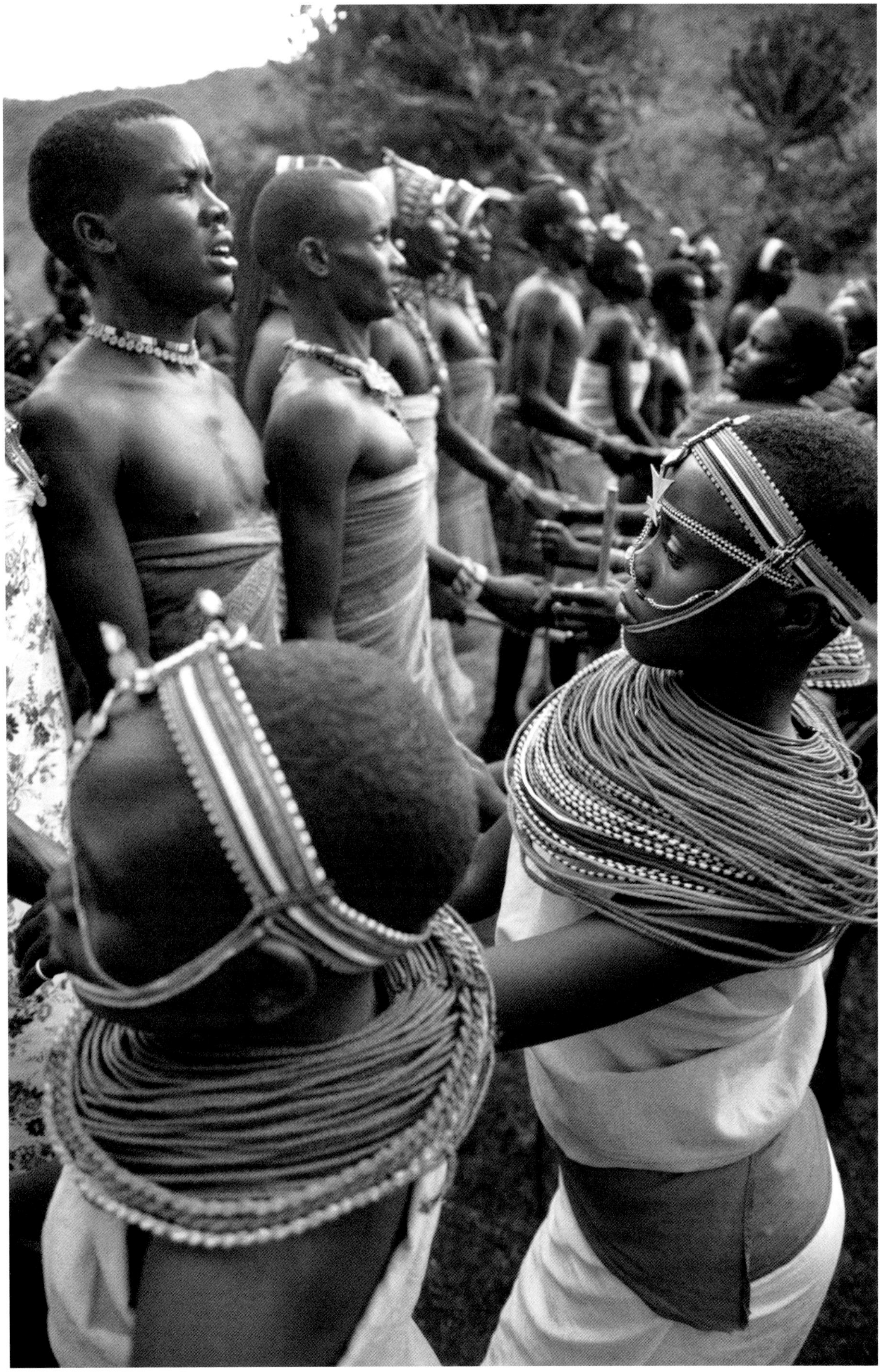

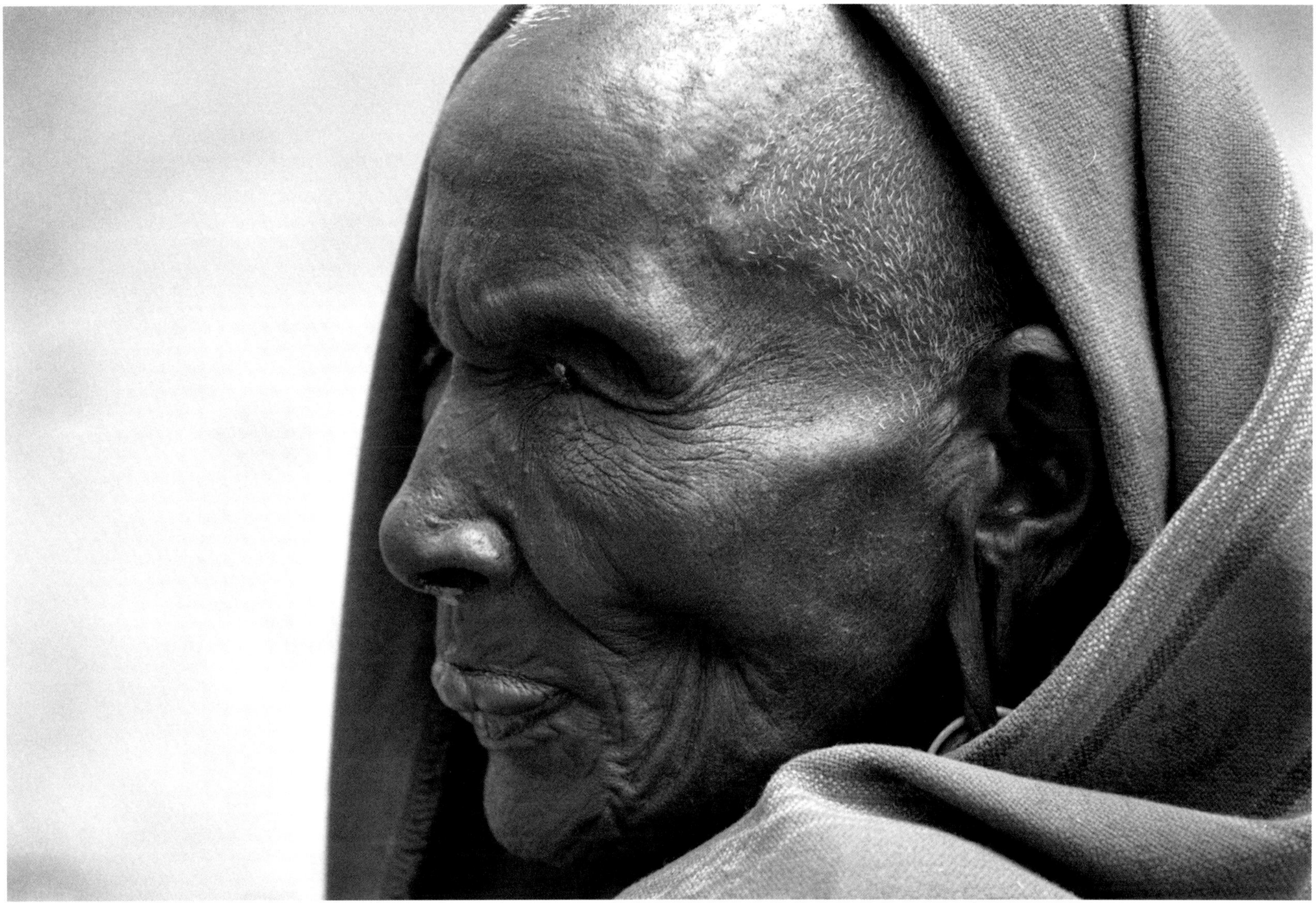

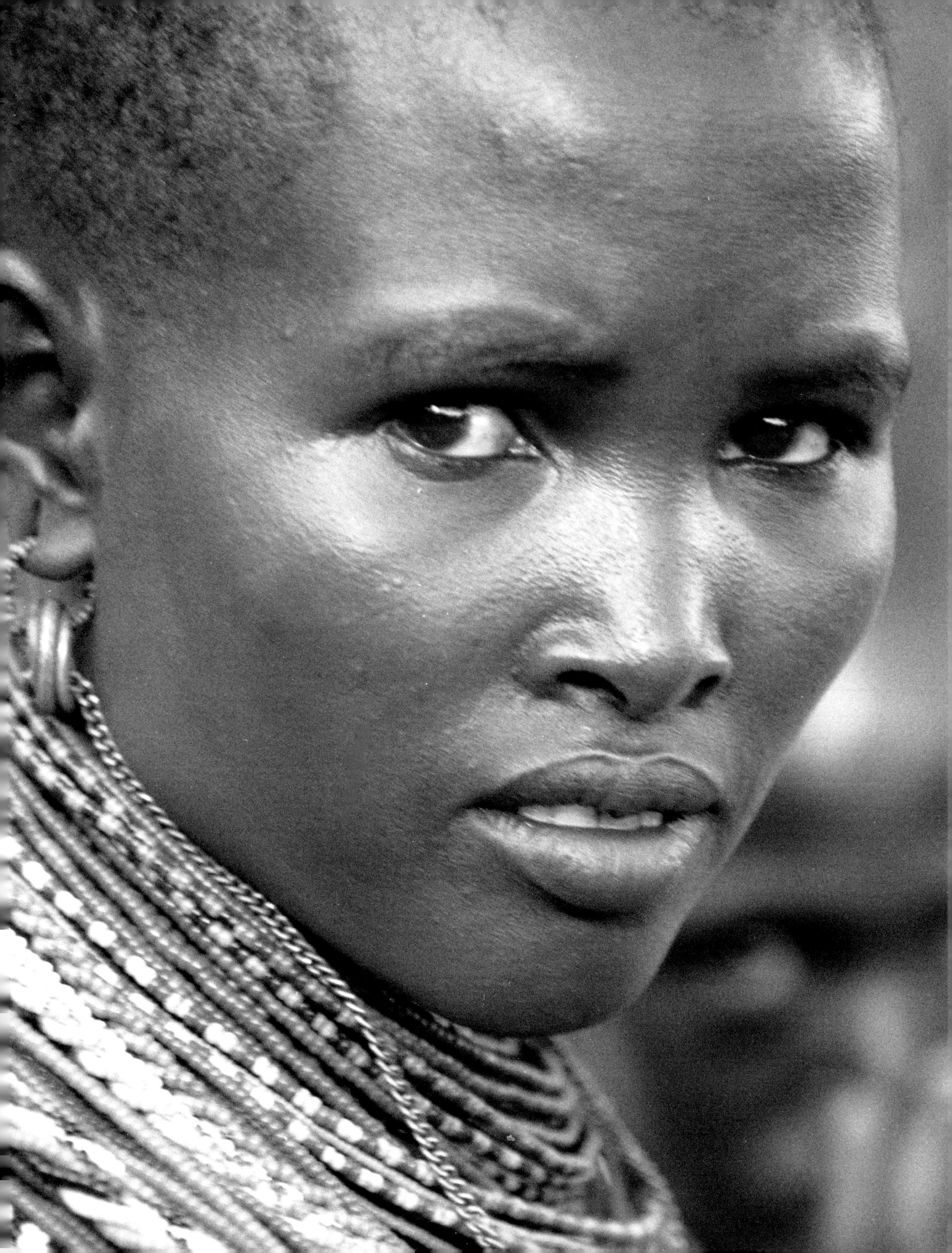

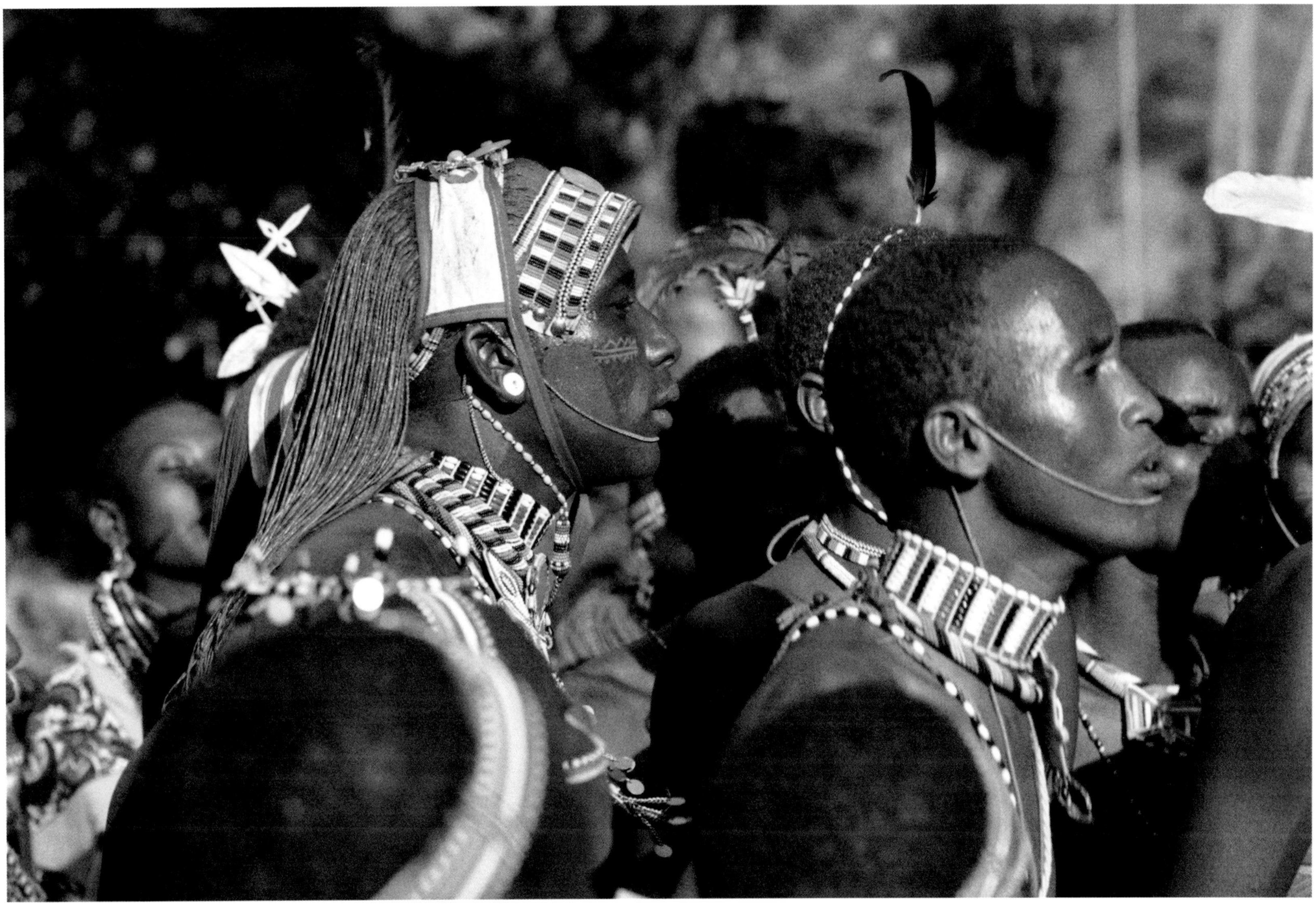

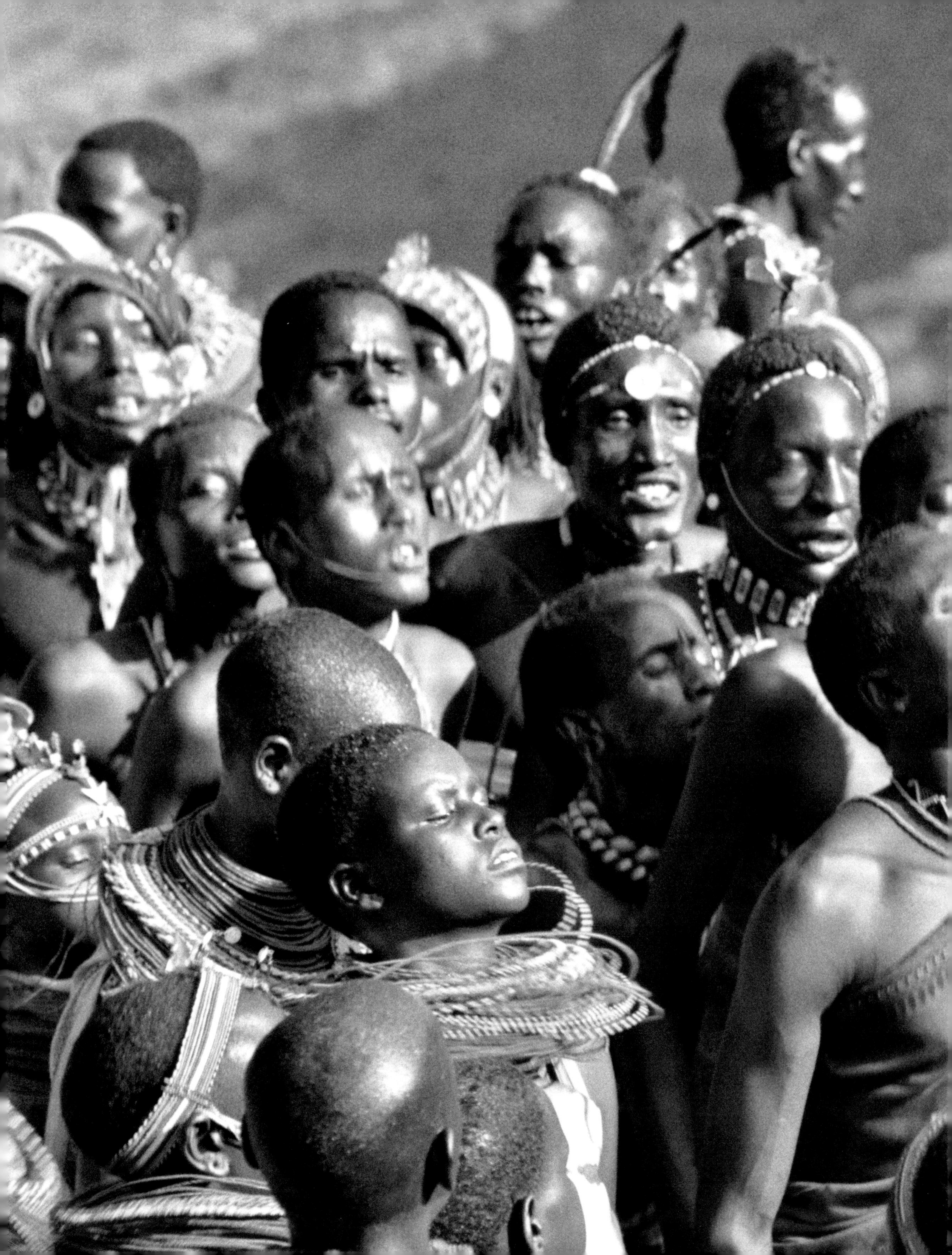

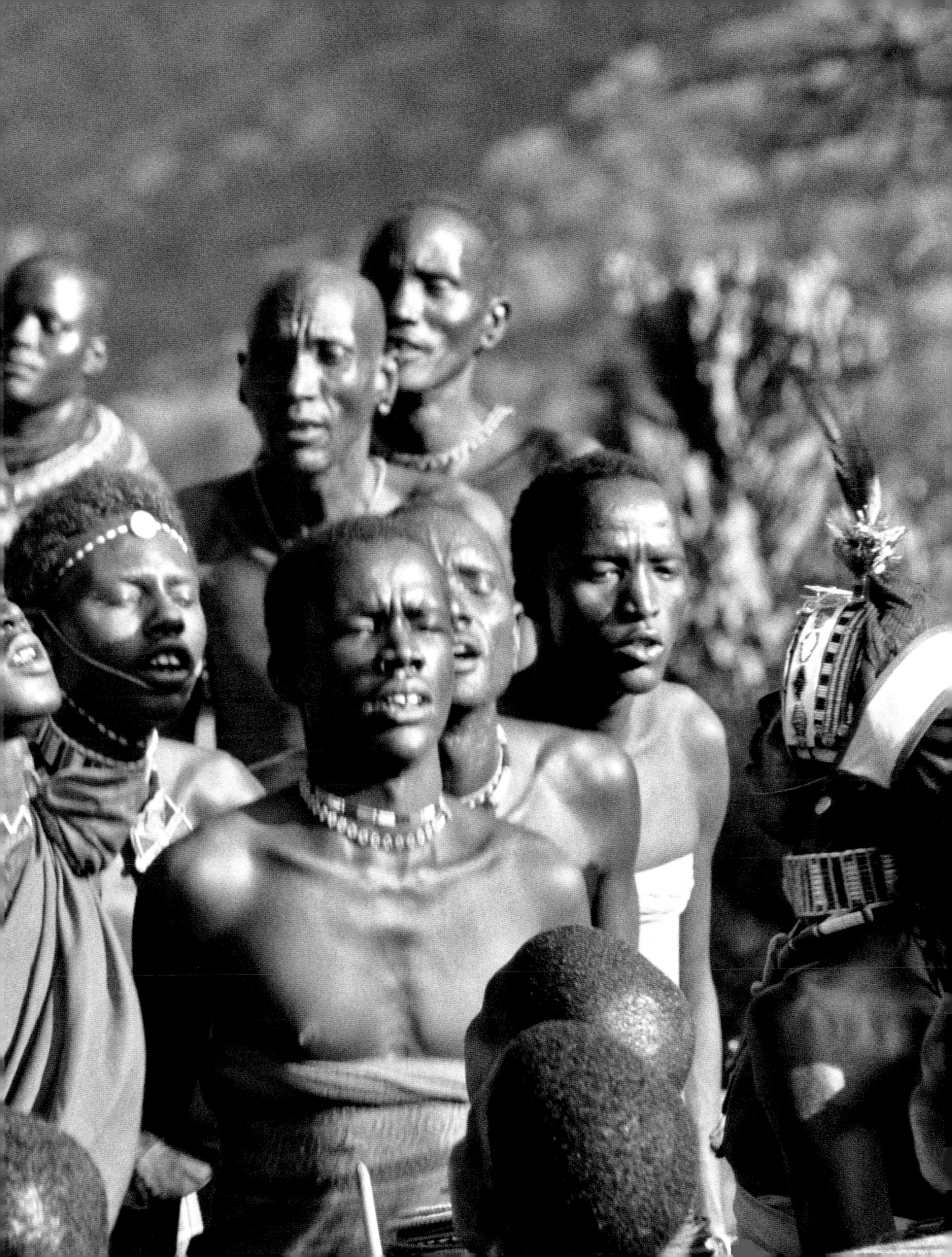

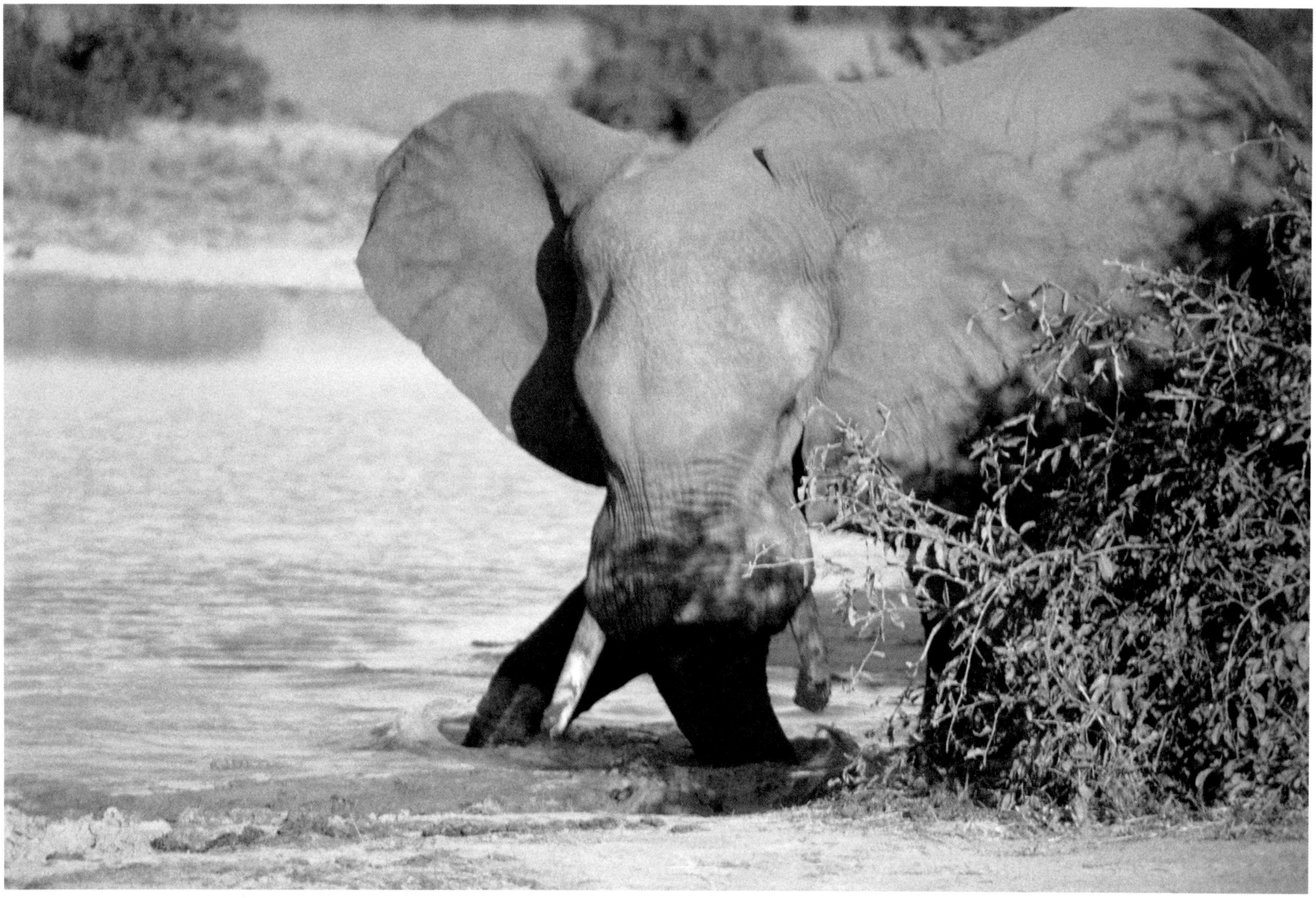

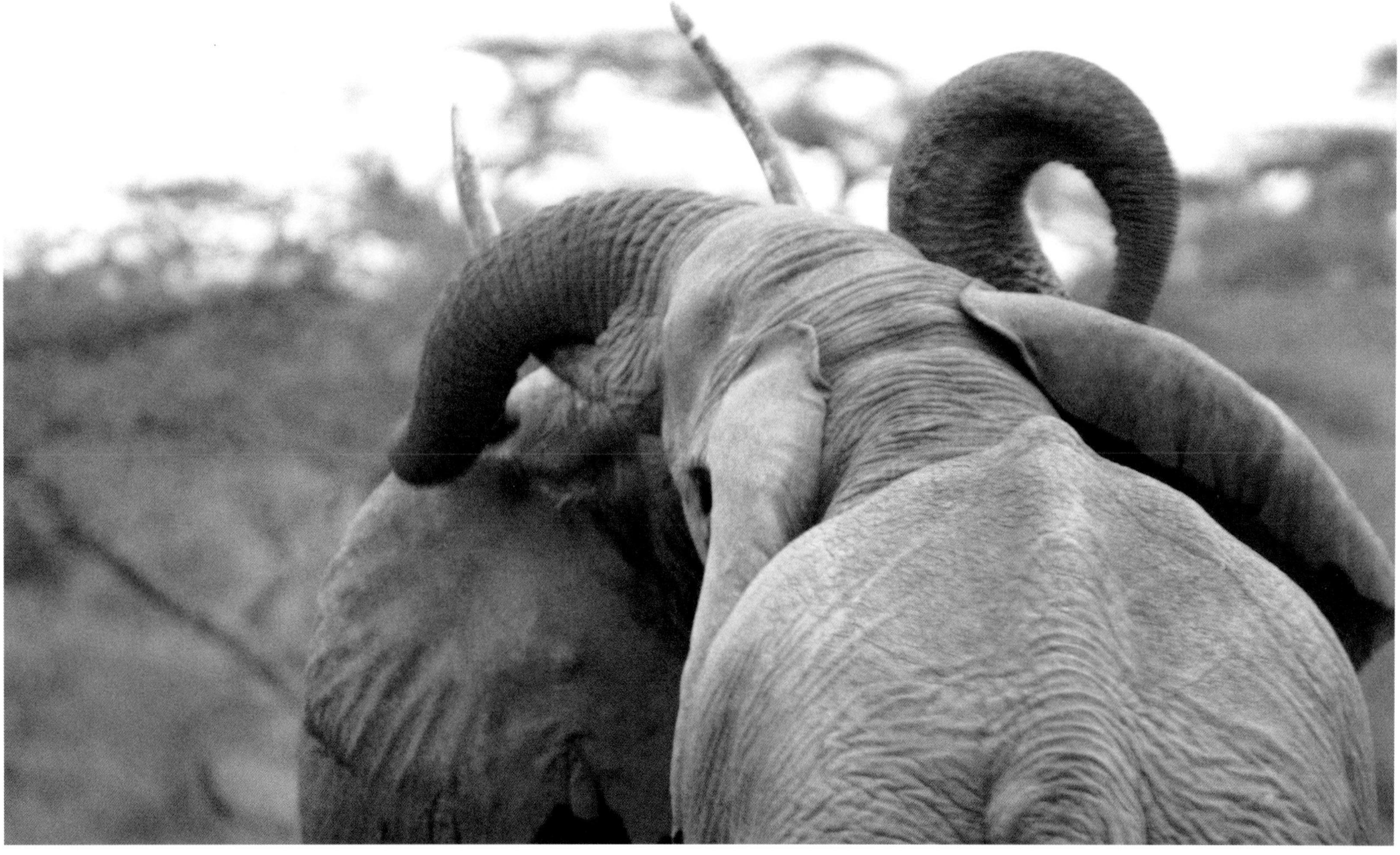

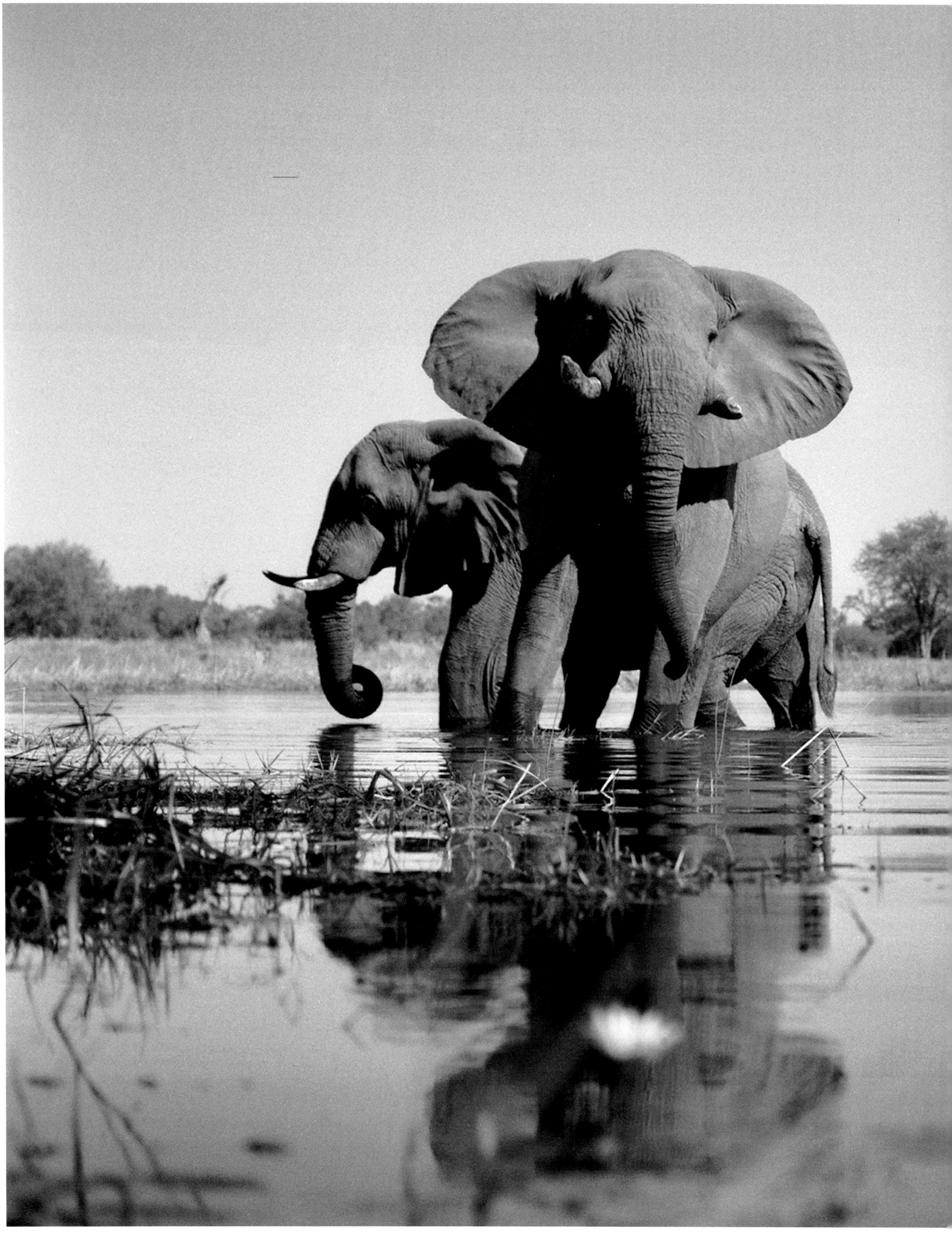

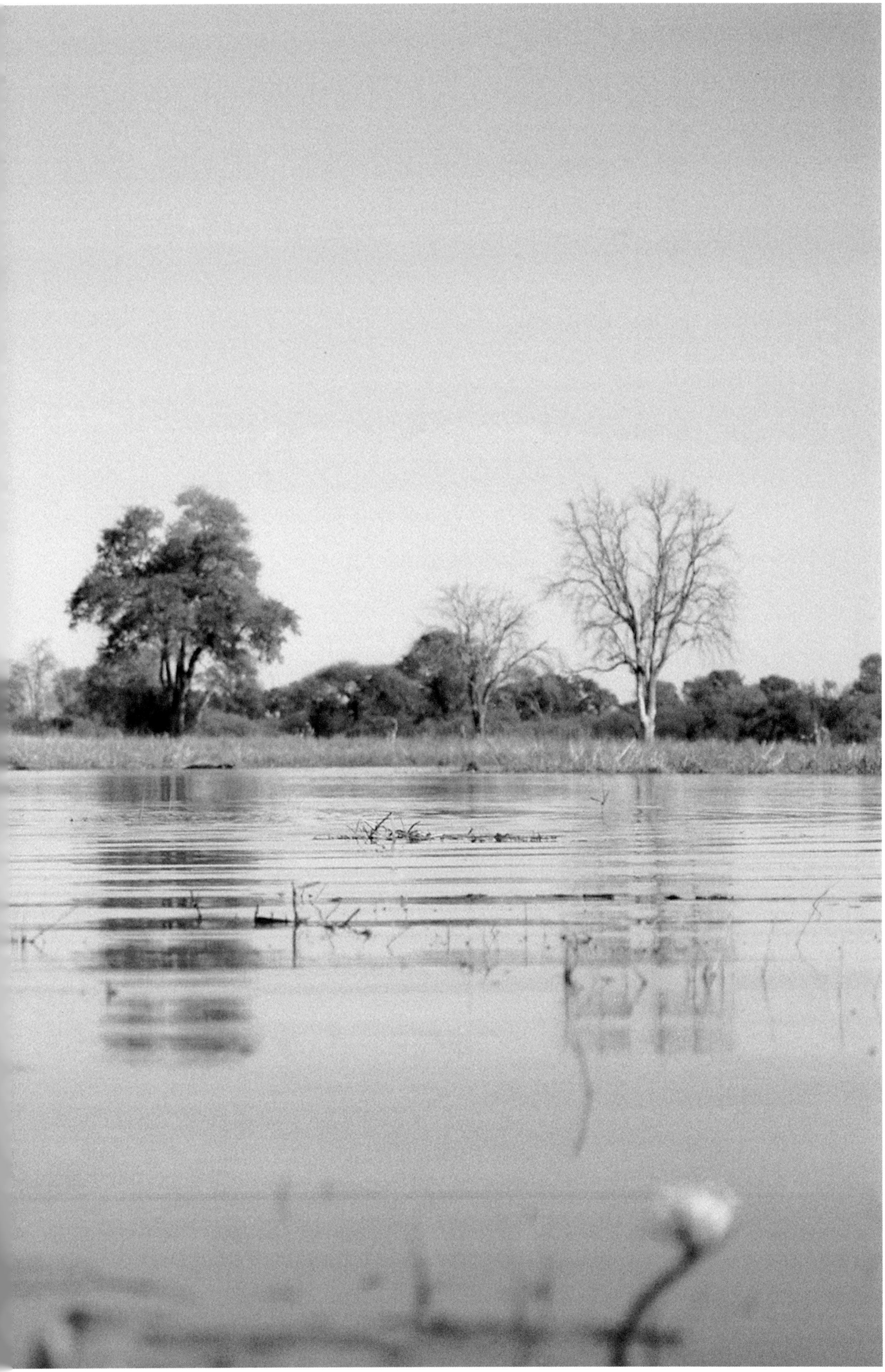

Western civilization raises monsters that neither human strength nor wit can overcome, whose depredations are a thousandfold more terrible than those of the river-horse on the banks of the White Nile.

**Sir Alfred E. Pease, *The Book of the Lion* (1913)**

# Lords of the Earth: The Entwined Destiny of Wildlife and Humanity

**Cyril Christo, Marie Wilkinson, and Lysander Christo**

In June of 2014, while Lysander, our eight-year-old, was watching elephants from the top of our car in the Samburu reserve in northern Kenya, a baby elephant, not more than a few months old, came to us and kissed the insignia of two elephants greeting, trunks wrapped around each other, on the side of our vehicle, acknowledging that the baby recognized who she was—an elephant. It was an ecstatic moment bonding us to this innocent being, but also a fabulous affirmation of our solidarity. Was the sight of our son the catalyst for this exquisite event? Was it the presence and relative safety of the Samburu Reserve and the Samburu people who still honor the elephant that allowed such an uncanny encounter? A baby elephant once left its mother to stroke the entire length of our car in Amboseli in 2006, when Lysander was only one year old. Seven years later, a baby elephant reaffirmed its place in the world and said hello to the human species and opened its heart to those of us who can only marvel at the power and wonder this species instills in all of humankind.

Kenya transfixed me, as it does so many, ever since I first set foot there at age 15 when I climbed Mount Kenya, struggling in pouring rain through the vertical bog of mud for nine straight hours. Kenya is derived from the Kikuyu word *Kerenyaga*, meaning mountain of splendor. To fall asleep at 13,000 feet and then the next day to be awed by the peaks of Batian and Lenana, named after Maasai medicine men, will remain the preeminent memory of youth, because to climb Mount Kenya was an immense rite of passage. Its shimmering snow, now threatened by climate change, was a challenge that formed the genesis of my fascination with Africa's life forms. The vines dangling from the rainforest canopy at the base of the mountain, the giant lobelias glistening in the early mountain dew like shrouds of ghosts of long-gone men, these are visions that haunt one for a lifetime. Later Marie and I would climb Kilimanjaro in June 2000, seduced by the same growths, bringing in the dawn of a new millennium. Kilimanjaro was first discovered for Europeans by the German Lutheran missionary Johannes Rebman, who thought the mountain was a cloud. He was so awestruck that he knelt and prayed to the glory of God. He saw the mountain on May 11, 1848, which was interesting for me because May 11 happens to be my birthday. He asked the locals what that substance was on the summit and they answered that whatever it was turned to water and that those who had climbed to the top had frozen their limbs in the effort. The substance could only be snow. It seems like an apparition, almost a ghost: the magnitude of that venture and its sentinel presence, like a messenger overlooking the place where man was born, transfixes one's place on Earth forever. Between the snow and its famed glacier vanishing owing to the vagaries of an overbearing civilization, bringing once eternal waters to its elephant herds below, and the tribes and fauna at its base, Kilimanjaro is fast changing like the rest of an inimitable and increasingly fragile continent—the heart of the world.

One of the most transfixing texts I have ever read on Africa was written by Henno Martin, a German native who, during World War II, survived in the wilds of Namibia for two years to avoid imprisonment. His book *The Sheltering Desert* published in 1983 questioned the priorities of advanced civilization. He saw firsthand what it meant to live in the wild, watching leopards and hyenas hunting and scavenging in the deserted wilderness: "The conditions of civilized life were dangerously unbalanced; they demanded primarily an antlike cooperation, yet in man there was a subconscious urge to live the life of a beast of prey. It seemed quite likely to us that one day our whole civilization would be destroyed by this contradiction.... We had slid so readily into the life of primitive hunters that we came to the conclusions that underneath the veneer modern man still had a 'Stone-age soul', which was difficult to reconcile with the civilized life he was leading. Could that contradiction be resolved? In view of man's steadily increasing powers of destruction it was a vital question."

In northern Namibia, the isolated and seminomadic pastoralist "red ochre" Himba people live surrounded by the chromatic rapture of the Namib desert, whose bewitching boulders and sands are the world's oldest, dating back 55 millions years. Ungulates like oryx and giraffes can go without water for weeks, although it seems a little bit of a miracle that they can survive at all. Despite the fact that the desert's name means "place of no people," the Himba are able to survive in what seems a combination of paradise and inferno. Traveling through the dry riverbeds of this region, where lions, rhinos, and elephants still roam, means moving through a landscape of utter magic. Largely avoiding the modern world, the Himba keep their goats, sheep, and cattle in enclosures called *kraal*, in line with their herding ethos. One fellow called Rutjani said "it does not seem strange to me that I should protect animals. I have learned to do so from my parents. If they go we will suffer a great loneliness of the spirit."

Traveling in the near-lunar landscape of Kaokoland twenty years ago, we were charged at full speed by a mother elephant accompanied by another member of her family and a calf. We had turned a corner and taken her by surprise. The other adult fled parallel to our car, escorting the calf away, while the mother bore down on us, maybe at 40 kilometers an hour, ears flailing like two mad sails. We didn't have time to turn around and backed up as fast as we could, hoping we wouldn't get stuck in the sands. After a few hundred yards she slowed down and eventually stopped before returning to her family. It was the closest call we had ever had.

In this unforgiving, sidereal world of almost Martian beauty we watched women leading their cattle to the Kunene River on the Angolan border. It was here, on ground as sacred as memory itself, that we learned about a megadam the World Bank was slated to build, 535 feet tall, at a cost of $500 million. The Himba, who regularly pray to their holy fire, would see their way of life radically upturned by this Moloch of the modern world. For a people who depend on the humblest of seeds, seeds collected by ants underground during the rains and brought to dry above ground, this invention of technological society would assuredly doom one of the most timeless civilizations on Earth.

As one elder exclaimed, "the Kunene is a living organism and needs to be protected. All will die under the water, the Baynes dam will affect us. It's our grazing area, farming is our livelihood. Different species, wildlife, most graves will be under water." Another elder expressed his great concern, a concern sounded all over Africa by traditional tribes whose world is being eroded by the extraction and subjugation of machine-made society. "We want to

Man is an actor. He acts all manner of men, and each one is a lie. Only the animal in him is real.

**William Saroyan**

remain in our culture like our forefathers. We feel the dam is our death. We want to live under the trees. We don't want their promises. Hospitals, schools are promised if we agree to the project, but the existing clinic has no medicine. The land is our bank. We don't go to ATMs. The money is in our land and the forest and livestock. We don't want our bank under water. The holy mountains and all must be treated with respect."

On our last day with the Himba, a blazing meteor descended into the lower atmosphere like the body of a supervening being presiding over their homeland. Was it an omen that a world unlike any other would be ravaged by modernity or a warning that this place, its remarkable antediluvian sands, was sacred and would not be destroyed by the whims of the outside world?

The tribes in the Omo Valley in Ethiopia are the most mystifying in Africa and are trying to hold on to a land many did not even know was called Ethiopia only a generation ago. When we visited the Mursi, Marie had to stay in the jeep because the gun-toting men, who have harbored guns since the Italians were driven out of Ethiopia in 1941, had seldom seen outsiders. Often they would use guns to attack officials of the state, and the situation we found ourselves in was a fragile one, one not likely to be duplicated in the future. One can only imagine what Richard Burton, the British explorer, must have felt when he arrived in Somaliland in 1854 and promptly received a spear in his upper cheek from one of the local warriors. And while it wasn't quite as turbulent with the Mursi or the Surma, one can only hope that they will be able to hold onto a semblance of their identity and withstand the onslaught of the modern state, which is trying to move them to make way for the Gibe III hydropower dam, whose waters will enable sugar plantations in the area. Sinohydro from China, with its $46 million dollar contract, installed and manufactured hydraulic gates, hoisting equipment and other steel structures that have upturned this part of the world. Globalization is in full swing even in what was once the most remote region of Africa.

When we arrived at the village of Tungit, a Surma village, the people there, who are renowned as hunters, were already in the process of being missionized, although the women have kept their famous lip plates and scars. The day after we arrived it poured rain, but it was supposedly only the small rains. We witnessed the practice of bloodletting, which a young boy performed after piercing the neck of cow held by a naked elder. They drank the blood in a ritual which has endured for centuries. Prospectors with wooden pans looked for small nuggets of gold in the nearby river. But everywhere there were signs of Ethiopian soldiers, the tribal way of life slowly giving way in the face of a totalitarian regime. Before we departed, hyenas called and yelped to remind us of the primal Africa that still beckoned from the darkest night on Earth. It is the kind of town the French poet Arthur Rimbaud would have appreciated in the late nineteenth century as he engaged in gunrunning to escape the confines of his civilization. When we left Tungit, swarms of bees and the song they carried in their memory crossed our path like immemorial sentinels that still guard the outback of this primordial land.

In Finnish mythology there is a minor god called Surma, and its name means death. It can only be hoped that the ethos of a tribe unlike any other will not entirely disappear to make way for the sins of the machine-clad world. Perhaps the Surma tribe's sky god, Tuma, will still be honored in the future. In this unique corner of Africa, the tribes were always able to repel the Muslims and the Christians, a feat achieved by only a few of them.

The military has also been accused of displacing and intimidating the tribes. It is a significant development in the name of progress, which homogenizes and sacrifices the irreplaceable, whether it be human or nonhuman life. Around 200,000 people could be affected in the Omo Valley, and another several hundred thousand across the border on Lake Turkana in Kenya. It is no exaggeration today to say that human rights are being trampled along the entire length of a valley that once appeared to us as the most pristine and unadulterated in all of Africa. A quarter of a million hectares of this World Heritage Site will drown under the weight of corporate and foreign profits.

A few months before Lysander was born, a woman in the US came up to me by the sea near New York and asked me if I had heard of the incredible story of a 12-year-old girl near the provincial capital of Bita Genet, 350 kilometers southwest of Addis Ababa, who was kidnapped and was going to be forced into marriage before being saved by three lionesses. It seems that the vast majority of marriages in Ethiopia are the result of abductions by men who take children from homeless women or drug users and sell them. The black market for children is a serious issue worldwide. This particular girl was walking home from school when she was approached by seven men. She went missing for a week. As one of the 15 million child brides in Ethiopia, her situation was not unique. If she had not been found she would have lived a life of beatings, rape, and unwanted pregnancies. The local police followed leads on the kidnappers and rushed to the men's last known whereabouts in the forest. When they finally reached the jungle, they found three lionesses guarding the girl. She was found by Sergeant Wondimu Wedajo, who testified that they "stood guard until we found her and then they just left her like a gift and went back into the forest. Everyone thinks this is some kind of miracle because normally the lions would attack people."

Tilahun Kassa, a local government official, verified Wondimu's story that her captors wanted to marry the girl against her wishes. The policeman said that the lions noticed that the girl was being beaten and came to her rescue by chasing the men off.

Wondimu said some believed that her moans and whimpers were mistaken "for the mewing of a lion cub, which could explain" why the lions "didn't eat her." The youngest of four, the young girl was "shocked and terrified" by the incident and was treated for her wounds. After being taken to the hospital, she was eventually reunited with her parents and siblings and saved from what would certainly have been a life of misery.

Some may say that it was a miracle, but I believe it is time to learn from the animals. That even predators can show compassion should be evidence enough that humanity, too, needs to change direction with regards to what remains of the natural world. Lions who are being persecuted by the hundreds every year are on their last legs. They are not just remarkable killers—or so we have been led to believe. Elephants, too, are capable of astonishing acts of altruism, as we have heard from indigenous people over the last generation. These are beings that have influenced us over the course of our evolution as few others have done. On their shoulders and those of other species lies a large measure of the future of an entire continent.

In Africa, like nowhere else except perhaps parts of the Amazon and Indonesia, the clash between the modern world and the original ways of our ancestors is coming to a head. But it is in Africa, too, that some of the megafauna on whom early man depended still roam the great outback of the vast continent. In the next few decades, the destiny of the last vestiges of an incredible heritage in the body of human and nonhuman evolution will be played out. What remains of Africa will truly dictate where our species is headed. If the great expanse of Africa's outback is homogenized like the rest of world, we will have lost the last refuge of its kind. This book is meant as a prayer to what is left of the most authentic kind of life, both human and nonhuman, in the place where humanity was born.

In 2010, after visiting the white lions of Timbavati, the most sacred animal in Africa, we had the rare privilege of seeing a white lioness eating a kudu at night in the wild. White lions are sacred to the Shangaan people. We then drove to Gemsbok National Park, where we chanced upon a rabbi from the Middle East, who told us he could no longer bear the conflicts of his homeland. He wanted to grow dates in Namibia because the conflict, war, and oppression of his native country were not things he wanted for his family. He needed another setting in which to find a proper home, and he found it in the vast, variegated beauty of the oldest desert on Earth, in Namibia. He spoke of the Talmud and explained that the word *pil*, meaning elephant in Hebrew, was the root of the verb *pela*, to wonder. The root of the religious and the sacred. If elephants and the other great beings with which we evolved were to be lost, then we would lose our humanity forever because we would lose our ability to honor something greater than ourselves. In honoring a being so inimitable in the great history of evolution, we learned to feel humility, something sorely lacking in our relationship to nature. That is why mankind has to act now in deference to the other species of this world. It is why this decade is so vital.

In his book *A Guide for the Perplexed*, Werner Herzog wrote of the ruins of Germany after World War II and takes us on a grand tour of his visionary films. At one point, after being mystified by the great animals in the caves of Lascaux, particularly its exquisite lionesses unmatched in the history of human expression, Herzog writes that "I do not want to live on a planet where there are no lions anymore." Continuing in this vein, his book reveals itself as a small manifesto for the continuity of life, both human and nonhuman. The unique stories we have heard of animals saving humans in the wild are emblematic of the bond we share with those beings who have evolved alongside us for countless millennia, beings we cannot afford to lose.

In 2000 we had the privilege of visiting the oldest peoples in all of East Africa, the Hadza, who lived much as their ancestors had lived 10,000 years ago, just east of Lake Eyasi in the Yaeda Valley, in northern Tanzania. Like the Bushmen of the Kalahari, their way of life had not changed much until the 1970s. Just 50 kilometers south of the famed Olduvai Gorge, where Louis Leakey made some of the key discoveries of early man, the land feels like an antediluvian garden. Tales abound about how, over the centuries, the Hadza had fights with their pastoralist neighbors, most notably the Iraqw, Isanzu, and even Maasai. Other neighbors were the Sukuma, who would trade metal hoes so that the Hadza could use the metal arrows to hunt elephant, but today that is no longer practiced.

While the Hadza hunted elephant like the Wakamba and Waliangulu of southern Kenya, it has been many years since they have done so, and the little game they depend on is getting scarcer by the year. The Sukuma, who are agriculturalists, are gaining on them as trees are yearly being cut. Another tribe, the Mang'ati, are destroying the surrounding water holes and also reducing the forest. Shy and wanting to keep to themselves, the Hadza still honor their ancestors, and one cave full of spirit walkers, or *wajini*, in the shape of stars was shown to us, with an altar to supervening forces that preside over the ways of those still living in freedom and in consonance with the elements, the trees, the birds, and the heavens. The dances the Hadza enacted honored the spirit world as a consciousness that lifted the eyes from the everyday world towards the invisible realm.

Here in Africa the horizon is teeming with a vastness unmatched on Earth. Although relations between men have changed, some of her people still know that, in contradistinction to the ancestors of old, a great demon, or *shetani mkubwa*, has overtaken the land. Just as *tamaa*, man's greed, had destroyed the elephant, now it had taken root in men's hearts everywhere. If the ancestors who watched over men did not welcome you to the land, you would be killed. It was a lesson that was eternally felt in so much of the bush, as Isak Dinesen made clear in her masterpiece *Out of Africa*: "God and the devil are one."

Our guide Patrick Texier, a Frenchman, had walked the entire length of the Amazon decades earlier. He honored the still raw, unrelenting beauty of the bush and the spirit of these ancient peoples. About 1,000 Hadza still lived near the salt lake, about several hundred to the west of the lake, the rest residing on the east side. Collecting honey, digging tubers, picking berries, and hunting game has been their mainstay for countless generations. In 1999, it was among the Hadza, the oldest hunter-gatherer people in all of East Africa, that we saw some of the oldest hunters left on the continent, along with the Bushmen. Increasingly corralled into smaller territory, the Hadza were being surrounded by farmers everywhere and forced to inhabit a small fringe of land to the east of the lake. There was nowhere for the Hadza to turn to. Like the Bushmen, they have been insulted and ridiculed by their neighbors, and even arrested by rangers for carrying their only means of survival, their bows and arrows. Once we followed a gallant young hunter named Kaonda, whom we accompanied on foot as he tried to find possible prey in the form of either boars or antelopes or whatever the spirits could provide. They occasionally hunted elephant, but never used the tusks. Like the Waliangulu up north in Kenya, they didn't understand those who killed or needlessly slaughtered the elephant for the most useless of objects, the teeth of the great being.

They showed us the cave of their ancestors' spirits, the *wazee wa zamani*, the people of long ago, who protected the living from evil. We were awed by the lifestyle of those living on the edge of a fast-fading universe, a world of sincere and simple needs, a community that honored the world and the trees, and of a people distrustful of those from the outside, encroaching on an increasingly fragile Eden. The Hadza were being overtaken by a fast-moving, incomprehensible world, where spirits did not flicker by the night fire under the sheen of the moon, but were extinguished by the impulse of a mercurial madness made of metal that had changed modern man's ethos and that was closing in on the Hadza people, who, many millennia ago, had emerged on the vast plains of East Africa.

When we first arrived, several of the men were making arrows, as they had done for countless generations, molding the wood over the fire with their teeth, bending the body of the arrow until it was straight and wrapping quail feathers at the tips for balance. Kaonda, one of the younger hunters, took us on a walk in the acacia forest one afternoon. All was still, like a stark primeval painting full of potential, when in the blink of an eye he saw a giraffe whose head just appeared over the tree tops. With bow and arrow in hand, he tore off into the bush and followed his prey. He was a hunter of consummate persistence and vision, whose place in the world was becoming more tenuous with each passing year. Something ineffable disappeared into the void of the bush that moment, like a signature memory from the beginnings of the first hunters' steps eons ago, chasing a dream as evanescent and necessary as origin itself.

One of the most bewildering moments with a tribe came just before 9/11, when the world's horizon still seemed a little more stable. We flew over the fantastic sweep of northern Kenya's landscape, scanning the Chalbi Desert for signs of the wandering Rendille. There seemed to be nothing in the enormous stretch of earth below us, just heat and sand as far as the eye could see, over the boundary with southern Ethiopia. And then, like a fabulous mirage, there they were, hundreds of camels spread out like a vast tapestry amidst fragile veins of waters undulating like a gargantuan liquid fan in all directions. When we landed among them, we felt we were approaching another planet. Dry, forbidding, and sublime in its vastness. Young Rendille men came to touch our plane as if to verify it was really part of this world. Their smiles in the midst of this blisteringly hot environment was a testimony to a tribe that lived in perfect adaptation with its camels on a seemingly infinite plain. The young men were going out on the land far from their homes, looking for water and surviving on nothing but camel's milk, superior in every way to cow's milk and lower in saturated fats and higher in iron and vitamin C. On one occasion, awed by the group in front of us, we wanted to take a picture of some of the young men with their camels in the background. One of the Rendille men, wearing nothing more than a simple loincloth, took his herding stick and waved it in front of the camera to keep me from taking a photo. There was no harm done, but it was a warning to me. Our guide told us later that the young man was concerned that our camera would turn the camel's milk to water! The trust, the fortitude, the love for their herds, the initiation the young men had undergone for weeks away from home to become men was a wonder to behold.

The people of Kenya everywhere shared with us their concerns about climate change in the early part of this century, and slowly we came to learn of the Samburu people's extraordinary relationship with the elephant, a bond that seems to transcend biology to a level of sympathetic resonance and mind that is remarkable, and almost inexplicable. One story, legendary among the Samburu, tells the story of Lesematia, a Samburu man who was inducted into the British army in the Ethiopian campaign of 1941 against the Italians. At some point he lost a leg fighting the enemy and would have to use crutches for the rest of his life. Twenty years later in north central Kenya, late one afternoon, Lesematia was walking on his way to his uncle's house on his crutches. Suddenly, two lions appeared, maybe two brothers, one from either side of him, closing in on him, because he was crippled and slow-moving. Often older male lions help each other in their later years, pairing up, especially since they no longer have the help of the lionesses to hunt. There was nothing Lesematia could do. Helpless, and knowing he was going to die, he called on his great totem, the elephant. He prayed for help from *Ol tome*, the classic term for the elephant in Samburu, and within a few minutes three bull elephants came out of the bush and surrounded Lesematia. The lions did not stand a chance against even one elephant, let alone three! The elephants spent the entire night watching over and protecting Lesematia from a lion attack. The next morning the lions gave up on Lesematia, on their desired prey, and retreated into the bush. Lesematia took up his crutches and slowly made it to his uncle's house!

To this day the Samburu say that those who kill elephants for ivory or sport are cursed eternally, invoking the wrath of God. *Shiftas*, or outlaws looking for ivory, had long denuded Mount Ngiro, their sacred peak, of elephants. The elders we met all longed for the old days when elephants were plentiful. Despite the beauty of the hills, we felt the enormous absence of the herds who used to roam there. The near-omnipresent stream of water dribbled down the hills like a magic presence from the sky. In the beauty of the dry undulating landscape, one could only wonder how much more magnificent the hills would have been with elephants roaming freely in this Edenic landscape. Years ago, during the heyday of the colonial invasion of Africa, Joseph Conrad wrote in his masterpiece *The Heart of Darkness* (1899): "The word 'ivory' rang in the air, was whispered, was sighed. A taint of imbecile rapacity blew through it all, like a whiff from some corpse.... And outside, the silent wilderness surrounding this cleared speck on the earth struck me as something great and invincible, like evil or truth, waiting patiently for the passing away of this fantastic invasion."

As we learned in March 2011, at Mount Ngiro, the Latimi and subclans Talas and Kuro have the supernatural ability to control and command elephants. Their psychic connection is of an order which is becoming increasingly rare in our mechanistic world, a capacity which was far more common in the olden days when electricity and the confabulations of the mechanical realm did not rule over every facet of our lives.

These moments of bewilderment and fragility highlight some of the wonder and extremes that the wilderness offers to those who are open to the heart of Africa. There is in the core of the African continent—humanity's original home—a universe of freedom that can be experienced like nowhere else in the wild. That wild has inspired the human imagination and especially the childhood mind to take in the full spectrum of the larger world. We learn to read and write with the legion of Africa's animals and landscapes as a backdrop to our imagination, beings we honor in our memory because it is the place where humanity first emerged. Africa's peoples have a critical role to play because her tribes and languages are consonant with the emergence of language, myth, and human evolution itself.

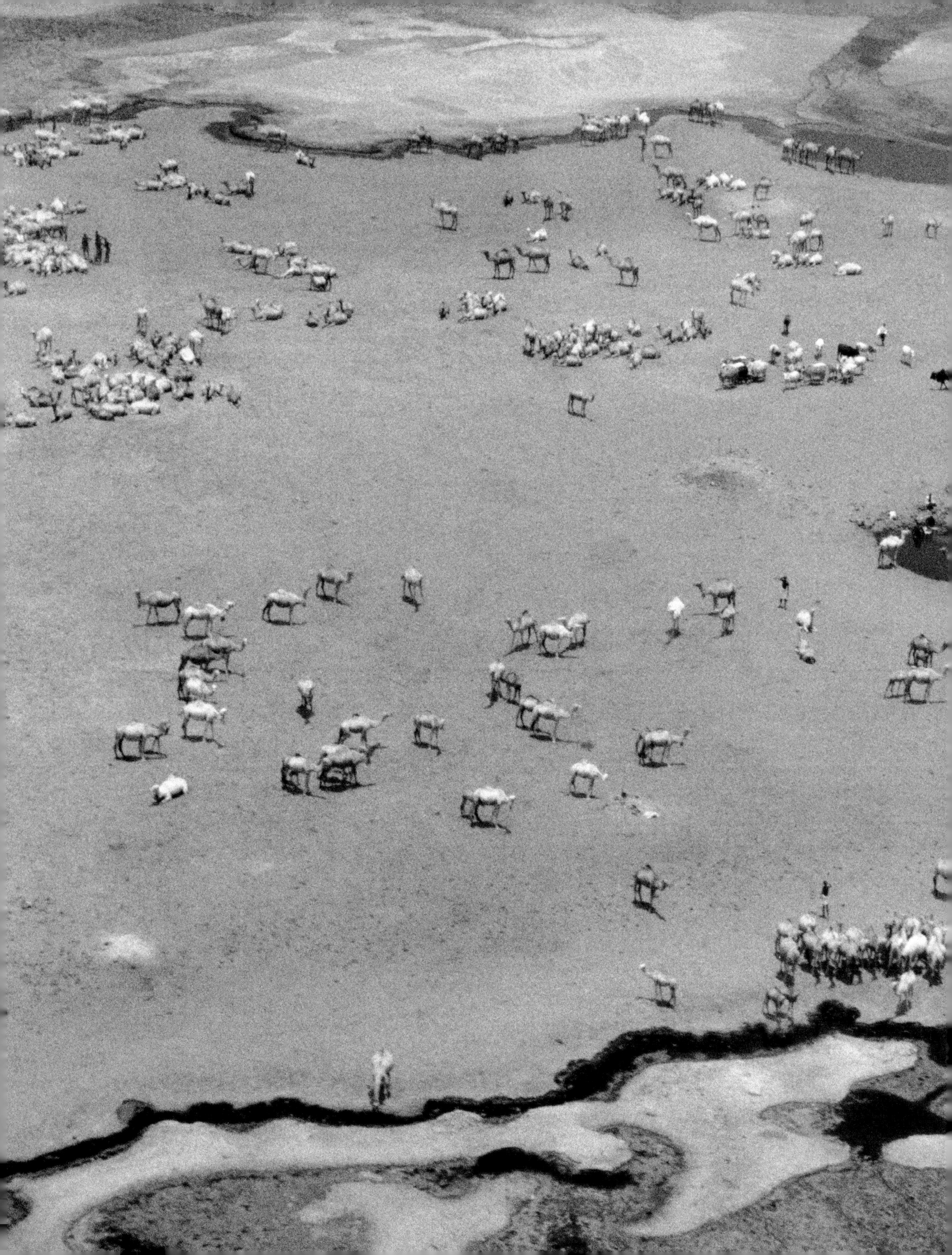

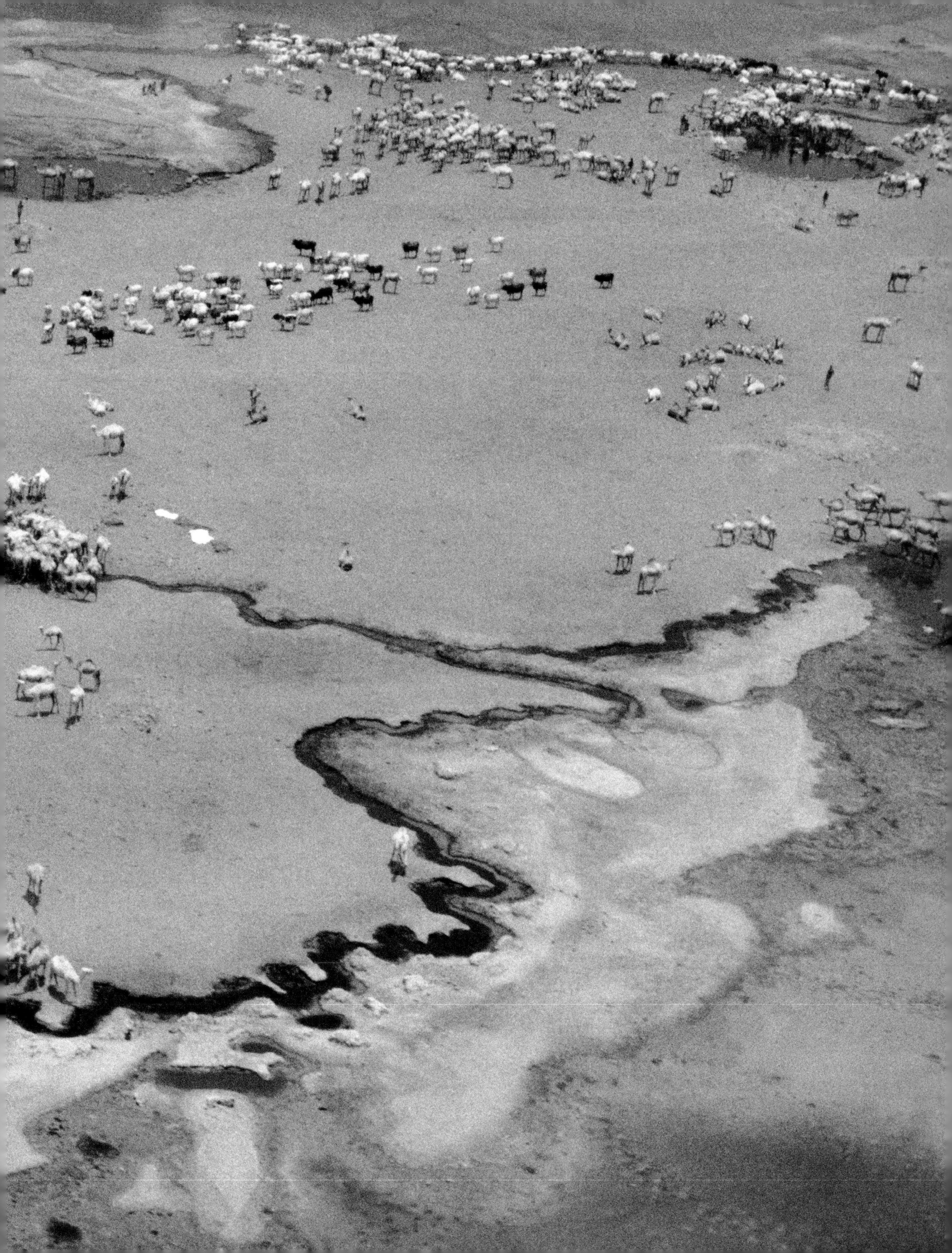

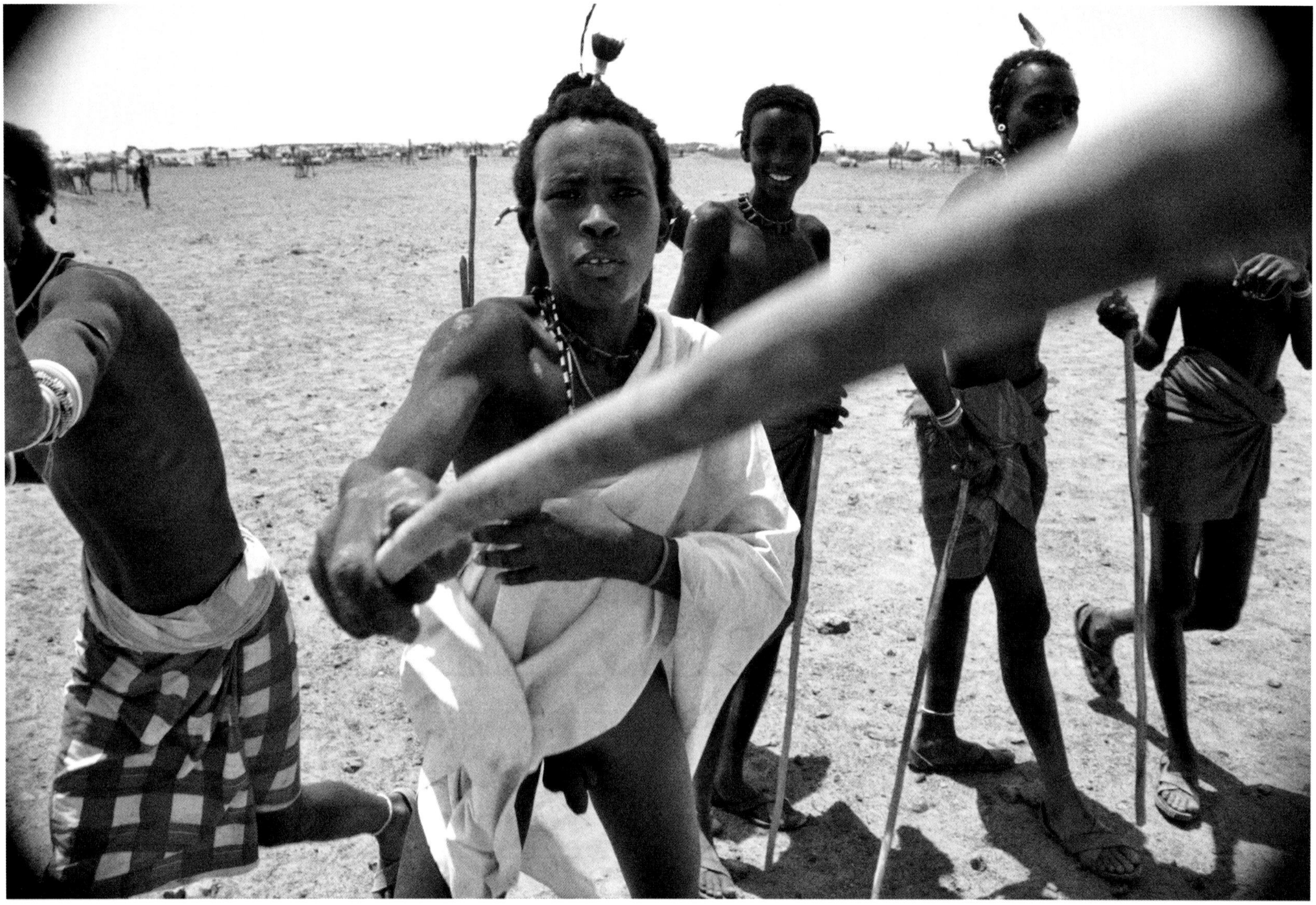

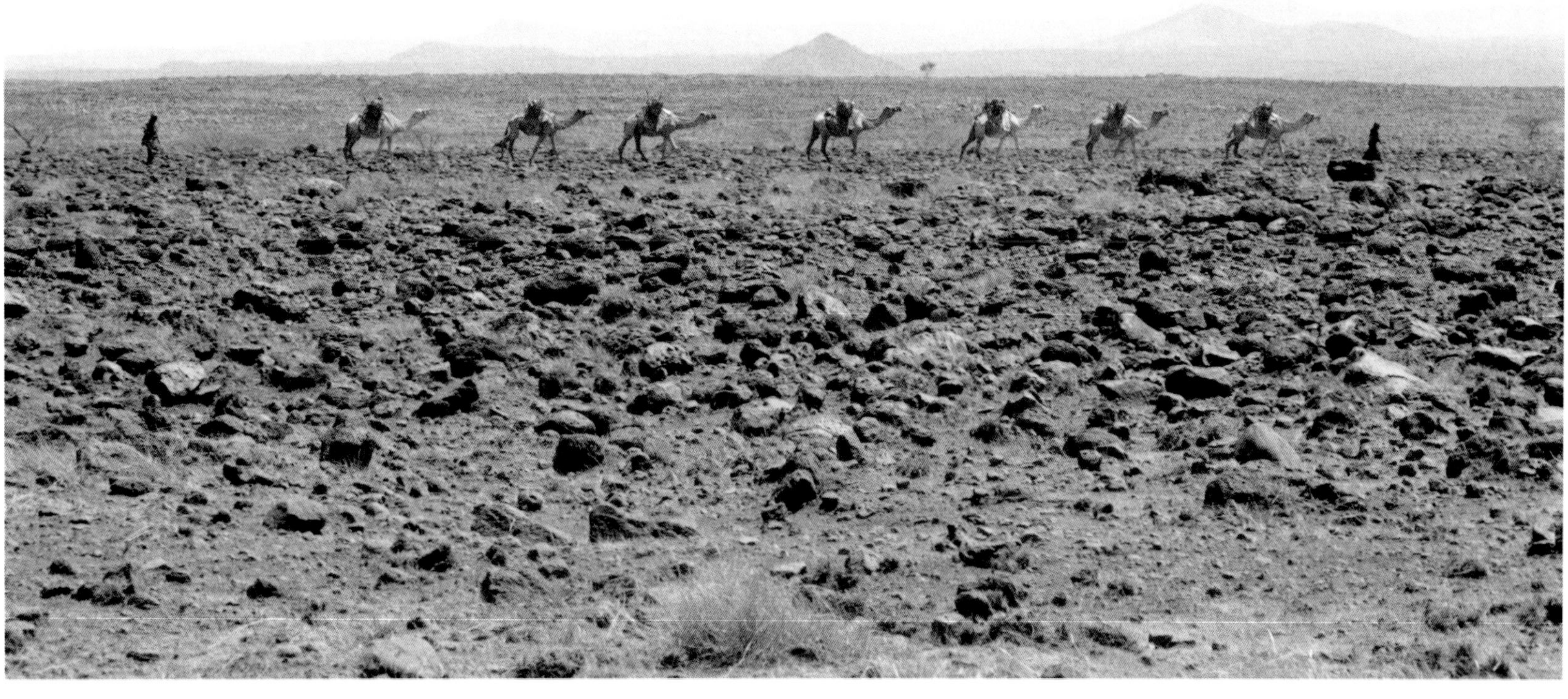

The fragility of Africa's soil, her forests, her peoples and animals is one of the urgent themes of our time. This dedication is meant as an alarm call to what we have to salvage because Africa inhabits us as our original home. Patrick Hemingway, who knew the elephant so well, especially in East Africa, once told me from his home in Montana that "Africans used to be tolerant of elephants. Everyone wants to escape the reality of what Africa was." Today, in the mad modern rush to the cities, urbanized Africa has little connection with the wild. "My money is that the elephant will soon be gone," exclaims Patrick. On the other hand, as the esteemed paleoanthropologist Richard Leakey wrote, "As an expert in evolution, I can assure you that the extinction of the elephant is no more certain than the extinction of man is certain." And yet the two are inextricably bound. If Africa's tribes are homogenized and lose their connection to place, what indeed will remain of the original ethos of the most ancient continent?

It is on Africa's soil that humankind emerged, among a myriad of other species on which we depended for food both physical and spiritual, and which precipitated the social cohesion necessary for our evolution. Today, the giraffe has been added to the list of endangered species, along with the cheetah, the black and white rhino, the wild dog, the mountain gorilla, chimpanzees, pangolins, lions, the gelada baboon, the Ethiopian red wolf, Grevy's zebras, giant sable antelopes, and a myriad of other mammals and birds such as the hooded vulture and the Northern Bald Ibis. Africa is the birthplace of memory, language, mythology, imagination, and civilization itself. Unique cosmologies occupy the aboriginal mind, and much of mankind's origin myths were generated by humanity's proximity to and dependence on animals. Africa is home to around 2,000 languages, about a third of all languages spoken by humans. Of the hundreds of languages that are endangered, many will disappear in the coming century.

The Maasai, perhaps the most iconic tribe in East Africa, have no word for nature, a concept that implies a separation between mankind and the larger universe. Instead, they use the term *enkope Ngai,* meaning the beauty of God or Creation. For the Maasai, there was no tension between the human and nonhuman world. The knowledge and wisdom of indigenous peoples all over the world is increasingly crucial to the conservation of life on Earth.

Species like lions were our competitors, but some groups like the San Bushmen, who "climbed the threads to God's village" during the oldest ceremony on Earth, the trance dance, had a unique relationship with the lion. The lions, honored as great hunters, would drink at night, and the people would go to the waterhole during the blistering hours of the day. There was no animosity between the two species. According to carbon dating of some San sites which are over 80,000 years old, the Bushmen have long evinced a unique truce with the lion that facilitated both species' survival. As Laurens van der Post speaking of the San Bushmen wrote, "The essence of his being, I believe, was his sense of belonging: belonging to nature, the universe, life and his own humanity.... Where we became more and more abstracted and abstract, he drew closer to feeling and the immediacy of instinct and intuition.... He was never imperilled as we are by numbers, and the blurring of the human spirit which their collective standards and approximations exact today."

Today, as a result of trophy hunting and loss of habitat, the lion population has dropped almost 90% in the last generation. Elephants, who used to wander freely across the plains of Africa in the hundreds, have been severely reduced in number, and continue to be killed by poachers and trophy hunters. 60% of her elephants have disappeared since the 1970s. 40% of Africa's giraffes have vanished in that time, with only 80,000 remaining on the entire continent, and the lion is down to maybe 16,000 according to Lion Aid, whereas there were still over 150,000 when I first set foot in Africa as a teenager in 1975. While trophy hunting has been debated for decades, its impacts cannot be overstated. Many areas have been denuded of their greatest populations due to poaching of late, not least of which is the Selous, which lost 60% of its elephants in the 2010s. Trophy hunting, which was allowed in the greatest reserve in Africa and thus encouraged poaching, did not help the situation. To detract further from the karma of that ineffable reserve, Tanzania has decided to build a dam in the larger hunting part of the Selous, where major logging of trees has already occurred. Bringing Tanzania up to par with schemes to modernize and provide electricity to its population undermines an essential environmental tenet of the founder of Tanzania, Julius Nyerere. How will Africa keep up with modernity and hold on to her inimitable environment?

It seems wherever trophy hunting has been allowed, poachers have followed and wreaked havoc on entire landscapes. The ones who have suffered the most from this exploitation are, of course, the animals. Elspeth Huxley, who knew more about Africa than most, had this to say about trophy hunters: "It's rotten to the core, like everything else about this modern civilization. Sport! It's no more a sport than shooting sitting pheasants, if as much. There's only one sporting way to hunt big game, and that's the old way, the way natives follow—to hunt on foot with spears and bows and arrows, weapons a man can make himself out of materials ready to his hand. It's a battle of wits between one man and one beast: a test of which can command the greatest cunning, the keenest senses, the highest skill. You say it was man's skill that invented machine guns, aeroplanes, bombs, and poison gas. Why don't you tackle elephants and rhinos, then, with those products of human skill? You wouldn't pretend that was sport; but why is it more unsporting to bomb a herd of elephants or turn a machine gun on to a pride of lions than to drive up to them in a motor-car and shoot them with a high-powered rifle?"

There is an inimitable bond between the first peoples of Africa and her great fauna, with whom our species emerged, species who are increasingly endangered by poaching, blood sport, loss of habitat, the bushmeat trade, and climate change. The great complex of mind and body that is the titan of the elephant was ransacked last decade. Already the great tuskers are on their last legs, and many elephants are not growing tusks any more. We have reached the point as a species where we are not just influencing evolution. We have created a "reverse evolution" that will affect all of earthly life.

It is with our interdependence on the other that we have become most fully human. Years ago, while going to Ethiopia to see the tribes of the Omo Valley, one of the cradles of the human race, the cover of *Time* touted the possibility of singularity, the possibility that, by 2040, the human mind would merge with that of the machine. In a time when the organic world is giving way to the synthetic, and is being challenged in every corner of the world, perhaps it would be better worth our efforts to reexamine, honor, and salvage the extraordinary kaleidoscope of life that surrounds us here on Earth, as the life-giving matrix that created humankind. Synthetic and artificial intelligence will not save us from ourselves. Our morality, our ethics, indeed our survival is intimately bound to the soil, and the ecosystems on which we have depended for millennia. Even the insects, perhaps, of all species, especially the insects need to be saved for the maintenance of the planet. The satellites we have sent to space will give us images of other worlds, but we are still desecrating this sphere as never before in human history. We have received images of the Martian soil, most recently with the Perseverance rover, but the world of Mars is desolate and dry. Will we render Earth as lifeless as Mars? The elite may take rides in Earth's atmosphere, combusting fossil fuels to gain different perspective of our home planet, but the rest of humanity has to learn to endure the ravages of this immensely fragile home and transform our behavior before it is too late.

Upon arriving in Africa, butterflies, bees, and dung beetles are among the first insects one encounters when one sets foot on her soil. And yet almost 30% of the world's insect population has diminished in the last generation. Human and animal life cannot continue without the insects. In Africa, as everywhere else on Earth, life depends on the smallest and seemingly most humble of beings as much as on her greatest creatures.

We are looking for another planet to live on, but it is here on Earth, and specifically in Africa, that our ancestors learned to walk upright amidst an amazing variety of megafauna. Some of Africa's first peoples, as native peoples all over the world, still harbor an ethos that we in the dominant society have forgotten and would do well to heed. They do not sacrifice their wildlife for vanity. Rather it is the bushmeat trade that is imperiling much of her wildlife. Globalization schemes, mineral extraction, and land grabs by foreign governments exert enormous pressure on the agricultural base in Africa, while Africa's peoples continue to cope with climate change, increasing population growth, and desertification. This endangers Africa's ability to feed itself, with consequent impact on her forests and wildlife. As Gillies Turle states in *The Art of the Maasai* (1992), "We need to move beyond repeated mistakes, stretch for the safety of common sense before short-term political expedience eradicates the human potential. Otherwise humans will duplicate on a global scale what the improvident behaviour of elephants achieved in Kenya's Tsavo National Park: a massive population increase during good times with the consequent destruction of finite resources and nowhere else to go, the animals enforced their own inevitable die-off. We see their bones everywhere, but can we hear what they say?" Africa is the very cradle of humanity, and it may very well be the litmus test for humanity as a whole.

During the supermoon in August 2014, our eight-year-old son Lysander remarked: "We have landed on the moon, but we have not yet landed on Earth." On Earth, our species began barely 250,000 years ago, and in less than 250 years we have jeopardized its life force. Today, only 23% of the world's surface is considered wilderness, as opposed to 50% 300 years ago. We are on our way to homogenizing the entire face of the Earth. As Romain Gary,

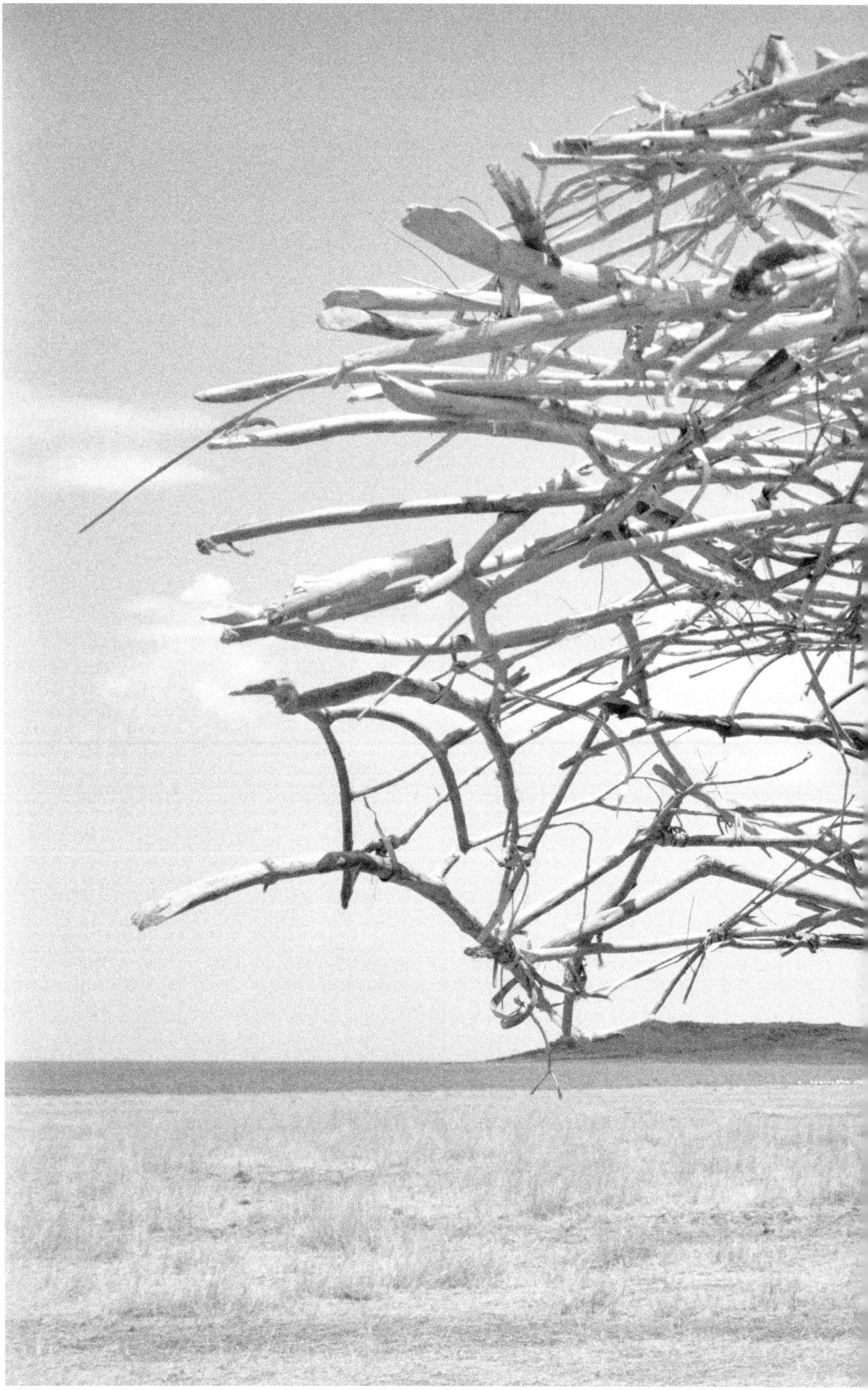

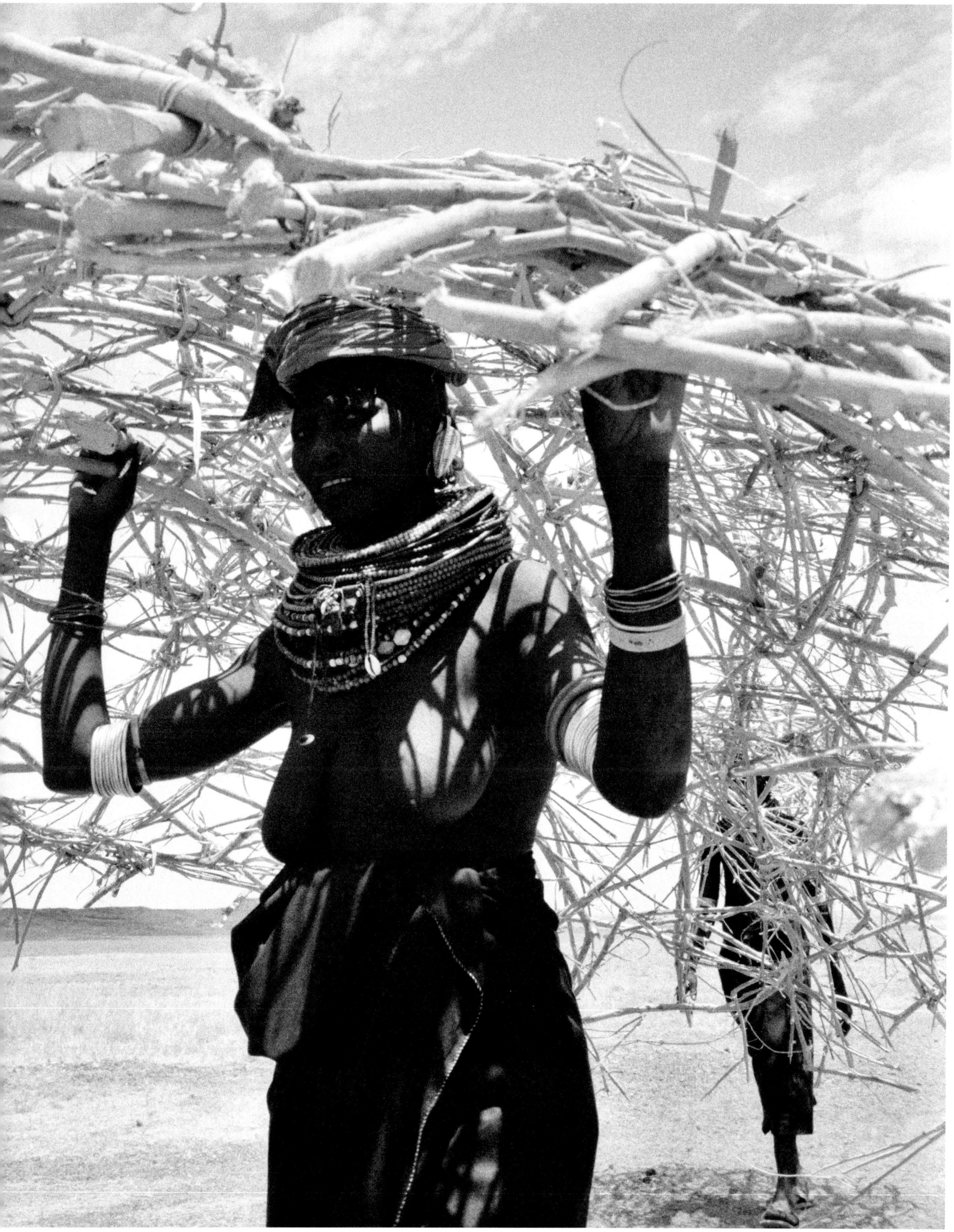

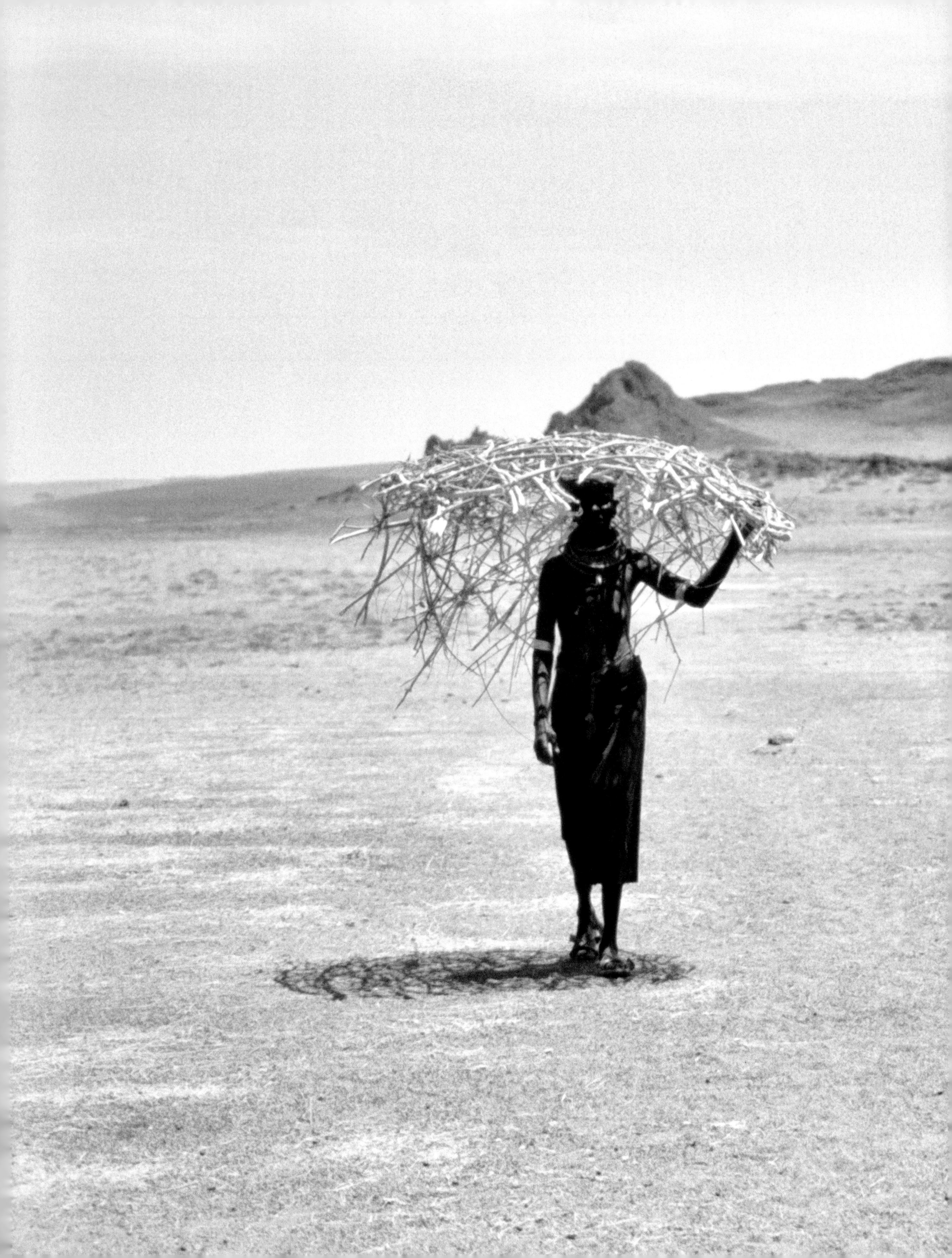

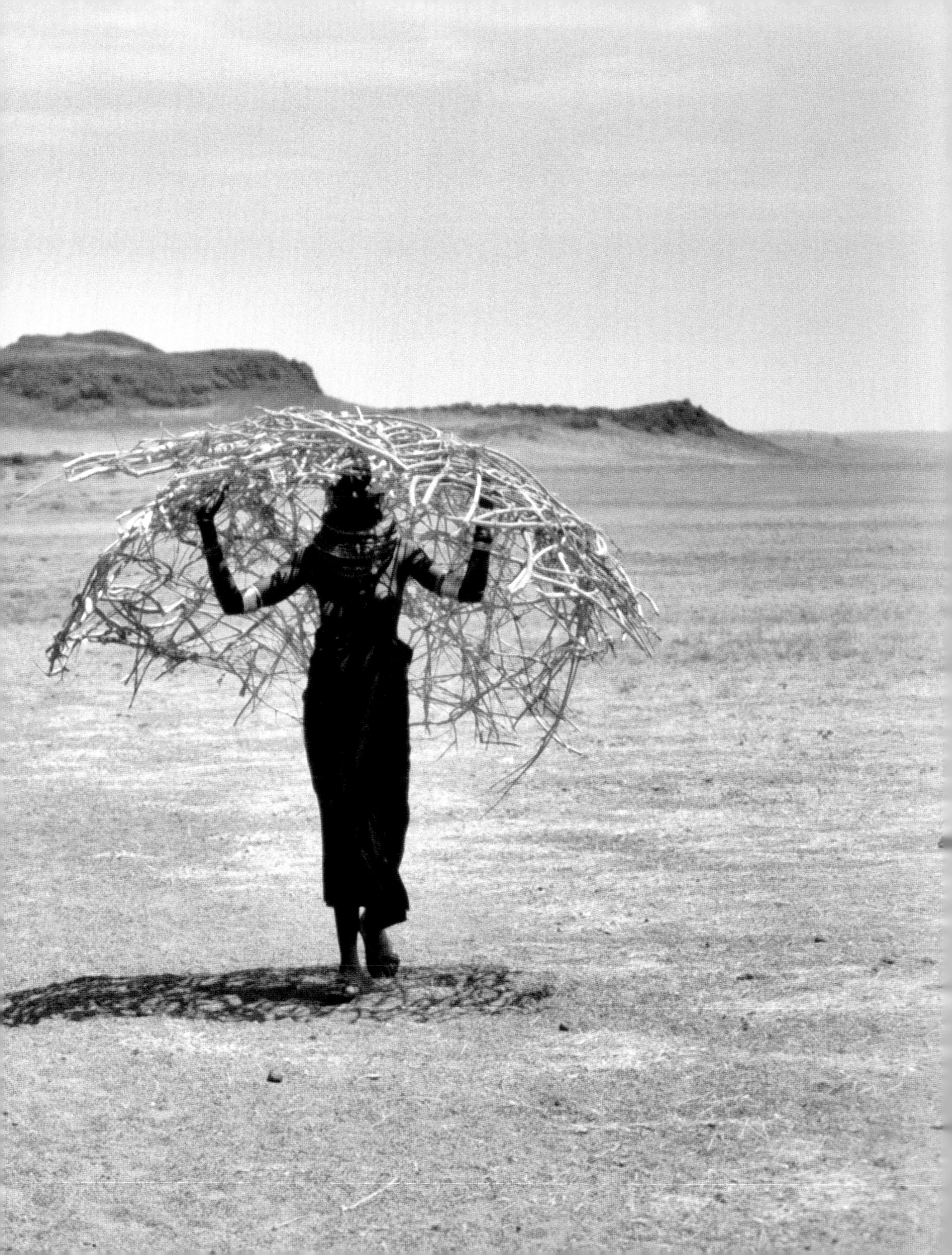

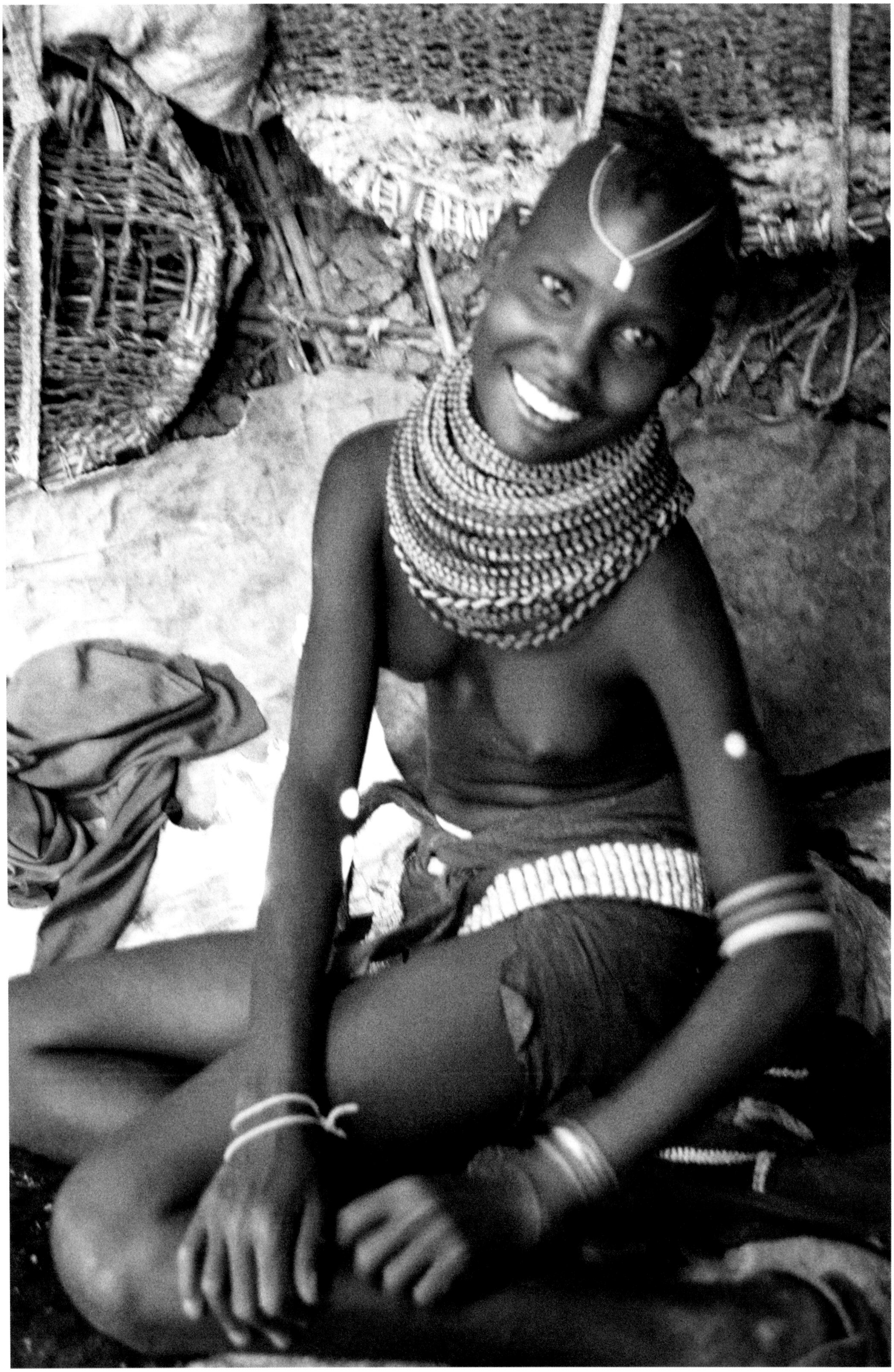

the prophetic French writer, noted, "The only thing we do know is nature has no favorites among the species." *Lords of the Earth* is an attempt to underscore the enormous indebtedness our tribal collective self, some of the indigenous mind of humanity in Africa, has for the other beings with whom we emerged in a hope that both will be salvaged not only for their sake but also for humanity's spirit, wonder, and ultimate place on Earth. That a language is being lost every two weeks should make humanity shudder as much as losing a spectacular bird in the wilds of the Congo, Australia, the Amazon, New Guinea, the Arctic, or even the Antarctic. Ways of honoring the world, nature, and species is something native peoples have embodied in the very core of their myths, dances, rituals, and souls. In redeeming ourselves from the iniquities of industrialization and globalization, the first peoples of the world have to be given fundamental rights. It is very late in the game, as this decade of the twenty-first century may be the final one in which we can salvage what is left of tribal humanity and Nature. The two have until recently been one and the same. Over 70% of the world's animal population has disappeared in the last 50 years. The UN has not been able to reach any of its 20 fundamental targets for saving the biodiversity of the planet. Life on Earth, both human and nonhuman, is reaching a tipping point.

Each human language is a species of consciousness unto itself, a miniature cosmology and template for addressing origin and animals that manifest themselves in the world. Without them, we lose our ultimate being. Animals were also key to addressing and honoring the ground of the ancestors which the juggernaut of modernity is eradicating. This decade has an immense responsibility to honor the Convention on Biological Diversity, which seeks to salvage the remaining life forms of the planet. Native peoples should be measured as irreplaceable, just like the species they have always lived alongside.

It is in Africa that Marie, Lysander, and I have witnessed some of the planet's most ineffable wonders. It is among some of her first peoples that remarkable legends persist about our origins and our relationship to the other beings we have evolved with. The present phase of the massacre of the innocent, in the body of the elephant, is the ultimate test for our species. Our ability to walk, survive, and even dream alongside these lords of the Earth is fostered in Africa like nowhere else on this planet.

How strange indeed, how apocalyptic an attitude was the behavior of the colonial invaders of the "dark" continent, who first beheld the great fauna of Africa and whose first impulse was to destroy them, as Ernest Hemingway once wrote in *True at First Light*: "He's your lion and you take your time and be in shape to shoot him … I did know that the white people always took the other people's lands away from them and put them on a reservation where they could go to hell and be destroyed as though they were in a concentration camp." By contrast, Carl Jung once remarked that animals were "the priests of God." In Africa, during his life-changing 1925 safari, Jung learned of a manifestly different way to relate to the lion. One day, he saw lion tracks outside his tent and was taken aback. His helpers, the natives, were astonished, but they supposedly smiled and said: "It is not bad, it is our lion," underscoring the power the lion holds on Africa's identity and conscience.

How many times have we been captivated by the lion, the very voice of Africa. In 1929, Martin Johnson admitted that "a lion does not, except for food, kill nor fight nor interfere with other living creatures. That is more than can be said of most human beings." In his book *Bwana Game*, George Adamson once superbly remarked: "According to Korokoro, the lion's roar translated into English goes: who is the Lord of the Land? Who is the Lord of the Land? … I am … I am … I am."

Competition for land and especially trophy hunting have decimated the lion population. It started in antiquity, when one Roman emperor imported as many as 6,000 lions from Africa just to see Christians being eaten by them in the colosseum. Pompeii even staged a battle between 20 elephants and 600 lions! Today, there may be no more than 3,000 male lions throughout Africa and 15,000 in total. When I was 15 and heard my first lion roaring in the Chyulu Hills of southern Kenya, there may have been over one hundred thousand. Over the years, Lysander, Marie, and I have been transfixed by their voice, their roar being the loudest sentinel voice in Africa, awakening the entire horizon to its presence. The lion's place in the world alerts you to some antediluvian shudder and wonder, like a stalking specter. They impressed Lysander by calling lions "the ghosts in the grass." They are regal in sight, hearing, power, courage like few species on Earth. Their being in the world, taking only what they need, has always been in contradistinction to the menace and deceitfulness of our kind.

The Mama Simba group of women in Samburuland in northern Kenya now recognize that the lion must be preserved, not just for the tourist revenue the lion brings, but also but for the immeasurable ecological and spiritual place the lion holds in the larger ecosystem. In a time when so much of the lion population has been lost in the last generation, and when 7 out of 10 trophy hunters come from the United States, their work is an emergency call to save one of the central icons in the ecology of Africa and the human imagination.

In 1998, while observing the trance dance, Marie and I heard wondrous tales of San Bushmen elders "transforming" into lions, whom many considered their peers, their brothers. Their relationship to the lion goes back at least 60,000 years, the oldest continuous human–nonhuman bond on Earth. As opposed to the dominant society's venal and mercenary bloodlust towards the lion, the Bushmen had an almost metaphysical relationship with them. Many Bushmen told us that "lions bring freedom. When lions roar you feel scared but you also feel happy." One story was told to us by an elder named Bom, who still carried a scar from an old lion that had jumped on him when he was a young man. He wore the scar proudly, as if it were a talisman. One day, in the early morning, after one of their famed all-night trance dances, Bom and his friend heard a lion roaring. The roar dissipated, but not before everyone had been alerted to the animal's proximity, and the senior men went out into the bush to try to find its tracks in the vast Kalahari sands. They found lion paw prints not far from their camp and followed them for a distance, and then saw that, amazingly, the tracks had become human footprints that had made their way towards the next Bushmen settlement a few miles away!

Isak, a companion of Roy Sesana, who headed the First Peoples of the Kalahari in Botswana, reminded us that humans "were on loan to the Earth" and that the "lion is a guardian, a protector. Lion is a good omen. The lion is our forefather, our ancestor."

Laurens van der Post expressed his love for the lion decades ago: "I would find myself intensely grateful that I was living in a day when such a sound as that lion's roar had not yet vanished from life. For people so shackled with negative aspects of culture and civilization as we war-time soldiers were, there was in these sounds and sights something of the nature of a prayer for a way of life for sheer living's sake which is Africa's great gift to the modern world."

In 2002, we once followed two male brothers on the Zambezi who were about to cross the river. We waited an hour to see what they would do as the dark obsidian silence of sunset took over the land. They hid behind some bushes ready to make a quick getaway. Our guide waited too long, and to my consternation vanished before we had a chance to see what would have been a miracle moment, two lions, perhaps refugees from Mugabe's regime, swimming across the river that separates Zimbabwe from Zambia under the spell of a full moon. That same year we were privileged enough to witness Kamunyak, the blessed one, in Samburu, Kenya, adopt a young oryx baby, maybe three weeks old, as it astonished biologists and reminded everyone the world over that the lion could indeed lay down with the lamb!

There have been ineffable moments in the bush, like the time we heard the stories in 2010 of the mystique of the white lions of southern Africa, perhaps the most revered and sacred animals on the continent to the Shangaan tribe of Timbavati. Seeing a wild white lion eating a kudu was a miracle to behold. Lysander felt something of the spirit of Aslan from Narnia come to life. The Shangaan believe that if the white lions were to disappear the entire ecology would collapse. The lion's place in the ecosystems of Africa are certainly under siege, and how humanity responds to the lion crisis will be a decisive testimony not only to the future of an entire continent, but to the legacy of what our killer species is capable of on this Earth.

In Gemsbok National Park between Namibia, Botswana, and South Africa, we were transfixed by numinous tales that go back countless millennia. We heard stories of changing climate patterns and of shape-shifters who still honored the lion. We were told how one must never stare directly at a lion and that if one met a lion in the wild, one had to walk away from the lion obliquely. We headed into the desert and witnessed wildebeest, giraffes, and oryx for a week, but no lions. It was not until three hours before sunset on the last day of our stay, when we were supposed to head back to the gate and meet our Bushmen hosts, that we saw the tip of a black-maned lion's head peeking up out of the red dunes. We waited for forty minutes, after which our guide told us we should head back to camp. Marie, who watched the lion move and was reminded of similar motions from our own cat on numerous occasions, decided we should wait just a little longer. Suddenly, the male lion sat up and watched us and was soon joined by two females who caressed each other, with the male looking on like a true nobleman over his harem.

Then two more joined the others from behind the sands. The intimacy of the moment was heightened as the male decided to walk by our cars, joined by the four females in single file, a fantastic procession to end an otherwise uneventful week.

We followed them for several kilometers until they came to another dune, as if poised to watch the resplendent African sunset. What is remarkable is that we had decided at the last minute not to join our Bushmen hosts at the gate as we had planned, but to spend time with the lions, the famous black-maned lions we had come so far to see. Our Bushmen host was a man, and he had with him four women friends, just like the male lion! In some ineffable way, it felt like the spirit of those Bushmen had somehow been transferred to those very lions there in the back of the beyond, where mystery and synchronicity collide. In this age of the synthetic and artificial intelligence, it is lessons such as these in the wilderness of silence that will ultimately be regarded as among the great overarching and sentinel voices of our time.

Elephants have always amazed Lysander, but the lions have been consorts to the cats we honor in our own household, the cats that mesmerized an entire civilization called Egypt. We tend to look for the marvelous in the grandiose and majestic, but it can also be found in smaller species like the wildcats, servals, and caracals, supreme marauders of the night. For millennia, humans and lions have had a truce with one another, as Elizabeth Marshall Thomas learned from her time with the Bushmen in the 1950s. The Bushmen had a living arrangement, a truce with lions, as the first peoples of Africa, unmatched on Earth. The lions' chorus would intone with several groups of lions following each other with a deafening roar, one behind the other. It was sounded not just for other lions, but for the Bushmen as well! To let them know that they were powerful hunters and that they both depended on the same food. They let the world know that humans and lions were living in proximity to each other and in fellowship!

Our species is trying to meld with the machine, with artificial intelligence, with robots, at a time when we need to restore our relationship with those beings who have helped define us spiritually, ecologically, and morally for as long as our species has been on this planet. The Ju/wasi Bushmen once said that humans and lions are not enemies until we make them so. We have coexisted, and we can again if we stop persecuting them for vanity. Trophy hunters, most of them Americans, as well as Europeans and now even Chinese, looking for lion bones to pass off as tiger bones to make tiger wine, are impacting the genetic pool of lions and indeed most trophy animals. One day, such depravity will be outlawed worldwide. But what will be left of the wild? With climate change, lions may very well face a more difficult future. We already know that heat is affecting the very rare wild dog's hunting behavior and that their pups' chances of survival are plummeting. Will the same happen to the cheetah's ability to reproduce, and the leopard's, and the lion's? How will climate change affect reproduction over the coming generation, both human and nonhuman?

One thing is certain, without the other species we will simply cease to be fully human. The fad today of transhumanism and the possibility of downloading the brain into a machine is a sad response, a far cry from what we have always had recourse to over the last 250,000 years and what we should be returning to: our organic self, myth, and story. It is perhaps why Lysander once exclaimed that "Africa was the introduction to the alternate Self," the other, much older, non synthetically derived, organic connection to the other beings of the world, the bedrock of the life force. If we lose the animals, gadgets will be all we are left with. Communing with the other than human has always been one of our key reasons for being on Earth. Africa was our original home, our first mentor, where humanity's communion with the other began. Some animals were food, but hunting embodied a sacred rite of passage. They were meant to be honored. It is perhaps why people who have gone there and been moved by her peoples' spirit, there where our heart was born, recognize in the animals a part of their very soul.

The Maasai used to pit themselves against lions, but only for the valor and prestige of their clans. Woe betide a modern trophy hunter to fashion his own spear and try to go after a lion for the sheer sake of hunting. The Maasai, who knew the lion best, have now become lion guardians across East Africa. In contrast to the moral cowards who killed for fun, for pleasure in fact, the Maasai risked their lives either alone or in groups, to confront an equal warrior, the lion. In this time, we are killing the supreme hunters, they who have always been our supreme teachers. We desecrate beauty with vanity, grace with perfidy. If humanity is to survive, we must hold ourselves accountable. The time draws near when we will find out decisively if we are the saviors of species or their slayers. The tribesmen of Africa, who lived in a balanced ecosystem, were assuredly the lords of the earth they watched over. Colonialism and the homogenizing and destabilization of Africa's cultures and landscapes accompanied the massive destruction of her wildlife. The times we came upon rhino in Namibia will haunt us forever. For there was a time when rhinos were the lords of the Earth. Seeing white rhinos, sometimes ten at a time, in the haunting ebbing lavender desert light, harkens to the times when the giants of the rhino family, Elasmotherium and Deinotherium, ruled the world. The rhino situation was so bad last decade that some thought of exporting rhinos to Australia and Texas. With heat waves and megafires upon us, how will the great mammals survive? Where will the smaller ones hide?

"But lions know that whatever is roaring from the sky is not quite a lion. Why, then, do they answer?" asked Marshall Thomas. Perhaps because the noise sounds like a lion. Perhaps a lion god wants to know where the lions are. "Where are you?" the lion god thunders. The lions on the ground think for a moment "Is he talking to me?" So each lion takes a deep breath, and they roar with all their might. "I'm here!" each answers, "Right here." "When the god speaks to lions, may there always be lions to reply," wrote Marshall Thomas.

In Africa, elders are often called the elephants! It is a bond that goes back hundreds of millennia. Early hominids depended on the waterholes elephants dug, and their meat supported us as far back as human memory allows. The elephant line goes back over thirty million years, when the first ancestor was barely bigger than a small pig. It is Romain Gary who knew the horrors and the camps of World War II and who exclaimed that "Where there are elephants, there is freedom." It is exactly our freedom as a species that is on the line. Some say that to get from the piglike ancestor of the elephant, Moeritherium, to the modern day elephant, it took 20 million generations. In less than 20 years' time, most of the world's elephants could be gone forever. It would be a crime for which evolution will not be able to forgive us.

When Nelson Mandela died, it was as if an ancestor, a deep all-abiding voice and conscience for the life force, had departed forever. In East Africa, people called him *Ndovu wetu*, our elephant. Today, it is not only the struggle between humans that challenges our kind, but also the even greater menace of humanity's separation from the totality of the biosphere, our place of origin, and the organic world as a whole.

My grandfather, one of the key generals in the French campaign in North Africa and one of the liberators of Paris in World War II, fought for freedom from tyranny. One man he knew was Romain Gary, who also lived through the horrors of the war. His masterpiece *The Roots of Heaven* appeared in 1956. Its protagonist Morel was an advocate of the rights of the elephant worldwide. Today, the continued butchery and trade in the body parts of nature's greatest terrestrial monarch, the elephant, shames our children. The renewed slaughter of the innocent after the ivory ban in 1989 threatens the greatest land mammal on Earth. The one-off sale of ivory by CITES in 2008, followed by the global economic downturn, spurred the rising middle class in China to buy ivory, igniting the second phase of the elephant massacre in our time since the 1980s. In 2016, a census revealed that one third of Africa's elephants had been destroyed by the ivory traders of the world. The population may now count little more than 350,000 savannah elephants, with no clear discernible population for the much more secretive forest elephant, who may number no more than 50,000. They are the great gardeners of the second largest rainforest on Earth.

The present fight for the elephant is a litmus test for the larger conservation effort worldwide and for what remains of the world's species. The elephant today is the greatest canary in the increasingly fragile coal mine of the biosphere. I believe that civilization will stand or fall on the back of the African elephant. We have been privy to accounts, oral traditions, and lore that should inspire us about a truce, a harmony that once existed between Africa's tribes and the rest of creation. The great lord of the Earth used to walk in relative peace with the people of Africa. Seas of elephants used to roam Africa like a giant wave of moving mountains, wandering across the savannahs, or in clandestine fashion like the rainforest elephant inside the dense jungles of the interior.

As Gary wrote, "Still, I am confident that there is something more behind this drive for the preservation of the earth and its inhabitants than an exclusive preoccupation with a continued presence on this planet." Romain Gary articulated like no one else in the twentieth century how vast the elephant's being impacted the psyche of the human species. He understood that it was not just one species that was at stake, but an archetype of being, freedom itself, the ability to walk on Earth as a sovereign individual. "On an entirely man-made planet there is no room for man either," wrote Gary. There is a spiritual bond, a conscious and unconscious bridge between ourselves and the others, especially the elephant, which exists with few other species on Earth, except for the whales and the great apes, with whom we share self-awareness. That bond is one of mind, and it is this unique element that the native people of Africa have understood for generations.

At fifteen, I did not realize how one species, an imponderable giant, opened up an entire continent to the world, a continent which helped open the floodgates of slavery to the European powers and especially America. But the elephant also influenced the imagination and the mind like few other species in human history. Their relatives, the mastodons and mammoths, may still have been roaming the tundra of the northern hemisphere during the building of the Sphinx. We now know that the great temple of Angkor Wat in Cambodia was built with a workforce of several thousand Asian elephants. Their very flesh helped humans survive spiritually, morally, and ecologically for countless millennia.

Almost an entire continent, it is fair to say, has been molded by the elephant. Some estimates say over 20 million traversed the savannahs and forests of Africa in the early 1800s. In the mid-1980s, perhaps as many as 60,000 elephants a year were destroyed for the Japanese market. In 1989, thanks to the remarkable efforts of Richard Leakey and an international ban on ivory products culminating in the ivory burn in Kenya, the market largely closed on ivory. But with the one-off sale of ivory by CITES in 2008, organized by southern African states and coinciding with the global recession, the Asian lust for ivory, largely led by China, created a feeding frenzy for what many had thought had been a problem of the past. In 2011, as many as 25,000 elephants were massacred for ornaments for the Oriental market. The lie that elephants simply lose their tusks seeped throughout the Chinese conscience like a river of blood soaked in the ivory trade. Some serious collectors are actually banking or hoping on extinction, so that their supply of ivory can accrue in value! The insidiousness of what is plunging a stake through the heart of elephant society is also unraveling human civilization. We are drunk on perfidy and massacre. If what the local Africans say about elephants is true, their fate is indeed our fate.

Already when a teenager I longed for what Laurens van der Post called the "first things of life." I was initiated in the central Rift Valley at Nakuru, where I had camped for a brief month, but a month filled with the blaring sounds of hippos, the wondrous swarms of flaming pink flamingoes, and the intimations of leopards by the lakeside that still haunt me to this day. It is not a religious point of view, but the roots of the archetypal psyche in Africa that so influenced Carl Jung, as he testified in his book *Memories, Dreams, Reflections*: "The more familiar I became with city life, the stronger grew my impression that what I was now getting to know as reality belonged to an order of things different from the view of the world I had grown up with in the country, among rivers and woods, among men and animals in a small village bathed in sunlight, with the winds and the clouds moving over it, and encompassed by dark night in which uncertain things happened. It was no mere locality on the map, but 'God's world,' so ordered by Him and filled with secret meaning."

Carl Jung saw Africa as the birthplace of the mind, where the undifferentiated psyche still contained the moorings of a primal consciousness. He first went to Mount Elgon, which harbors the famed Kitum caves, carved out by generations of elephants looking for salt minerals. It was there that Marie and I saw newly initiated young Pokot boys coming out of the bush, with their goat skin vestments and sisal-cactus face covers swinging back and forth, in imitation of the elephant's trunk, deriving inspiration from the elephant's power and presence. A band of sixteen had walked out into the bush and survived for several months on their own. Few people have seen the elephants on their nightly migrations to the caves, on what seems like a pilgrimage to the interior of the Earth. It is as if they had a sixth sense that enabled them to escape detection. But the evidence is there for all to see. Carl Jung, who grasped the great fundamental theater of the African mind, would have been mesmerized by the elephant's great trumpeting and its silent steps, the great song lines of their passage. For I believe that the elephants molded not just the continent, but influenced our entire passage on this Earth, ever since the Old World migrated across to the New World millennia ago. They are the great architects of time and collaborators in our very evolution.

As Marie and I began to help sound the alarm and draw attention to the elephant crisis back in 2009, along with an army of concerned conservationists and ecologists, we started to get a glimpse into native peoples' profound respect for the greatest land mammal on Earth. We also heard stories that went beyond a totemic relationship and hinted at a much deeper level of mind than most ecologists and early explorers of Africa had hitherto alluded to.

Jung, as the great discoverer of the psyche, had come to realize what lay hidden and was in a sense "incomplete" in Africa. Jung did not spend ample time probing the deeper mysteries of a continent where consciousness was born. He was still too much under the influence of the nineteenth-century idea of the Great Chain of Being. European man was bringing a light to humanity that the native mind had not yet tapped into, or so he thought.

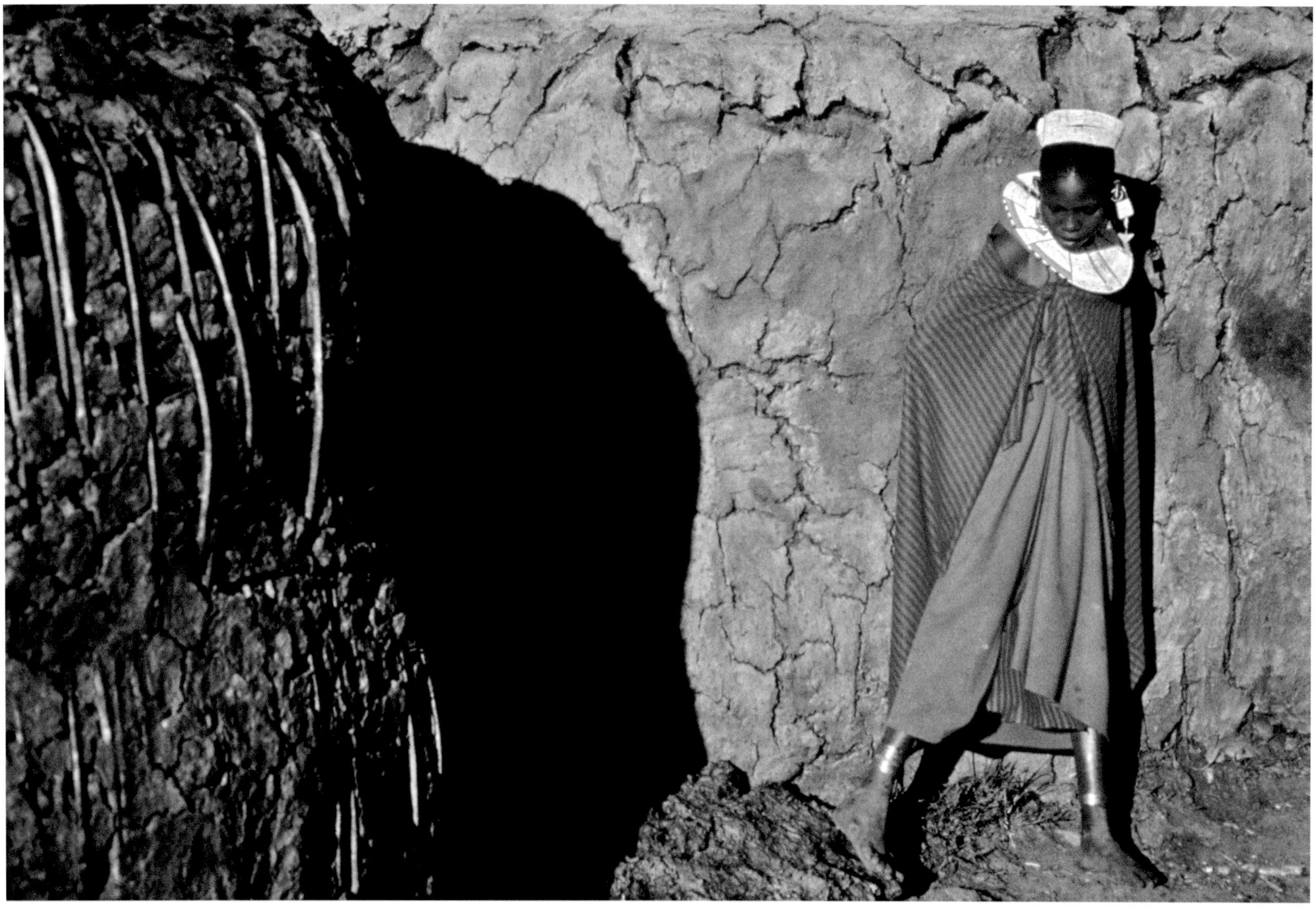

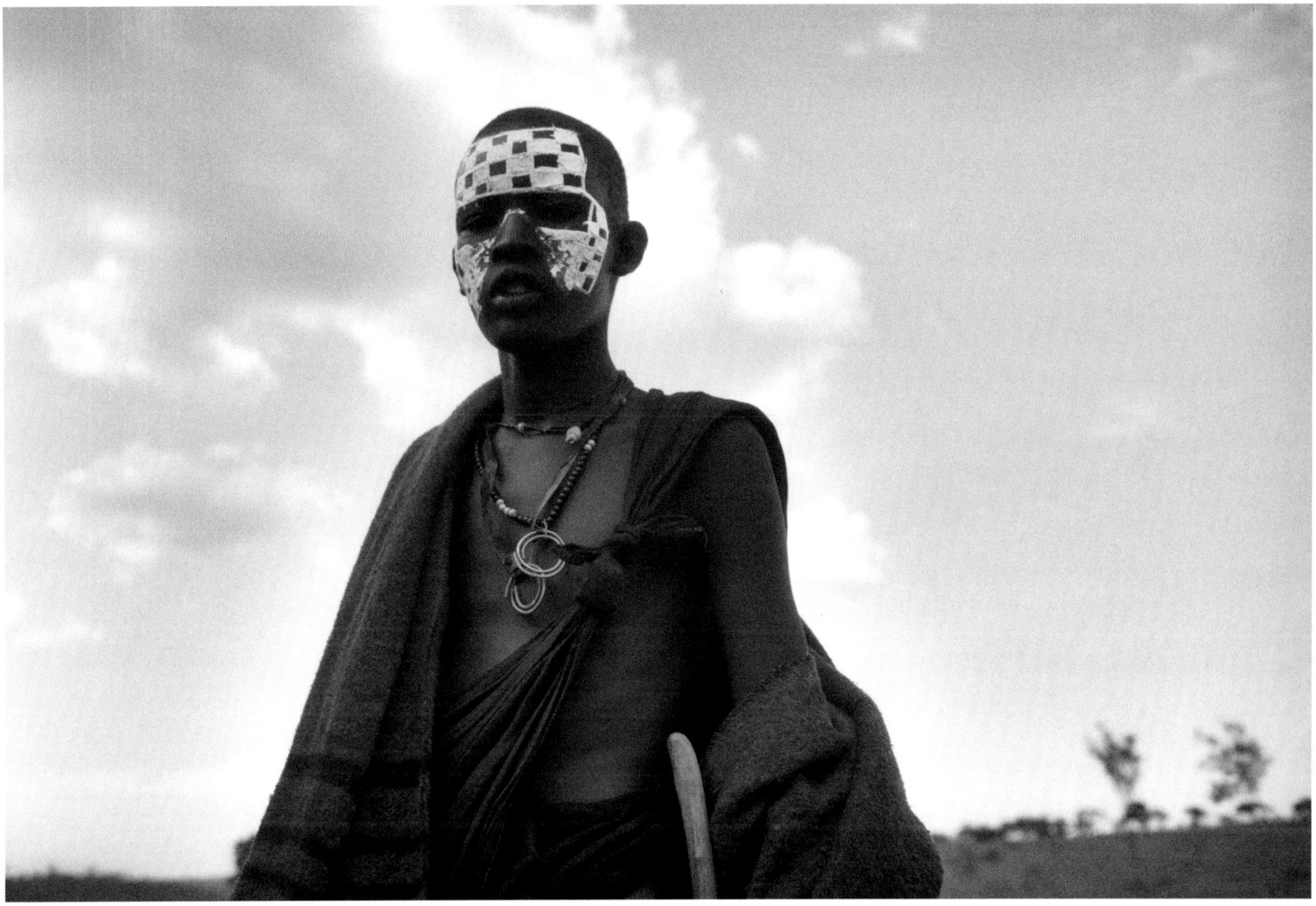

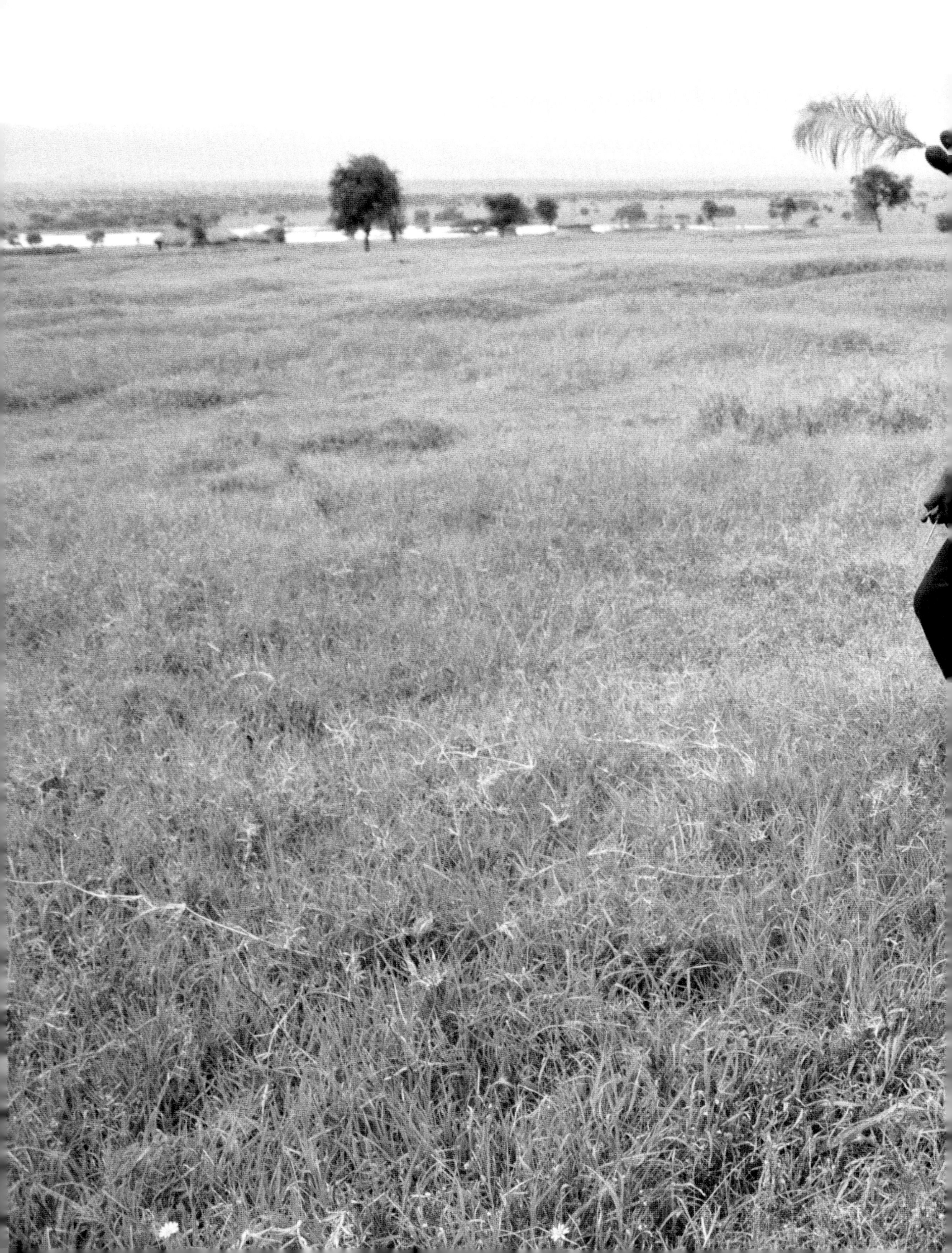

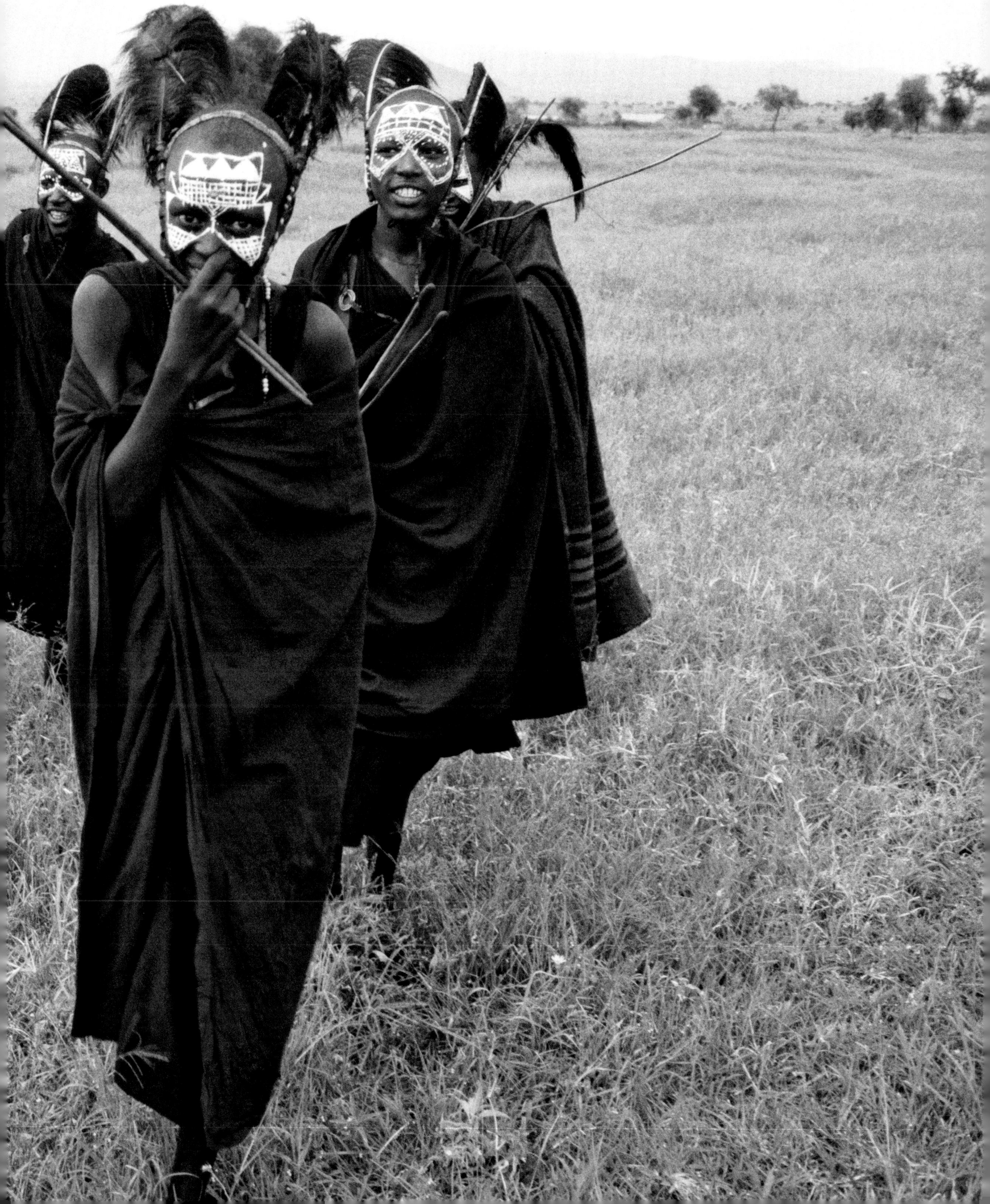

But Jung's trip to Africa also prompted him to free his "arrested being." Raised in the confines of metropolitan reality, Africa shone a light on aspects of the primal undercurrents of thought he could not have imagined in Europe. That "stillness of eternal beginning" seduced Jung, as it would later writers such as Beryl Markham, who wrote in *West with the Night* (1942): "Competitors in conquest have overlooked the vital soul of Africa herself, from which emanates the true resistance to conquest. The soul is not dead, but silent, the wisdom not lacking, but of such simplicity as to be counted non-existent in the tinker's mind of modern civilization. Africa is of an ancient age and the blood of many of her peoples is as venerable and as chaste as truth."

The trip through the Chyulus, sleeping in tents among elephants, in the days when there were still visible herds, continue to reverberate like a primordial landscape. We must have changed tires five times a day going over those volcanic hills, whose rocks humbled our trajectory as we moved towards the ocean and the red, red earth of Tsavo, whose elephants seemed to have been painted by the Creator himself. Camping under the stars, under the same skies that had inspired George and Joy Adamson during their honeymoon, makes this area of the bush, with its rolling igneous rocks overlooking Kilimanjaro, one of the great refuges of the world. Lions roared not far from our fire, a memory grafted from another time.

It was in the Chyulus, on that great serpentine volcanic spine overlooking Kilimanjaro, that we were many years later to hear one of the greatest lion stories ever told by a former hunter, Koni, of the famed Waliangulu tribe. Known all over Africa as the greatest elephant hunters of their kind, the Waliangulu depended on the elephant for their very survival. To hear their testimonial is to go back in time to the roots of how we survived as a species because, in some very essential way, humanity, in the early days, fed on the body of the elephant, the meat that it provided. At a kopje rock outcrop overlooking the Chyulus, one late afternoon on a day in June 2012, on a boulder seemingly molded by antediluvian giants and glowing in the spellbinding amber light of Africa, Koni told us the story of his grandfather Tise, who had been hunting many years ago before the ivory ban was introduced in Kenya. During a drought long ago, Koni's grandfather had not caught any antelope for over a week and had been living on honey which he provided for his people. He returned to the bush, and late one night, as he lay in his makeshift hut, he heard a strange noise coming from a local lion. Something bizarre reverberated in the lion's throat, something he could not identify. Koni's grandfather decided to go to sleep by the fire and was woken up by a lion who looked down at him in obvious pain. The lion gave his paw to the hunter with a porcupine quill stuck inside it. He tried to extract the quill with a knife, but was unsuccessful. He proceeded to extract the quill with his teeth! The lion went back into the bush and disappeared. The hunter still could not find any game and brought honey back to his people. A few days later the hunter spotted what he was sure was the lion he had saved. The lion looked at the hunter and then went off into the bush. Every time the hunter stopped, the lion stopped as well to make sure that Koni's grandfather was following him. Finally, after a few kilometers, the hunter came to a clearing, and next to the lion was a newly killed giraffe. The lion went on top of the giraffe, as if to tell Tise that he had caught the giraffe for him, to thank him for having saved his life! Tise took some meat and brought it to his family without explaining what had happened. Everyone walked to where the giraffe lay and fed on the prey. Tise told his family never to hunt a lion, even if they were hungry. The lion is like your family! A curse on those who hunt lion. Today, nobody will hunt a lion because they are friends, hunting partners! Before that event, the Waliangulu used to hunt lion, but since it happened, no more. The most magical human–lion interaction story I have ever heard.

This remarkable story is unique, but it also demonstrates the truth of a time when lion and man understood each other's powers, when two great killers respected the potency and mind of the other. In a time when the lion population has been depleted by over 90% in the last few generations, emergency action should be taken all over Africa to salvage the remaining animals. Loss of habitat and poaching for trophy hunters has vastly denuded Africa of its greatest carnivore. Lions killed when they were hungry, but, as Elizabeth Marshall Thomas noted during her time with the San Bushmen, there was a truce between humans and lions in the days when hunter-gatherers still depended on the wild for their survival. The beauty of this story lies in its mythic undertone, a concordance between two species that have been wary of each other for hundreds of millennia.

Already among tribes like the Barabaig in the enormous Ruaha National Park in southern Tanzania, conservation measures between Panthera, the Ruaha Carnivore Project, and Lion Guardians are bearing fruit. Given that the Barabaig, like their cousins the Maasai, would have competed with or killed lions to save their livestock, cattle, and goats, reinforced boma structures were erected to help the lion hold on in one of the largest reserves in Tanzania. A new realization is emerging that tourism, essential for the money it brings to local communities, is crucial for the survival of the greater ecosystem.

Koni recalls his former hunting days when his father, who had five wives, would take him before an elephant, pull back, and leave him by himself in the presence of the tusker. His father would tell him to get ready and, when he shot his arrow, to never shoot high. He admonished Koni to aim his arrow at the area where the stomach starts and the last rib met. When asked why he did not aim for the heart, Koni explained that "to get through the heart was not easy and one might hit another organ, but the moment one hits the stomach the elephant will not walk any farther" and would succumb to the poison. Whenever you shot an elephant you always had to make sure there was a tree behind you. You had to be about fifty meters from an elephant and run behind a tree. Always go back to the place where you shot the arrow, the sharp part would stay in the elephant, but the stick would be left behind. After the arrow had been collected, you tied a little grass around it and, tightening it, it was believed spiritually that you were tying up the elephant's leg and it would not go very far. Then you can start tracking it because you know it will not escape. The poison was made from a tree: in ten minutes the poison would go all over the body, and it would not move any more and would automatically start falling down. If it did not fall down, it would still start to sweat and sometimes regurgitate water from its stomach and shower himself. To show that he was the one who killed it, he would cut off an ear, cut it in two, punch two holes and make a rucksack out of it and wear it. Then you would cut a piece of the trunk and apply some blood across your forehead. You cut the tail and have it stand upright on your belt. Then you cut a piece of meat from the head and hang it with a piece of rope on the left shoulder and sing on the way back home. He would get all his clothes off and, standing on top of the elephant, start singing and walk down its back all the way to the tusks. He would take the piece of the trunk he applied to his forehead and put it back near the elephant's stomach. Then he would go back home with a piece of meat. When he got within fifty meters of home he would make sure there were no women who could see him. He would sing and know that now he was real man. His father would know the right song to sing. Then all the mothers and women would sing and celebrate. Everyone would surround him and take him home. Oil would be poured all over his body. He would be told by the village: may all the elephants wait for you, may they never charge you, may peace surround you for all the elephants you kill. In the morning, everyone would leave to go to the elephant. The warriors would have their own home on one side, and everyone else, the fathers, the mothers, on the other side, and in the middle the feast of the elephant took place. They would skin it and then make a long rope from the bark of a tree on which they put all the meat. The meat would be hung up, and oil would be given to the women so that they could prepare the feast. After one week, all the meat was gone. They would move again to a new place. Whenever the men kill, the whole family goes to that kill. The Waliangulu had no permanent home. They moved every ten to fifteen days for their entire lifetime.

> *Two things: the oil and the meat. The Waliangulu don't do anything with tusks. They didn't need it. They even threw it away. You only need the meat. The oil … the women cook it, and they take the meat and crush it, and it becomes light. They put it in a pot with meat and oil all mixed together. Salt was not added so you would not feel thirsty. A big pot of honey … meat was given until everyone was satisfied. Everyone drank a cup of honey … the honeycomb was put on top of a bowl and what seeped inside was collected and drunk. When you ate oil with meat you took in that spirit … when an elephant sees you it will never run away … it will wait for you, it will never get upset … you take your chance and you kill it. We never eat any other food … only meat … never other food.*

When asked about the modern poaching crisis and the desire for ivory, Koni responded:

> *That comes from greediness of money and lack of spirit from the earth. In the old days, we didn't know about the tusks, the only thing we needed was meat not tusks. Somebody who gave you meat from the elephant was a friend. By keeping the elephant we keep the bond between us and our ancestors. The spirit of our ancestors lives in the elephants. In the old days, the Arab could send other tribes called Garama found on the coast, those were the ones who could take the tusks. Because they could keep cows, sheep, and goats and because they could trade tusks for the oil of the sheep. That's how they lived. The Waliangulu*

*never knew tusks were being taken to sell; they knew that tusks were made into necklaces, but not that they were worthy of any money. I believe one hundred percent nothing will be left under the sun, if you cannot stop the Japanese and the Chinese who are buying the ivory, the elephant will be past and history, just like a long time ago. The elephant will not be present anymore. The greediness, the selfishness of money has entered people's spirit, they don't see the beauty in the elephant and the goodness of having an elephant. They even don't need the meat, which is one hundred percent more worthy than that tusk. Today's peoples, today's men are the worst generation ever. If they could stop it, things could be better. The Waliangulu believe if you don't stop doing something it will come back one day and knock on your door asking you why you did it, and you shall not have an answer for it. Get ready to face the consequences.*

*We have one belief, that if you killed a lot of elephants, when you reached a certain number you will start shaking your legs and your body all the time for no reason … you will be running mad automatically … you start talking to yourself because you will have gone beyond the limit number you are supposed to kill. We believe the elephant's spirit needs revenge and by avenging themselves the spirits are making you mad!*

*The Waliangulu also believe that even after the death of the elephant, those who killed more elephants than they were allowed, they are already mad, the very old men, even to date, they are out of their minds. They say we killed elephants, look at how we are, please stop killing, you continue killing you will be like us or even worse than us. We have learned a lesson. We did it, we celebrated, but today we are crying! All of them stopped killing elephants, they don't even want to see anybody else killing elephants.*

*There are those upcoming boys who are being influenced by the money, they are still killing elephants. Some of my boys almost inherited the hunting way, and then I spoke to Richard Bonham about his boys, and because he knew that if they continued hunting like I did they will lose their life, they will lose their value for the earth and lower the dignity of my life as the protector of the elephant. I can give the example of my uncle today, who is mad. If you continue hunting the elephant, you will be like that old man there. All the big hunters, the Ndorobo, the Somali, the Giramaa, all those who have the habit of hunting, if they all come together and have one voice for saving the elephant, and have one voice for being the protectors of Mother Nature, everything will come back as how it used to be. In our time of hunting, you hunted one elephant, these days you use anything that comes to you, from snares to arrows, and some even have guns, they even end up killing three in a single day, and they even go for the kids, the young ones, and that is destroying tomorrow's future. I am trying to appeal to those who buy this ivory, it could be stopped, if no one could cry for the elephant, there will be no more elephant in a few years to come. We are asking the heart of sympathy, for the elephant, for the heart to get to the people and people to understand what is so good about the elephant who is the mother of our own tribe. Let's save the elephant and it will save our future and us.*

*The elephant, which sleeps standing up, slowly you walk up to it, hold the tail, and pull out several hairs. By the time he turns around you are gone. Then you go and make a bracelet, and at the same time, if you put some on your wrist, it is a medicine, it stops your hand from aching from shooting arrows too much during hunting. His father did something miraculous, he tied two tail hairs together from an elephant while he was standing, he went a few meters ahead, shot them, and went back home. He said to the other men around, I have done one thing, I've already shot an elephant, I've put a mark on it, I've tied its tail together. All the elders and hunters said you can't do that! But they saw what he did and he was made a king of the tribe!*

*My grandfather Tise, a prophet, and Galo Galo and Bakuna, the champions, they tracked elephants on the wind side so the elephant could not get their scent, when the elephant relaxed or slept, they sat close and around 1 o'clock, when the elephant was sleeping, very slowly went to the tail, held the tail and one of the hairs and tied two hairs. His arrows that he left behind, he went back slowly, took out his arrow and shot it. When I darted the elephant, I just went back home and told my brothers and neighbors, I tracked an elephant this morning and I already darted it, and I already marked it. Which mark did you do, they would ask. I tied two tail hairs together. One of the neighbors said no, you couldn't, you're lying. I said, OK let's track it. I already darted it. Then they went to where the elephant was darted. They followed the elephant tracks. They found the blood. After an hour the elephant was there, dead. They found his tail where the hairs were tied. I was made a champion. I was celebrated. We sang.*

> *Also, whoever found the afterbirth, the placenta of an elephant, was made a medicine man for sicknesses regarding women. The placenta is respected because it generates life. When a woman is expecting and is having difficulty delivering, she is given a part of the placenta that has been boiled to eat. The mother drinks the soup and even if she is having difficulty, the baby will reposition itself and the mother will give birth in a very safe way. That is why the female elephant is so respected! That is why female elephants are never killed! Waliangulu hunters had to kill 99 elephants, but you do not kill 100. You don't go past that mark. After you have killed 99 elephants, you gave up your bow and arrow because you have finished your task. If you kill 100 elephants, another elephant must kill you because you have gone beyond the number. You can't go on killing your whole life! Those poachers who kill for ivory are cursed. They may fight amongst themselves, the penalty for killing an elephant will go to their family. One day these people will kill themselves! These people who kill without care or any regard, one day they will turn on themselves and kill themselves. They may have a clash within their community. One day this curse will turn back to them. It may not happen to that person immediately, it does not matter how long it will take. One day the spirit of the elephant will go to these people and make them have a clash within themselves! We will win the battle for the elephants because nature created elephants for a purpose. The purpose of nature will win and we will be the winner. Poaching in our day is a very serious issue. If the government does not take any measure to protect the elephant, in the future there will be no more elephants.*

I asked Koni what would happen if we lost the elephant in 2014:

> *That would affect all Kenyans, the wildlife, including elephants, if they are all being poached and killed, the tourism sector will be finished and many Kenyans with their dependence on the tourism industry. The children will lose schooling fees and food … it is a very serious issue. A lot of elephants are killed, it is reported to the authorities, we don't see anything big being done because the poacher will run away! We don't see the government taking this as a serious issue. It is not good at all to be making powder out of the ivory. I want this issue to be stopped completely. Kenya is trying to stop the corruption but it is a very big battle. We can win the battle, if we fight.*

In 2014, in Tsavo, near the Galana, we had the privilege of meeting an 80-year-old former Waliangulu elephant hunter named Koja Badiwa Barofa, who told us:

> *When you were sick, the people who killed many elephants, when they were about to die, they would lift up their hands waving like an elephant's trunk to let people know you were a great hunter. Then they would take you to the bush and bury you. Before we went out to hunt we would pray, so they would not have any problems with the elephant. After prayers, they would check the arrows, if they were sharp enough, and then they would go out with the bow making sure that the bow was strong enough. One man would carry ten to fifteen arrows. When we saw an elephant we would aim for the stomach because in the stomach there is a lot of fat and the fats would make an elephant die quickly. Once one arrow was put in the stomach, then the elephant would make a rumbling sound and you would know that that elephant was going to definitely die. Where the arrow goes into the elephant is where the black blood would start coming out. They would track the blood and within minutes the elephant would be down.*
>
> *A man could not even touch a girl, unless he killed an elephant, or a buffalo or a rhino. Then you are allowed to get married or have a relationship with a girl. We would find a lion with a kill and share the kill with the lion; they would chase away the lion, they would not take all the meat, but leave some for the lion. There was a friendship with the lion. There were words, prayers we spoke to the lion with a kill, and he would walk away. Asking the lion in a respectful way so the lion could move away, but not very far! We would leave the tail and some other part of the meat, because if you took the tail, the lion would not eat the meat! If you took the tail, the lion would follow you wherever you went!*
>
> *When we went hunting we went four or five together. We went to look for waterholes. That is where we would have our camps waiting for the elephants to come and drink. If we didn't get elephants, when we*

*woke up, we would separate, two would go in one direction and two others in the other direction looking for elephants. We were very interested in elephant tracks, how big the tracks were, and also we would have to know which way the wind was blowing before going to hunt. The wind was very important so the elephant could not get our smell. We also depended on shoes made of leather from elephant or giraffe or buffalo. Before we went out we would throw the shoes and the shoes would tell us which direction the elephants were! The direction the shoes face is the direction we always follow. We had trust in that shoe! If you went in the opposite direction of the shoe, some got injuries or did not come back. We also depended on Venus, whichever direction it came out from is the direction we followed.*

*If we went out five times and didn't come across an elephant, we would call the whole family and go to the oldest man, and the whole family would gather in that house. The man would make a traditional brew. The hunters would hold up the brew to the sky, to show that they were praying to God to help them to kill an elephant. We used the fruit of the sausage tree and honey, and mixed them for a brew.*

*It will be very bad if we don't stop the poaching. The poacher is like a robber. We used to hunt, and after the hunting was stopped in 1977 we continued hunting, and were caught and jailed. After we were released, we realized that it was not good to kill the elephant! We were taken to Arusha in exile. The same thing should be done to poachers. The only way to save the elephant is to employ more rangers, so they can be everywhere in the park!*

The red dirt of Tsavo is still blistering from the die-off of tens of thousands of elephants in the early 1970s who had overrun the vast carpet of the outback due to the stress and overpopulation of a species corralled into smaller living areas as a result of human encroachment. In the old days, herds of hundreds would stop traffic and the trains on the Ugandan railroad. Those were the times when travelers would have to wait an hour or more for giant elephant herds from a timeless era to pass by.

The link between humanity in Africa, the original land of milk and honey, and the greatest land mammal ever to walk the Earth is a primal bond forged from the roots of our beginnings. Something imponderable, a mythic membrane, joins our psyches. When we were in Ethiopia right after 9/11, we heard stories about climate change from several tribes, from pastoralists like the Mursi to the Surma and the Hamar. As fiercely proud and independent peoples, their pastoralist ethos is perhaps humanity's most resilient. Pastoralists forged alliances; everyone was a potential ally to be able to survive the harsh arid realities of their environment. When we first listened to the tribes of Ethiopia and Kenya over 20 years ago, we were told that many believed this time to be the "time of confusion" because many of the foundations of society, like the predictable and steady rains, were being undermined. It was like the "dark side of the moon" where one was deprived of clear voices and signs relevant to survival. According to John Reader, "The nomadic pastoralists have developed the only feasible strategies by which people can sustain themselves exclusively from the resources of arid regions. Their population density is low, but that is a measure of the environment, not a defect in the strategy of nomadic pastoralism. But what of the future? It is unlikely that any other means of exploiting the food potential of the land could actually support more people. Enterprises such as large-scale ranching or irrigated farming might produce more cash from the land for a few individuals, but neither activity would employ as many per square kilometer as nomadic pastoralism supports … there is hardly a system of human existence more highly developed than nomadic pastoralism."

We learned that the hallmark of the pastoralists was an ethos of peace. Peace was grounded in a position of always being able to defend one's livestock, and when that thread of continuity was broken, arrogance set in and intertribal raids ensued. Moral superiority issued from a defensive posture. Peace was broken by going on the offensive and taking more than the land and cattle provided. Pastoralists lived in a resilient and mobile relationship with the land. Their wealth derived from the renewable resource of the ground and the rain, wealth that could be admired by all who had eyes to gaze on the patterns of the cattle's back or the ineffable presence of the clouds that brought the life-giving rains. Unlike the technological society where wealth was often acquired by theft or deception, the pastoralist creed was one of true wealth, wealth that is expansive and not driven by arrogance. The elephant, by its very nomadic being, worked in tandem with the pastoralist creed.

We did not see elephants on our two trips to southern Ethiopia, but they lingered in the background of our conscience like the march of some ineffable presence that seeped through the landscape. Much of Africa, it is fair to say, was influenced by the great stature of the elephants. The rainforests of central Africa depend heavily on the forest elephant for seed dispersal and pathways. Elephants inspired empires as long ago as ancient Egypt and later Rome, where elephants roamed North Africa and the Middle East until the fourth or fifth century AD. All over the continent elephant migration paths and therefore corridors infused by elephantine memories have been forged by its behemoth strides. In northern Kenya, we heard allusions to elephants in Turkana stories, where the elephant fought against the malefic forces represented by Satan and the Creator had sent the elephant to do battle with him. Satan's thunder was countered by the elephant's trumpet calls, and the elephant emerged victorious. Satan vanished and the elephant reigned over the world as the representative of the Creator. It is difficult to imagine elephants in the dry, unforgiving, lunar boulder landscape of northern Kenya. But they were once there. Elephants were honored and respected by the Turkana, according to Kenya Wildlife Service officer Patrick Ikaale. During wedding ceremonies, songs were performed to praise the elephant. Seeing an elephant meant rain was coming. If it was seen in the direction of the rising sun, it meant that heavy rains were expected and possibly a downpour. The elephant was seen as the only animal next to God. Elephants were protected because if they disappeared the rains would go away, causing great suffering and starvation to both livestock and wild animals.

Clan elders punished anyone caught hurting or killing an elephant. A clan elder would punish the guilty party by giving a fine, which was in the form of either animals or millet. If the guilty party failed to pay the fine, they were sent away. Indeed, throughout Kenya one can find the expression *Ukiue Ndofu, utalaananiwa,* which means if you kill an elephant, you will be cursed. In the light of the recent elephant massacre, civilization itself should beware lest it lose a species of imponderable significance to the ecology and spirit of the world, a species without whom the soul of humanity will never recover.

In 2001, at Lake Turkana, the famed Jade Sea, we met an elder who was a witch doctor bearing an ostrich feather on his head. As he told us in his hut, "we go with the animals, we are nomads and are afraid of enemies, the Pokot." As the anthropologist Pat Robbins remarked about the Pokot, "Parents of firstborn girls … have powers to chase away large beasts, such as elephants or lions. For instance, if a band of men encounters an elephant on the path, they will ask each other, 'Which of you had a daughter first?' One of them will reply, 'I did.' He will climb a tree, make a noise liked a hyena, and the elephant will run away. If a man whose firstborn was a son tried this, the elephant might attack! The elephant knows." This relationship with virgin girls and their connection to elephants would become increasingly significant, as we would learn later with the Samburu.

This elder came to live at Lake Turkana, whose vehement winds from the Indian Ocean inspire a mythic landscape at the end of time. "In the old days there was always rain, and we lived peacefully. Now there is a drought, because God is angry because of the intertribal battles that have been going on."

Much has changed since the northern frontier was considered the forbidden zone and the Hungarian explorer Teleki first "discovered" Lake Rudolf, as it was then called, in 1887. Occasionally, in the old days, according to the Turkana elder, when raids occurred between the Samburu and the Turkana and the Turkana stole cattle from the Samburu, the Samburu would retaliate by "directing" elephants to rampage or run through Turkana camps, wreaking havoc. How they were able to unleash such power from elephants is anyone's guess. How they communicated with the elephants is one of the great mysteries of African lore and one of the unknowns that continues to haunt us.

The Samburu have a connection with the elephant that is sacred. Ever since they came down from the Sudan to modern-day Kenya, their alliance with and reverence for the elephant has consolidated into a bond. For the Samburu, the elephant was not just one of their clans, a totem, but a brother, indeed an ally, who has helped them endure and survive for hundreds of years. What still lurks in the native imagination none of us can ever fathom, but it is a relationship that is sacred. The first inklings that something more profound resides in the indigenous conscience came to us on our first journey to Kenya with Lysander in 2006.

The Samburu's relationship with the elephant is unique in all of Africa. For most tribes, the relationship with the elephant has been eroded over time, but not with the Samburu. We went to Samburu territory in the fall of 2006 and marveled at our first white rhinoceros. Lysander was just learning how to take confident strides in the bush.

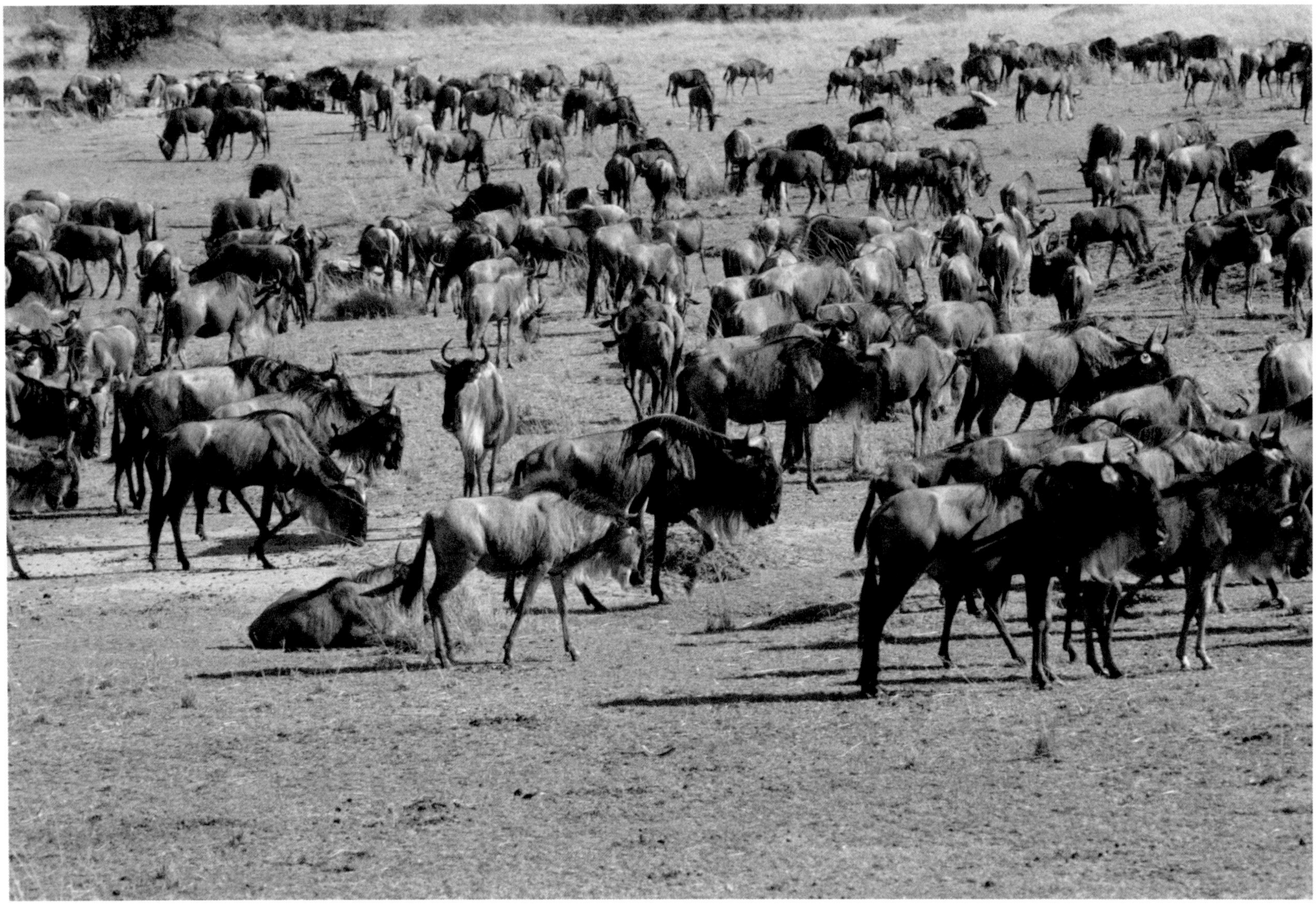

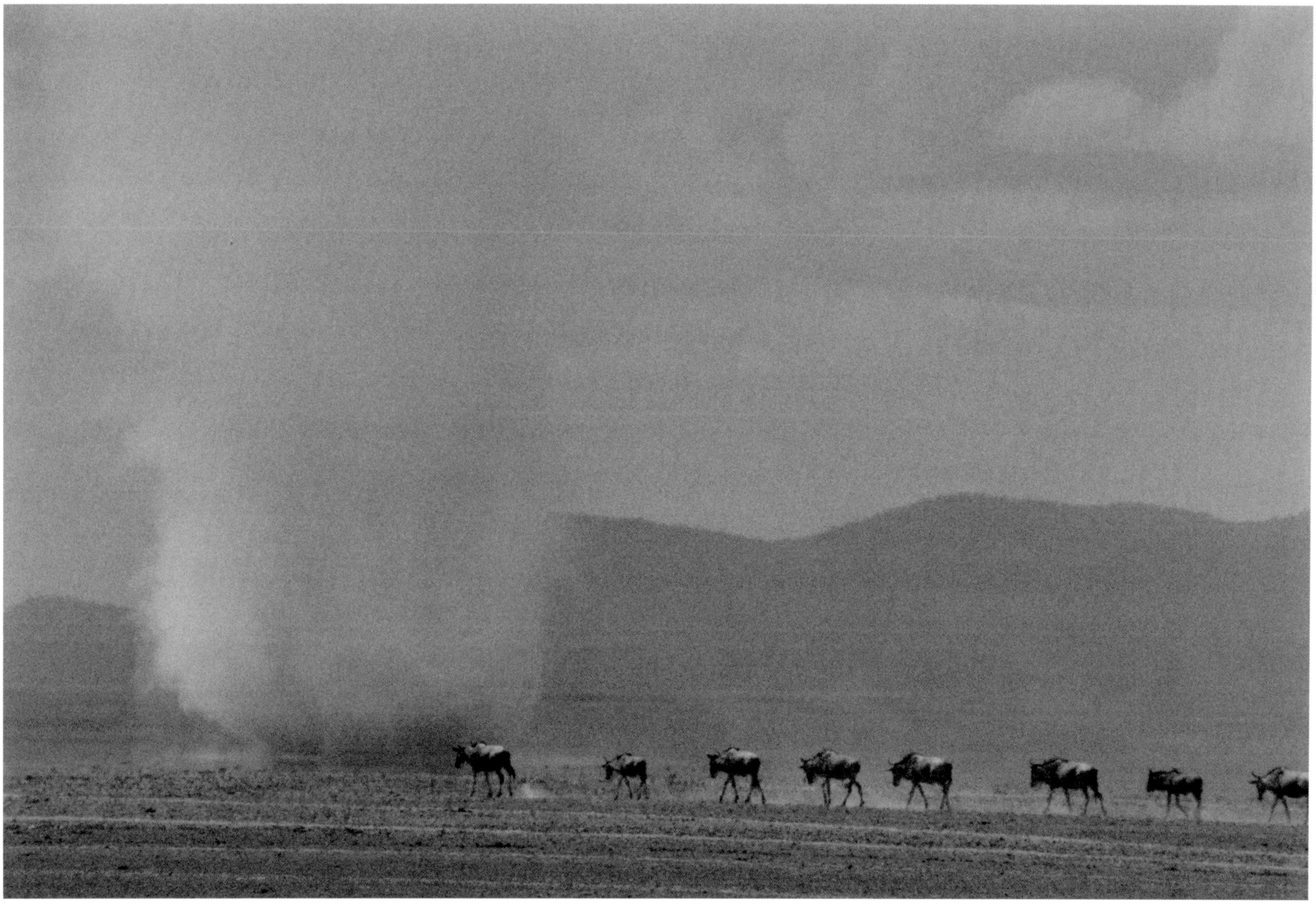

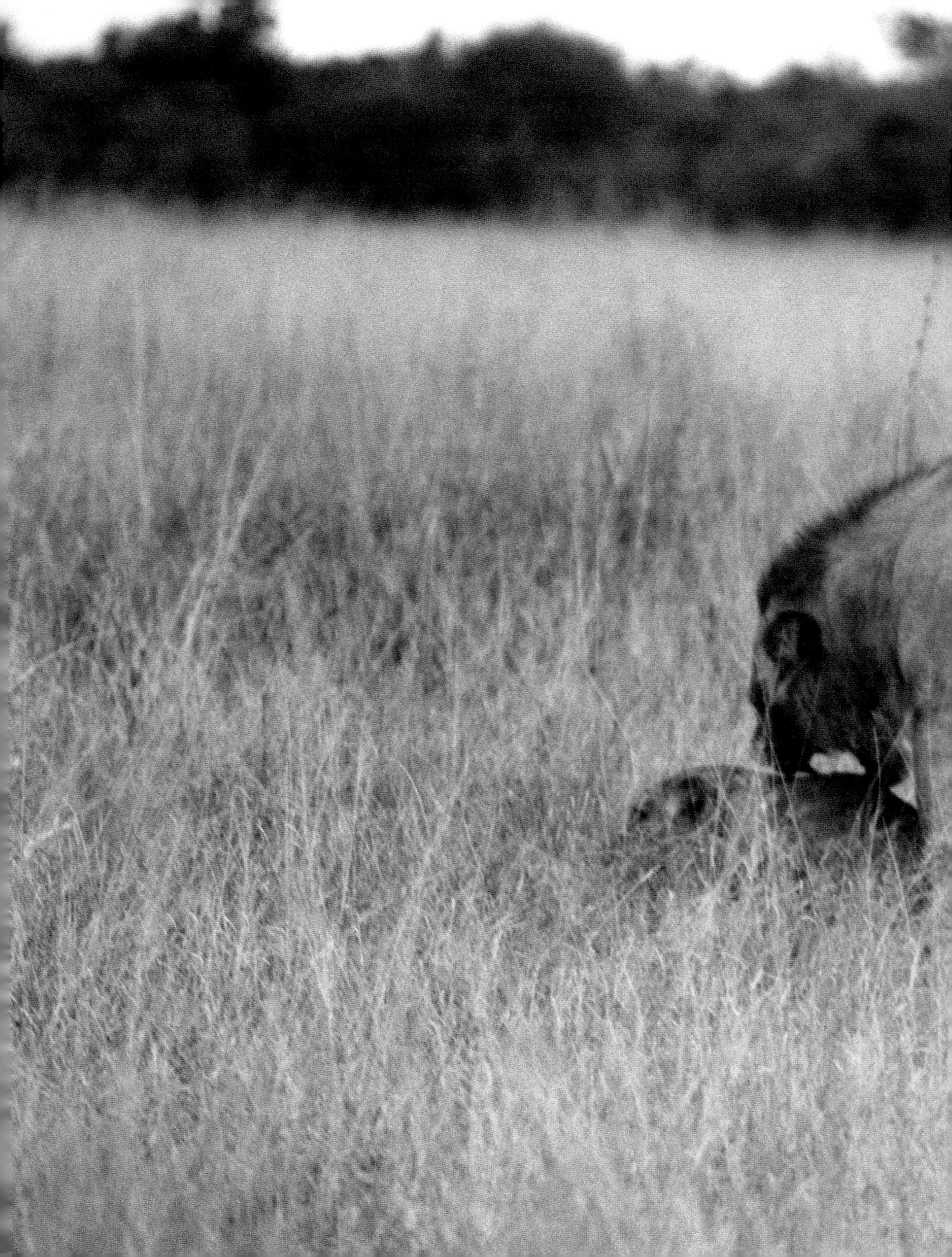

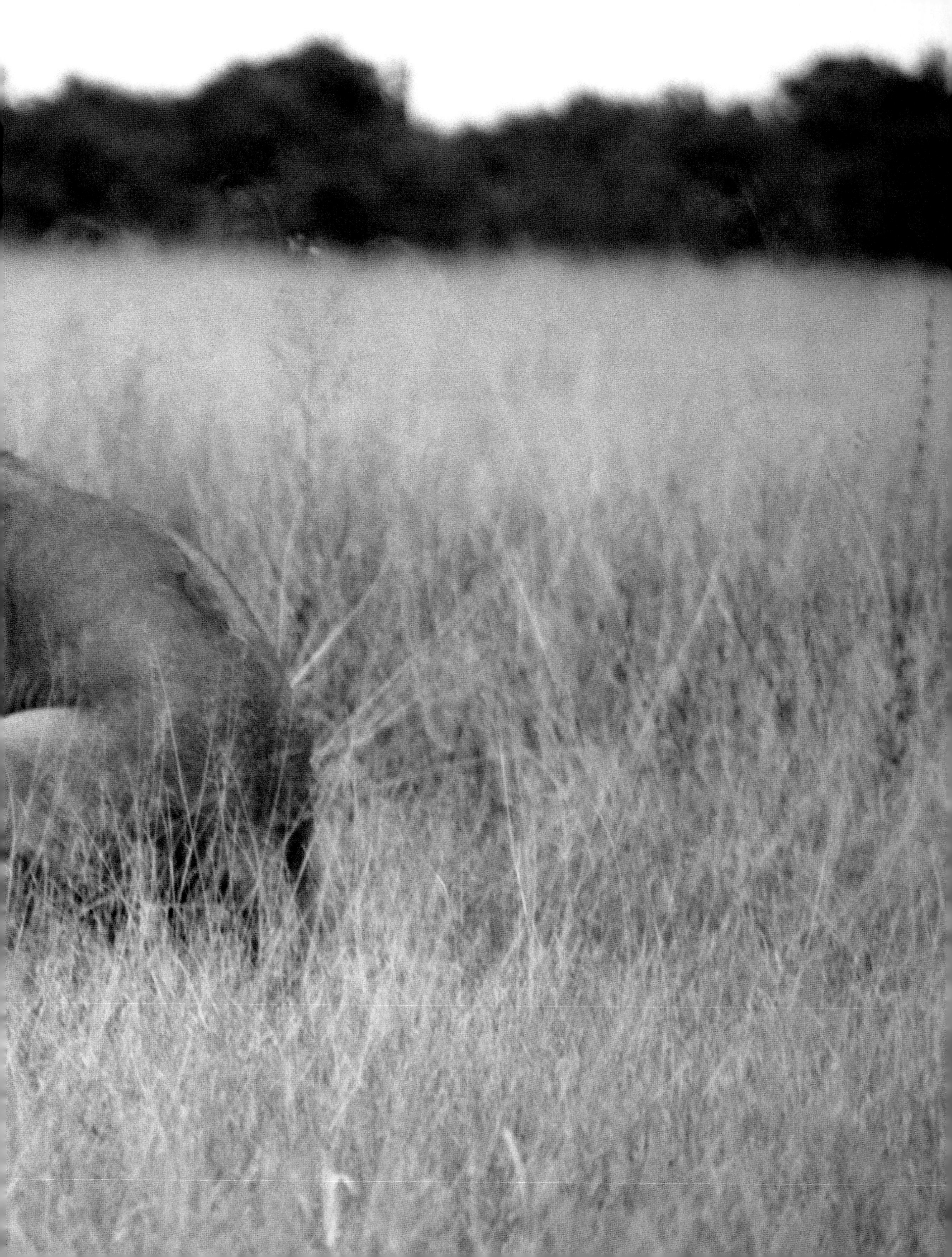

One afternoon, I left him with Marie and went to a Samburu outpost just outside the Lewa Conservancy. I was told about a plant, a humble shrub that supposedly cures cancer, a plant that is perhaps not known to science, but that is well respected by the tribe. One of the junior elders was talking about the rains and how changes in rainfall and increasing drought had made life quite difficult in the last few years for the Samburu. He mentioned how the government often ignored the needs of the pastoralists and marginalized them, while they were warred upon by Somalis and the Boran to the north, who historically had raided their cattle.

One story that suggests an almost psychic connection between elephants and humans occurred in the middle of the last decade. The Samburu have had a unique relationship to elephants for generations. It is a story that bears recounting because it is of an order of mind Jung would have been very fortunate to have heard. It tells of an elephant that had been bothering a local community in central Kenya. This bull had come to partake of a local community's corn, every night for several weeks. The villagers had used every means at their disposal to ward him off. They told the authorities that they wanted to see this elephant move away, but they were powerless to do anything about it. Firecrackers, gunshots, all sorts of schemes had been used to scare off the elephant, but every night he would return. The elder of the village was eventually asked to get wildlife rangers and see if they could do something about this intransigent bull. Rangers talked with the elders and said that they would be at his village the next night, ready with guns to dispose of the bothersome bull. That last night before the authorities came, the elder saw the elephant in the fields and, supposedly, told him using mental powers that he was bothering the villagers and that they needed their corn, that rangers would come for him the next day and shoot him if they found him feeding in the fields. His life was in danger. He needed to go away and never come back to this village. The next day, at the same hour when the bull elephant would have come into the fields, the rangers waited for the elephant's arrival. They waited several hours with gun in hand. They waited and waited. The elephant did not appear and never returned. He was never seen again.

Nonguta Leparashau, a Samburu woman, told us in 2014 how her people once adopted an orphaned baby elephant who had come down from the Sudan hundreds of years ago. Eventually, a bond was forged between the Samburu and all elephants, which led them to accept the elephant as part of their extended family:

> *The Samburu started living with elephants as brothers and sisters even though they are in the wild. The clan of the Lukumai could say something and the elephants would move away. Or a lady could ask an elephant to bring her firewood. We are really glad when others come to see our elephants. We are not ready to lose our elephants. When children go look at their livestock, they know how they can easily go to the side of the elephant and mingle with them. They are friends. Elephants don't kill if no one tends to threaten them, if you don't trouble them. That makes us love elephants. During droughts, elephants can sometimes kill acacias, the branches fall down, the grass grows under those branches and those can benefit us because the animals can feed on those grasses. Now when the acacias are producing pods, the elephants can shake the tree, the pods fall and when we graze our animals they can graze on the pods, and the animals are very happy. That's why we love elephants! When it rains, the elephants go to the dry river beds and dig small holes and when our animals pass by, they drink the water. Even if you go very, very close to them, you just go slowly by, they will not harm you.*

In one instance, the central government, feeling the need to bring the Samburu more up to date, planned on building a dam on their territory, which would have pushed the people off their land. The Samburu, who have an intimate knowledge of over 400 plants, would have been devastated. The people of the community were worried lest they should lose their homes and went to the local *laibon*, or medicine man, who said that he would take care of the situation. But how, people wondered? He was just one man. The medicine man insisted he would figure something out. The people left that afternoon, wondering whether they would be evicted from their homes. The next day several government workers came with their John Deere backhoes and trucks and proceeded to start the survey of the grounds, when out of the nowhere hundreds of African killer bees swarmed and stung the men, who hurried off at full speed and left their heavy equipment languishing behind. They came back several days later to gather their machines, but never built the dam!

Bees are small, but they too have a mind, a mind we do not comprehend. Somehow, on an order of symbiotic resonance we cannot fathom, the *laibon* had summoned the force of nature's mightiest soldiers, who sensed the Samburu plight and came to their rescue. In this time of enormous consequence for the bees, agriculture, and survival as a whole, whatever the *laibon* was able to touch within the larger psyche of the bees was unleashed at just the right time. A part of Samburu land was saved from a potential dam and the bee's territory was saved from drowning!

A few years before Lysander was born, we had been walking in the Matthews Range of northern Kenya, not far from the sacred peak of the Samburu, Mount Ngiro, where water, in the midst of the dry heat, miraculously continues to cascade down its exquisite smooth rock faces. It was at Kitich Camp that we walked amongst elephants, just after 9/11. We kept an eye out for a rather feisty bull called Mugabe and regaled in the elephants' presence, just as humanity had done millennia ago. It was there that we heard the incredible story of about a dozen young elephant orphans, about thirty years previously, in the heyday of the elephant slaughter in Kenya, miraculously attracted to the Matthews Range. They had gone there to seek refuge from the tyranny of the ivory trade wreaking havoc across Kenya and Africa in the 1980s. How they knew where to go is a mystery few of us can decipher. How did they know that sanctuary awaited them among the Samburu? The Samburu came down from the Sudan hundreds of years ago, but separated from the Maasai branch and stayed north, where they are bordered by the Turkana. In their migration they made allies with the elephant, with whom they walked like an extended human–elephant family. Somehow, the young elephants knew exactly where to go and the Samburu adopted them as a part of their own family. The elephants continue to reside there generations later.

There are mysteries in the world science cannot explain. Many are to be found in Africa. Some are hidden in the elephantine mind. We could only imagine them when we climbed the top of Kilimanjaro to celebrate the new millennium in 2000. Twenty-five years after climbing Mount Kenya at age fifteen, I returned with Marie to Africa's highest mountain, as the supreme sentinel of the birthplace of the human race. But today, the world knows that its mythic glaciers are melting and might not survive another generation. Only the black volcanic tuft will remain as a reminder of the havoc wreaked by our civilization. Kilimanjaro's snows have become an icon of a planet melting under the enormous weight of fossil fuels and the ignorance and arrogance of the human species. The earliest bones of hominid evolution are found between Ethiopia and Tanzania, the fossil relics of humanity's relatively short evolution. While mankind burns the global remnants of antediluvian forests, Kilimanjaro's snows are evaporating. What indeed will become of her iconic elephant herds and the fauna of an entire ecosystem.

Leaving base camp at 14,000 feet at 12:30 a.m., we reached the summit a good half hour before dawn. Many arrive only after the glaciers are already ivory white in their luster. We had the good fortune to see the ice change from magenta, lavender, pink to Arctic white. Slowly before daybreak, the clouds below us refracted the triangular shadow of Kilimanjaro as a gigantic beacon over the cloud canopy. Under the hallucinating spell of a full moon, a mirage-like deity crept over the horizon like a gigantic apparition. Between us lay infinities of time and space, eons since the first hominids formed to become the human race. On the summit of the oldest continent, for a brief moment, we felt we could touch the stars. Down below, herds of elephants were leaving the refuge of the forests of Kilimanjaro and making their way to the life-giving swamps of Amboseli, which depend on the runoff of Kili's snows. If the snows were to dry up, what would happen to the game and the village below? The Chagga and Maasai medicine men, legends say, would retreat into some of Kili's caves and meditate for months. Was it in one of those caves where Lenana, one of the most famous Maasai elders, over a hundred years ago, had a vision of the snake that would weave its way across the plains, foreshadowing the railroad from Mombasa to Uganda? It was there, atop the peak, that Ngai, the supreme deity of the Maasai dwelled and oversaw the ways of mortals below. Inside the mountain's being, the elders survived the elements, forecast droughts, and saw into realms beyond the ken of the rest of their people. They absorbed the teachings of the dark within and the light of the forests without, and became initiated to visions few are privy to. As more and more Maasai find themselves lured by the prospects of the modern economy, what will happen to traditional village life?

A thirty-mile circumference holds lions, rhinos, buffalos, hyenas, zebras, and elephants in the Ngorongoro Crater. Its geology, however contained, is unique on Earth, though fraught with the vehicular stress of tourism. Leaving the great caldera, we found an elder, Paramitoro Ole Kasiaro, who explained the changes that had

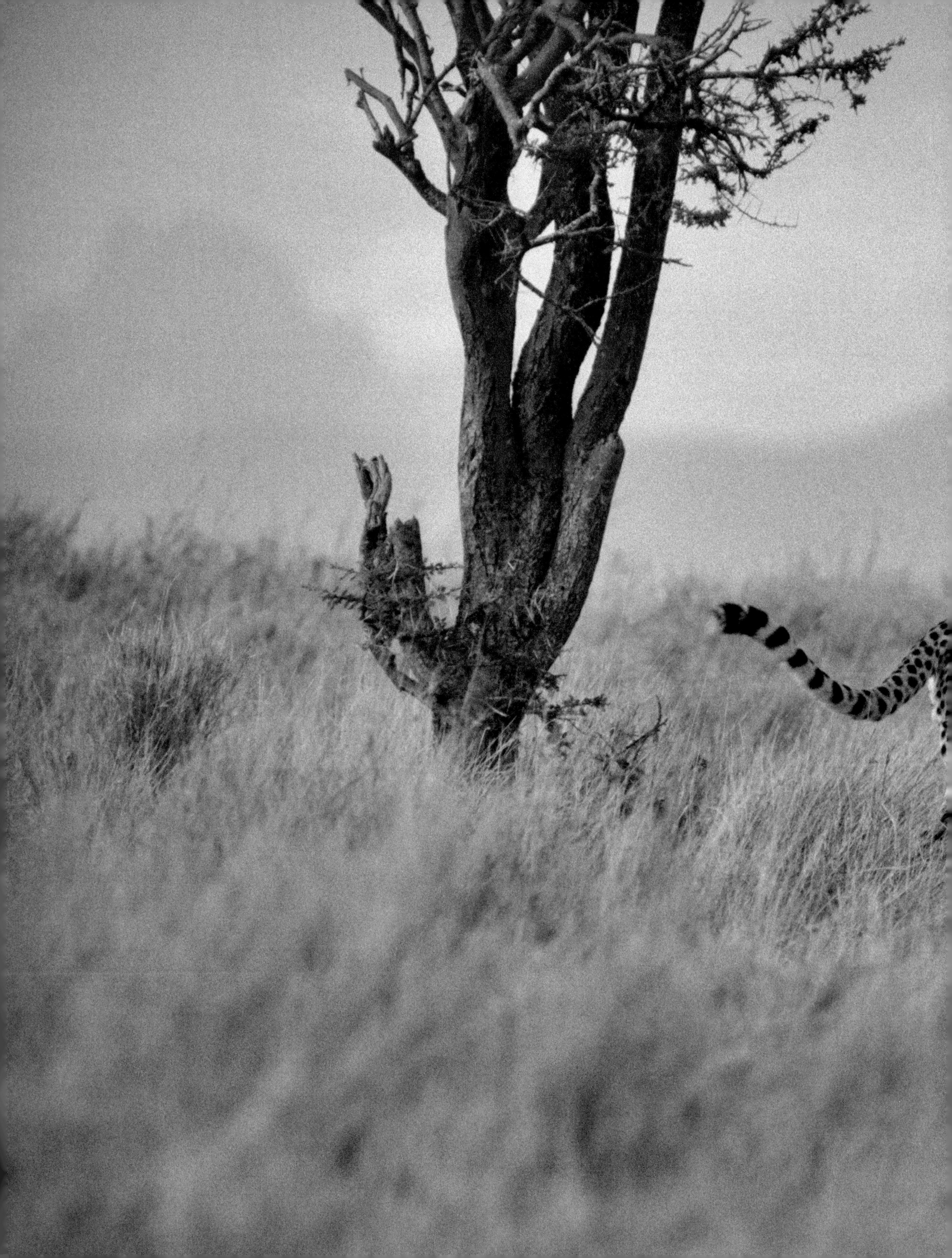

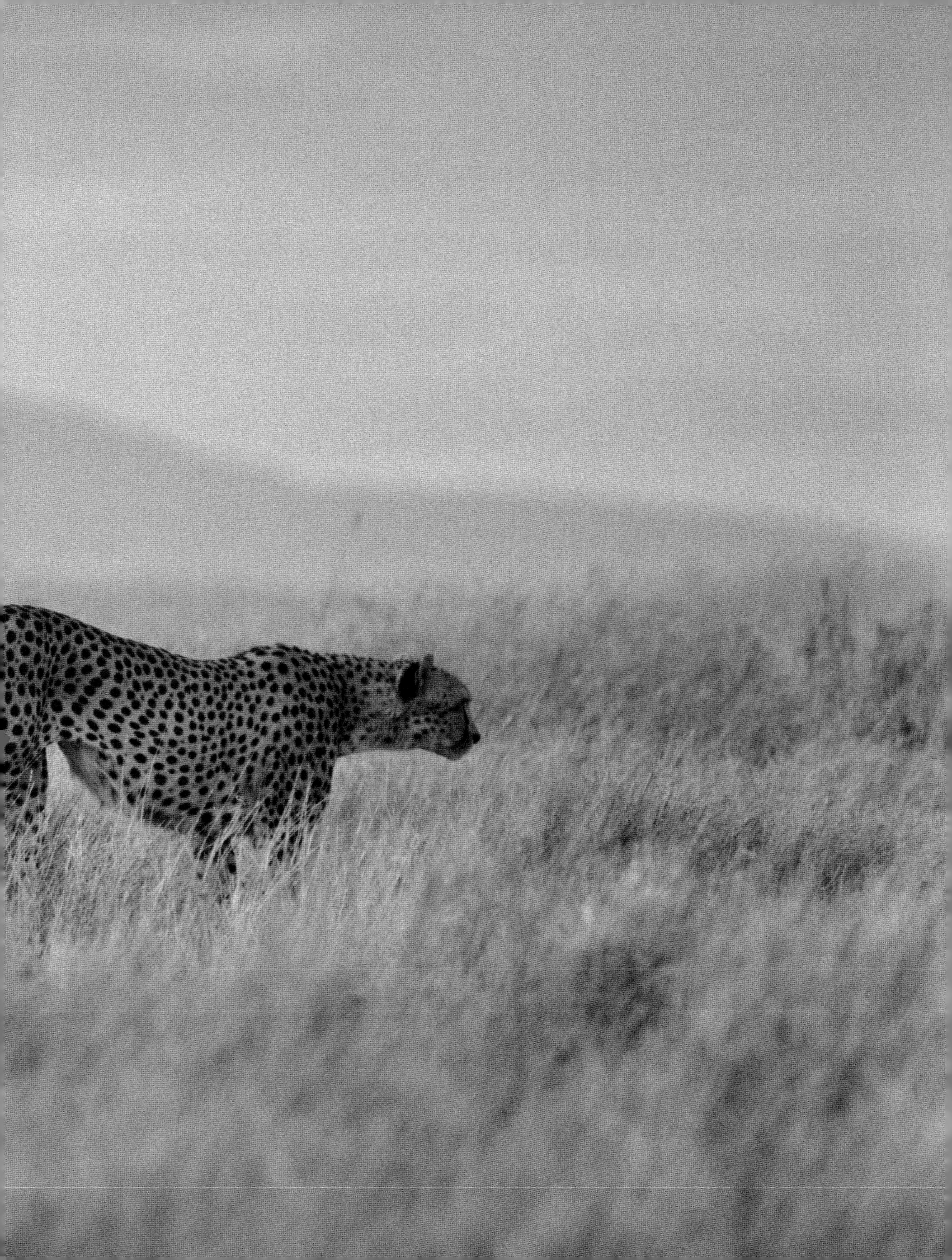

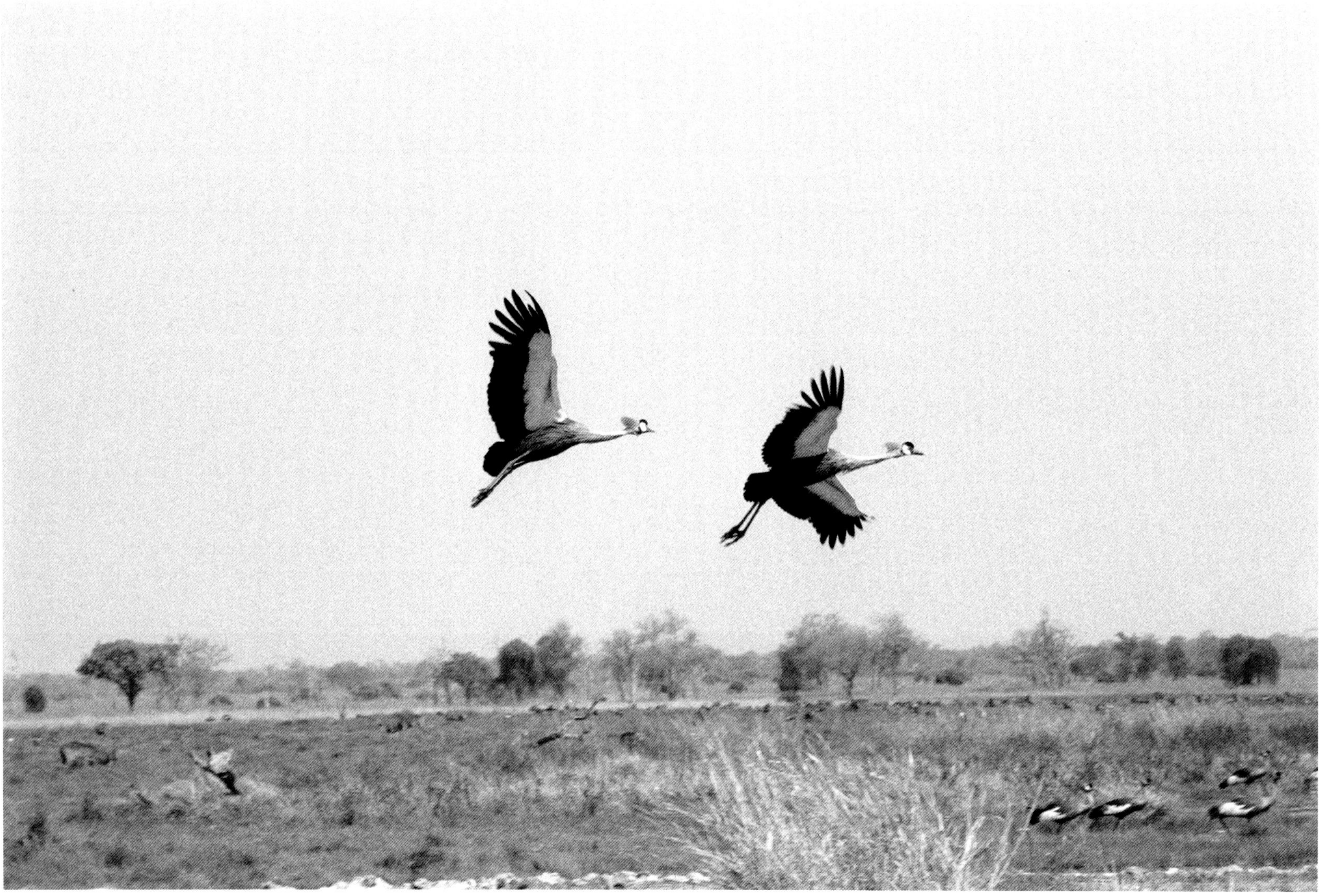

occurred to his people. The Maasai were evicted from the crater in 1974 by field soldiers armed with rifles and machine guns. When most of the cows who were made to walk up the slope turned back towards the crater they were shot. Today, a few Maasai can still take their cattle into the crater alongside elephants for salt and water, but they need a permit. Being a tourist takes no effort and no permit, but the Maasai have no say about the hundreds of foreigners who camp and litter the crater as if it were their private playground.

Kasiaro came from a wealthy family which once owned 500 cattle, until 1990, when disease killed most of the herd. Absorbed by the stalwart conviction in his voice, trying to ignore the squadron of flies that are legion in Maasailand, I listened to the changes that have been eroding Maasai culture ever since the first explorers made contact in the nineteenth century and since Arab traders were repelled by spear-wielding warriors. Kasiaro's pride recalls Beryl Markham's words in her 1942 masterpiece *West with the Night*: "What upstart race, sprung from some recent, callow century to arm itself with steel and boastfulness, can match in purity the blood of a single Masai Murani whose heritage may have stemmed not far from Eden?"

In his red shuka and sandals, which some say were copied from Roman centurions 2,000 years ago, I sensed Kasiaro's concern about where the Maasai were heading, Maasai who believe that the elephants are the only other beings besides humans who have souls. In an age so ruthless in its dispossession of the first qualities of life in favor of the trappings of modern luxury-based civilization, the Maasai, like indigenous peoples all over the Earth, were being increasingly torn between two very different worlds. The upstart race Markham was alluding to manifested itself more clearly in the recent human rights violations against the Maasai by Tanzania's government at the instigation of the sheiks of the United Arab Emirates, who wanted a personal hunting ground in the area just west of the Serengeti, in the Loliondo region, which caused dozens of Maasai bomas to be burned and destroyed. Such violations demonstrate a clash of civilizations at its most blatant. Paramitoro's nostalgia for the old days reverberated in his every word. He emphasized how his people still prayed to their trees and mountains, including the most famous one, the holy strangler fig tree on the crater floor, which is honored with milk, honey, and home-brewed alcohol, distributed in a gourd and poured around the boma where the cattle are kept. Trees have always been found where the Maasai settled. For decades, he exclaimed, Westerners thought that pastoral people were bad for wildlife and the environment, but the evidence suggests quite the contrary is true. Increasingly, conservation activists will have to work with indigenous peoples, they who have cohabited with the wildlife for millennia, if there is going to be any hope for Africa's fauna.

Since the old days in 1958, when the Maasai were forced out of the Serengeti, like so many indigenous peoples worldwide, to make way for Western conservation schemes, much has changed. The Serengeti, which means "extended place" in the Maa language, no longer extends for those who once lived there. Conflicts between the game and Maasai livestock have increased. Short-sighted managerial methods imposed by those who presumed to know better, the white conservationists, have created a theme-park mentality. Westerners who wanted to see elephants and lions have largely failed to grasp that the Maasai, like many tribes such as the Ikoma, who lived side by side with elephants, were part of the entire ecology. The Maasai even considered the wildebeest their "second cattle."

Paramitoro said his peoples were still resisting the "Western way of life" and the Maasai simply didn't see "the importance of education." When some Maasai come home after being educated, they no longer "fit in the environment of the place and don't cope with the tradition of the people." They were learning things that were not relevant to their way of life. Being subject to taxes and the entire system of money hindered the Maasai's ability to be sovereign on their own land. What was at issue, as with native peoples everywhere, was a tribe corralled into the modern global system. Fenced off from nomadic routes they had used for centuries, some had become panhandlers in a world that has co-opted life by the rules of the economic juggernaut. There were predictions that if the Maasai kept losing land they would be forced to become totally sedentary within a generation. Today, the spears of once-proud warriors cannot fend off those intent on profits. Shields will not ward off nor deflect the arrows of a world bent on the homogenization of tradition in the name of progress.

The Maasai have a distant relationship to the elephant because the elephant sometimes comes into conflict with their cattle and livestock. Even though they respect the elephant's strength, they are wary of its power. Paramitoro looked from side to side, as if searching for remnants of a world that had passed. Black sheep sacrifices are still occasionally made. In Kenya the government had opened Maasailand to land adjudication, which would curtail elephant migration paths and open their land to other tribes. The "uneducated" would naturally not know how to litigate or get title deeds to secure land. There would be no process of informed consent if land were taken away from them. Instead, "range schemes," pieces of land owned by foreigners for agriculture of cattle, have taken over Kenya and were plaguing Tanzania. Some Maasai have tried to get work in cities, but often they languished as security guards in a world they no longer recognized. If jobs were not available, shanty towns were the next stage in the acculturation and sedentarization of the Maasai spirit.

Years ago, in his *Autobiography of Values* (1976), Charles Lindbergh described how he came to East Africa and met a Maasai elder. He told him about his exploits and his plane that had traversed the seven seas and crossed continents, and about new ports for steel ships that would open the world to commerce. The elder listened and responded: "We have known a freedom such as you have never known." But today, as the population in Maasailand explodes and as globalization and cell phones intrude on a centuries-old tradition, the imperatives of the technological society are forcing their way on ancient customs. Wildlife is being impacted as much as the traditional way of life of indigenous peoples around the planet. Paramitoro explained that his people were accumulating many things in their homes, shoes, chairs, aluminum wares instead of their age-old gourds and other items the previous generations had used. These things that came from factories were polluting the air and "destroying the environment completely." Even modern cows had failed because they were not as strong, having grown up in factories as opposed to traditional ways of following the seasons and the growth of the grass. Once self-sufficient, more and more Maasai were slowly having to defer to handouts from the government, depending on the vagaries of the modern state, which was slowly eroding their sovereignty. A picture in the New York Times several years ago showed herds of cattle being taken into Nairobi to look for pasture and grass because of the drought and failed crops. What had caused the drought? Why were crops failing? Everywhere "coercively controlled monocultures" were giving rise to ecological violence and erosion. The worldwide "corporate monopoly" was fencing in both culture and crops and, by extension, wildlife. The homogenization and similarization Isak Dinesen had foreseen generations ago were overtaking one of the proudest people on Earth. In the big cities today, one can take to heart what Beryl Markham wrote in 1942: "You know then what you had always been told—that the world once lived and grew without adding machines and newsprint and brick-walled streets and the tyranny of clocks."

We learned from Louis Leakey's research on the history of the Kikuyu that, in the past, the Kikuyu people had sworn oaths with the help of the greatest bone in the elephant body, the atlas bone, which holds the head to the rest of the torso. More nerves went through the atlas bone than through any other. Considering the mindfulness of the elephant and what we are discovering about the compassion and uncanny intelligence of this species, it is no wonder that a seemingly inert bone could hold such talismanic power. What other secrets did the Kikuyu possess with regard to the elephant's power and spirit?

One miraculous story we did learn in Amboseli was from a half Sikh, half Maasai guide named Divan Singh. He told us of a Kikuyu woman who had been renting land and growing crops on a Maasai shamba, far from Kikuyu land. The story seemed like a fable from another time, on the order of myth. One night several years ago, near a town called Ndarara on the border between Kenya and Tanzania, a pregnant Kikuyu mother who was close to giving birth walked in the bush towards a mobile clinic at about three in the morning and was startled by a bull elephant. Her husband thought she had been killed and went back to her village to get help. He came back a few hours later seeing his wife lying on her side. Then he heard the baby crying, the baby was fine. He heard the mother, who was also fine. The elephant acknowledged them, shouted, and walked away. The husband discovered that the elephant had stayed with the mother throughout the birthing process and had gathered acacia thorn branches to make a boma enclosure to surround the mother to protect her from hyenas, lions, or leopards! The baby was called Njogu, which means elephant!

One moment we will remember was during Lysander's second trip, when he was only two years old, in Amboseli. Three young Maasai herders had been walking their two cows to the local waterhole. At first, three cows moved ahead of the boys, then one boy moved ahead of the other boy, leaving two cows on one side and the third behind his friend; then one boy was caught between two cows and his companion behind him and the remaining cow off to the side, until finally all three herders found themselves in-between with a cow on either side in perfect symmetry, just as a herd of elephants came out of the dust in the far distance behind them. That moment became what we would call the convergence of the tribes, the human, the domestic, and the wild, in coherent motion, like very few instances of peace and symmetry in the African savannah ever captured. It is perhaps no coincidence that the Maasai say that only humans and elephants have souls!

We had been hearing stories about the Samburu from Pacquo Lesorogol. In his book *Man on Earth: A Celebration of Mankind,* John Reader wrote:

> *A visitor might find a degree of contradiction in the restrained but obviously deep sense of religious devotion that the Samburu manifest. They live in a marginal environment, often at the very edge of starvation; a hard existence in which there is no room for anything not functionally appropriate. And yet, where one might expect a hard tolerant manner, with little evidence of sympathy or smiles, an air of grace prevails. Grace—there is no better word for it. When elders meet, their greetings take the form of responses—asking after the settlement, the family, the livestock, the land. The replies are positive (any manner to the contrary that need to be discussed will be broached later), accompanied by a slight bow of the head and the word Nkai, Nkai, repeated in supplicatory tones. On parting, senior individuals will offer blessings and again the response is Nkai, Nkai. So the name of god and the word for rain are constantly repeated in the Samburu community; it is impossible for them to speak of rain without there being some reverential connotation. Similarly, whenever they call for god's blessing they bow to the overriding authority of rain in their lives.*

What we did not yet know was how sacred the bond was between Samburu and the greatest land mammal on Earth. It was thanks to Pacquo Lesorogol in 2006 that we started to understand the enormous importance the elephant had for the Samburu. Pacquo was far from his native country in north central Kenya. James, a Maasai translated for us:

> *The elders said we should feel for the wild animals, especially the elephants. We are still concentrating on the elephants … because they can show us the time of the rains. Droughts have been increasing in number compared to 40 years ago. People have been increasing in number. The vegetation has been cut down, which increases the drought. The weather conditions have changed. Droughts have been increasing with each age set who have to be circumcised. But he doesn't know why. Whenever we get rain, we don't get enough. The laibons don't tell people when there will be drought because it will make them very worried. It's better to keep this a secret. They know there is something coming, but they don't want to scare people so they become afraid. Whenever they see something, they say that's already happened. Venus (Kiligin) sometimes crosses the plains from one side, whenever it passes a certain area, the rains will come … when it passes the other side, the rains will not come.*

During this passage of Venus and the coming of the rains, the elephant was and continues to be the clearest and most evident harbinger of the coming of the rains.

The Samburu confide that the elephant is an elder to us—it is taboo to hurt one. Like the Bushmen in the Kalahari, who consider the lion their brother, the Samburu have a bond with the elephant that is unmatched. As a Samburu tribesman once exclaimed, "the elephant was like our brother … we have to live together, not hunt elephant. That's what we say we were told at the beginning. That's what we believe. The elephant has always been, and will always be special to us. That is why we protect it now."

In 2001, a day before 9/11, far from the concrete mayhem and congestion of the urban world, we were lucky enough to be with the Samburu on Mount Ngiro, their sacred peak, a place that looms like a throne rising out of the parched landscape of northern Kenya. At the time, we did not yet recognize the enormous significance of the elephant to the tribe. We had been riding camels for a few days outside Emma Chen's wonderful Desert Rose camp. A year earlier a lion had attacked a camel on the same path. Being stalked by lions is surely one of the most haunting testimonials one can conjure in Africa. We were marveling at the rugged outback and acacia forests of northern Kenya when Marie had a near clairvoyant moment that seemed frozen out of time. It was a prescient foreshadowing of another order of reality. Marie and I were sitting under an umbrella thorn, listening to stories. It was a kind of utter peace that rarely occurs … as if we were suspended in another time, when she felt that something was about to happen that would change the world forever. Everything was still, the trees, the wind, as if partaking of another era. The world slowed down, seemingly in slow motion. Perhaps a portal opened up into another construct of time and space, indeed as if we were entering another era. Later that next day, while seeing the Samburu leaping their famed *empatia* dance, an entire village welcomed us to their sacred peak. To witness the power and the joy, to see those entering altered trance states, to see an entire village honoring the very principle of life, was to affirm a people for whom the reality of the sun was ever present. They leap, like their cousins the Maasai, to honor the life force of the trees. To become like the tree, to not dry up. The Samburu and Maasai jump to honor that which is alive and which grows tall towards the presence of the ultimate reality, the sun. What we were to learn that night issued from the opposite spectrum of reality. Shortly after, all the Samburu had returned to their homes. That night we received a call from our hostess, Emma's mother, in Nairobi. She had heard that someone had just attacked the World Trade Center. Marie had, somehow, prophetically seen through the veil.

"Elephants have a very good brain to think," one young Sonjo tribesman told us at Lake Natron in 2011. In the heyday of poaching a few years ago, of which Tanzania was the epicenter, we heard a remarkable story of how the Sonjo used to honor elephant tusks for rituals. In contrast to those who sought out elephants for their teeth, this tribe respected the very mind of the elephant and saw in the tusk something irreducible in its essence. One one occasion, rangers became aware that the Sonjos had found a tusk in the bush and decided to confiscate it, to the great sorrow of the tribe. That night the rangers put the tusk in a wooden safe, hoping to give it to wildlife authorities the following day. The next morning the tusk was gone. The Sonjo believe an elephant had smelled one of its own, opened the container, and retrieved the tusk, so that it would not fall in the hands of humans who did not respect their kind!

We had been driving from the Serengeti to the sacred volcano of the Maasai, Ol Donyo Lengai. En route along the Rift Valley, we passed by two young Sonjo teenagers dressed in calf skins and holding their bows and arrows, who had been looking for birds or lizards to hunt. "The elephant is very much like a human being. If there is something in the wind, an elephant picks up soil with his trunk and sees which way he needs to go. If he smells a bad smell, he tests the wind to see which way he should go. There is a relationship between the elephant and the human being inside."

In March of 2011, ten years after first journeying to the sacred peak of the Samburu, we returned to learn more about their connection to the elephant. We had driven from Kitich Camp, where we stalked elephant on foot in one of the lushest valleys of East Africa, approaching them from a respectful distance much as tribes had done for hundreds of years. In the Mathews Range in northern central Kenya, Patrick Reynolds astounded us with his knowledge of the bush, from its secret insect life to the great titans who inhabited the hills. Lysander indulged in a wild plunge pool, where elephants regularly came to drink and which seemed like an oasis from the olden days. The Samburu explained that in order to marry, the man had to find a small piece of tusk for the bride to wear on her necklace for the ceremony to be complete. Honoring the elephant was a communion, a great consecration to the totality of the life force. Once we had the opportunity to creep up on a lone elephant, watching it in the distance, mystified by its lonesome stature and gentleness. Most of the other elephants had long disappeared, hunted by the *shifta*, or poachers, looking for ivory, who ran roughshod over the land decades ago.

On our way out from the valley en route to the sacred peak of the Samburu, we were introduced to an elder Samburu woman who explained to us that the elephant was like a brother and that the young women had special powers over the elephant. She insisted that if we wanted she could command an elephant to pass in front of our tent the next day. It was a remarkable offer, but one we did not want to test out of respect for the tradition. In her voice there was a conviction of a bond founded on generations of reverence for a totem that was honored like no other.

Once at Samburu the waters of life flowed from the peak like an eternal fountain of youth. How the mountain was continuously awash with these springs was a miracle to behold. It is there at the top of the peak that their supreme deity Ngai resides. It had been a few years since elephants had been seen crossing the hills near Mount Ngiro, and their passage still lingers in the mind of the locals. Lysander was greeted by Mara the bush pig, who became his stalwart companion during our stay at the sacred peak.

We learned from several elders of their great migration from the Sudan. They told us that a mother and her children on the way down to the Rift Valley had been befriended by a herd of elephants who walked alongside them on their journey south, as if the Samburu were part of the elephant's very clan. It is perhaps easy to romanticize such stories and believe that they are nothing more than confabulations. But on our last trip to Kenya in 2014, some Maasai guides in the Chyulus, where we had spent time listening to the great accounts of Koni, told us of the time only a few generations ago when young Maasai children did play next to elephants and even went under their bellies to witness the elephant mother's full breasts with no apparent conflict. Since that time, before the recent episodes of elephant poaching, humanity and elephant lived in a much less stressed environment and were generally allies in the venture of life. Those who honor the elephant know how significant a species it is. Woe betide our modern civilization if we should become the agent of its demise. I truly believe that civilization as we know it will stand or fall on the back of the African elephant. Slavery and the ivory trade helped build the modern world, and both sins continue to ravage humanity's conscience and Africa's soil as never before.

The challenges of the ivory trade and the increased dissolution of Africa's wisdom and lore continues to erode a centuries-old knowledge base, wisdom which was handed down from generation to generation, knowledge of plants and the land and patterns of being, that we will all need to survive in the coming century. Conservation needs community-based approaches where the indigenous people are consulted and allowed into the larger conversation. Shared stewardship is the only model that will work. The exclusion of native people is a grave mistake and needs to be reversed.

The Ogiek community in Kenya is another example of people who have been ignored in the decision-making process, especially as they try to hold onto their Mau forest in Western Kenya. Forcibly evicted from their ancestral land by the thousands, the Ogiek, one of the oldest hunter-gatherer tribes in Kenya, told us stories of the times when they used to follow ancient elephant migration paths. They also ate the olerondo fruit just like the elephants, but today times have changed as they have become casualties of the modern state, living in ramshackle houses. As the indigenous inhabitants of the Mau forest, they have been victims of abuse and humans rights violations by the local government for years. As an interior ministry official in charge of security remarked, "You tell me that people can survive on honey and herbs. What a nonsense story. Nobody dwells inside a forest." The Mau forest is one of the very few remaining forests in Kenya, where the Ogiek used to gather honey and hunt antelope and hyrax. "There is no such thing as a forest-dwelling person—these are misnomers. The forest should not have people residing there. With the evictions, what we are stopping is destruction, by Ogieks, and by other Kenyans, and we make no distinction." Cattle grazers have moved in on the land and an age-old alliance with wildlife is being sundered, perhaps forever. The bias against indigenous people all over the world is one of the grave iniquities of our time. They who hold the ground as sacred are the best caretakers in the world; they should be permitted a stake and a voice in their future in this tumultuous time.

Conservation all over the world, not just in Africa, needs a bottom-up approach, a grassroots approach. Humanity needs a paradigm shift today. The first peoples have always been the best stewards and custodians of the land and the animals. For far too long native people have been the victims of conservation schemes, for instance by moving native peoples out of prime tiger habitat in India. Tribes from the pygmies in the Congo to the Penan in Borneo have been affected. When the colonial powers invaded Africa, the wildlife indeed became a game to be dominated for pleasure, for fun. Lions and elephants, rhinos and buffaloes were shot for trophies, no longer for self-defense or for rites of passage as with the Maasai. It is our perverted relationship to the wild that we must correct, for in the end it is not only the wild, what Mirella Ricciardi called "wilderness freedom," that is at stake, it is also the essence of much of the human family that is on the line, whether in Africa, the Amazon, the Arctic, the forests of India, Indonesia, or the rest of Asia, where the world's last tribal cultures are struggling to survive.

As Laurens van der Post pointed out in *The Dark Eye in Africa* (1955), "For Africa, from earth and beast up to the most intelligent of its indigenous children, is not letting this loss of soul take place without a terrible struggle." Africa's soil and her soul, her people and her inimitable wildlife are undergoing trials the likes of which she has never experienced. The Gibe III dam in Ethiopia, prostrate to the demands of modernity, could alter forever a millennia-old way of being for the tribes of the Omo River that will never be restored once lost. It is time to ask if the foundation of much of what makes Africa unique needs to be sacrificed to the Moloch of modernism and the profit system of globalism. Indeed, will Africa still be Africa?

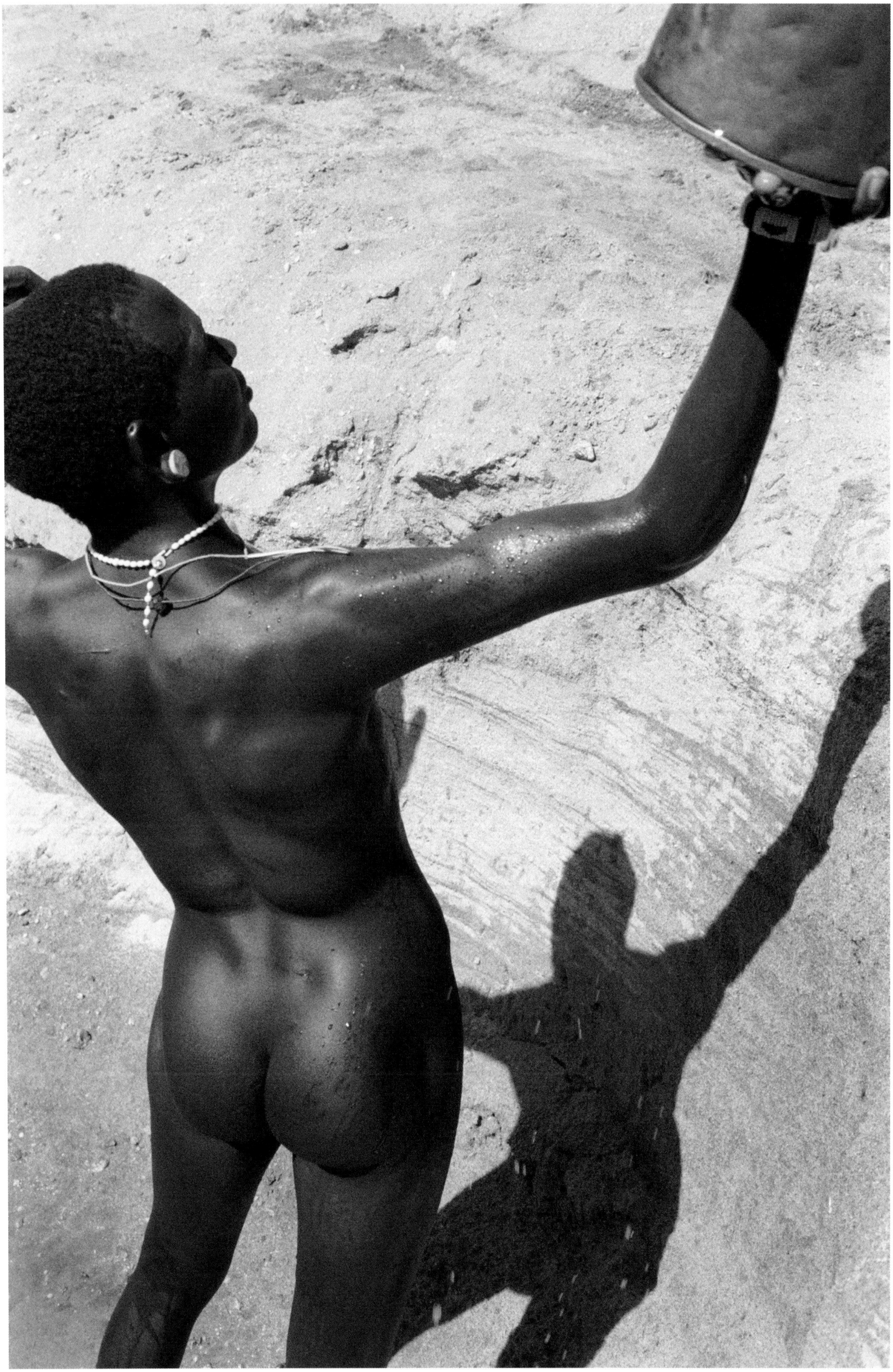

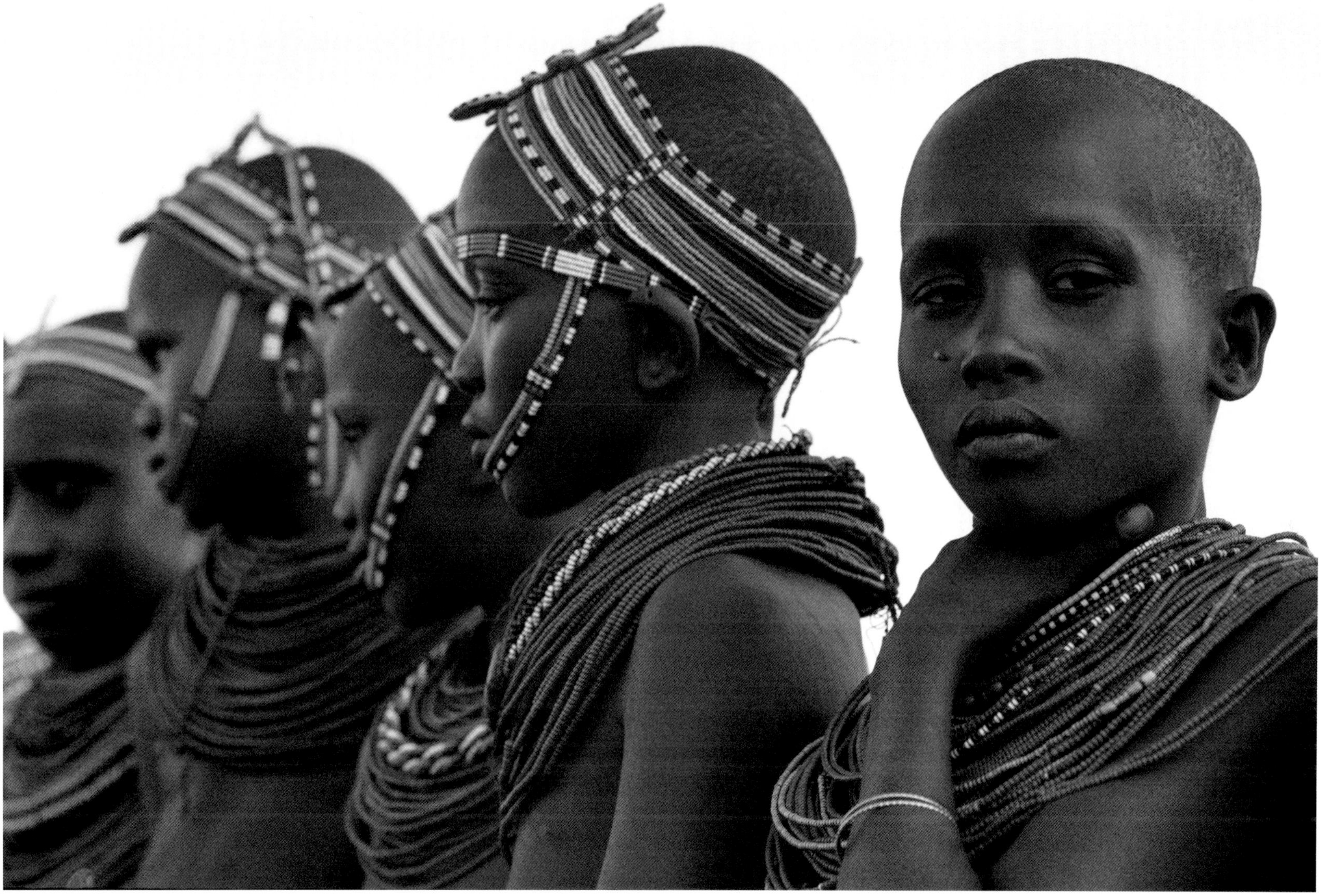

There may be those who say that amidst all the human suffering in the world, in the Middle East, in Ukraine, in refugee camps in Myanmar, and especially in Africa, why should humanity care about elephants and wildlife in general? We heard the answer in New Mexico, where we had the chance to meet a charismatic elder, a rebel soldier, Christian Bethelson from Liberia, who was involved in the revolution against and who fought the regime of the dictator Charles Taylor. He told a remarkable story of 1,200 men who fought Taylor's forces. They were taking a bypass to get to a town called Jonestown. Someone told them to look up, as there was "a huge creature just standing like a wall between the government's forces and the rebel force." Since his birth in 1958, Christian had never seen an elephant.

> *It was so astonishing! This was a sign of peace. So the 1,200 men all laid down their arms right there! Seeing an elephant was a sign of peace. The elephant brought a cease-fire and total peace. Some people did not believe the elephant was peaceful. Some of our men ran. One of the men who left us went to another front in another part of the country to fight and in the process got killed! The elephant is so connected to us. When I went to Tanzania many elephants came close to our vehicle. I could see elephants in a social way, which was so profound for me. I believe the elephant saw the tears of our women in the war and prayed for peace to come. Both sides did see the elephant. We laid down our arms. We need not disturb the peace of the elephant. We need to protect the land. We need to have a profound relationship with the elephant. Let's see how we are connected. The sense I got was I felt the elephant did care for our suffering, that women and children had been killed in war. The elephant said OK it's over and from that time on, not a single bullet has been fired at all in Liberia! Seeing an elephant made me change and made me peaceful and changed my life. The elephant was a peace ambassador.*

With regards to the Ebola epidemic that caused worldwide concern in 2014, much of the outbreak was in Liberia, where forests were badly decimated and where bats had lost their home. As Bethelson explained, "We have to preserve our forests so we won't get crazy. When we disturb the peace of the elephant like in the Ivory Coast, what happens, total chaos! Because the elephant was no longer friendly with the people. We had a lot of elephants in Liberia. What happened? We disconnected ourselves from nature. But now we know the significance of elephants.

How can you take the tusks of an elephant? In reversing the process of global warming, we have to stop hunting elephants! They mourn their dead! The younger ones respect their elders. We can't destroy the life of the elephant. I'm begging the world, I'm begging Africa to protect the elephant. If they can listen to me, can cease hunting, we will have a vibrant peaceful Africa because of the peace of the elephant. How will Africa survive? In Liberia the antelope, the chimpanzees have come back. Liberia used to be a very beautiful country of peace. There is no way we can survive without the elephant. There is no way we can ostracize the elephant from the face of the Earth! This act of killing elephants is not acceptable for a civilized society. The elephant has a right to live. No one has a right to kill elephants. It's always human rights, human rights, human rights, what about the rights of the elephant! It's always the human race, but the human race is destroying the planet! Why can't we start in a global sense to advocate for elephant rights and see how the world will turn!"

It was in 2008 that we started hearing about renewed elephant poaching in East Africa, especially in Tanzania. In 2009 we tried to encourage the media to listen to the massacre of the innocents in Africa, the second such time since the 1980s, when over 600,000 elephants were killed for the ivory market in Asia, led by Japan, which needed ivory for Hanko stamps used by businesses all over the country. No one listened. Even the New York Times told us they were not interested in elephants. The economic downturn, which helped fuel the lust for ivory, was more important. That the greatest being walking the Earth was to be rendered lifeless for small bars of ivory is beyond criminal. We imposed on the elephant what we had been doing to ourselves for millennia. I took the liberty of calling Elie Wiesel about the elephanticide and urged him to use his voice in protest against the slaughter. We talked about what had happened in World War II, and although he insisted there was no similarity, I responded that if humanity were to lose the elephant forever, the karma for the planet, for life on Earth would be worse than what we did to ourselves during the war. He acknowledged that to save the elephant is indeed' "an urgent moral imperative." I tried every major magazine I could, all of them rejected a piece on what was exploding in Africa, until the editors at Vanity Fair, after five months of urging on my part, finally accepted, and in November 2010 sent Alex Shoumatoff on a five-week investigative journey from Southern Africa to Central Africa and Tanzania. The result was the tremendous "Agony and Ivory" article which finally came out in August 2011, galvanizing the planet and the conservation world. The fight for the elephant prompted a flurry of responses ranging from WildAid to Save the Elephants and many other groups to campaigns inside China to alert people to stop buying ivory. Yao Ming used his voice from his days as a basketball player in the NBA to help a fifth of the planet understand that the future of the most magnificent being on Earth was on the line. By the end of the decade the tide had turned and China, the biggest importer on Earth, decided to close its markets in late 2017. The black market continues and there were collectors banking on extinction, so elephant ivory would jump in value. Such is some of the perfidy of our species, but while the peak of the massacre could be said to be behind us, there are still individuals who believe in slaughtering elephants for sport. In early August 2020, an American killed a young elephant in Africa with his shotgun. It seems that despite the shutting down of entire markets amidst a pandemic that has upturned the world, the germ of evil for those who believe themselves superior to the animals will never be able to be eradicated. We have embarked on the defining decade of human civilization. It is not enough that the Chinese and other Asian countries encage animals, whether they be wolves, foxes, bears, pangolins, bats, civet cats, or buntings in wet markets; their germs have infected the world. The animals of the world, their karma, have returned the favor to the human species for millennia of abuse. It is now time for humanity to acknowledge that it is but one of hundreds of thousands of species living on the only planet we know of in the universe that harbors life. And certainly the only planet in the universe with lions and tigers and bears! The climate within the human heart will have to be radically altered and finally learn respect in a way we have never done before. Otherwise what remains of the life force of Earth will bring us to our knees.

Climate change will have its impacts. In Botswana, in July of 2020, about 300 elephants died, their tusks intact. Southern Africa underwent tremendous drought. The stagnant pools of water helped create cyanobacteria pools which contain toxins that affected the elephants' central nervous systems. Animals all over the world, from the polar bears of the Arctic to the penguins of Antarctica, will suffer from man's ignorance of the atmosphere and what industrialization has wrought. Elephants may not be shot for ivory as they were in the last decade, but they may have a more indirect, long-term, and insidious foe in the form of a fast-changing environment. Whatever elephants have to endure in the bush will surely boomerang to the hundreds of millions of humans trying to cope in the heat of a novel planet. And some individuals continue to seek out trophies, as if it were a talisman, as if some aspect of an elephant could imbue their being with a manhood never there to begin with. The cowardice, malice, murder exhibited on the innocent is one of the hallmarks of our kind, and for this we will be branded as outlaws and pariahs among the species. It is evil incarnate. As the world tries to enact and abide by the Convention for Biological Diversity, the elephant sits on top of the pantheon of creatures looking at the human species and is wondering if we are up to the task. Because in the end, it will not be the stock market that decides whether we survive, but the ability to salvage what remains of Creation in this crucial time.

The bushmeat trade and poaching menace the world's wildlife as never before. Animal populations worldwide have lost an estimated 70% of their number in the last few generations. At some point in this time of the sixth extinction, mankind will have to realize that it cannot remain on Earth without the other species. Even the bees, especially the bees, are menaced. This is why this decade has to be the turnaround decade and why humanity has to come to abide by the Convention for Biological Diversity to parallel the Paris Climate Agreement. It will need hundreds of billions of dollars to save what is left of the forests of Earth and its species and what still survives in the oceans. Human consciousness began in Africa, but the struggle to survive will depend on a worldwide effort with the oldest continent at its heart.

I asked Pacquo Lesorogol, a Samburu elder, about humanity's future if we lost the greatest land mammal on Earth: "People too will be finished. There will be nothing to return to. The only thing left will be to kill on another. We will lose our minds." A hundred years ago, Baron Bror von Blixen, husband of Isak Dinesen, wrote in his book *African Hunter* (1938): "For some reason or other, fears of the total extinction of the elephant are sometimes expressed. Allow me to declare that there is no danger! If anything the opposite is the case. I cannot give any exact figures without reference to the elephant statistics, but there is no doubt that the race is increasing. Even today herds of a thousand strong are no rarity." When will our species ever see such herds again?

The lions, the elephants, the antelopes of Africa, their populations are at a crossroads before the juggernaut of the human species. Indeed, nature is what ultimately stabilizes the human psyche. The failure to honor a totem such as the lion by depraved trophy hunters, who shot 5,000 in the last generation, not only depletes the gene pool of Africa, it creates turmoil in the ecosystem and ultimately disrupts the stability of the native people of the continent. Terrorists and armed groups looking for money to fuel their insurgencies killed untold numbers of elephants for their ivory to fund their operations from Central to West Africa. The second decade of the twenty-first century was a demonic period of nearly unparalleled proportions. Locals, poor villagers, and unpaid park rangers were killing their greatest patrimony for ivory. Kony, the head of the rebel group Lord's Resistance Army, lusted for ivory for his operations to try to overthrow the Ugandan government. 1,000 traumatized children were abducted and co-opted into the LRA as soldiers. Even their parents thought their children had become devils. In light of such realities, the fauna of Africa has suffered beyond measure. It is a lesson humanity should never forget nor repeat.

The decimation of the black and white rhino for Asian superstitions about health should shame us all. They once dotted the landscape in the tens of thousands, like the graceful giraffe, which has in recent years also seen a 40% reduction in its population. Will the children of Africa be told that giants once roamed their motherland? Will they too be told, "This is where the wild things were?" Sadly even the "wooden elephants," the great baobab trees that have lived for thousands of years, are cracking under their own weight, due to climate change and drought. Just as several sequoia far away in California were felled by high winds in early 2021. This generation could be the last stand for the great legacy of the Pleistocene that created modern man. Without the other beings, what on earth will we become?

With the mechanistic ethos of maximum growth and profit, the second decade of the twenty-first century has clearly brought much of the organic world to the edge of a biological cliff. Native peoples were and are beholden to a complete cosmology, one that recognized bees as well as elephants and every life form as having an intrinsic and irreplaceable life force unique on Earth. Bees that yearly bring 170 billion dollars in revenue are being sacrificed to the toxins and pesticides of modern agriculture. Diamonds, which have created havoc from West Africa through the Congo to Botswana, where the Bushmen have had to suffer the shame and genocide of their peoples for hundreds of years, bring only 25 billion dollars a year. The Congo's estimated untapped mineral deposits of cobalt, gold, tantalum, tin, and gold may exceed 24 trillion dollars. Its lithium deposits, which are indispensable for cell phones, laptops, digital cameras, and electric vehicles, may top 1 trillion dollars. Indeed, how will the rainforest survive the onslaught?

In *Foreign Policy* magazine in the summer of 2018, just as the thickest ice in the Arctic was melting, with enormous implications for the planet, an article reminded us of the ethos and importance of indigenous knowledge to conservation and the future. Indigenous people form only 4% of the world's population, but are the caretakers of most of the world's biodiversity. Will the Selous in southern Africa, the largest reserve on the continent, be sacrificed for a dam and the blood wages of globalization and modernization? What will Tanzania turn to if it sacrifices its land for energy and money? How will the Uganda–Tanzania pipeline pollute these countries? Will the Congo rainforest be sacrificed for palm oil plantations and lumber, as has happened in Indonesia and the Amazon?

The elephant is the greatest stabilizer and fertilizer of land, both in the savannah and in the rainforest, and its present decimation in the ecosystem, along with the rampage of warlords across Africa, lusting for blood ivory, has dismembered an entire continent and threatens the planet as a whole. Indeed, if the peace of the elephant were to be restored and the ivory trade shut down once and for all, will the continent see less bloodshed? The potential loss of the elephant, an inconceivable loss, would mutilate our place on Earth forever. The physical desecration of this great animal is similar to the wars man has visited upon himself especially in the last century. The elephant is the greatest terrestrial buoy for the future of the human spirit. Lose it, and humanity's soul will no longer be recognizable. The native peoples, who know the elephant best and who have worshipped the spirit of the ancestors for millennia, will only have images on their cell phones to contemplate the vast beauty that once was, longing for the greatest pillar of life on Earth, the elephant.

The rainforest of Africa is the second largest on Earth. Species like mandrills, okapis, rainforest elephants, and countless others fertilize this vast green canopy that Africa desperately needs to hold onto. Palm oil plantations and lumber companies from Europe, Japan, China, and the United States are slowly eviscerating an area of woodland larger than western Europe for furniture and palm oil. Small-scale deforestation due to poverty is having an impact everywhere. This forest, too, represents the future of this continent and in large measure is an essential part of the future of the planet. In this decade we will have to measure whether humanity can salvage its original home. The Congo rainforest could be gone by the end of the century, which would affect the rainfall of an entire continent.

Africa's population could increase by a billion over the next two generations. What will be left of the wild? What will be left of the herds with whom our lineage evolved, the very species whose blood and flesh enabled us to survive? Lions, who orchestrate the grandest sound in Africa alongside the elephant, are disappearing fast, and could be gone within 15 years. No one will want to go to Africa anymore. Only the "Lion King" in cinematic form will remain. We have to heed the warnings. A pandemic of loss is stalking the world. What will the children of the future have to look forward to? Animals, their grace, their very being in the world, have always been children's first mentors. Without them, what will become of childhood itself? As Lysander, whose photograph adorns the cover of this book, once exclaimed when he was only ten years old, "Mining and exploding mountains is like playing with fire and right now in this day and age, people are blowing at the candle of life."

One story we recently heard was gifted to us by Elijah, a Maasai guide in the Chyulus, the volcanic region in southern Kenya overlooking Kilimanjaro. When I camped here aged fifteen, I saw once-plentiful herds of elephants feeding a mere hundred feet away. Elijah told us how the Maasai respected animals and that children were told never to disturb baby animals in the wild. "When the children go to graze and find a gazelle foal, or find a zebra colt, they don't harm them. When you go with your mother and somebody kills her, how do you think you will feel? The way I feel about you being damaged by an animal is the same way that an animal feels when you kill her baby. When the Maasai interact with animals, they have that feeling, we have the teaching from our parents. They are being taught, don't ever take even eggs from an ostrich or egg of any bird because you are destroying the family. When the children grow up and do something carelessly, that child will be punished, because he or she did something wrong. They should be responsible. They get along with this sort of wilderness and the wild will respect them." There was a bond between humans and animals, but one that is in jeopardy as the modern Maasai seek to increase their cattle, which is their wealth, pitting conservation lands against Maasai livestock who seek new pastures.

Elijah's story tells of a young Maasai woman, maybe ten years ago, who had given birth to her child. She was to walk from her house to join her husband in their new home. She was walking alone and out of the blue a male lion recognized that she was alone with her newborn and most definitely vulnerable. The lion started to walk alongside her at a distance, stopping when she needed to rest and escorting her over the distance that she was traveling. That night, in the middle of nowhere, she rested against a tree and the lion was by her side, making sure no predators would disturb her. He even fended off hungry hyenas and other marauding lions. The next day, after having walked maybe twenty kilometers, everyone greeted her and wondered about the lion. She explained that this lion was special and that he had saved her in the night. He had escorted her on her journey and kept her safe from hyenas and other lions. The elder of the village was very impressed by this unique and compassionate lion and decided to sacrifice a goat in his honor. The lion ate the goat and moved off into the bush. This almost miraculous tale of altruism is extremely rare, but one that should force us to rethink our relationship to the other and reflect on the consciousness that resides in the entire animal kingdom.

Not that long ago, animals were at the core of much of our being. Whether in stories of transmutations, or of myth and origin tales, children were introduced to life and many learned to speak, as our son Lysander did, learning the names of animals. Whether it is the Ogiek, the first hunter-gatherers of Kenya, who so depended on the African bee for their honey, or the Turkana in the north of Kenya, who hunted crocodiles, or the Bushmen's millennia-old kinship with the lion, or the Samburu's alliance with the elephant, humanity is indebted to the other species as part of its very flesh, its evolution, as the backbone of its very spirit. But the bushmeat trade, exacerbated by logging, continues to threaten hundreds of species, including the great apes, the chimpanzees, the mountain and lowland gorillas, and the bonobos. Can we even conceive of the day when we lose our closet living relatives? If the present pandemic does not threaten their survival then surely the unconscious habits of one species, ours, menaces them with the malevolence of the human strain and the continuing bush trade.

All over Africa, where national parks were created, the expulsion of its first peoples continues. Whether it be in the Mau forest of western Kenya, where the country's oldest inhabitants, the Ogiek, fight to retain their land, or in the Simien Mountains in Ethiopia, or in the famed Maasai Mara. Or in many parks in Tanzania, Rwanda, and the

Congo, where human rights violations have impacted the Batwa Pygmies. In all these place, indigenous peoples have been separated from their original home. Increasingly, as in other parts of the world where national parks have been created, pastoralists, farmers, and hunter-gatherers have become pariahs.

Africa and the rest of the world need to forge a new covenant between what remains of the wild and humanity, for the two must work hand in hand. Worldwide, the homogenization of space is gravely impacting the ability of animals to roam. Whether it is by blocking migration corridors due to encroaching human population or by growing avocados on plantations near the famed elephant herds of Amboseli, near Kilimanjaro, animal movements are increasingly being constricted. It is creating an artificial division between the human and the nonhuman. Originally, there was no such separation.

In this increasingly tenuous time, people will not be able to hold onto their myths and beliefs without the foundation of the land and its animals. This is the central challenge of our time, along with the enormous tribulations of climate change. Originally, humans and animals lived side by side. The first peoples of Africa have always known how to coexist with the other. Their stories are the world's oldest and their knowledge is slowly sliding into the backwaters of memory. The resources that the so-called first world demands from her lands are mere belongings and things, whether they be diamonds, or oil, or lumber. What we desperately, truly need and long for the most in the modern world are not commodities, but the wisdom to know how to belong and adapt to a new world. Indeed, we are indebted to the animals, which some of Africa's first peoples still honor as sacred.

What the first peoples of Africa have shown us is an elemental knowledge and resiliency we could well marvel at and which could well salvage humanity in the long run. The dominant society has become a desecrator of the organic tapestry Earth's first herders and caretakers have always cultivated and respected. The Maasai have a concept called *ngoki longoyek*, meaning the sin one carries from the eyes of those who witness one's arrogance. A curse may befall those whose identity is derived from conquest, from a reckless act of taking rather than an ordered existence on the land. The pastoralist ethos is based on an abiding respect for Earth's capacities for renewal: real wealth is regenerative. For both hunter-gatherers and pastoralists, true power derives from the capacity to bequeath knowledge of the Earth's gifts to the next generation. It is a lesson our vaunted civilization should heed this decade. The "blazing lights" of our civilization, as Isak Dinesen said, are dissolving age-old relations to myth, oral traditions, the Earth, and her animals.

Climate change, road-building, poaching, mining, dams, the bushmeat trade, and the forced separation of indigenous peoples from wildlife has altered the face of Africa and the planet over the last 50 years. The lion population may be as low as 15,000 individuals or lower, as trophy hunters continue to target the greatest animals of Africa for the thrill of killing. Some call it an addiction. Even the King of Spain has enjoyed killing elephants, and one Spanish hunter in particular killed as many as 1,300 of them! How in the twenty-first century can this ever have been allowed?

We began as a species in Africa, and many of those species that nourished us for millennia could be gone in our lifetime, and then there will be no ground of being to return to. So much has been depleted. If the last herds cannot be salvaged, humanity will have crossed the river of no return. Our species will have no recourse but to self-cannibalize. Like no other continent, Africa's enormous challenges and incomparable history encompass the breadth of humanity's experience on Earth and as such offers the opportunity to salvage a vestige of what supports the foundation of mankind, our relationship to the cosmos, and humanity's unique indebtedness to wildlife since the dawn of our kind. Africa forms the firmament of our origins, and will in large measure dictate our fate as a species.

Romain Gary, who fought for freedom in World War II, knew what was at stake when he wrote with inimitable eloquence about prisoners in the camps: "When I couldn't stand it any longer, I would close my eyes and think of the herds of elephants at liberty, running freely across Africa, hundreds and hundreds of magnificent animals that nothing can resist—no cement wall, no barbed wire, nothing: they rush forward over the great open spaces and smash everything in their way, and nothing can stop them. That's liberty, I tell you! So when you begin to suffer from claustrophobia, or the barbed wire fences, the reinforced concrete, the absolute materialism, just imagine this: herds of elephants charging across the wide open spaces of Africa. Follow them with your eyes closed, keep their image inside you, and you'll see, you'll feel better and happier, and stronger ..."

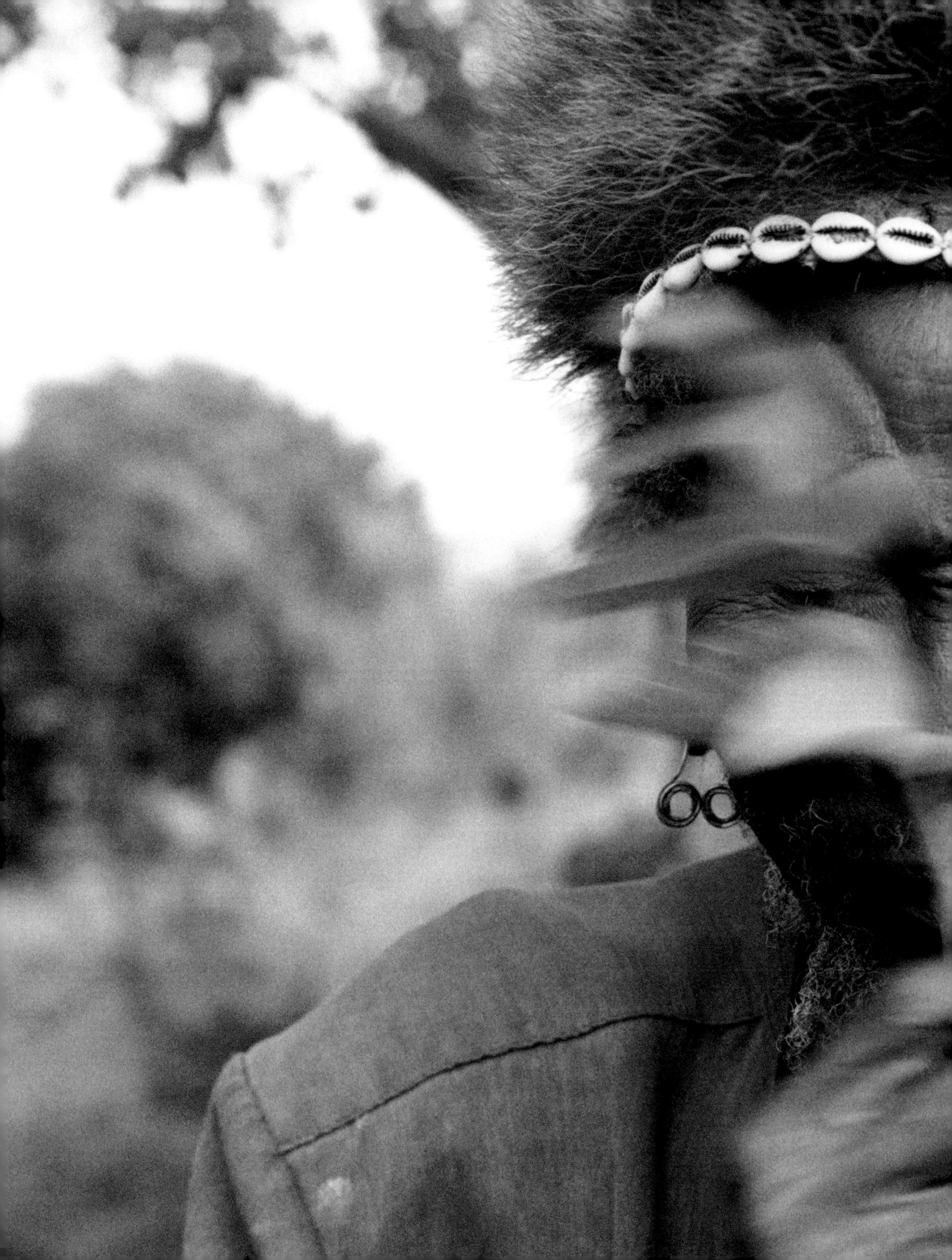

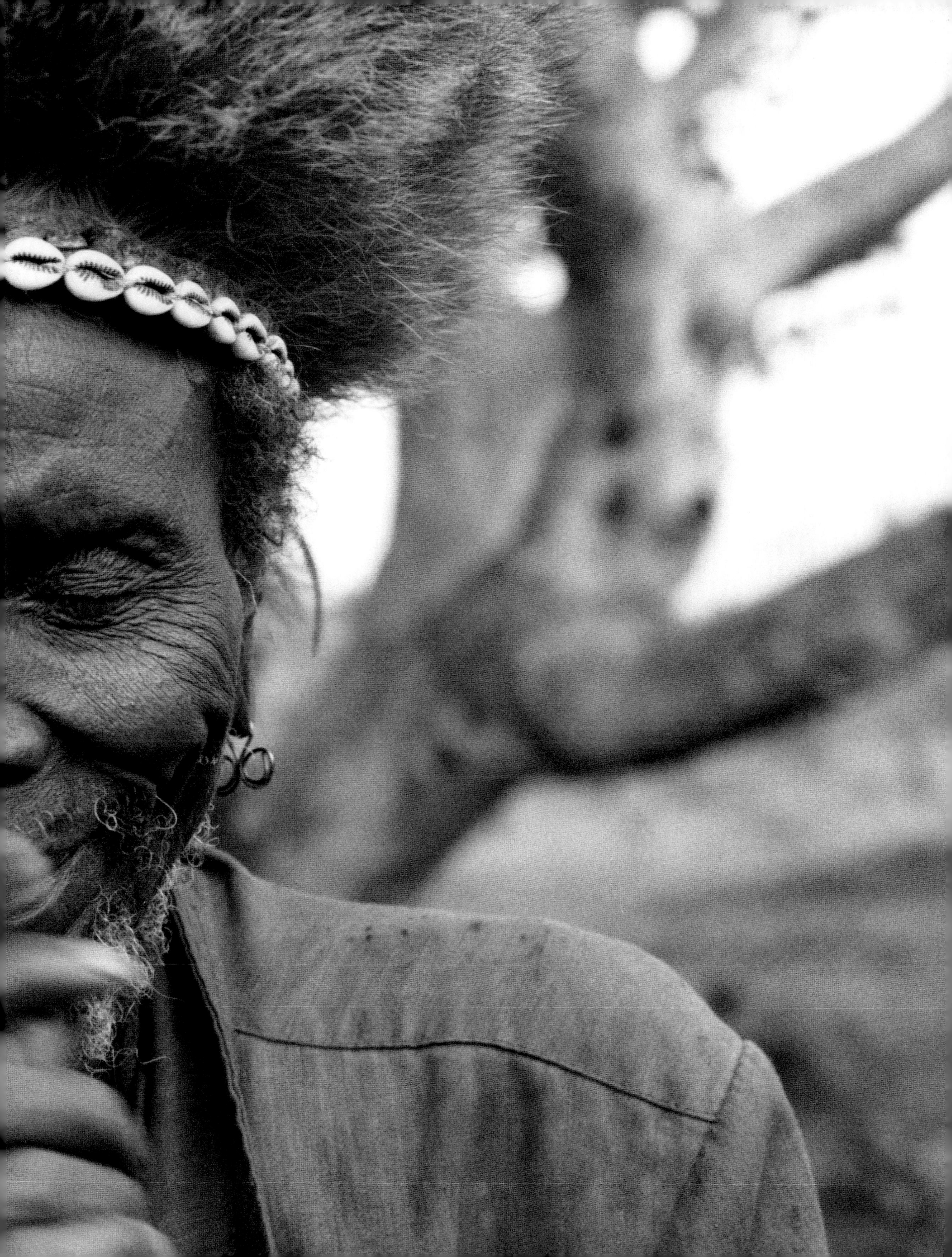

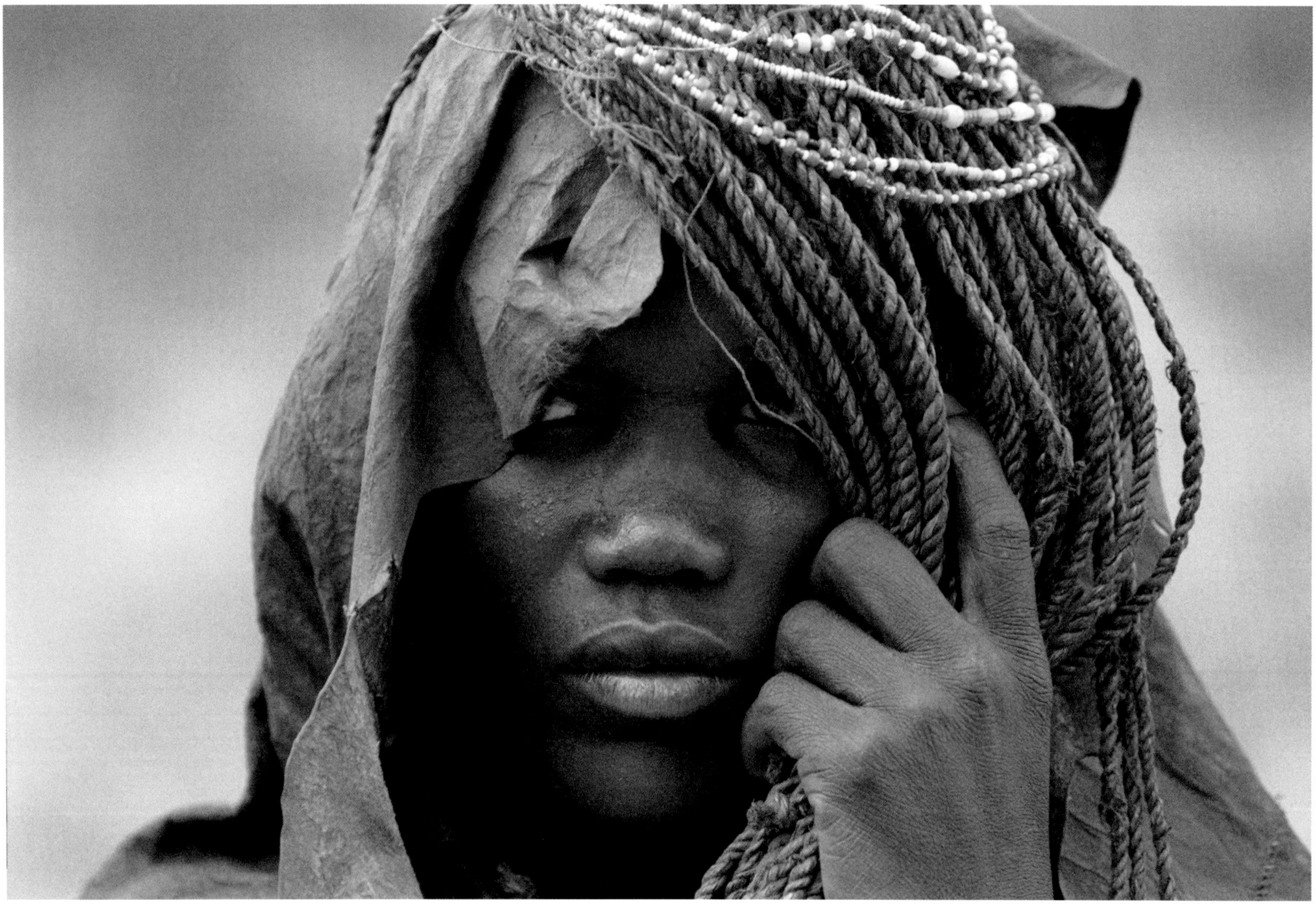

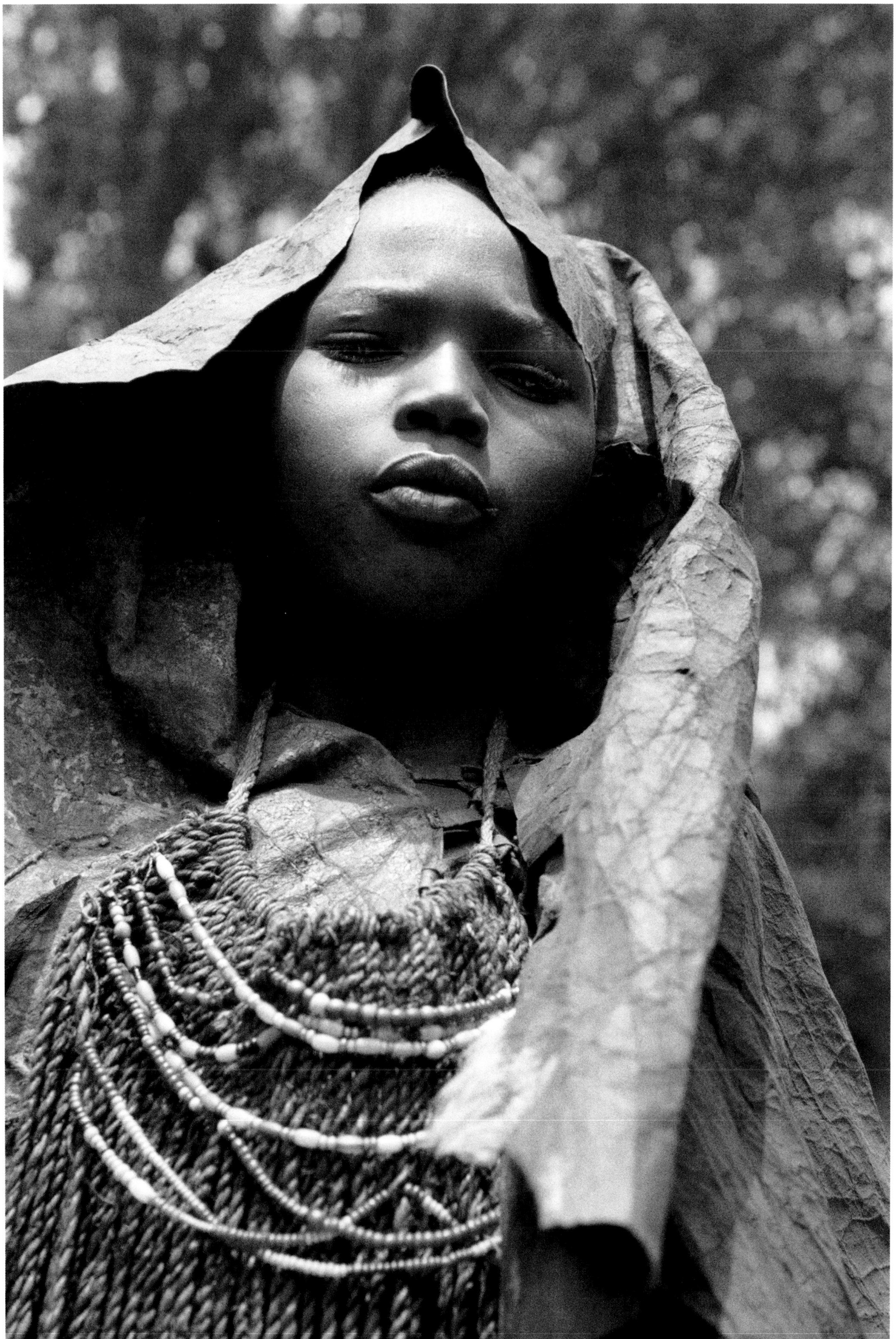

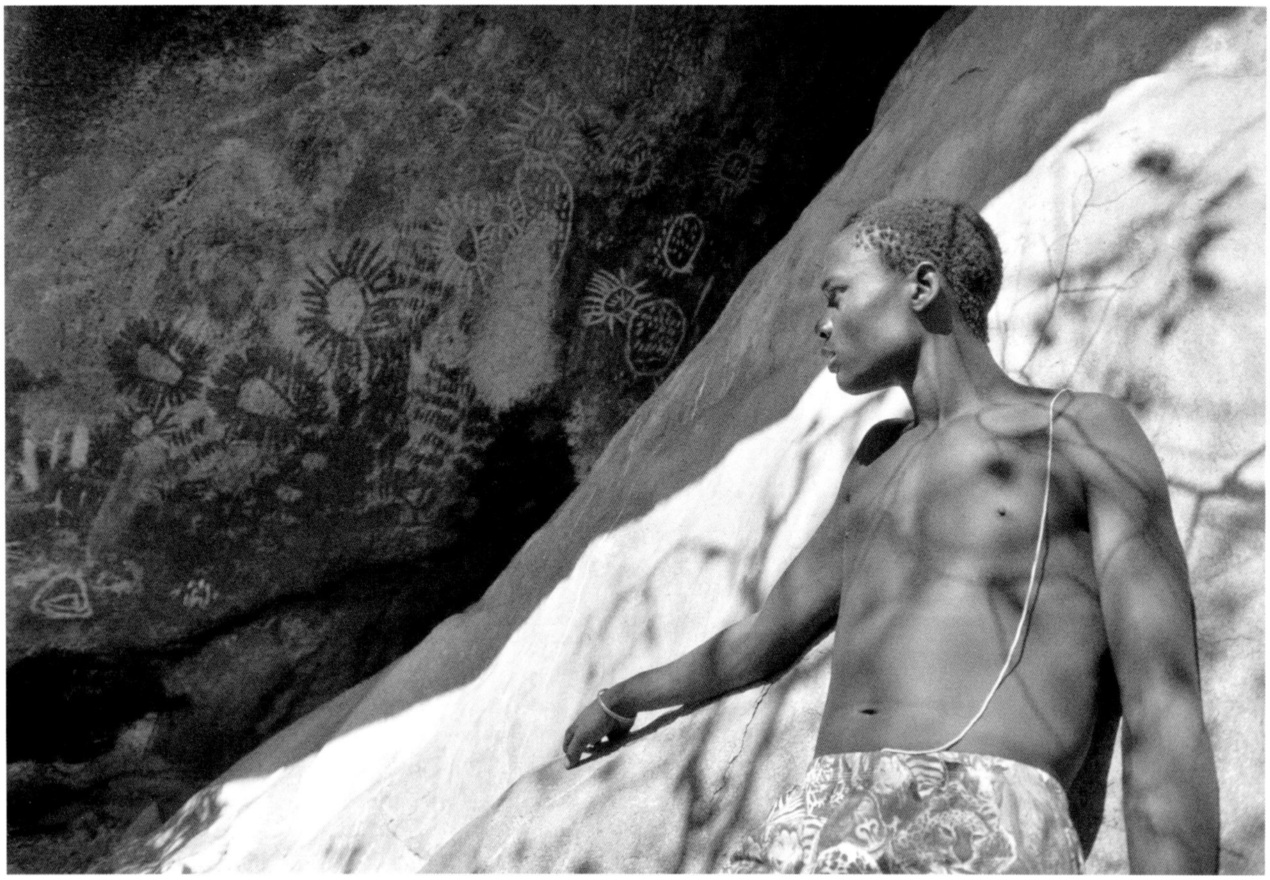

In the long years before them, will the Giraffes sometimes dream of their lost country? Where are they now, where have they gone to, the grass and the thorn-trees, the rivers and water-holes and the blue mountains? The high sweet air over the plains has lifted and withdrawn. Where have the other Giraffes gone to, that were side by side with them when they set going, and cantered over the undulating land? They have left them, they have all gone, and it seems that they are never coming back.

**Isak Dinesen,** ***Out of Africa***

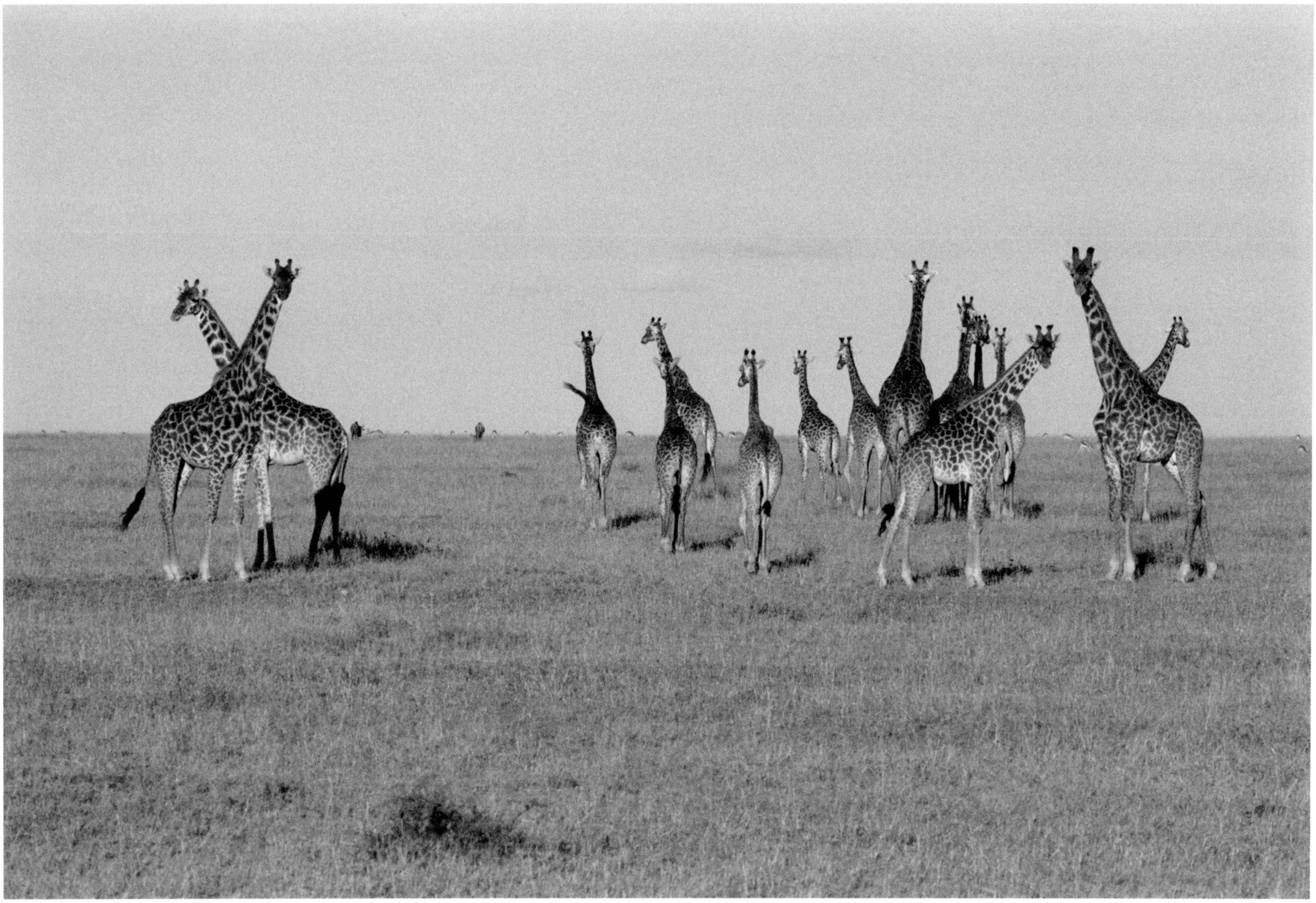

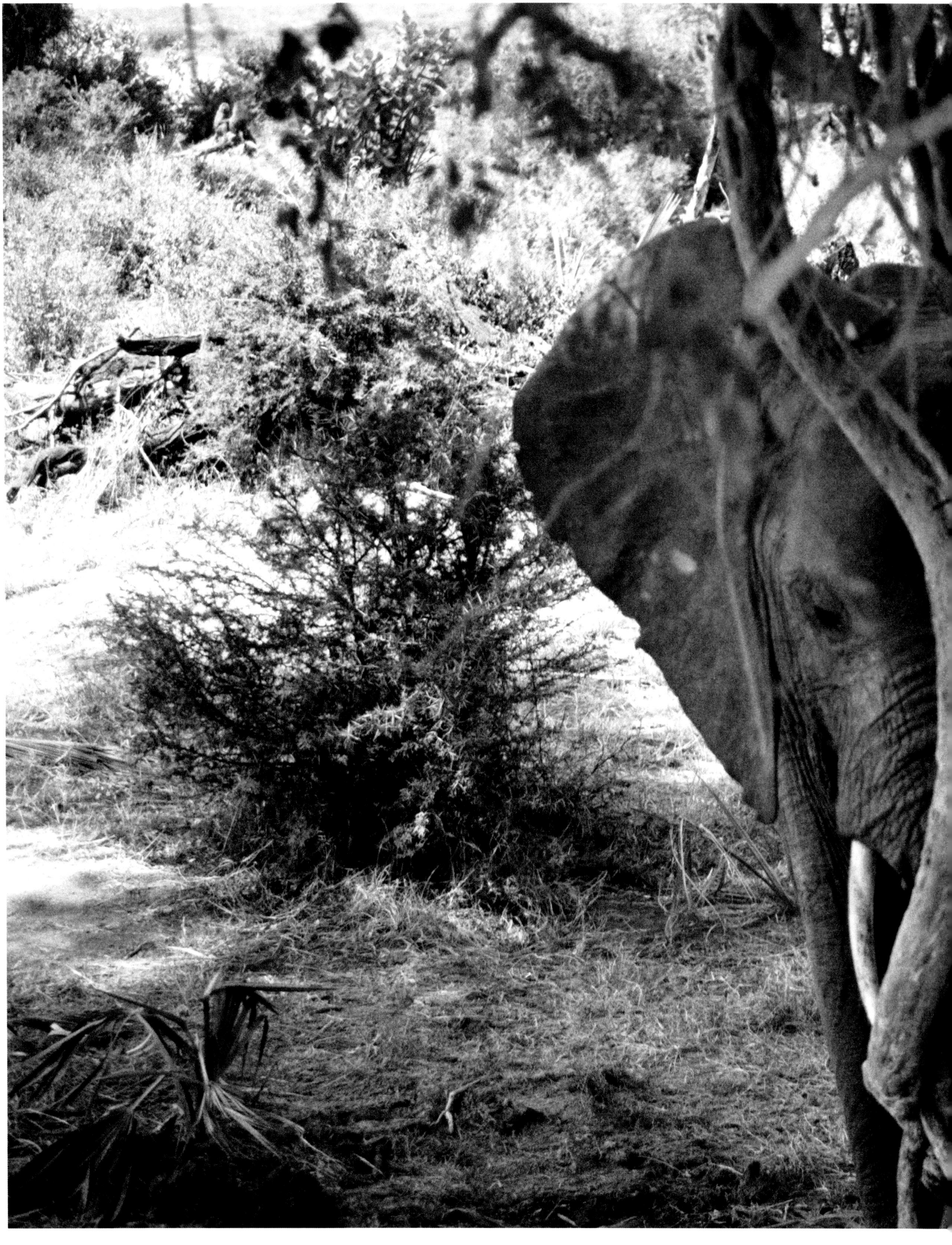

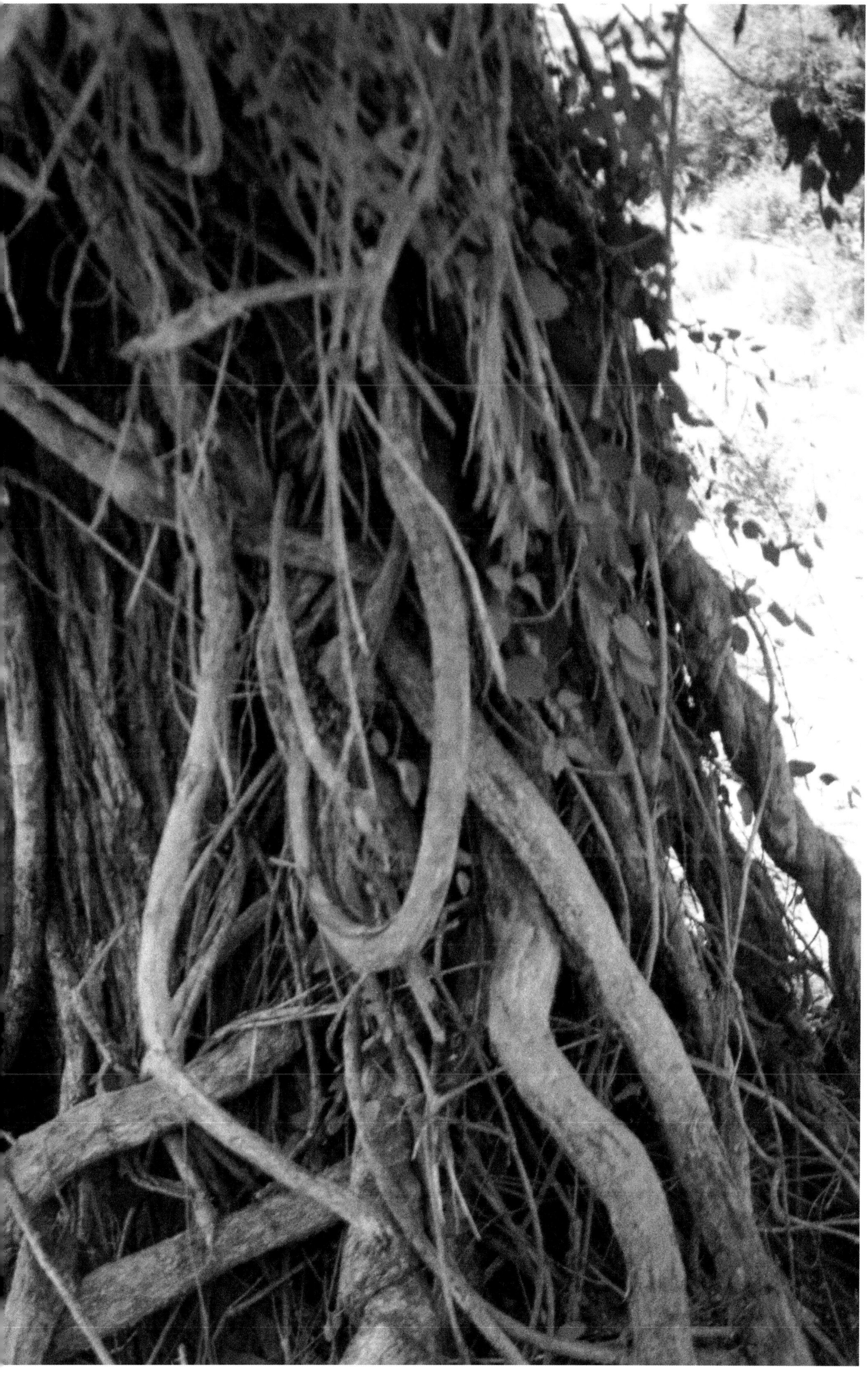

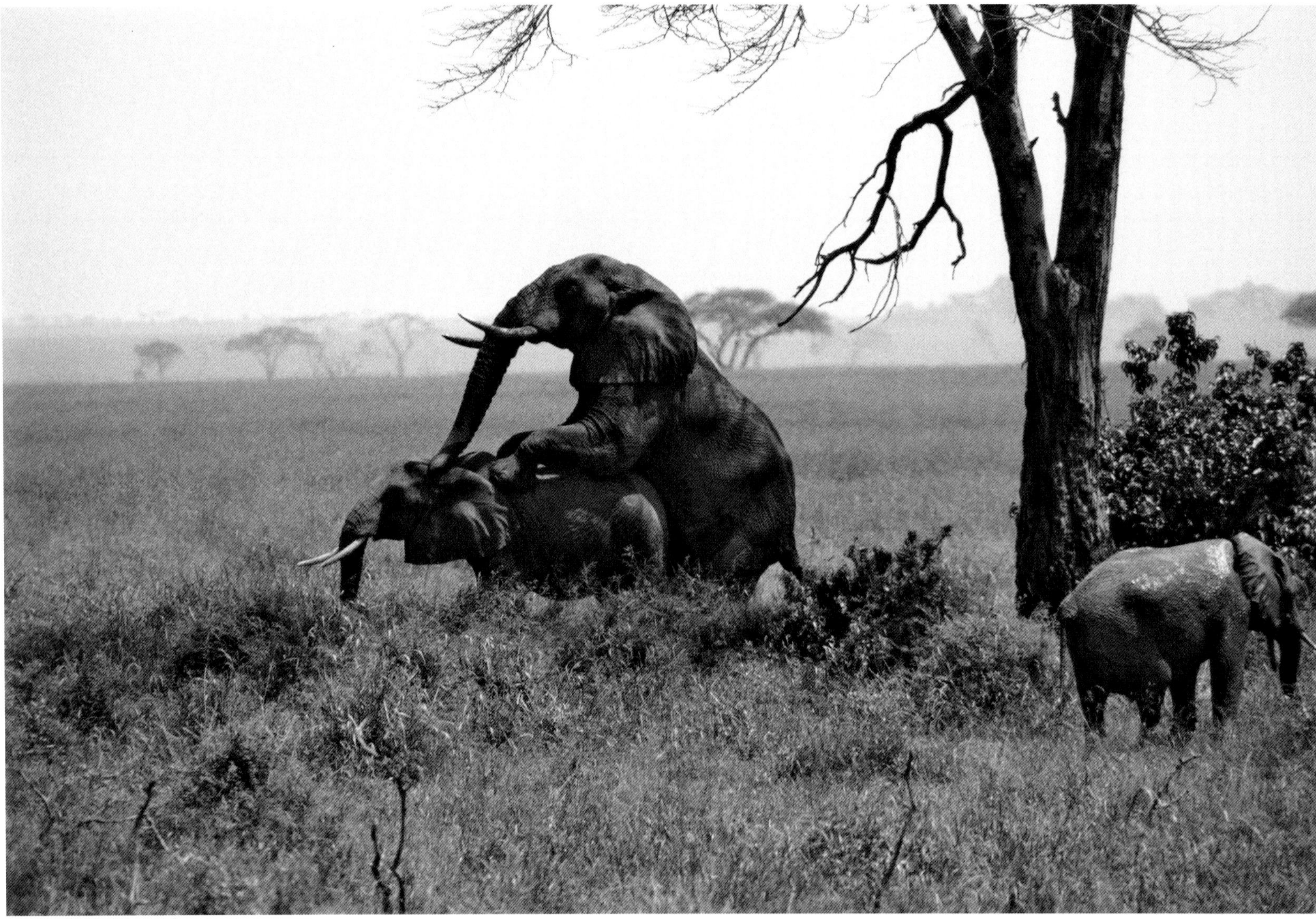

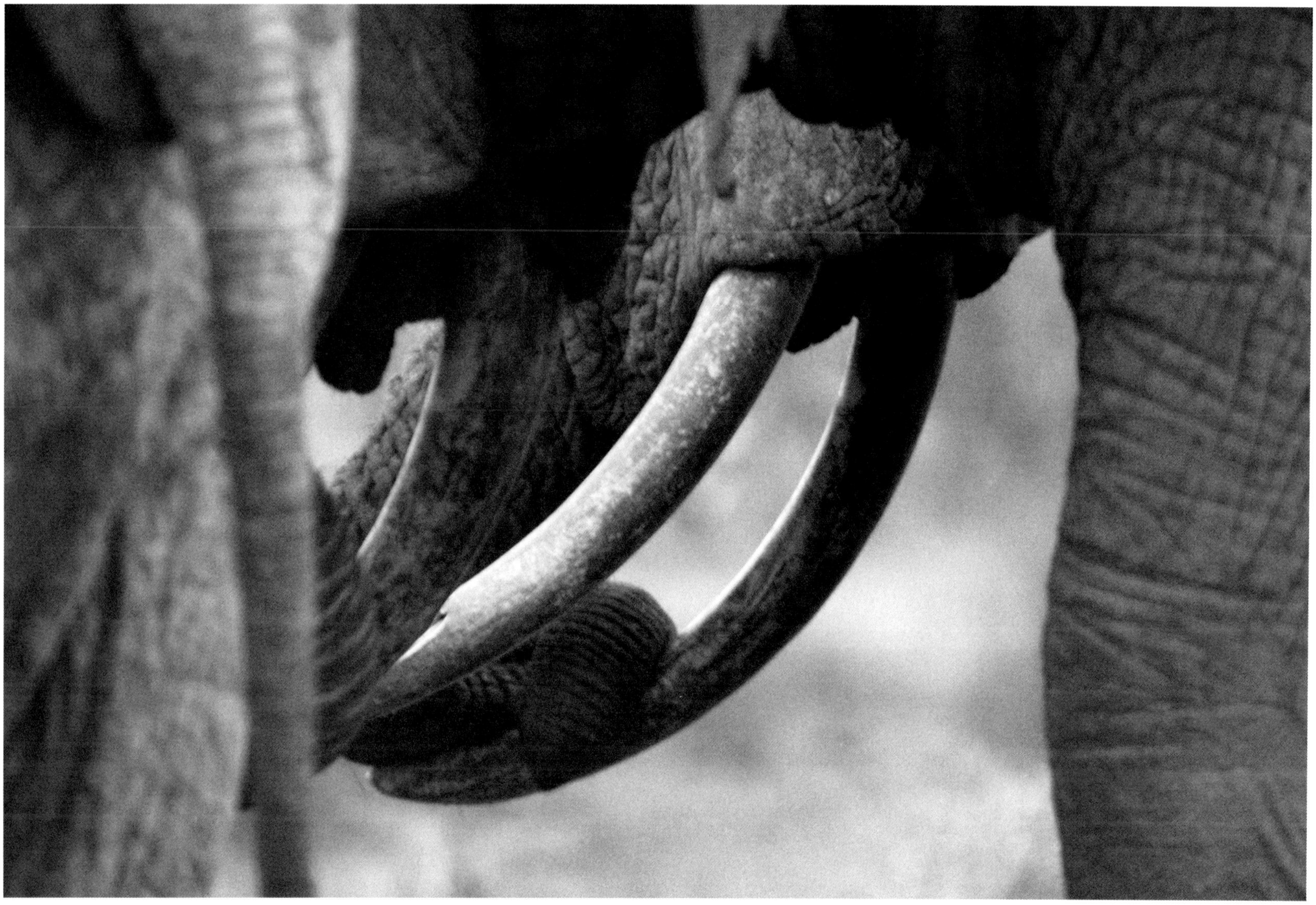

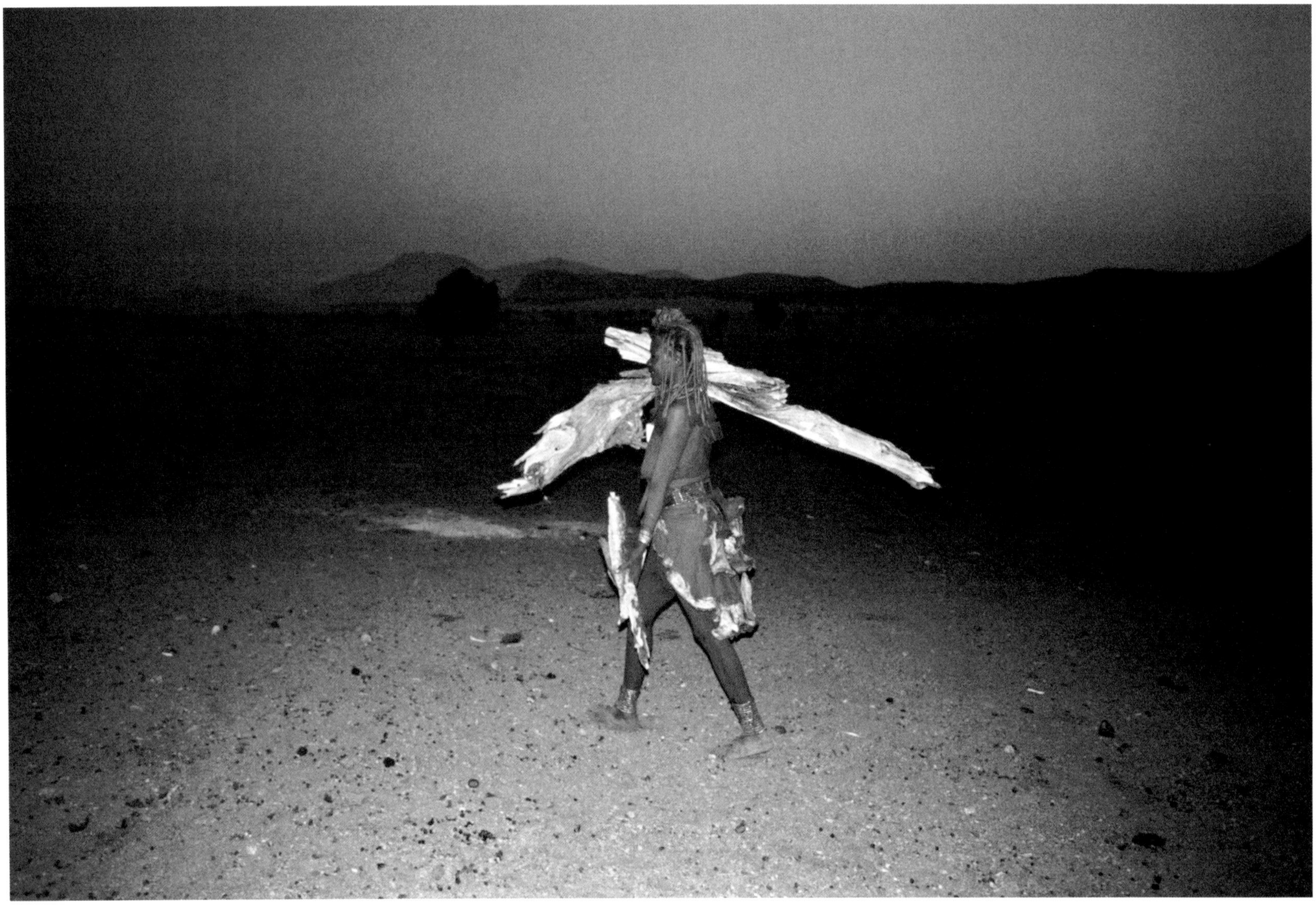

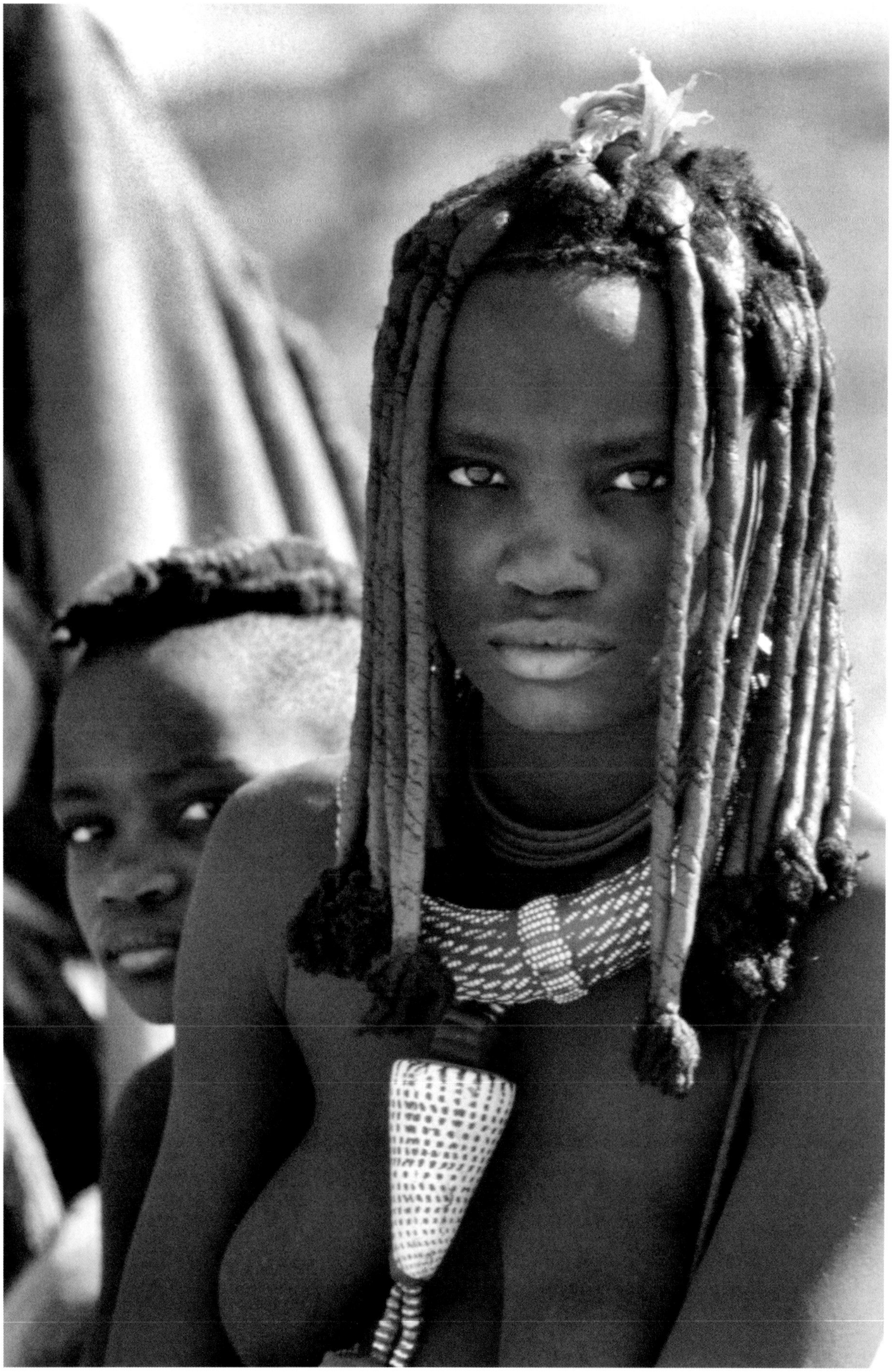

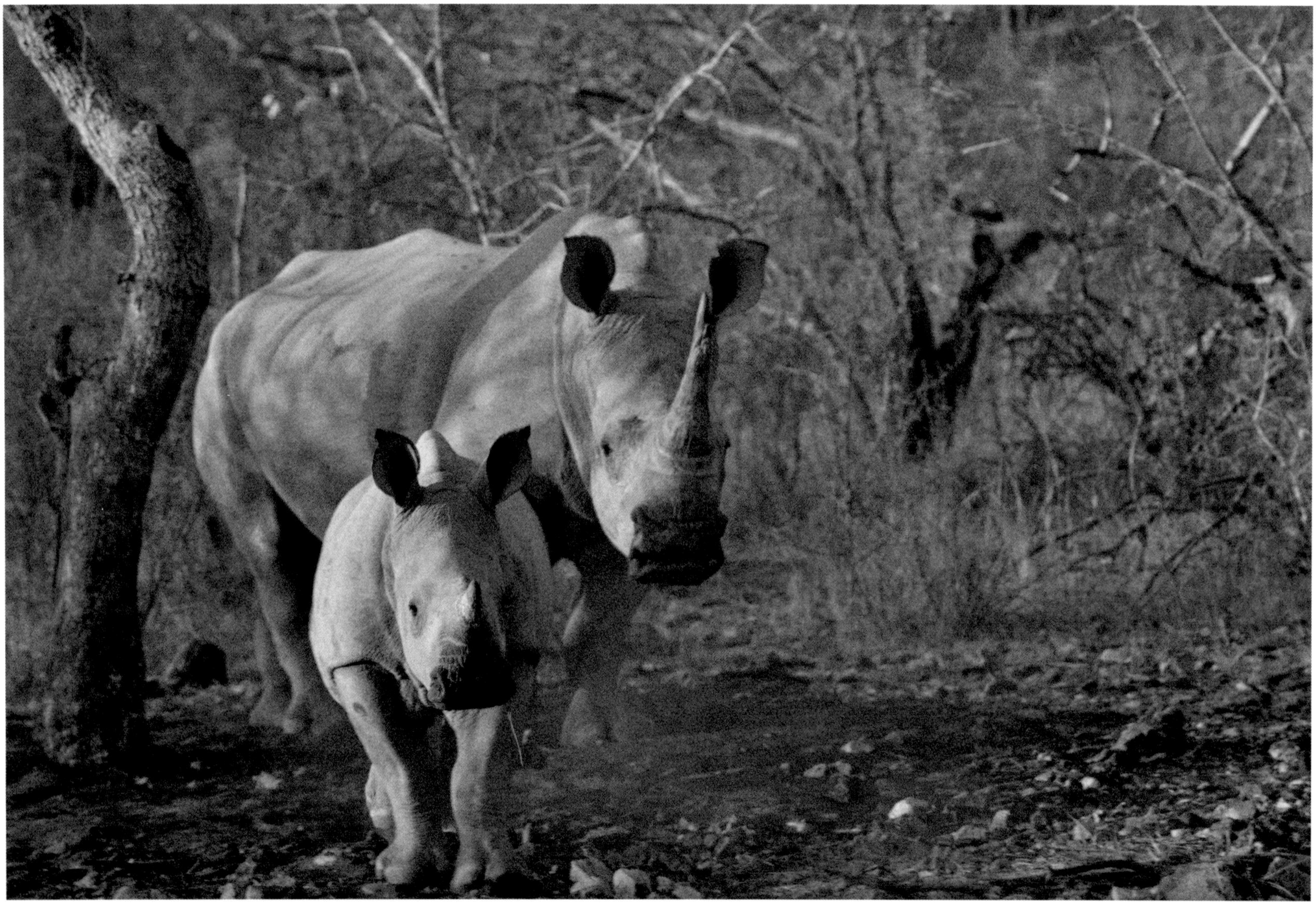

In the animal world the rhinoceros is Arthur and his horn Excalibur ... once you break through into the rhinoceros's idiom, discover what a rhinoceros mother would find beautiful in a rhinoceros son, the impression animal beauty makes on you is blinding.

**Laurens van der Post,** ***A Walk With A White Bushman***

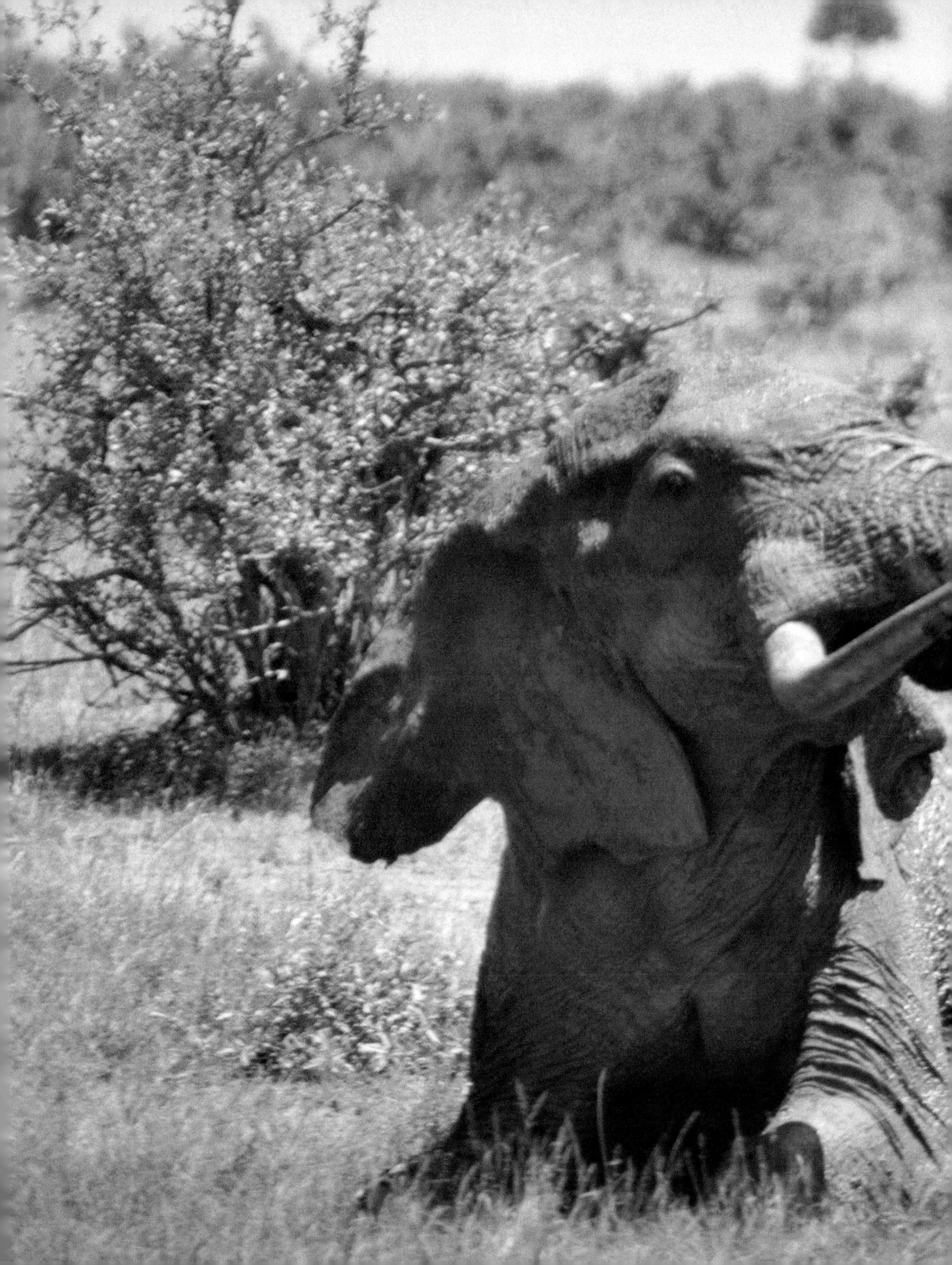

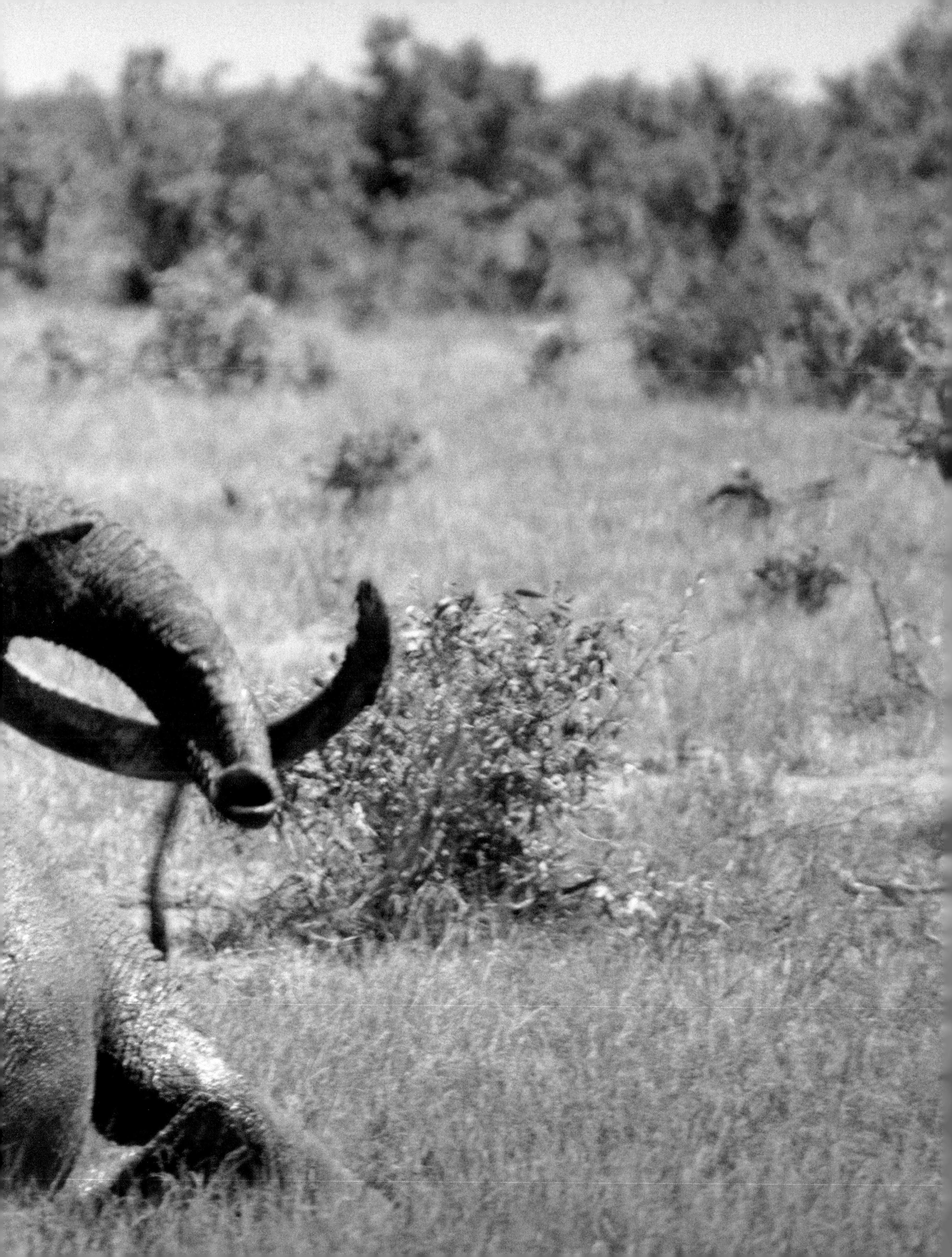

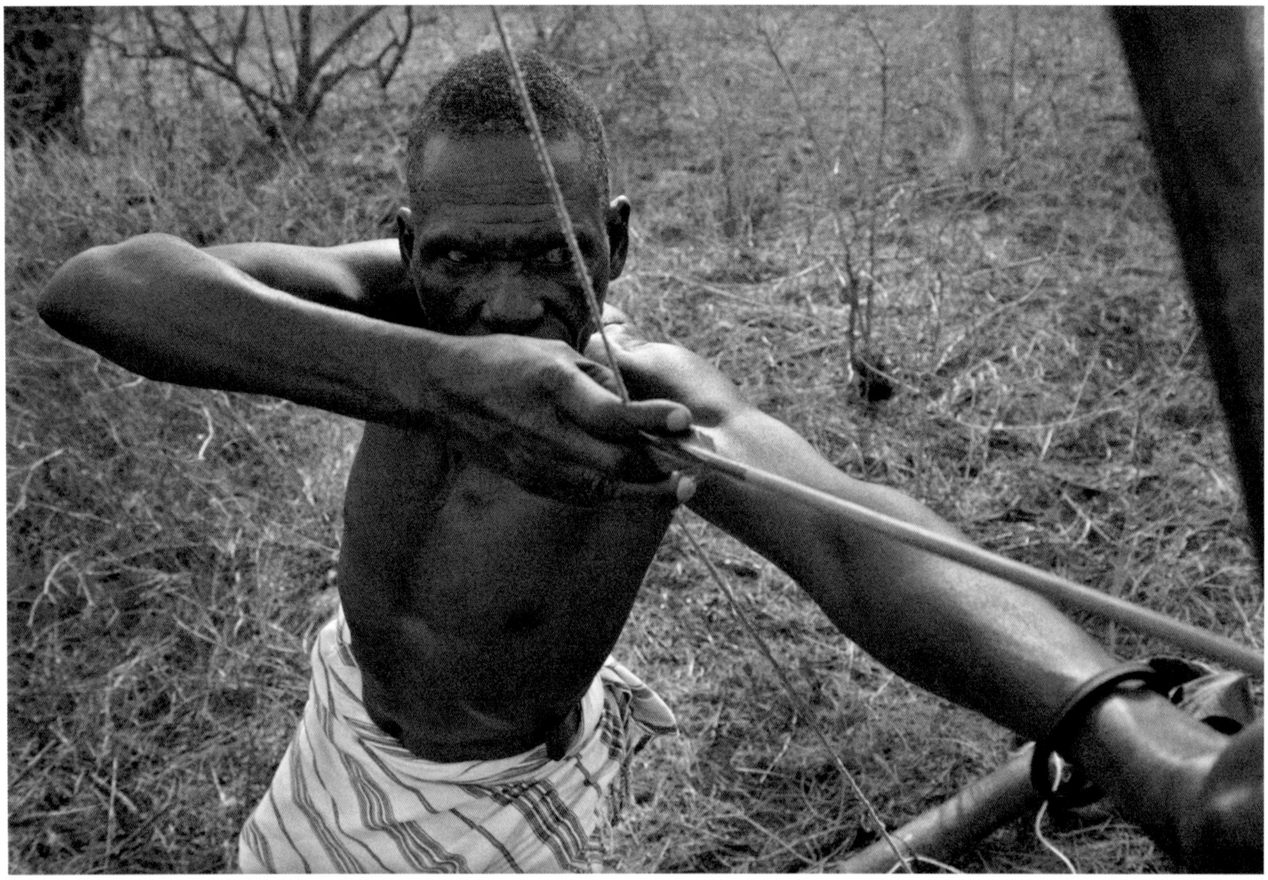

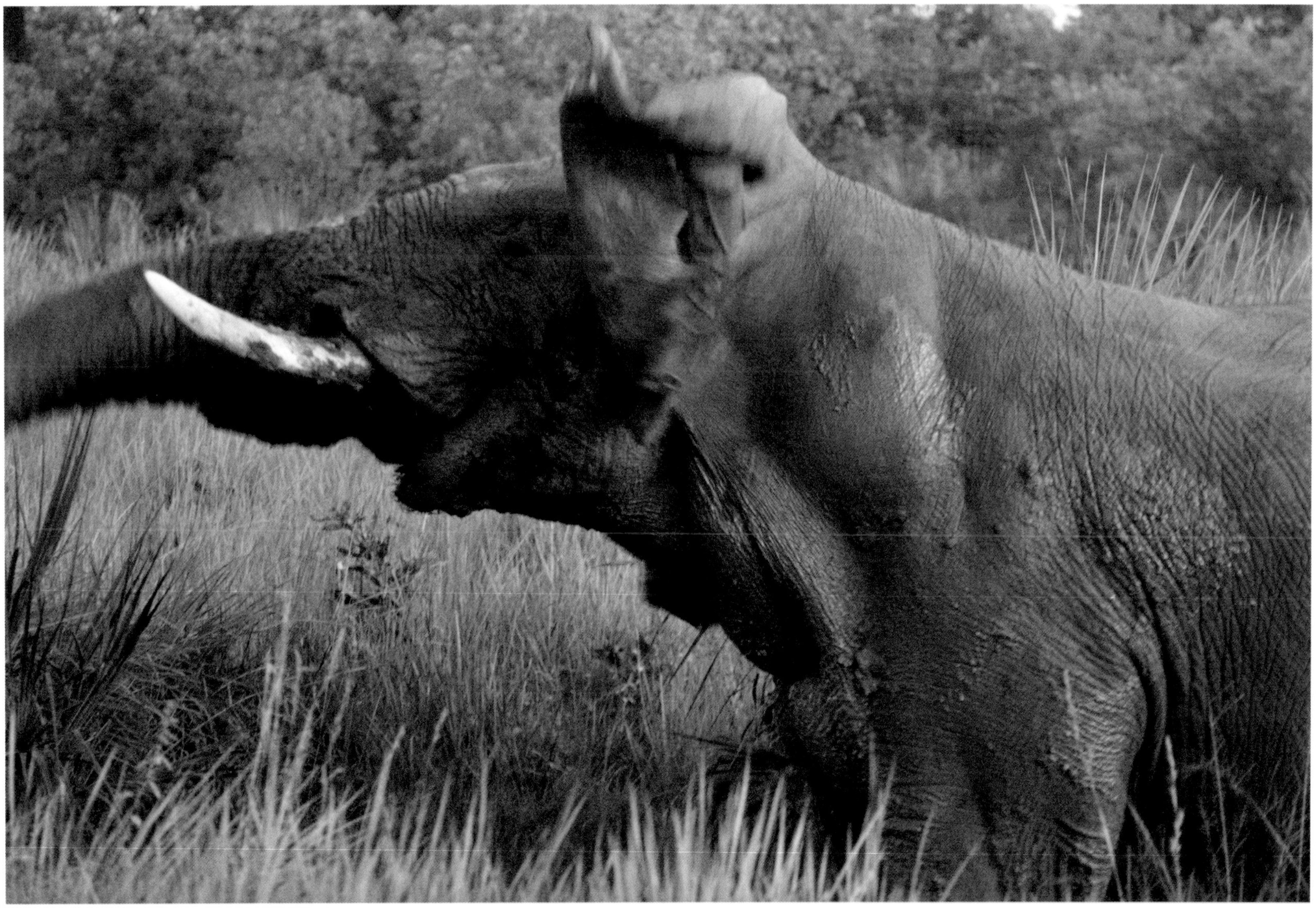

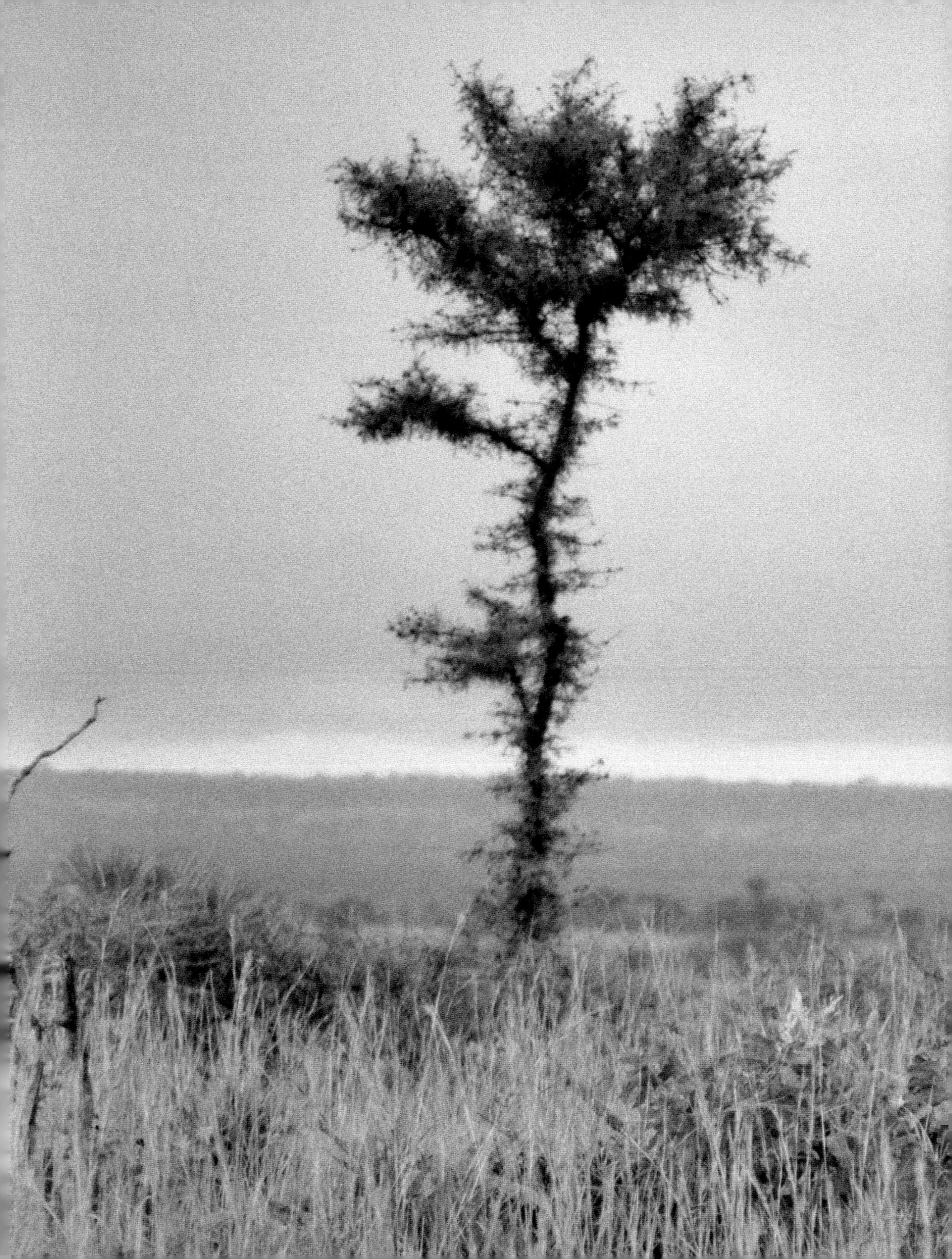

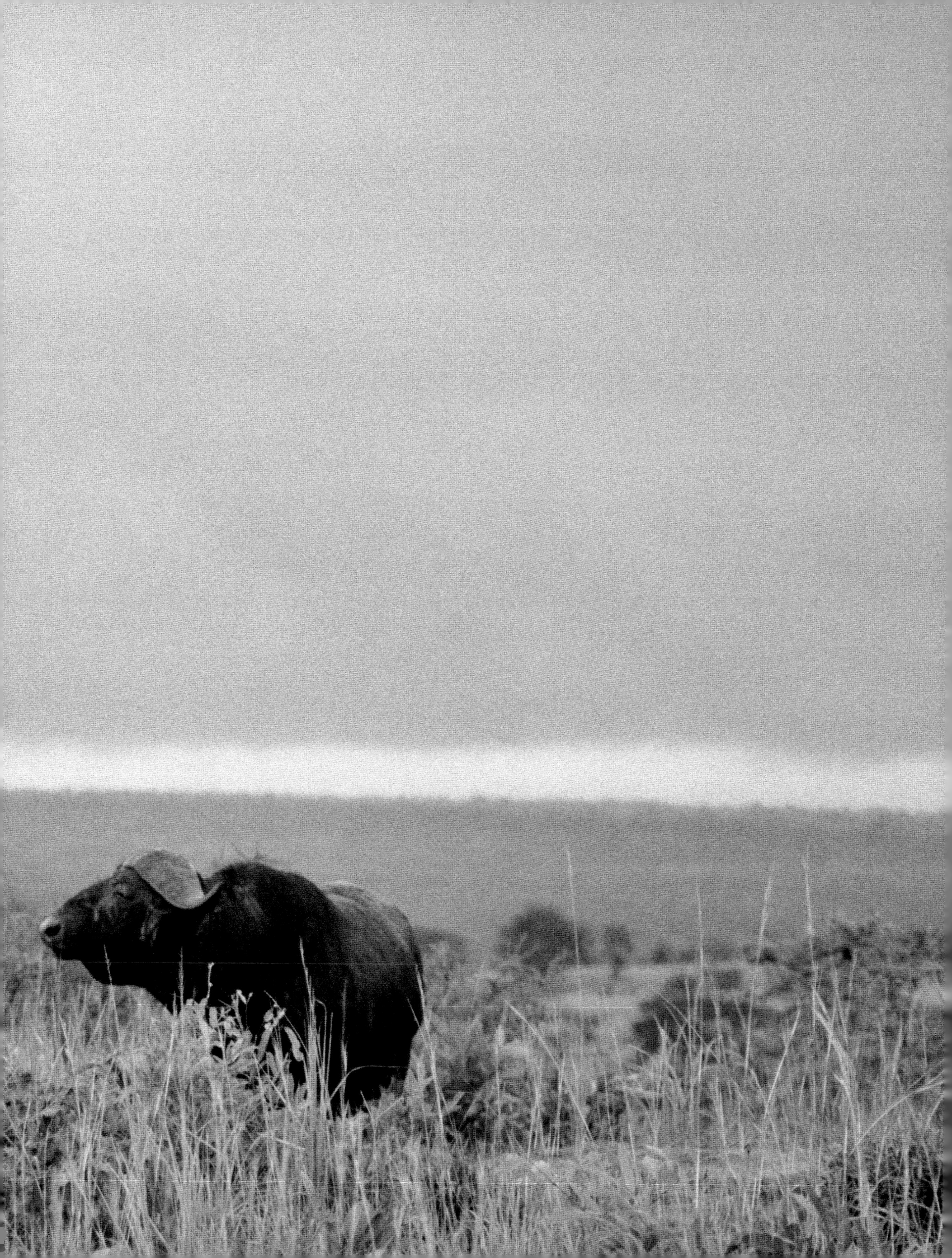

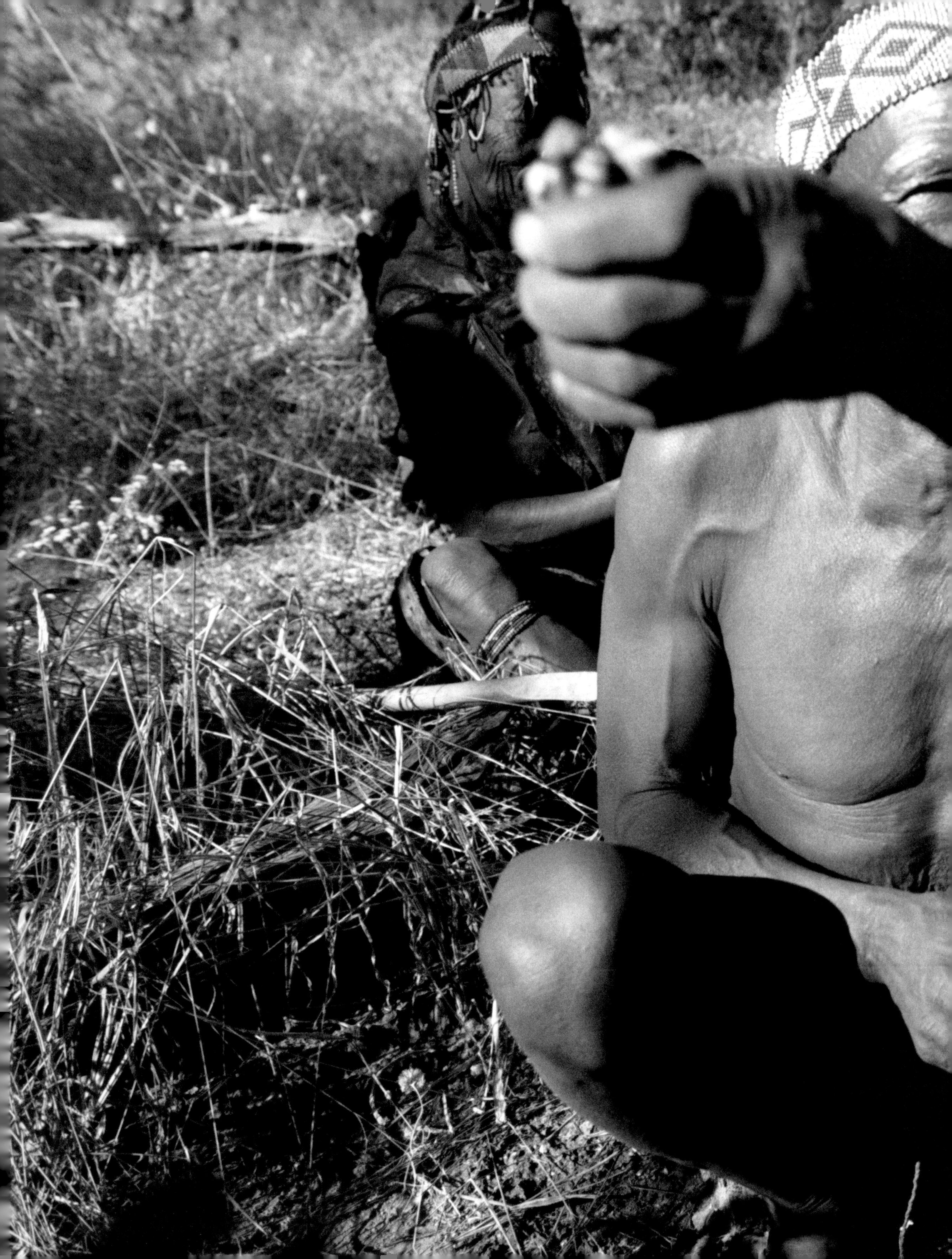

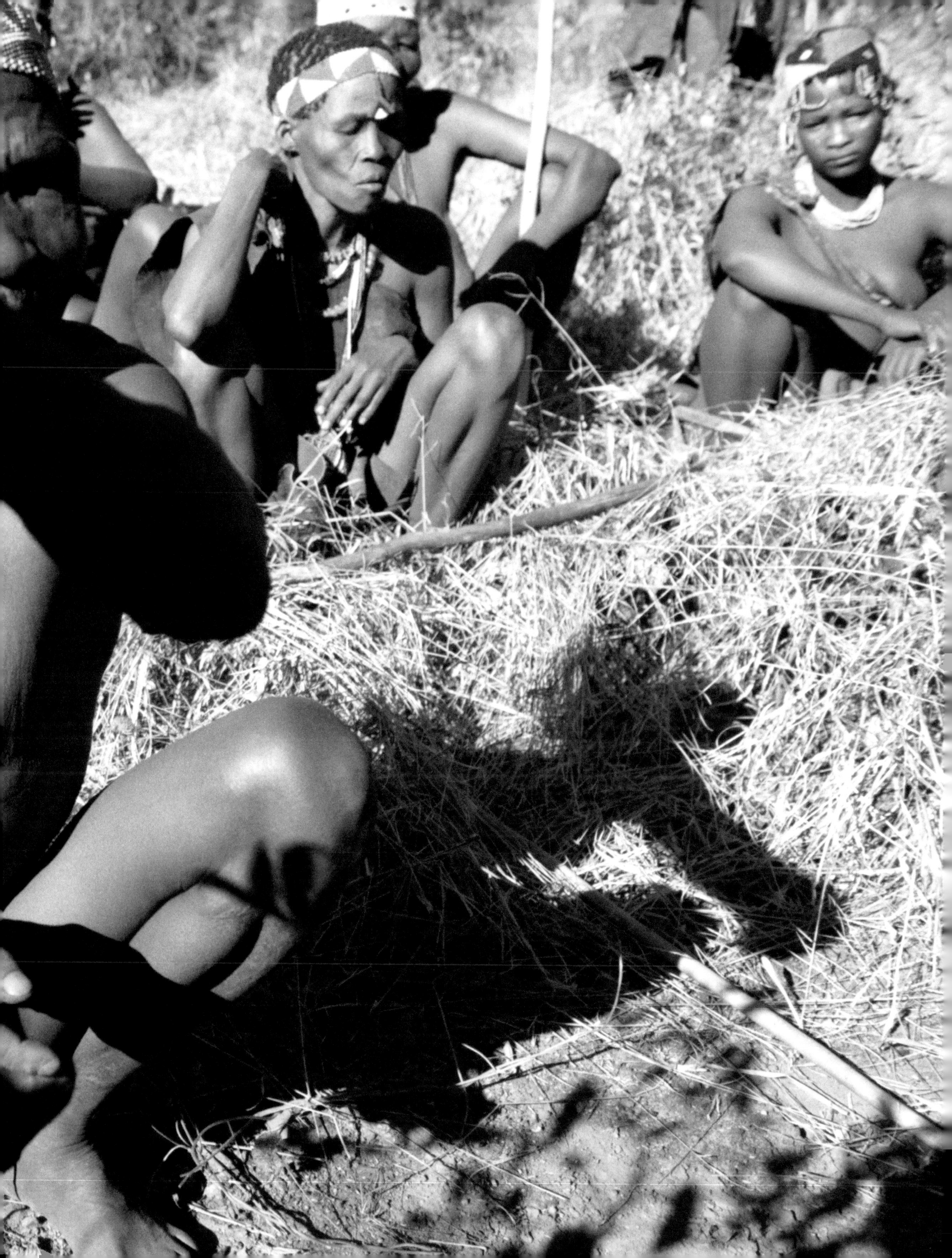

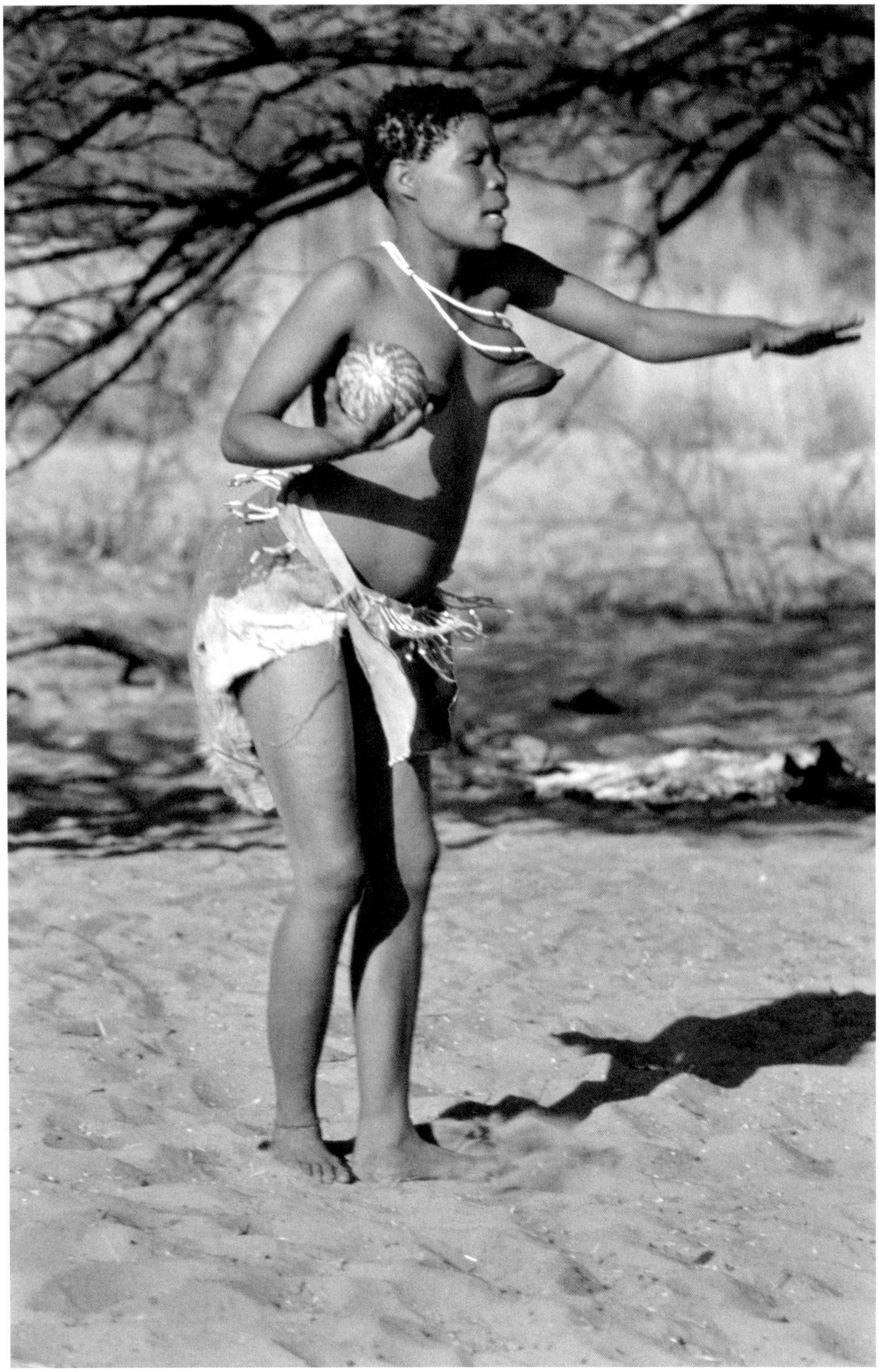

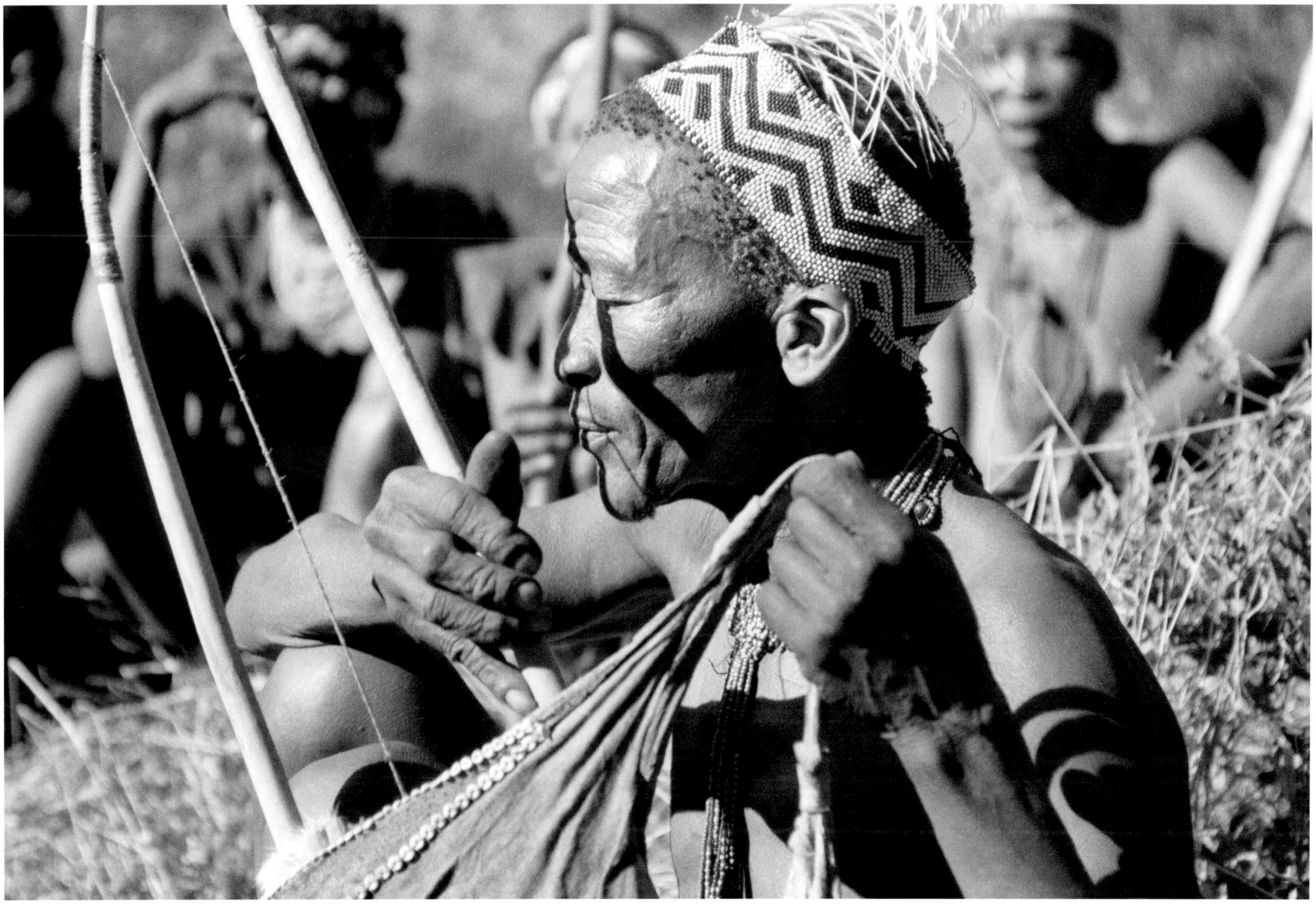

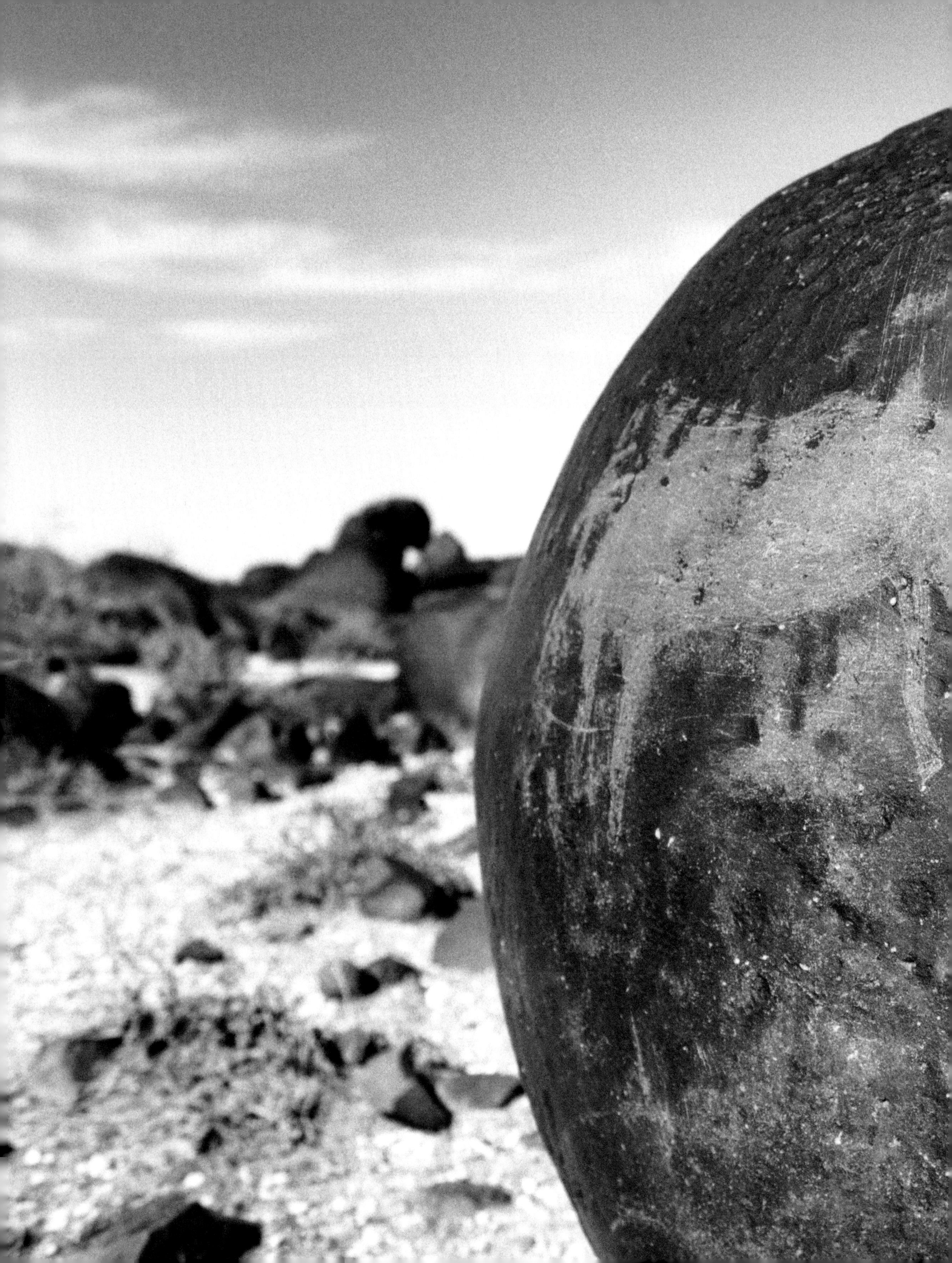

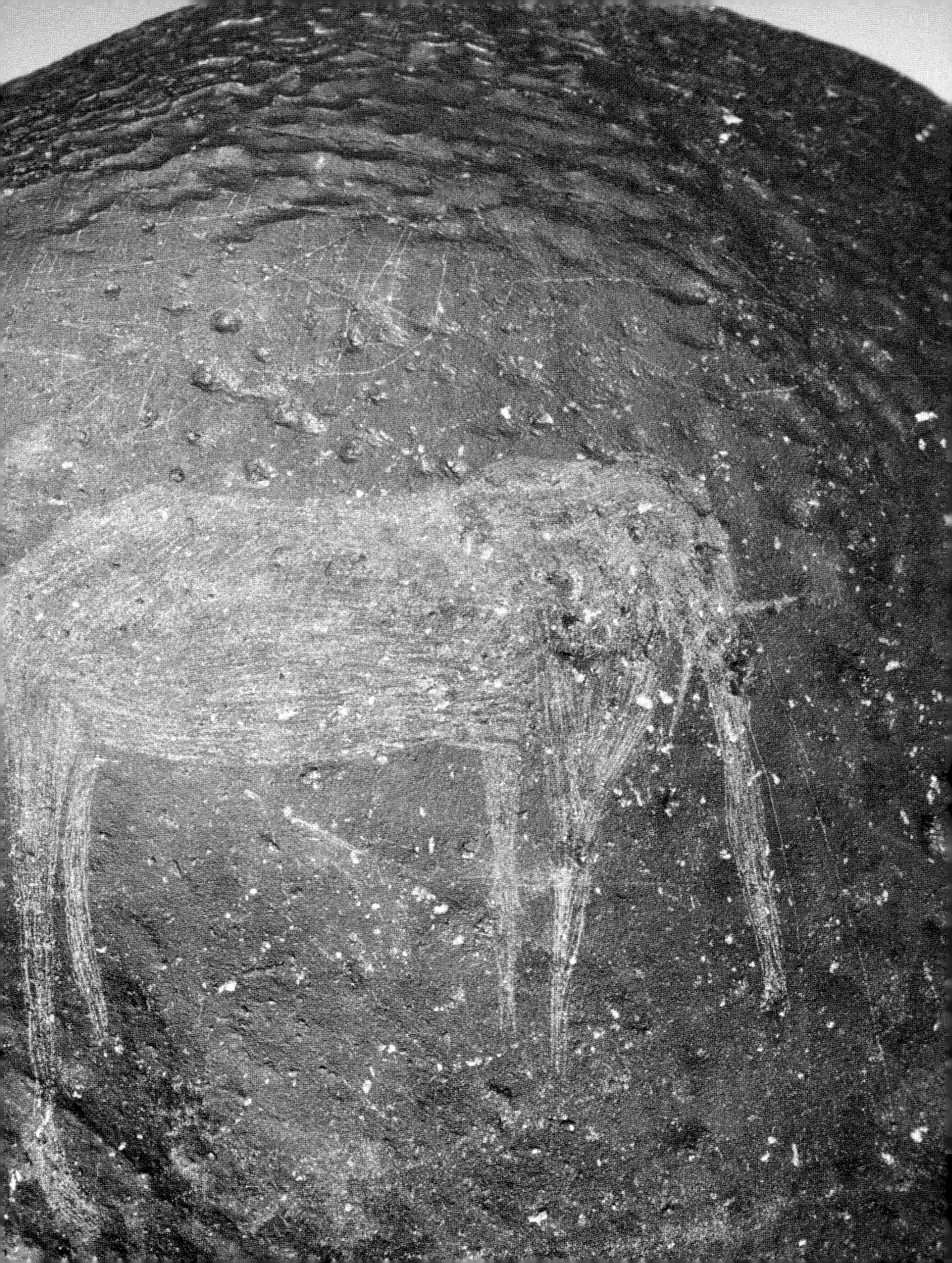

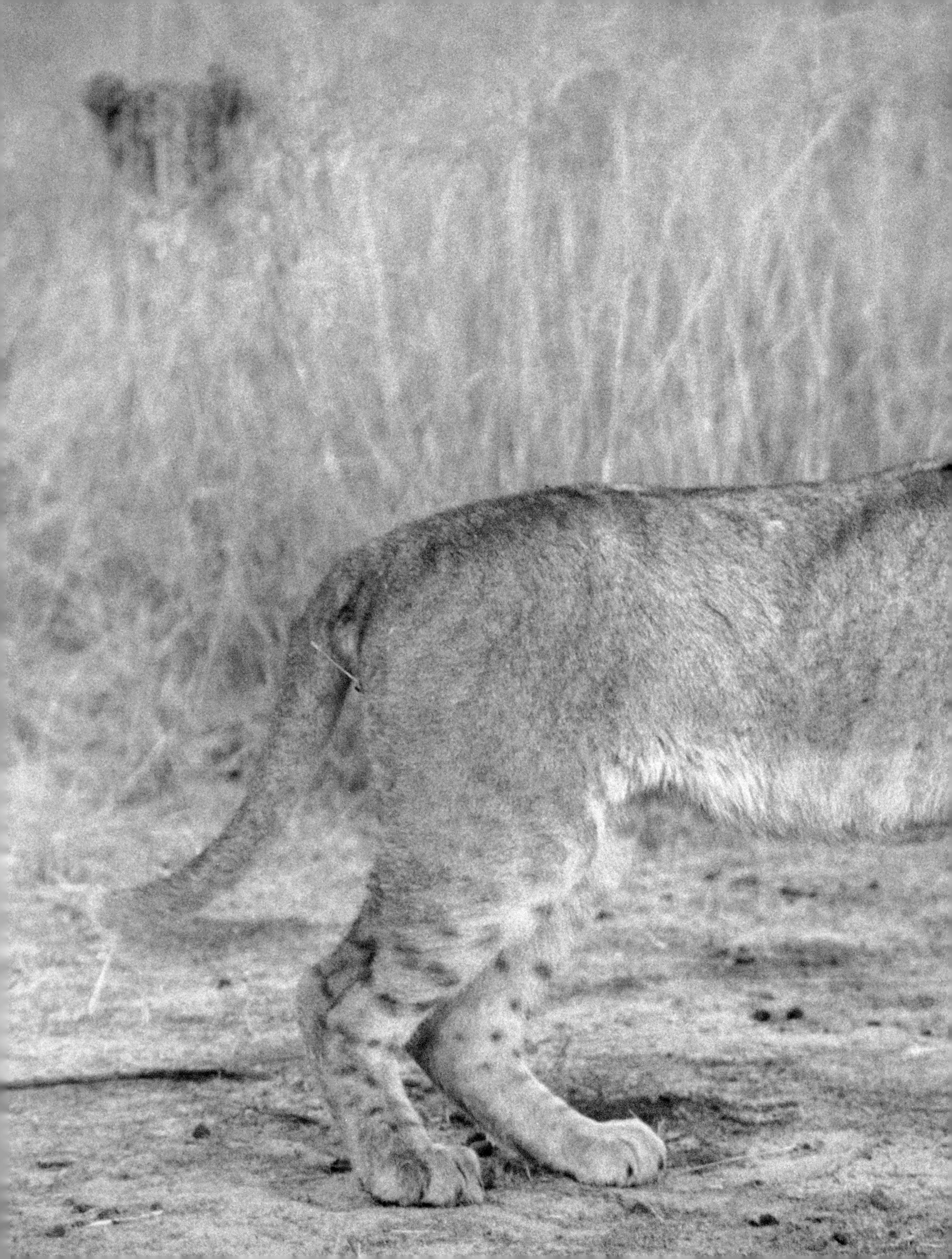

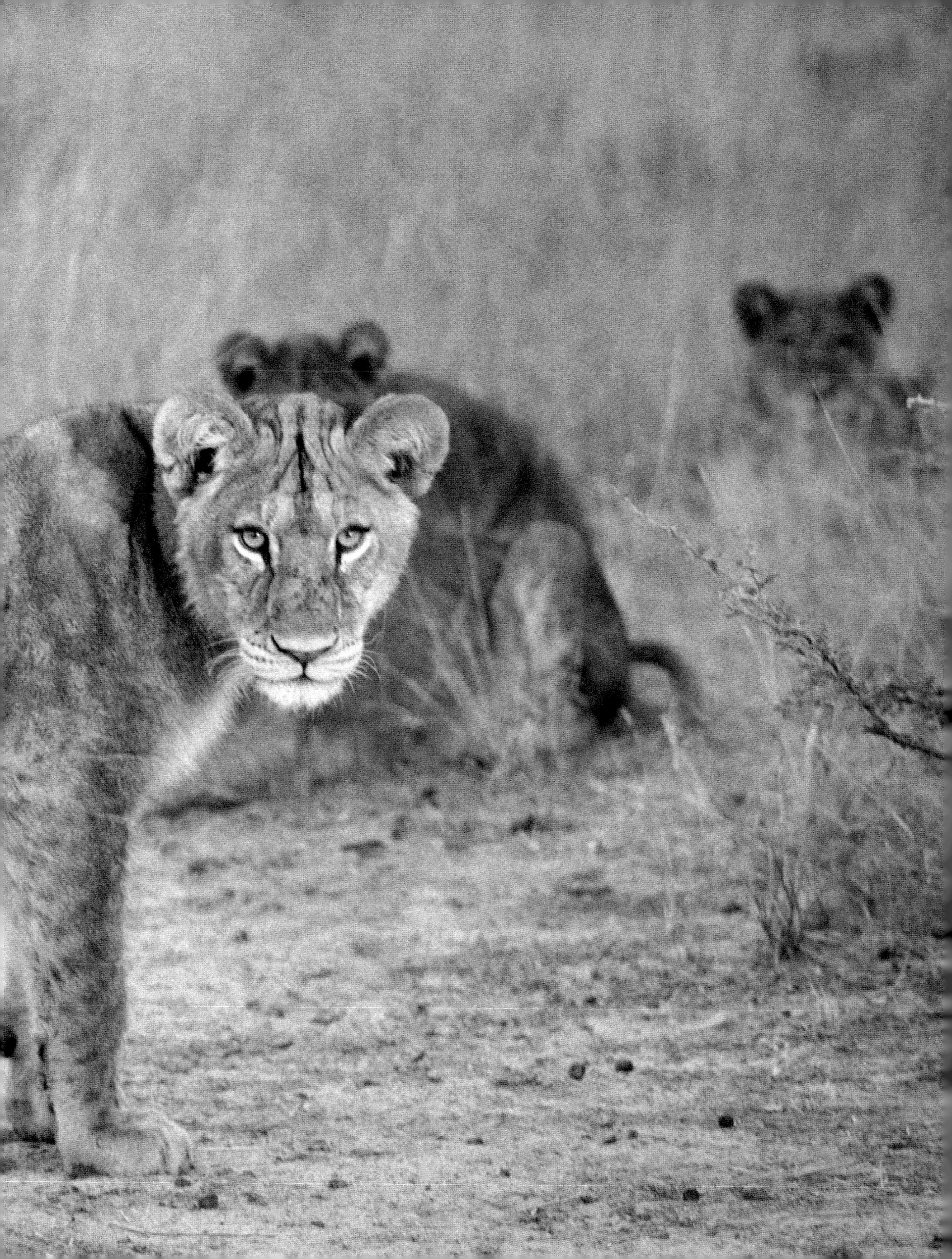

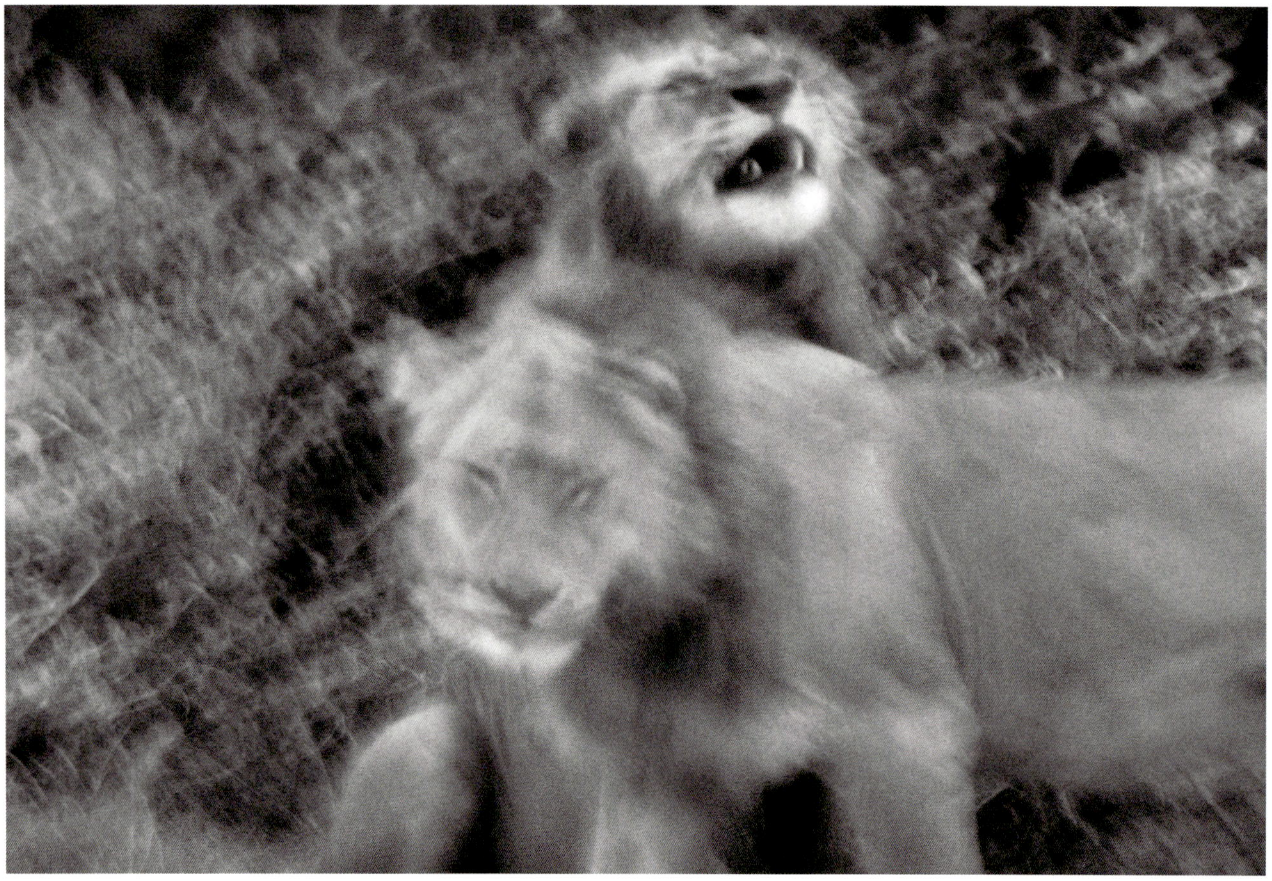

Only Nature is eternal, unless we senselessly destroy it. In fifty years' time nobody will be interested in the results of the conferences which fill today's headlines. But when, fifty years from now, a lion walks into the red dawn and roars resoundingly, it will mean something to people and quicken their hearts whether they are bolsheviks or democrats, or whether they speak English, German, Russian or Swahili. They will stand in quiet awe as, for the first time in their lives, they watch twenty thousand zebras wander across the endless plains.

**Bernhard and Michael Grzimek, *Serengeti Shall Not Die***

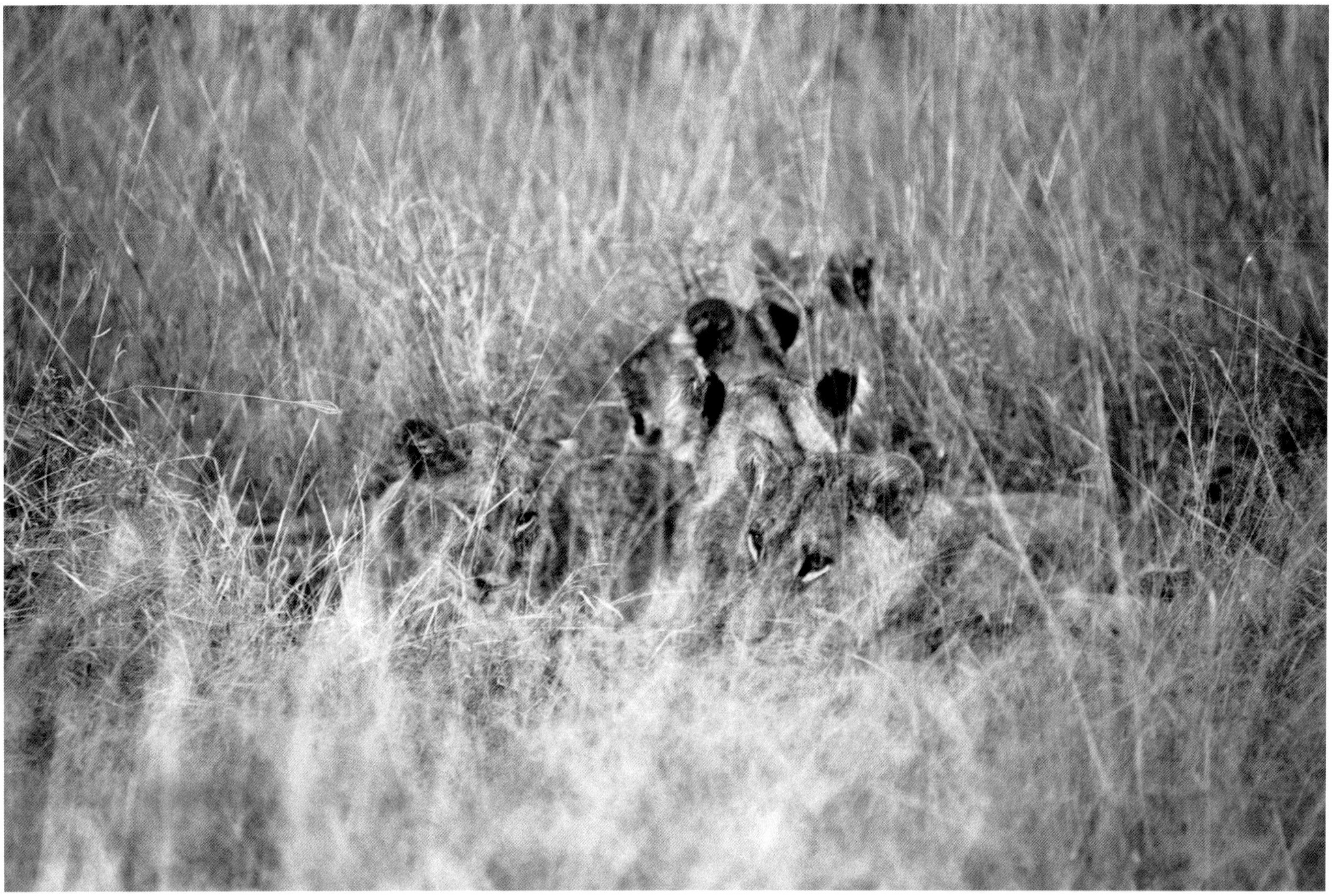

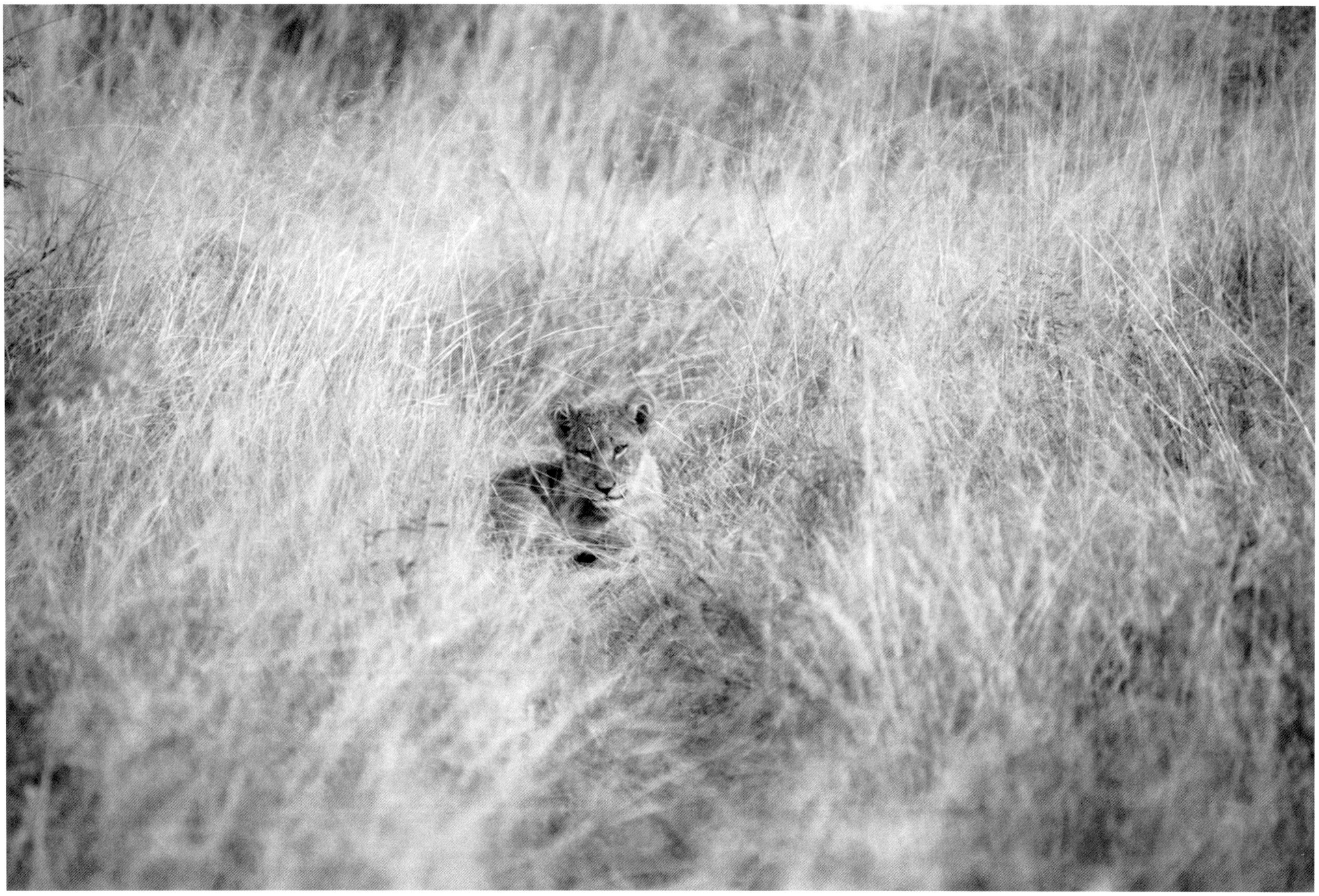

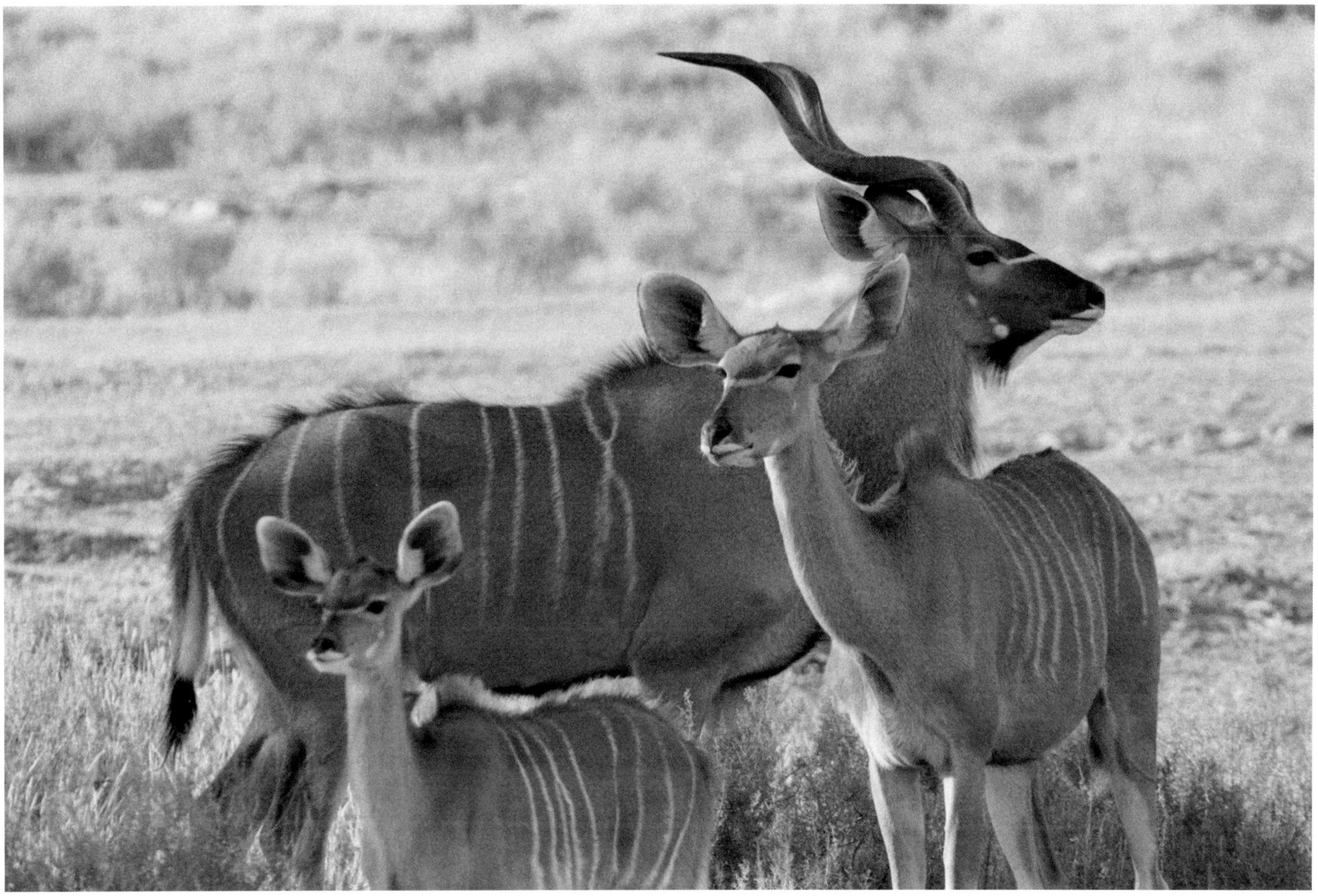

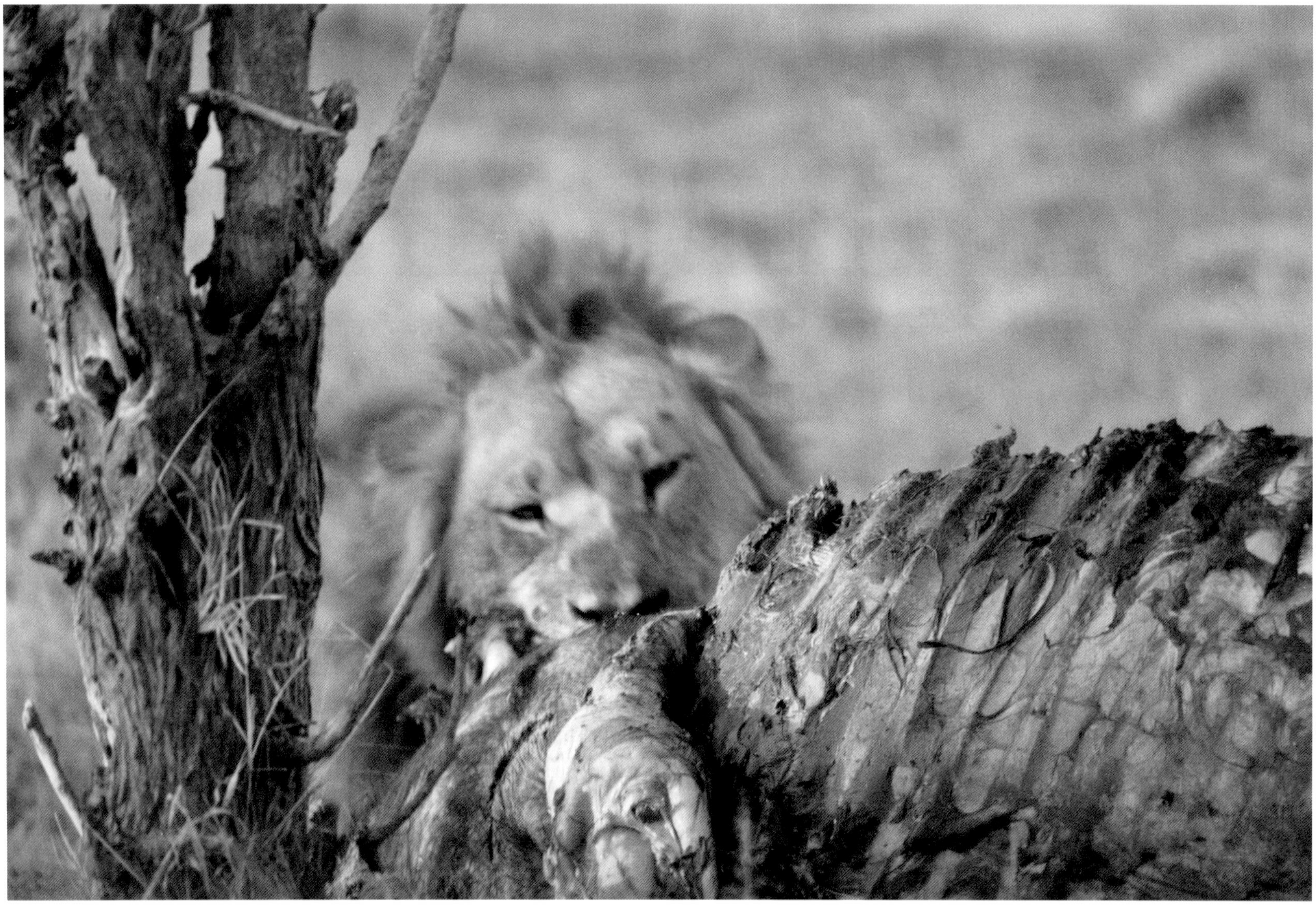

The animals could not, I suppose, be said to be living at peace with one another, because predators were constantly hunting their prey, but only when they were hungry; species did not do battle against species, or herds vie with each other for power and glory; no animal oppressed or tortured another; they shared the pastures, the bush, the shade and foliage of trees, the salt-licks and the drinking places without dispute or rancour. They did not, as Walt Whitman put it, whine about their condition, weep for their sins, or agonise over their duty to God.

**Elspeth Huxley, *Out In The Midday Sun***

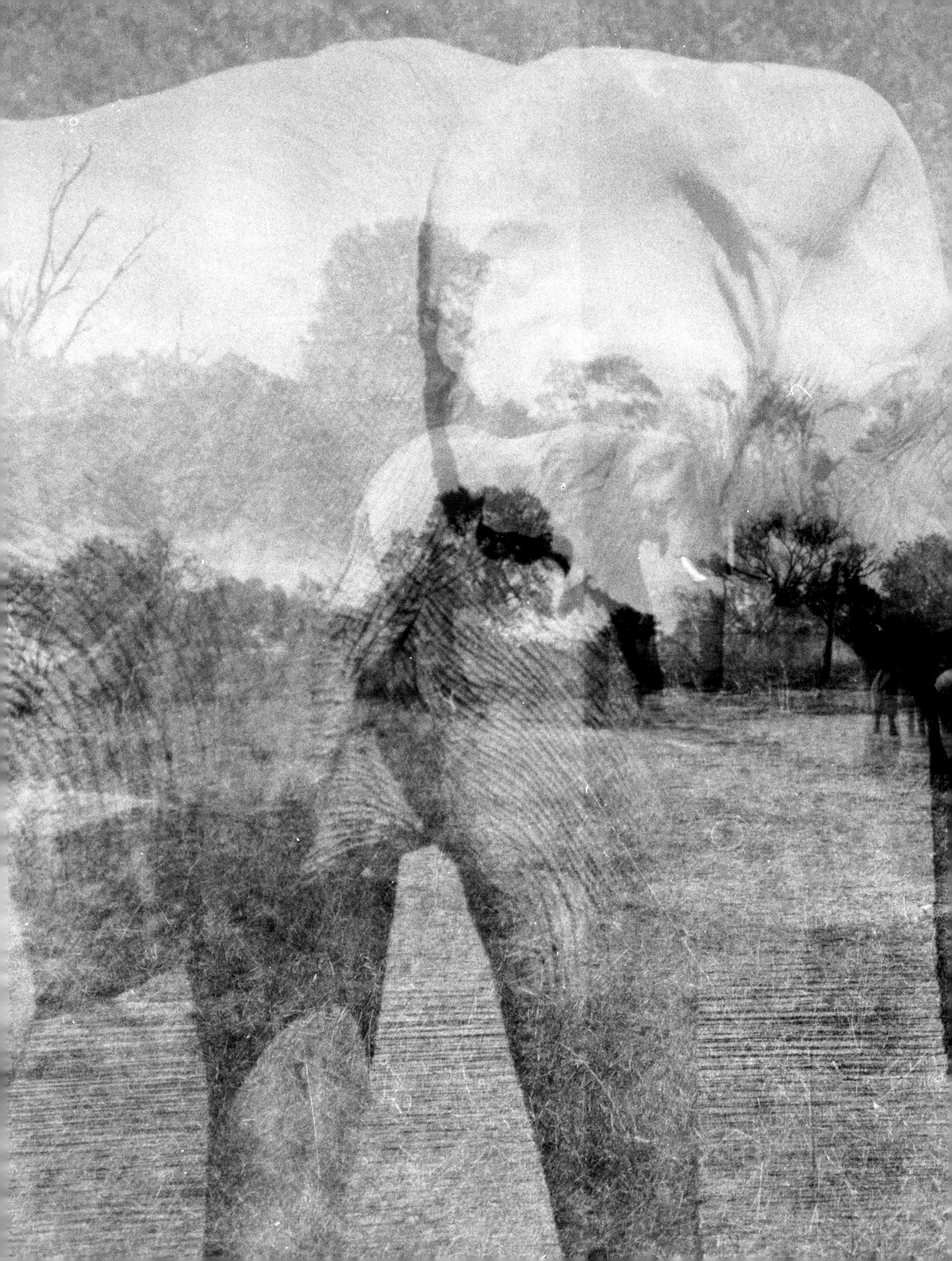

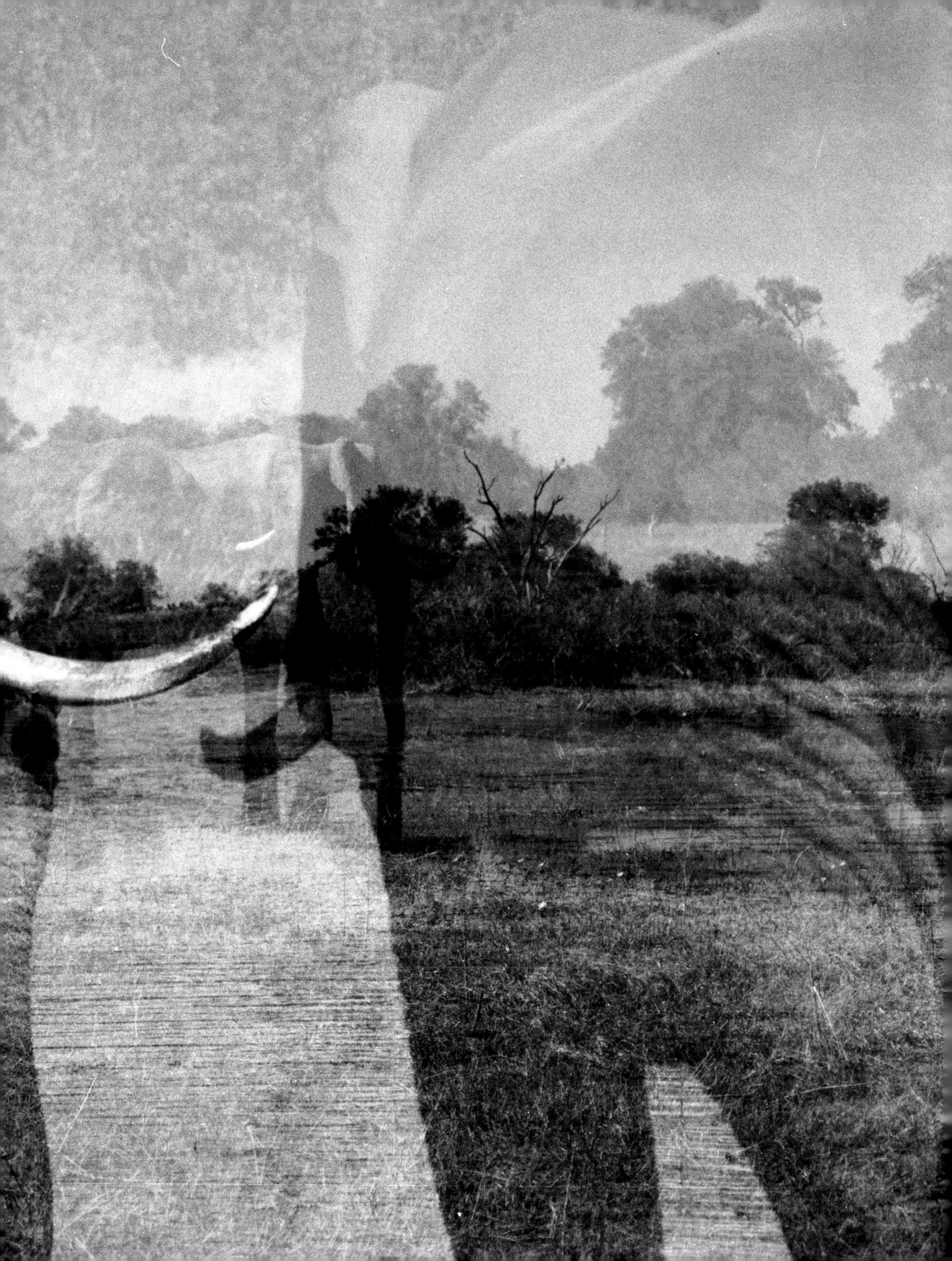

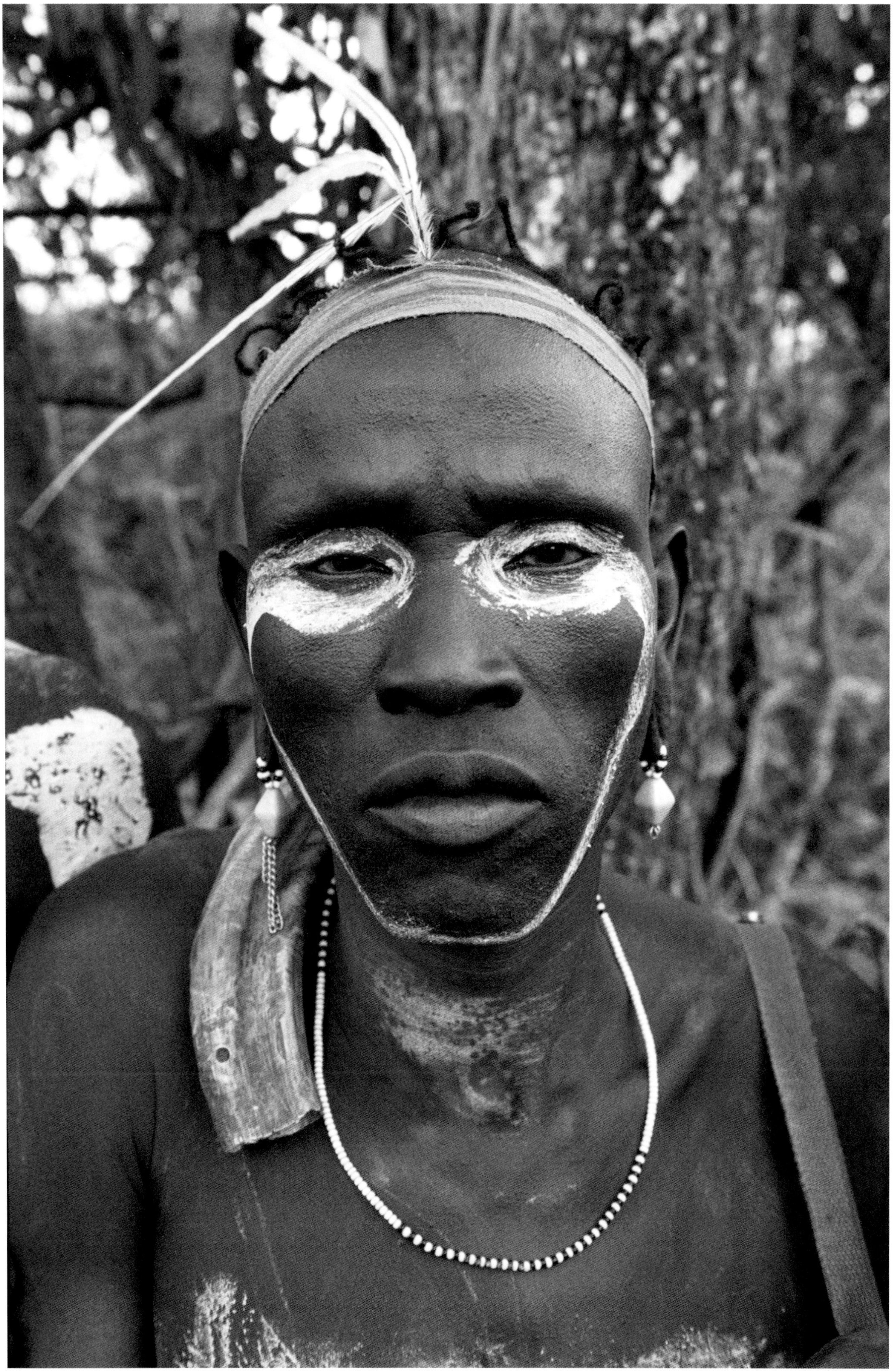

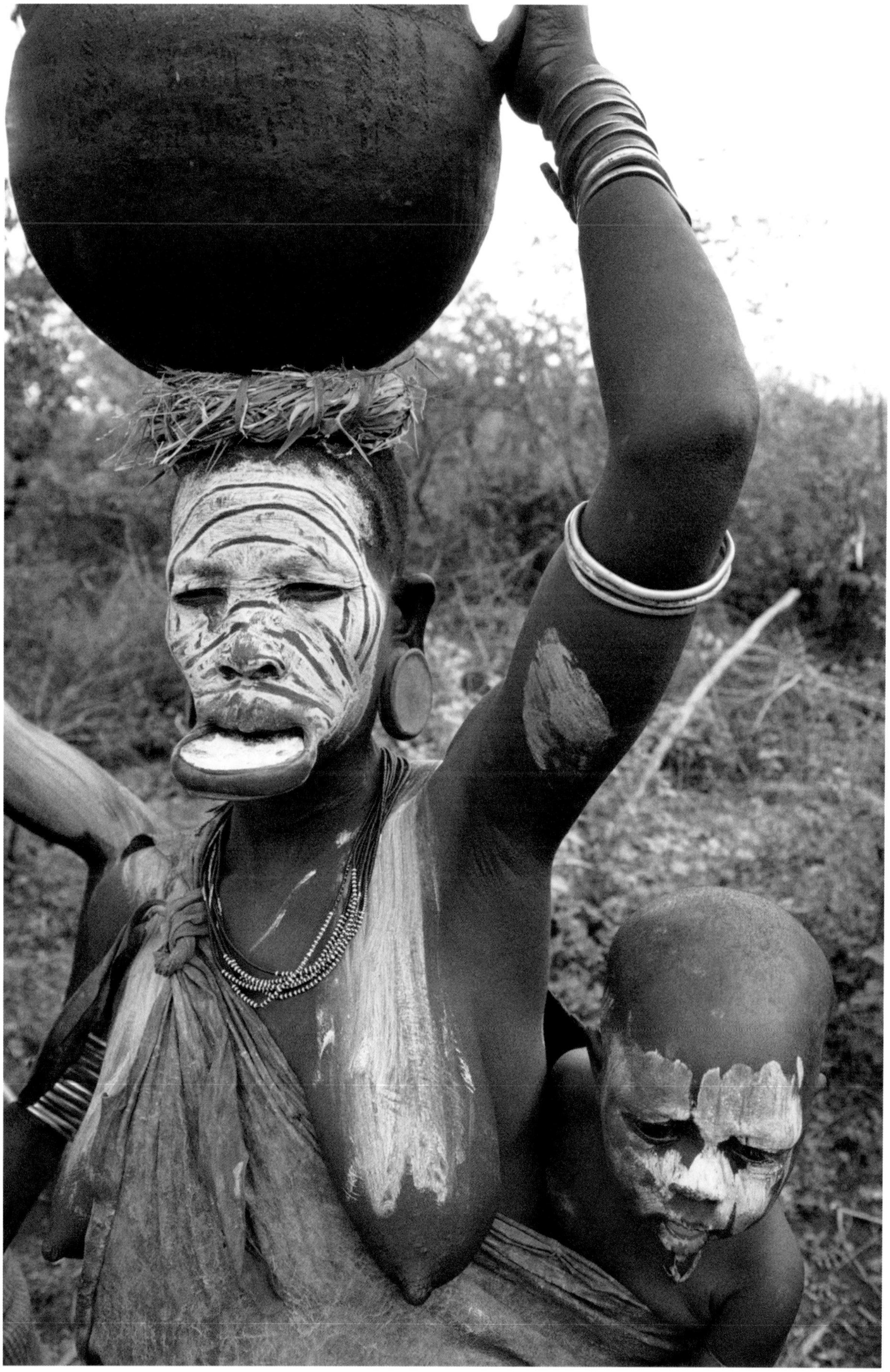

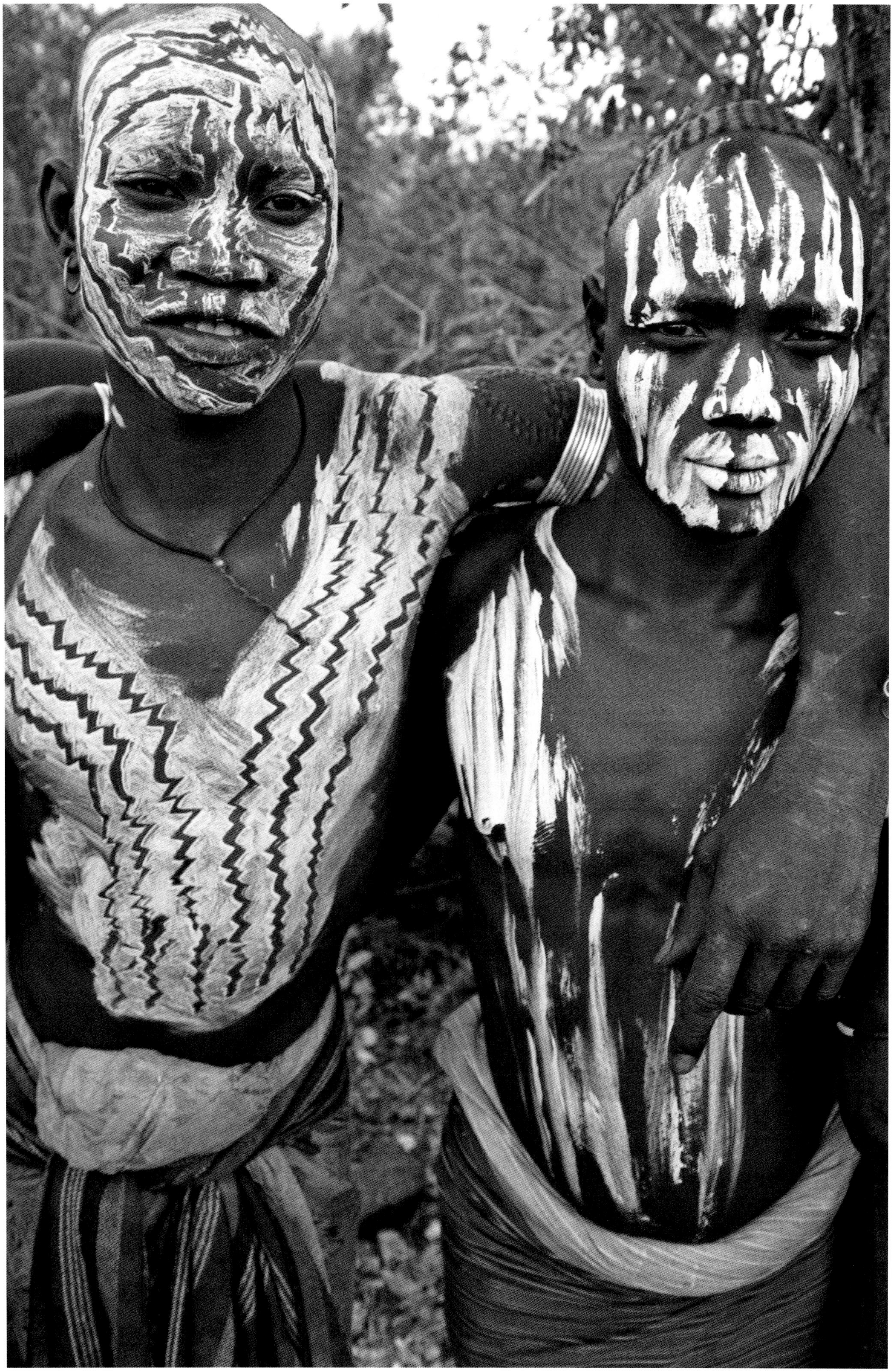

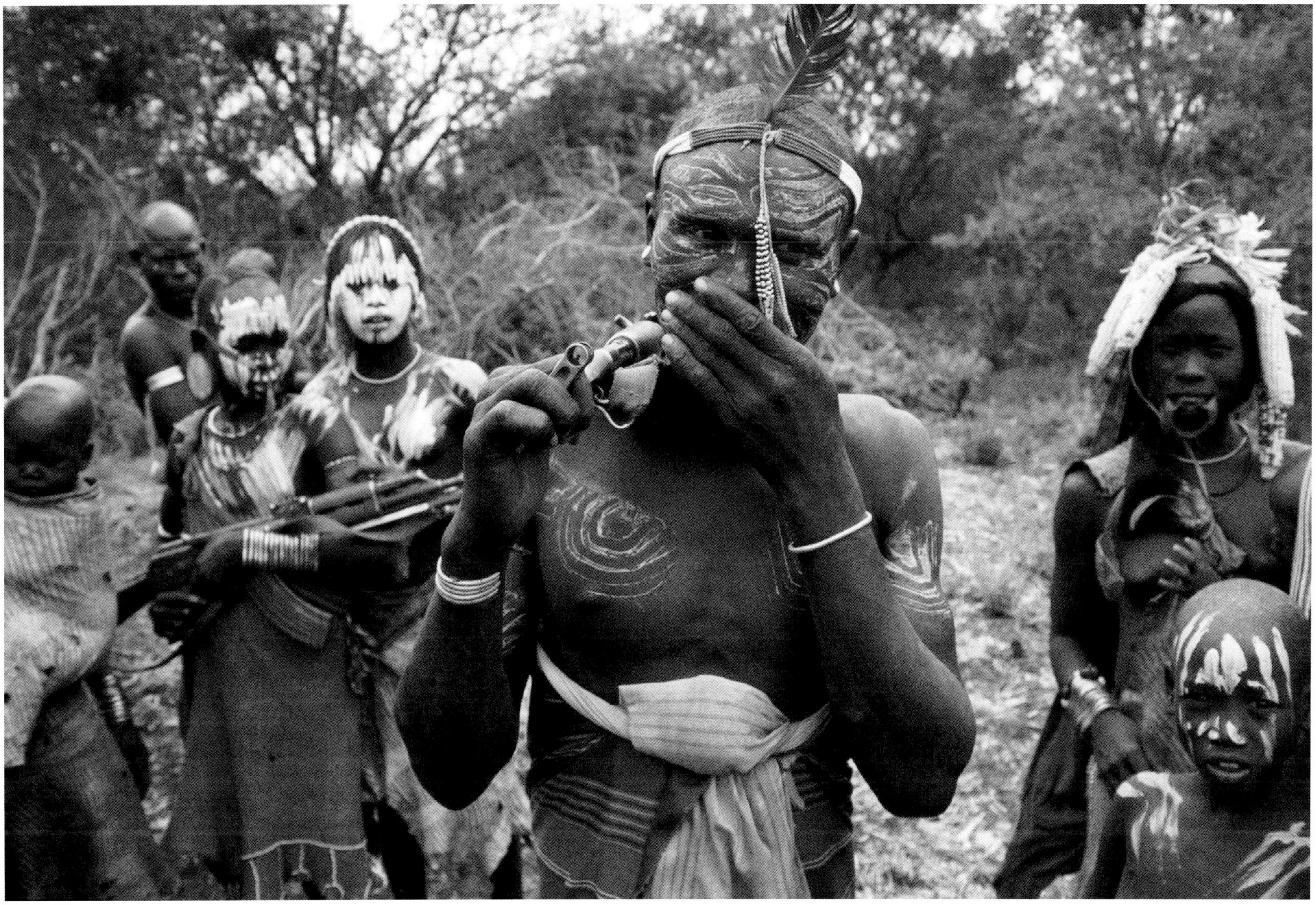

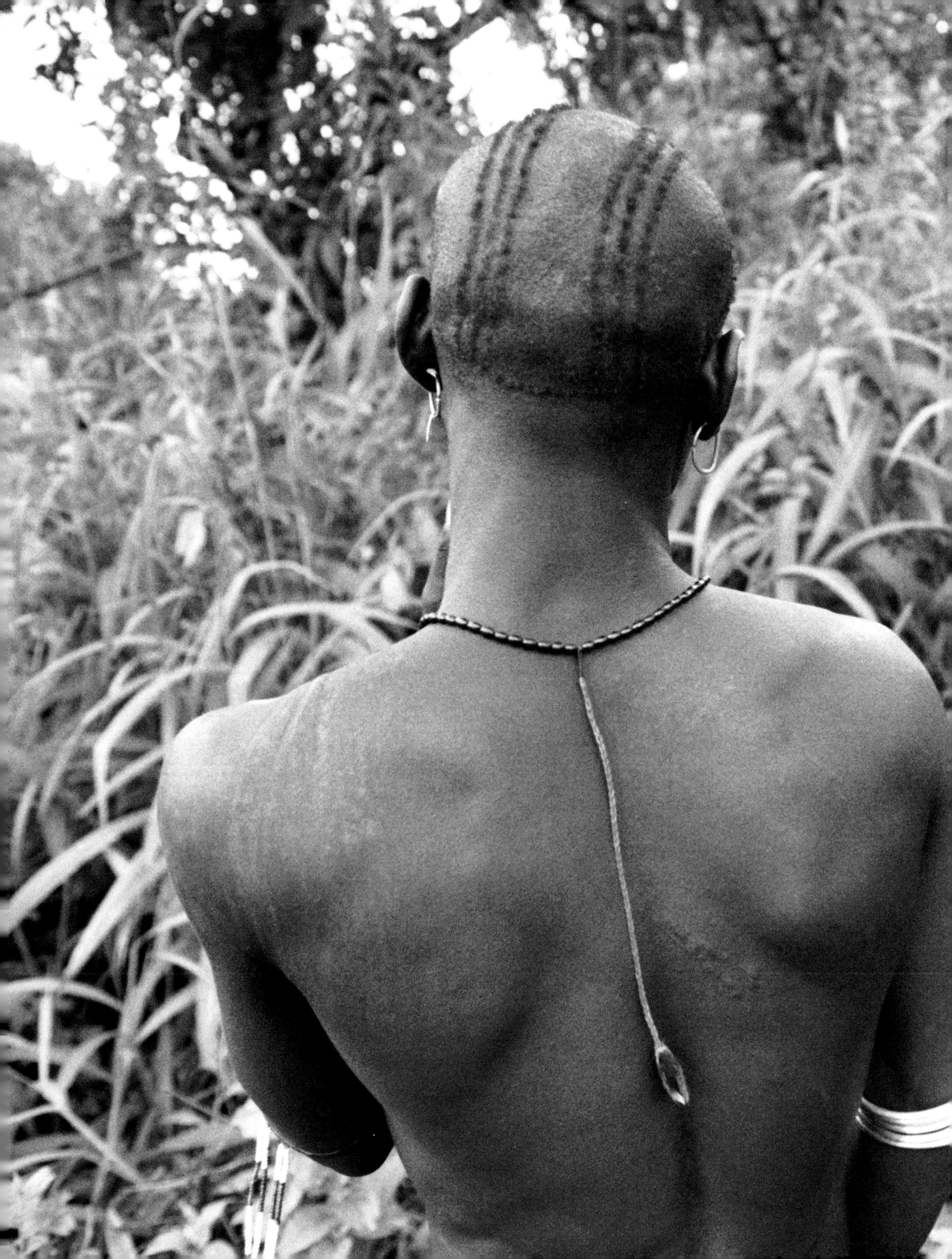

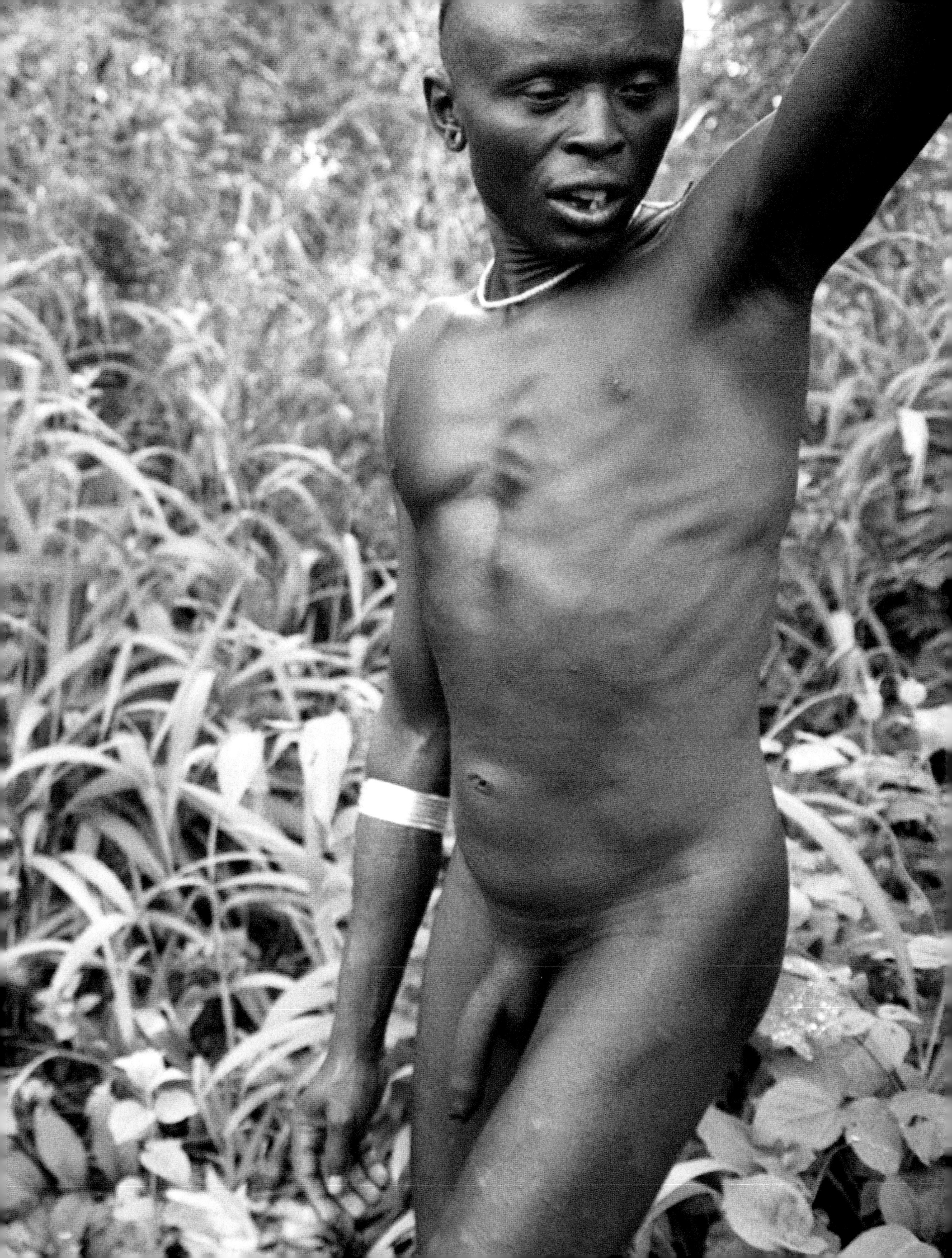

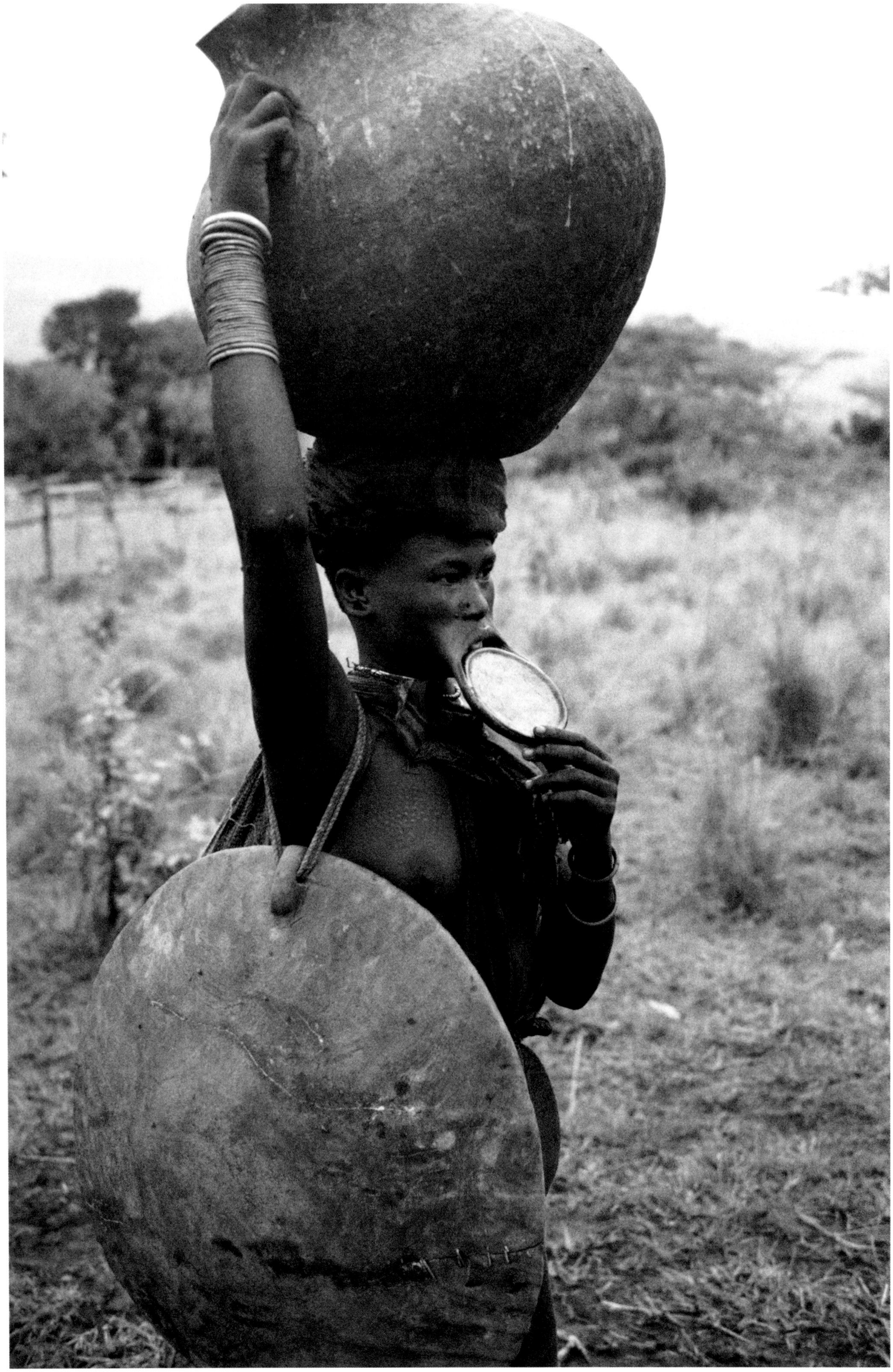

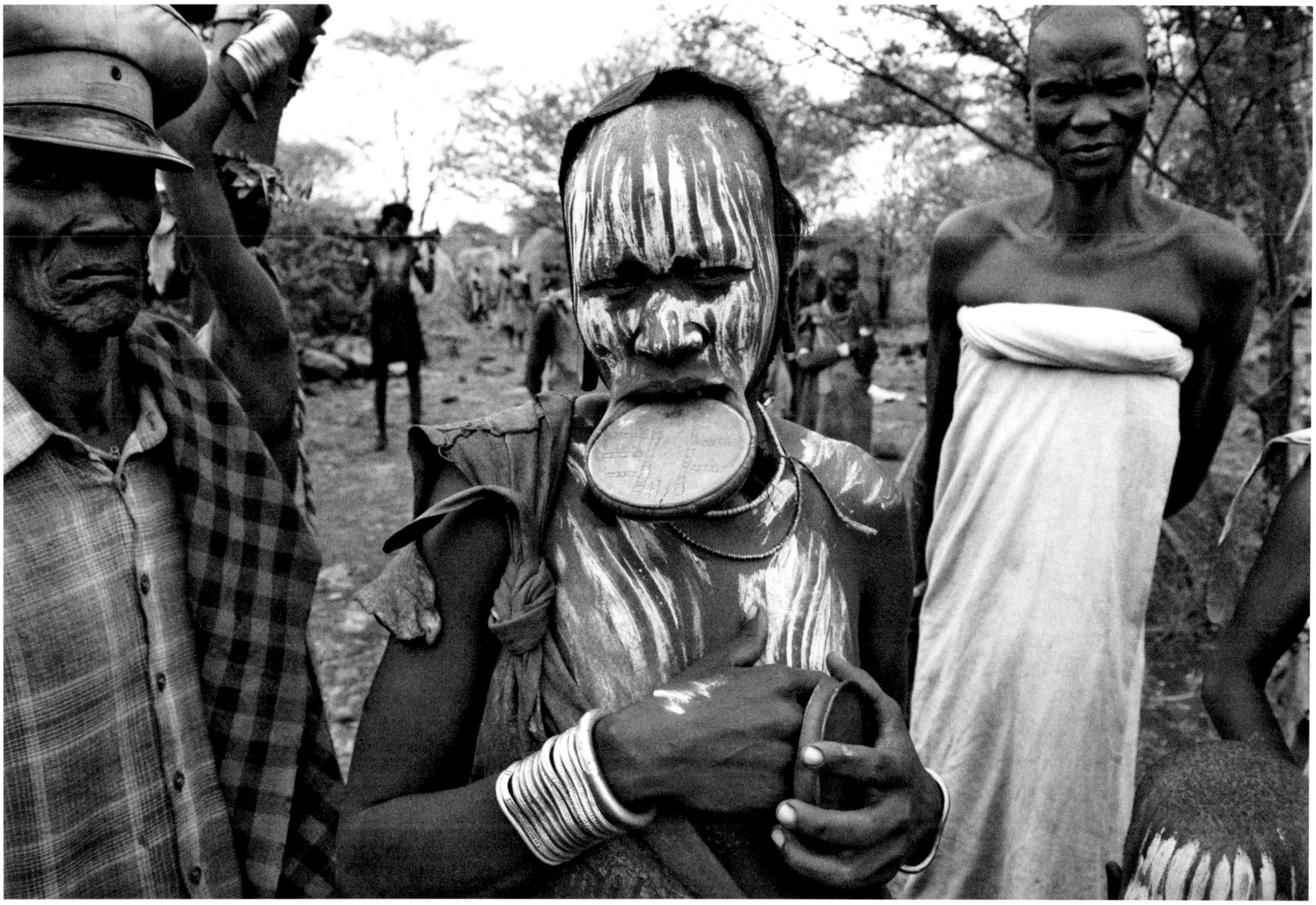

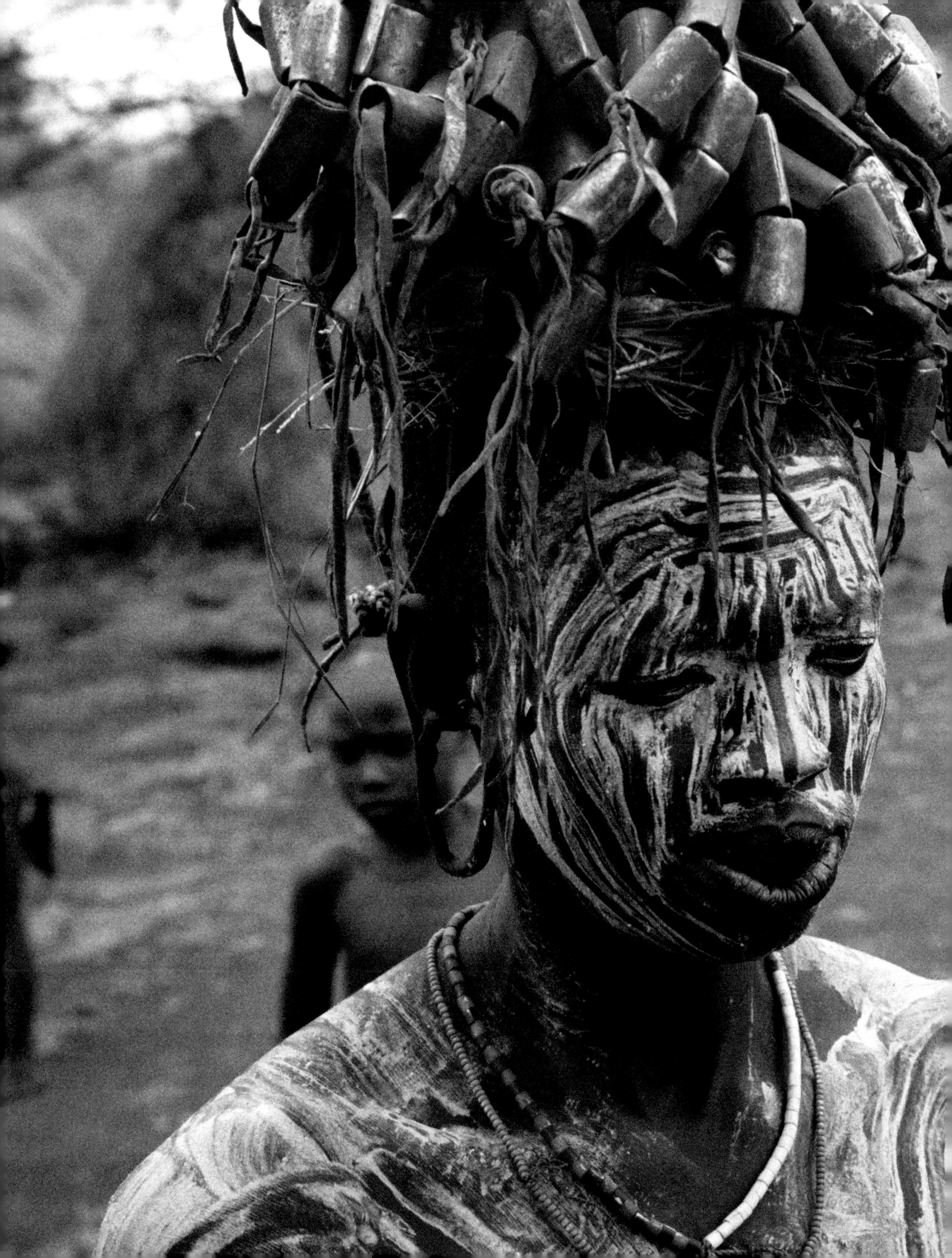

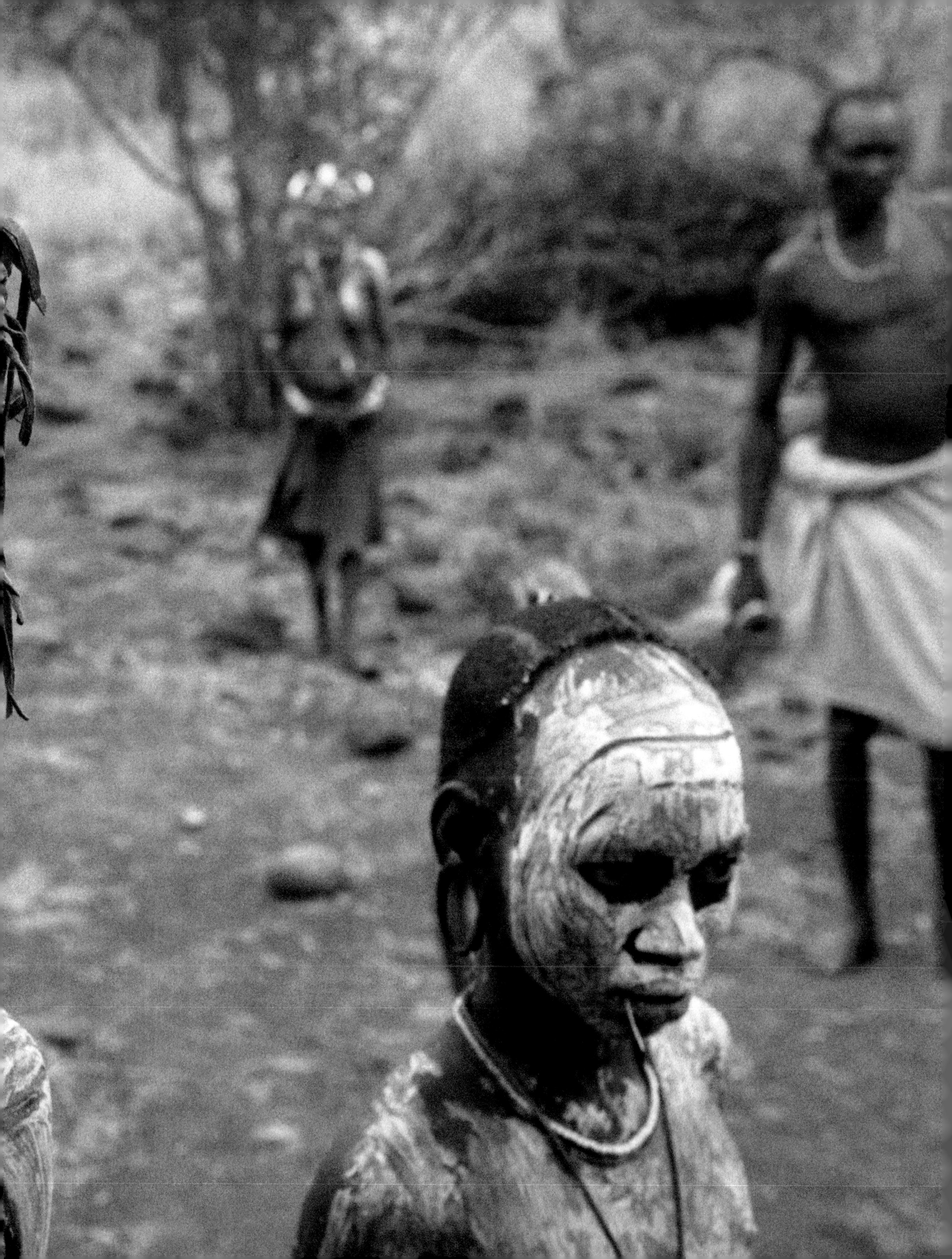

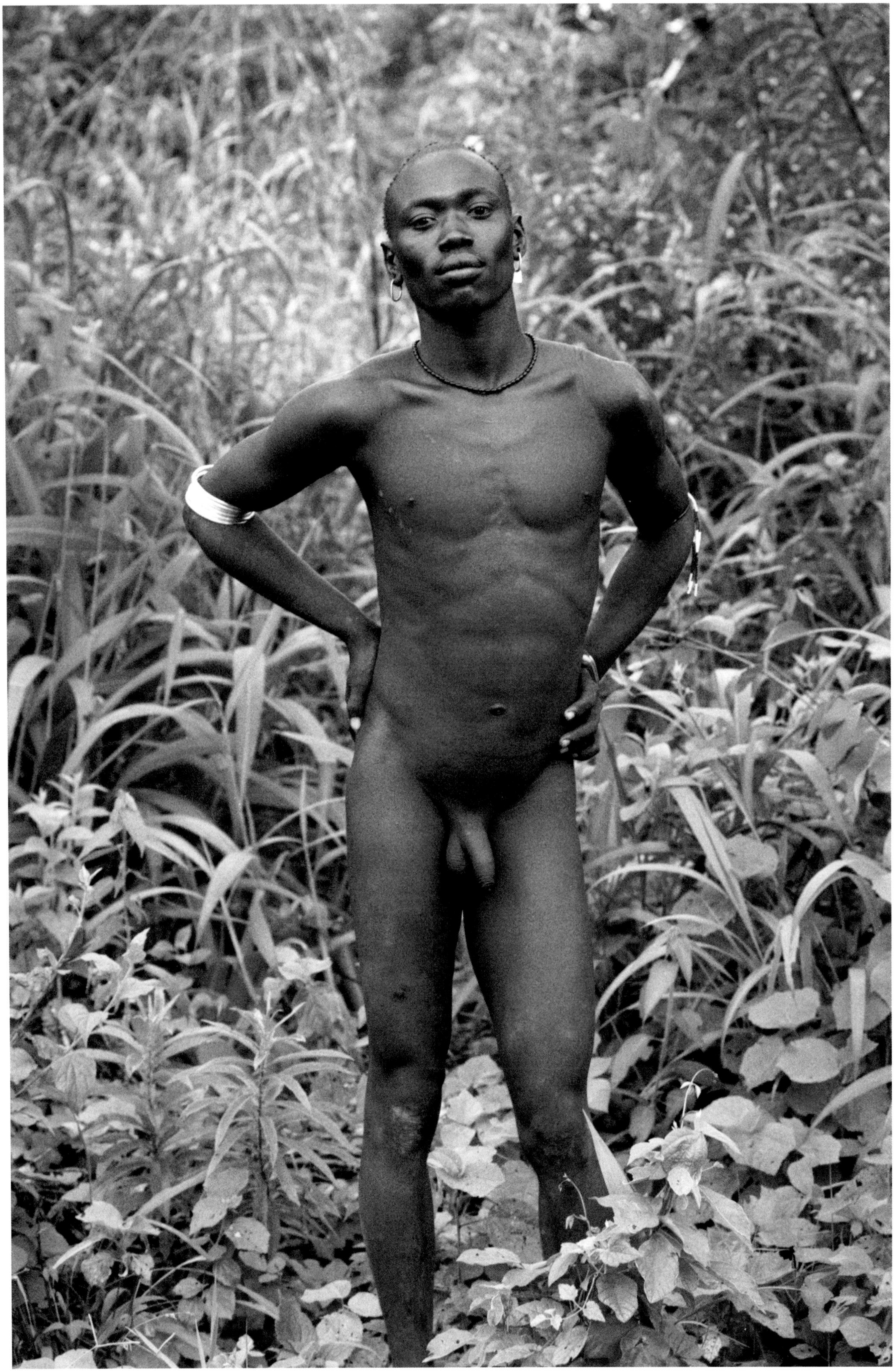

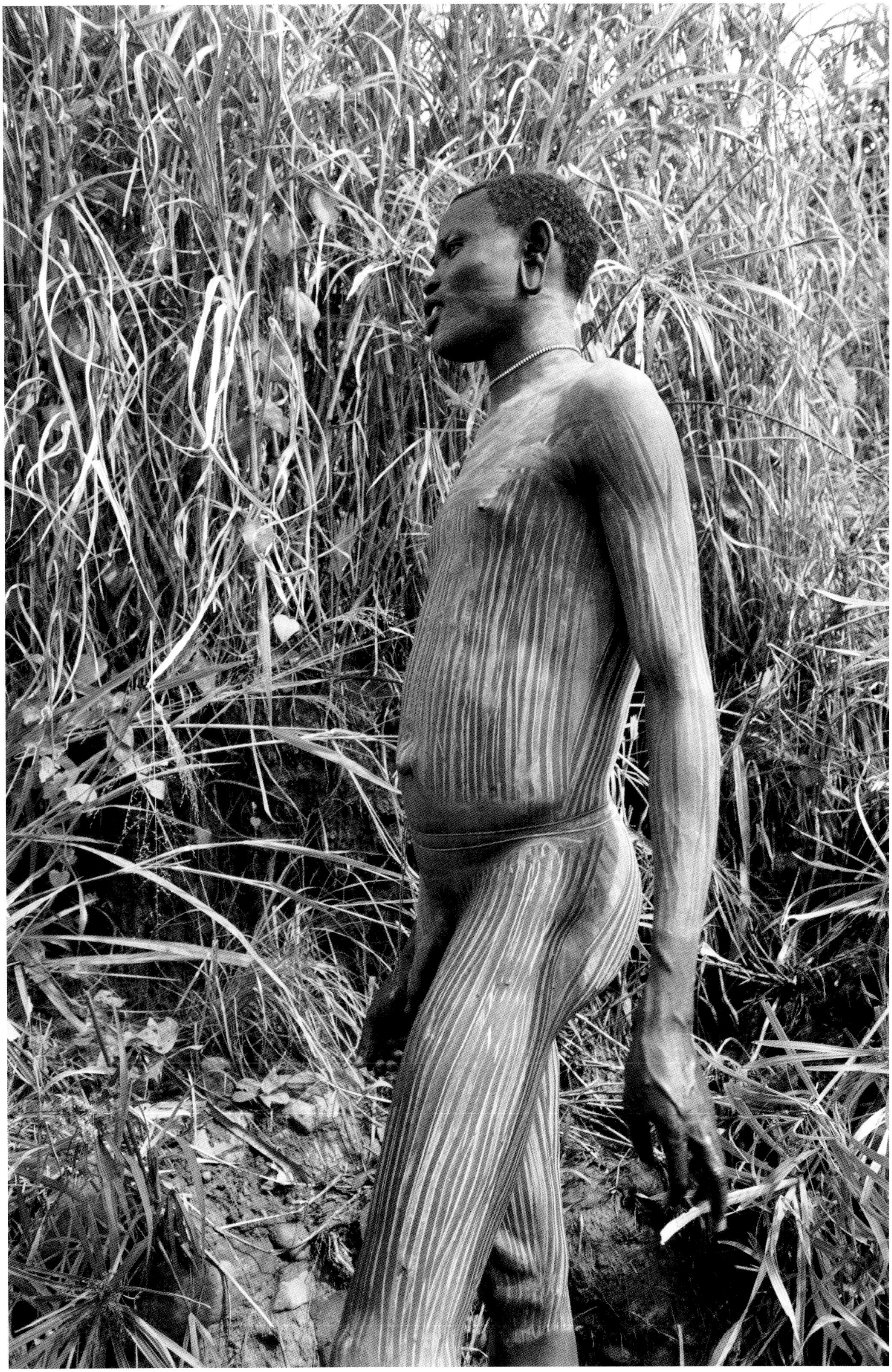

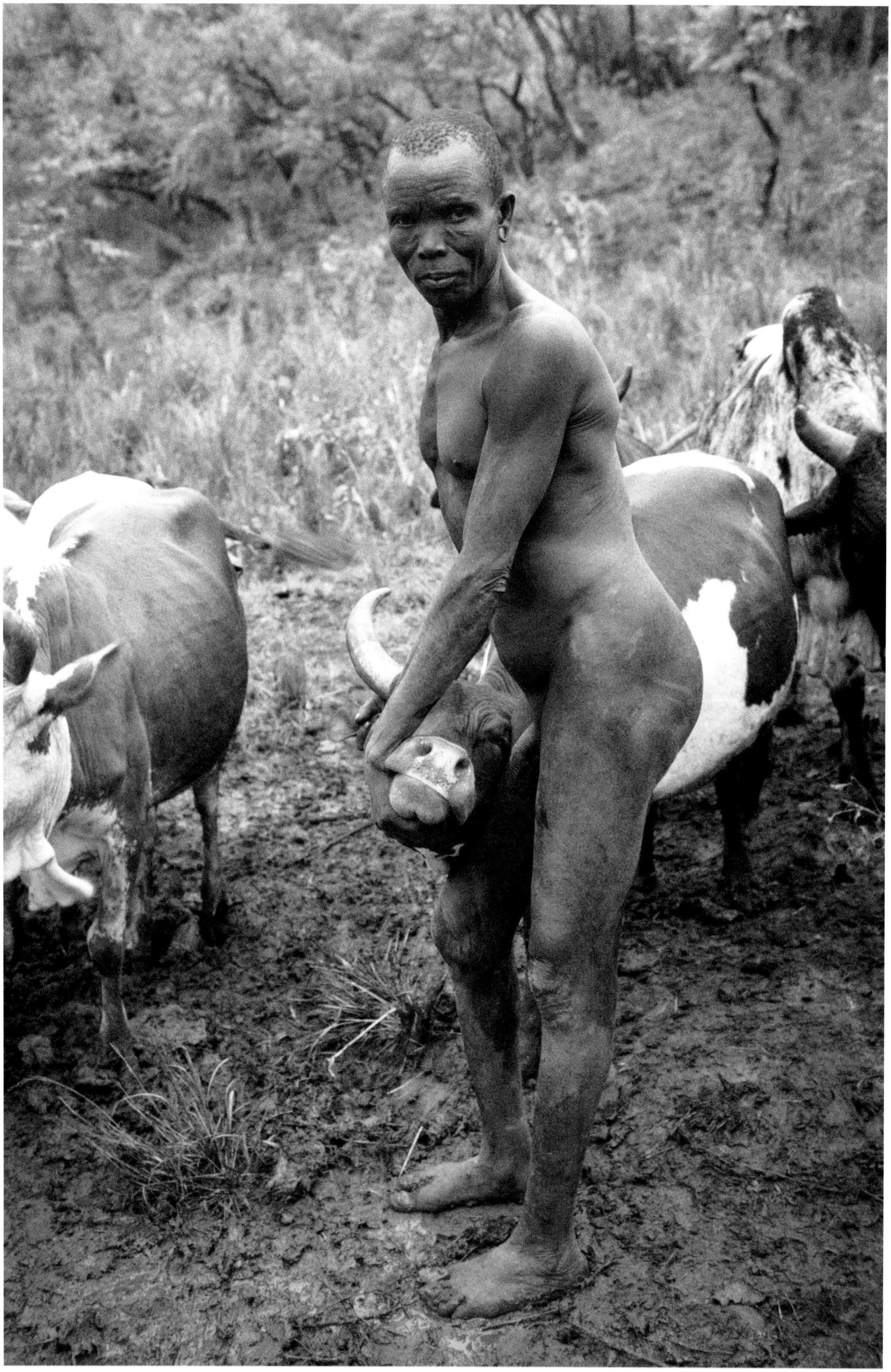

... there is a void in the life of the African, a spiritual emptiness, divorced as he is from each world, standing in between, torn in both directions. To go forward is to abandon the past in which the roots of his being have their nourishment; to go backward is to cut himself off from the future, for there is no doubt about where the future lies. The African has been taught to abandon his old ways, yet he is not accepted in the new world even when he has mastered its ways. There seems to be no bridge, and this is the source of his terrible loneliness.

**Colin Turnbull, *The Lonely African***

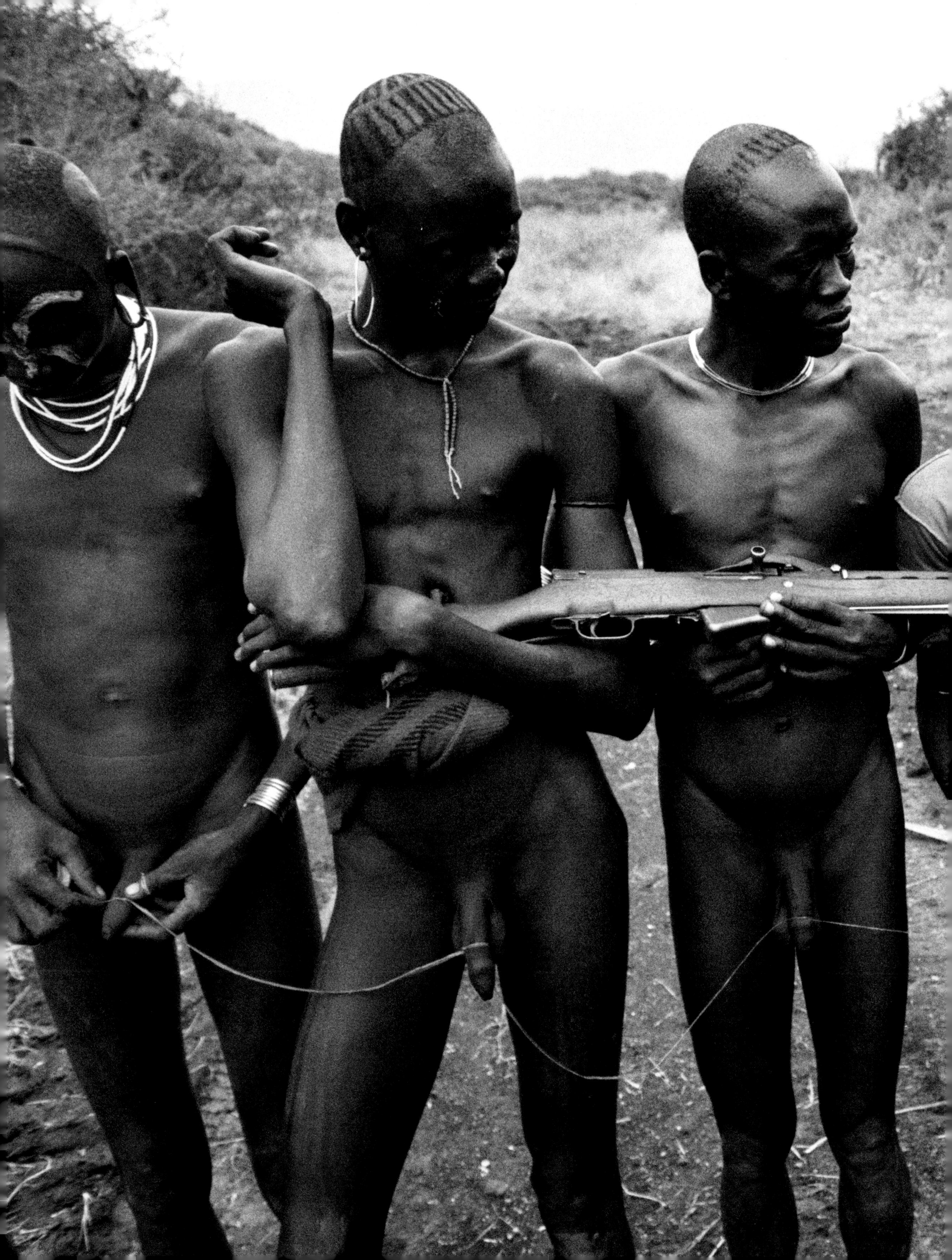

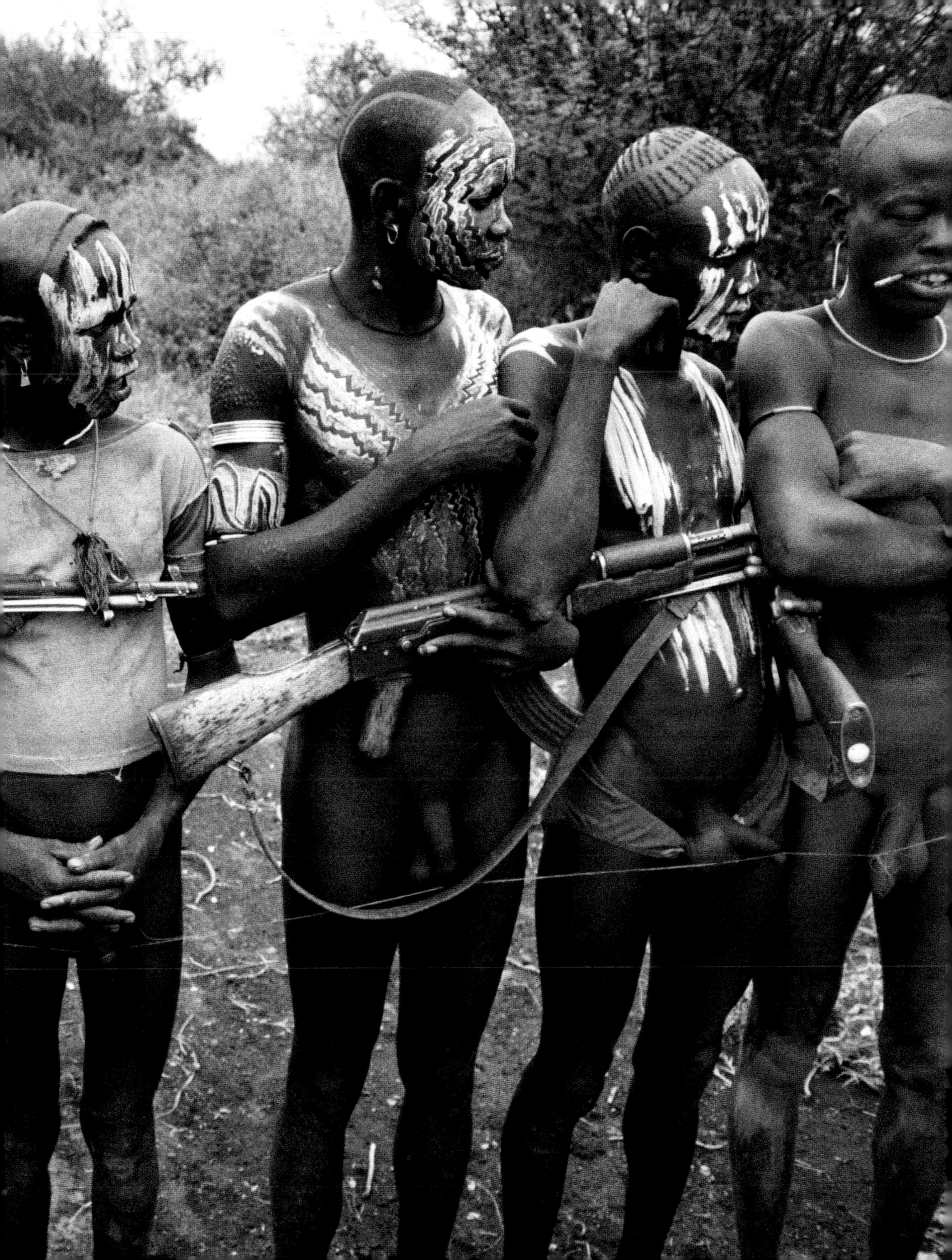

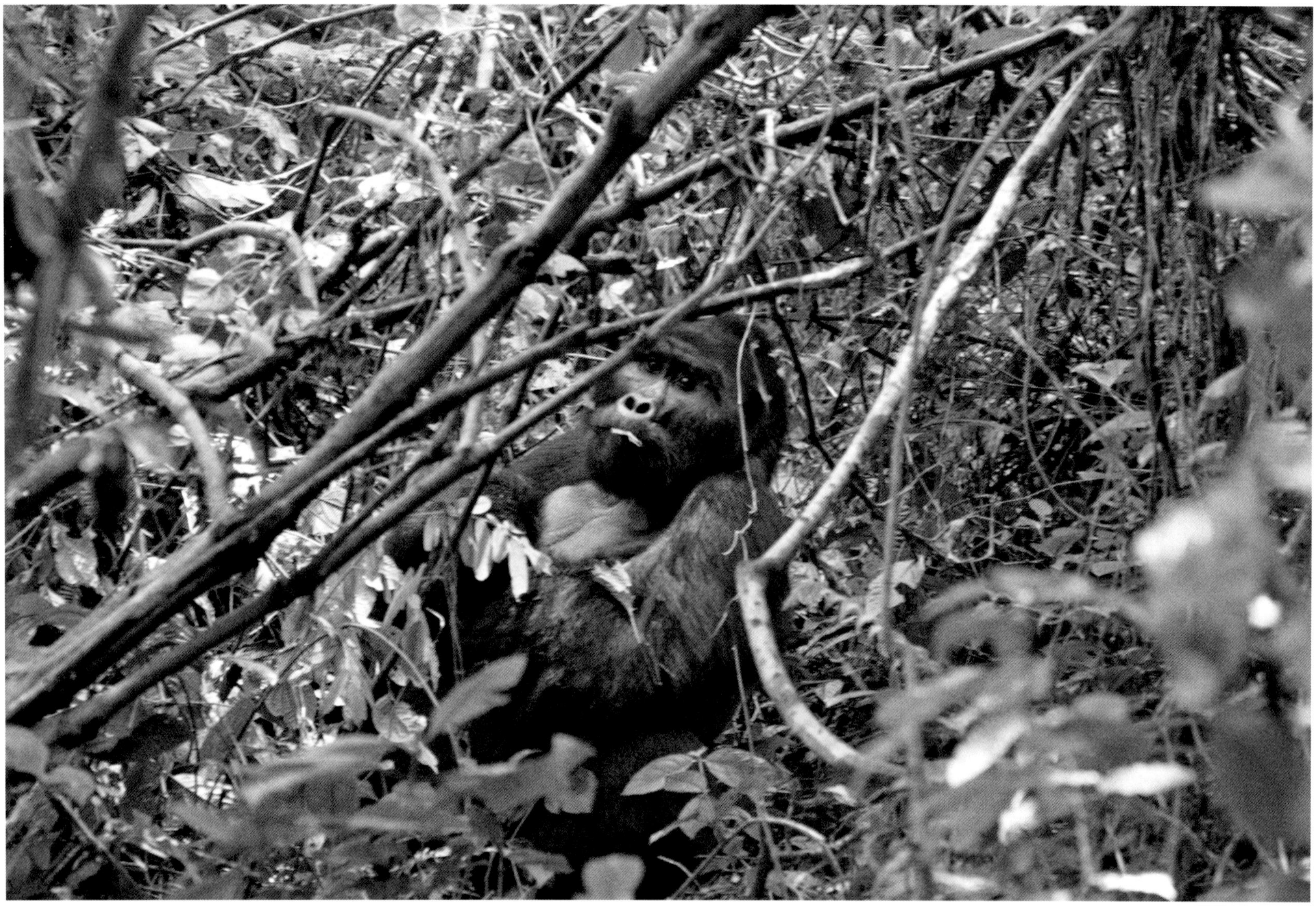

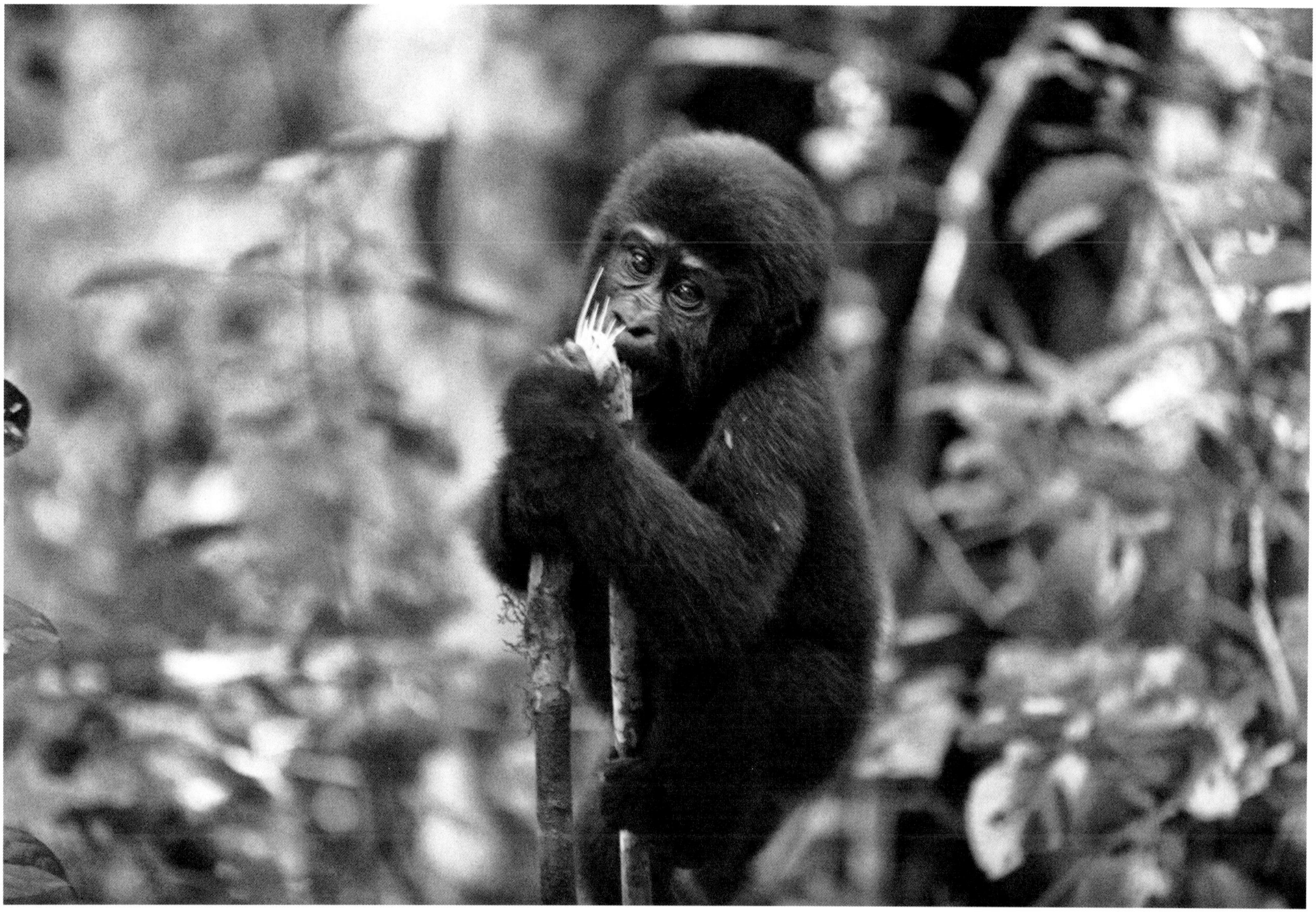

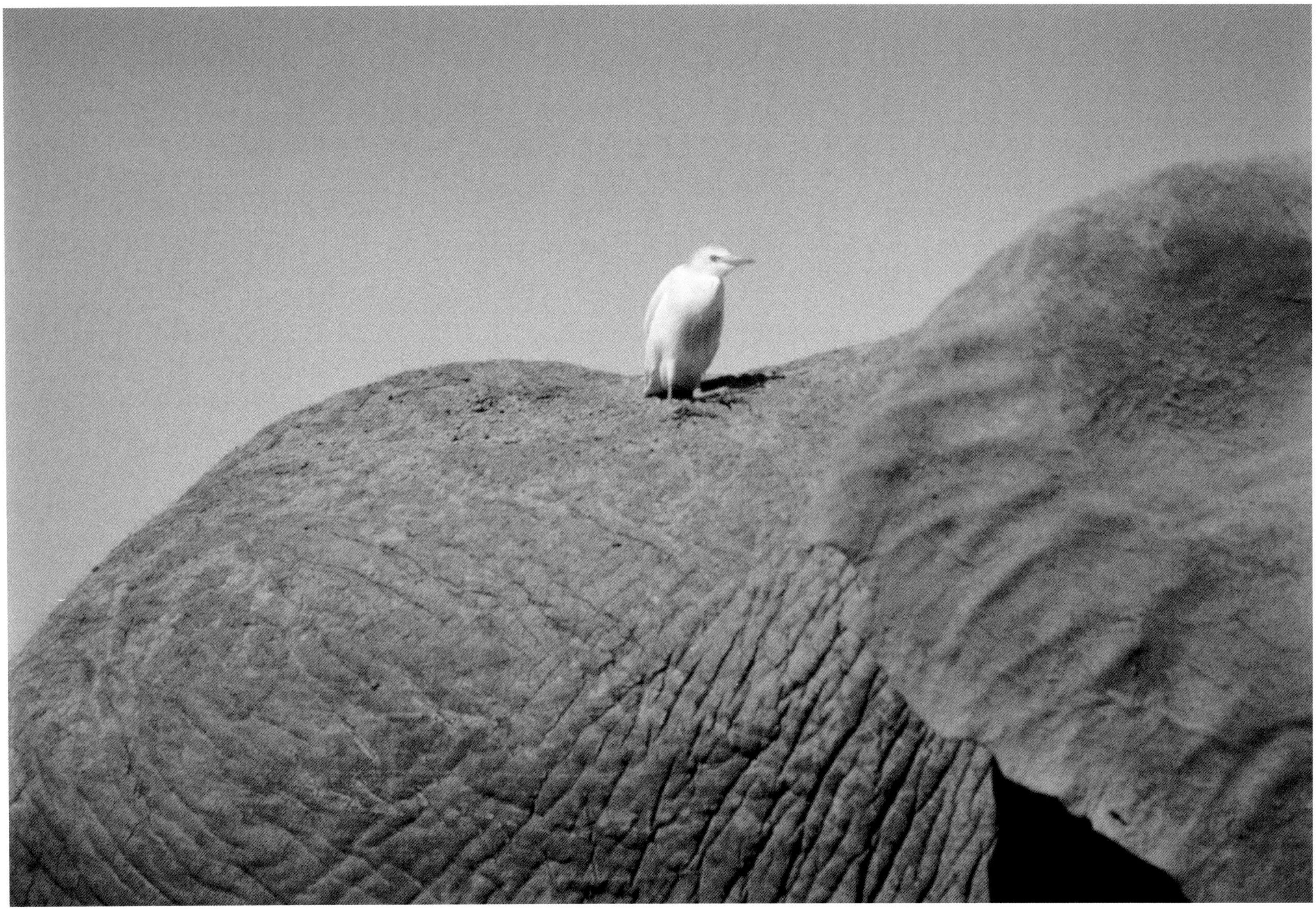

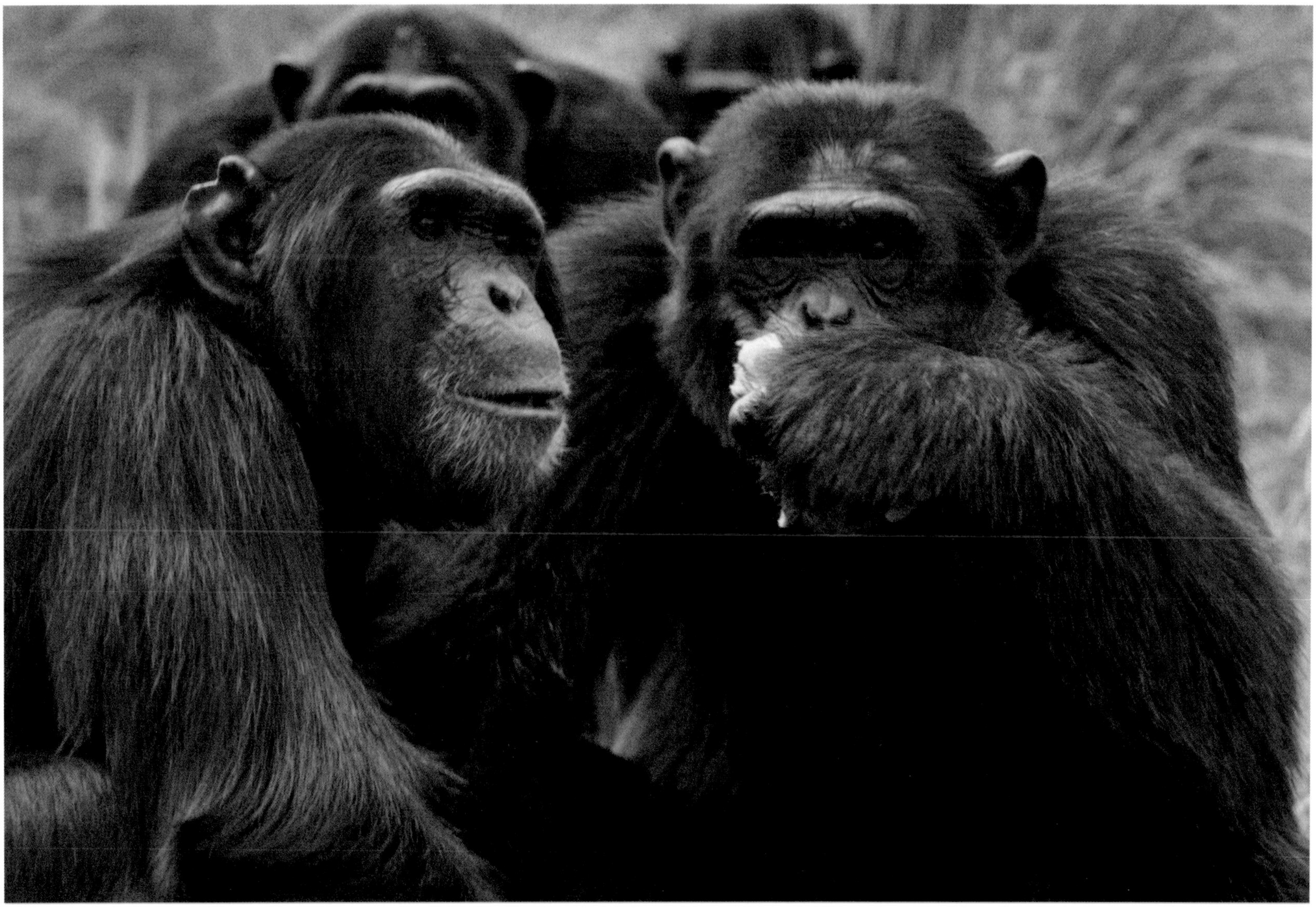

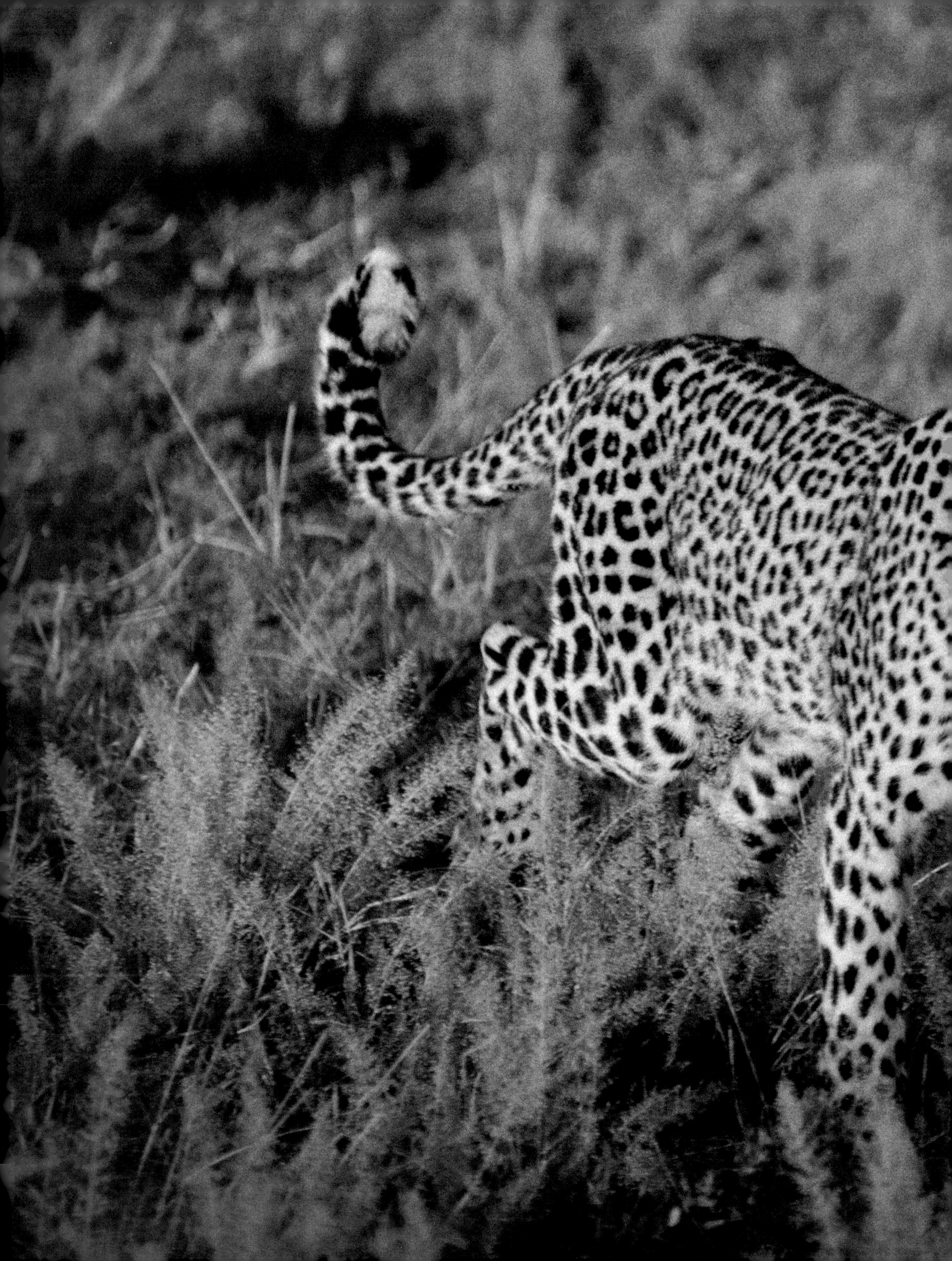

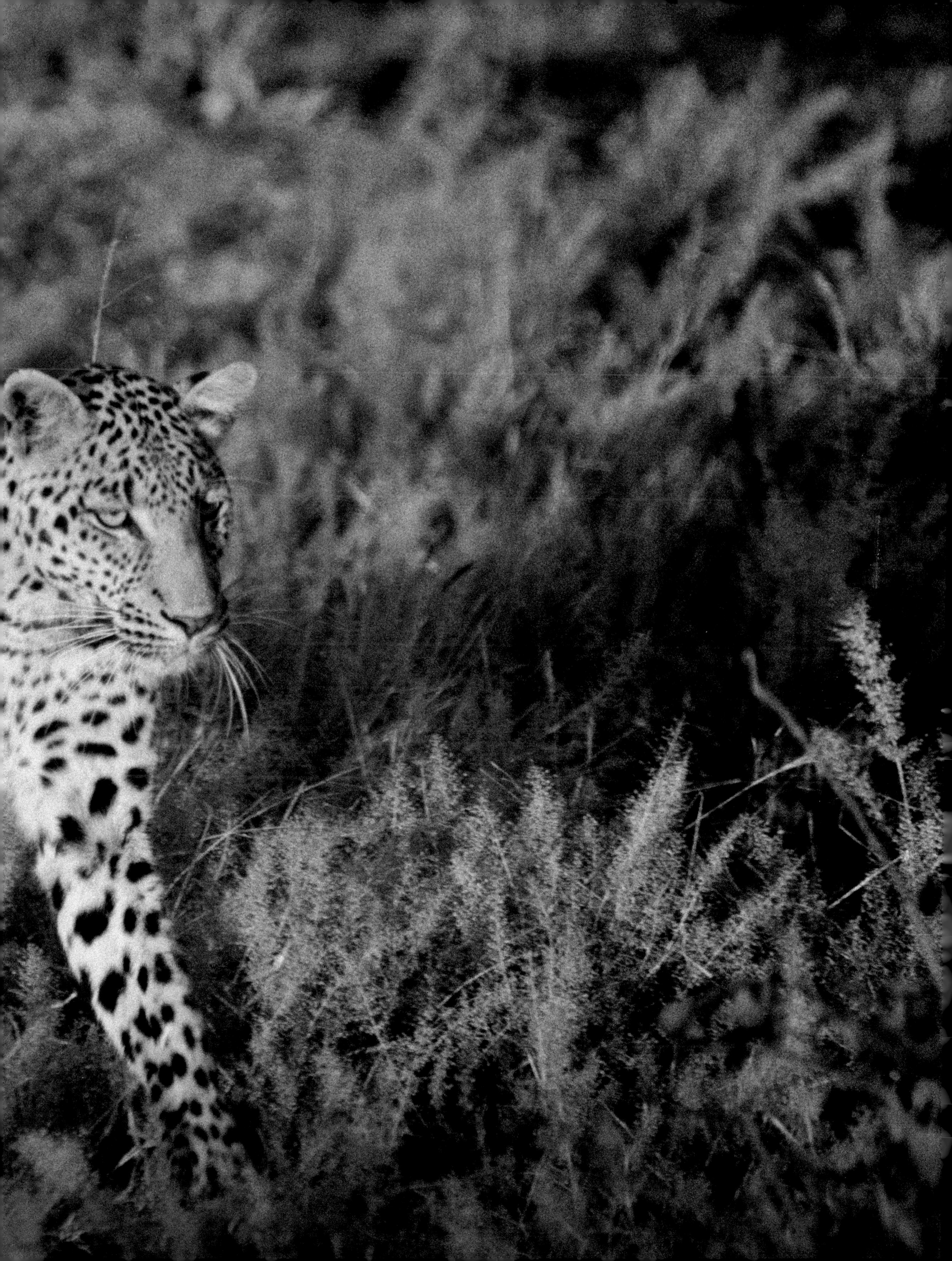

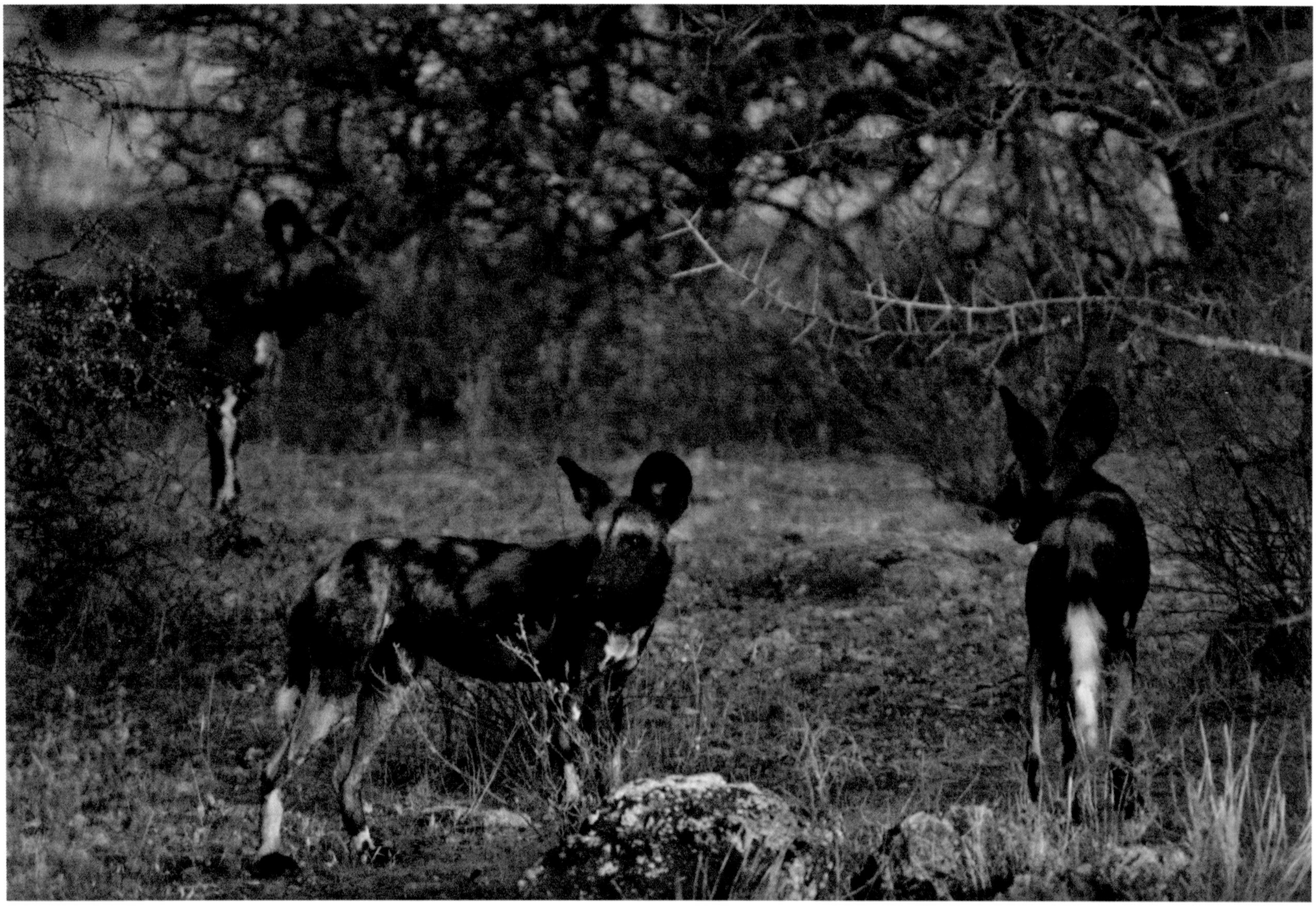

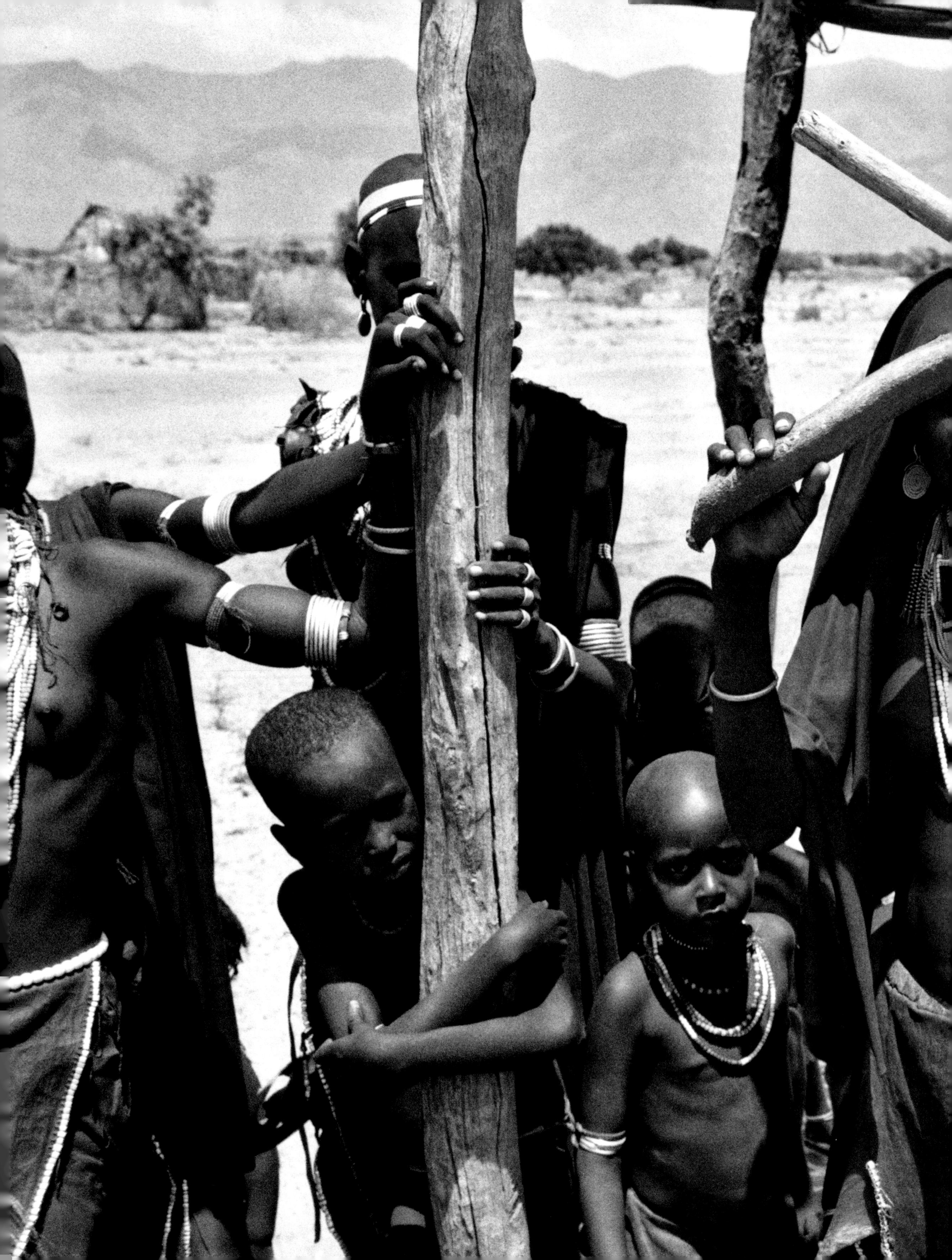

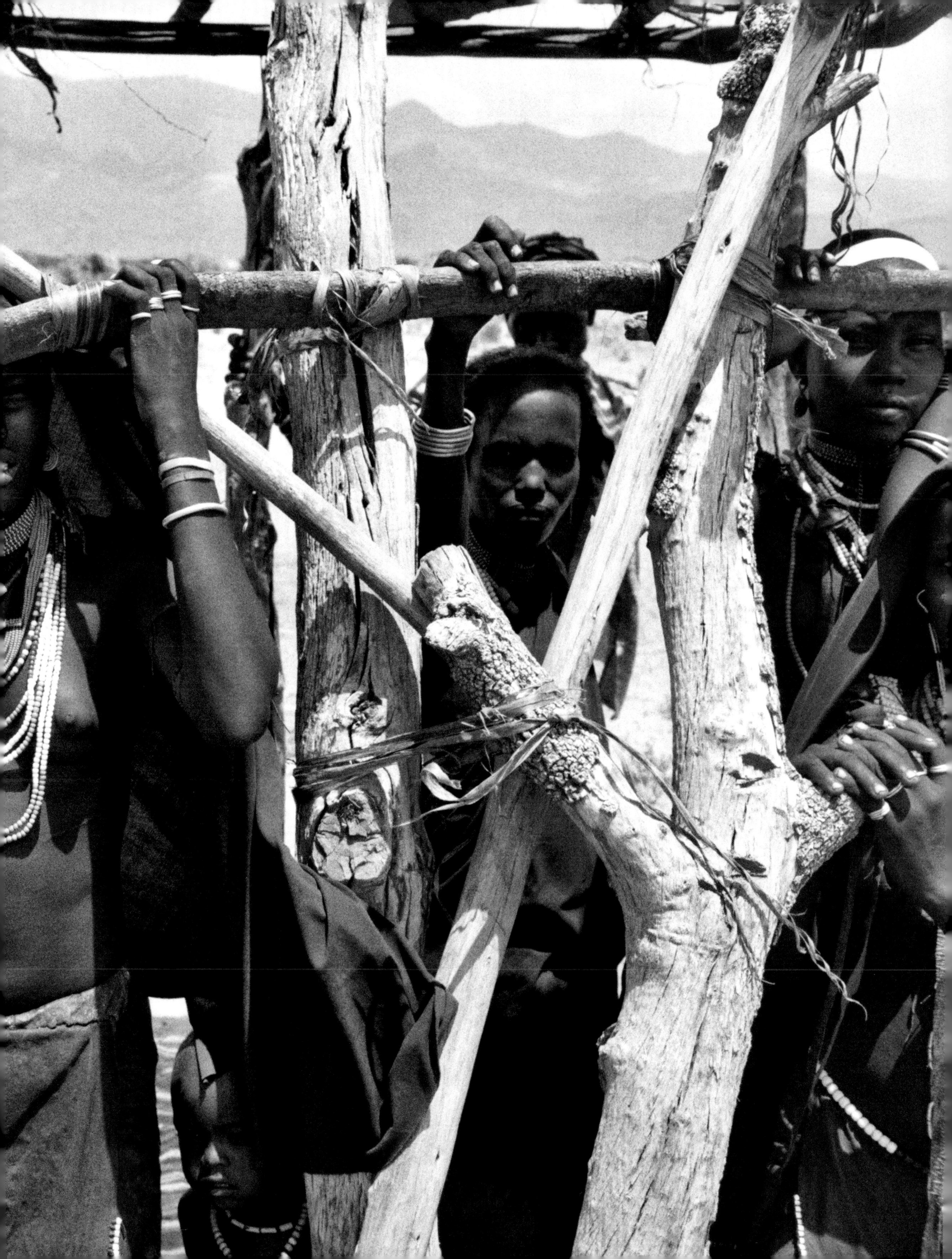

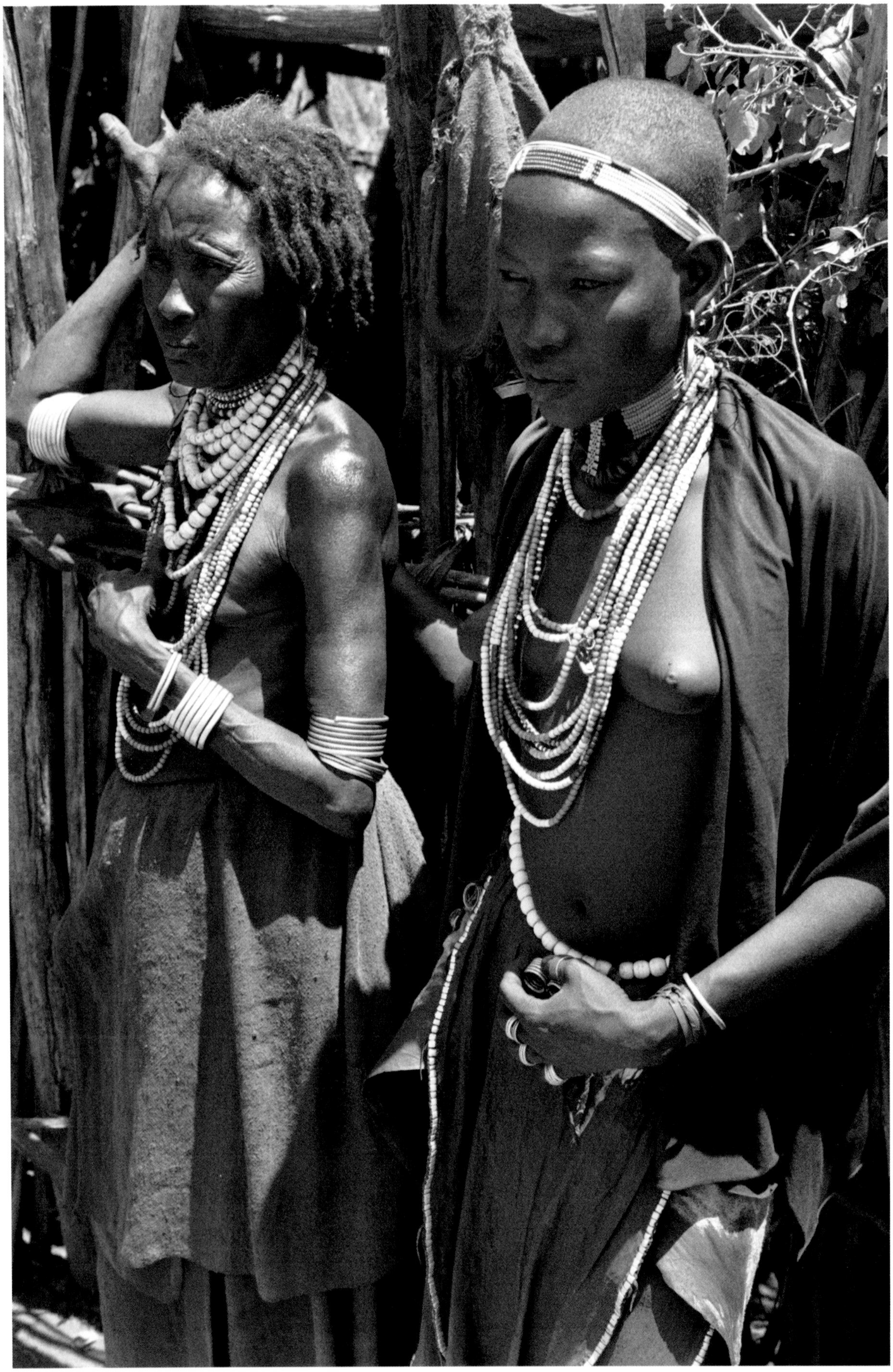

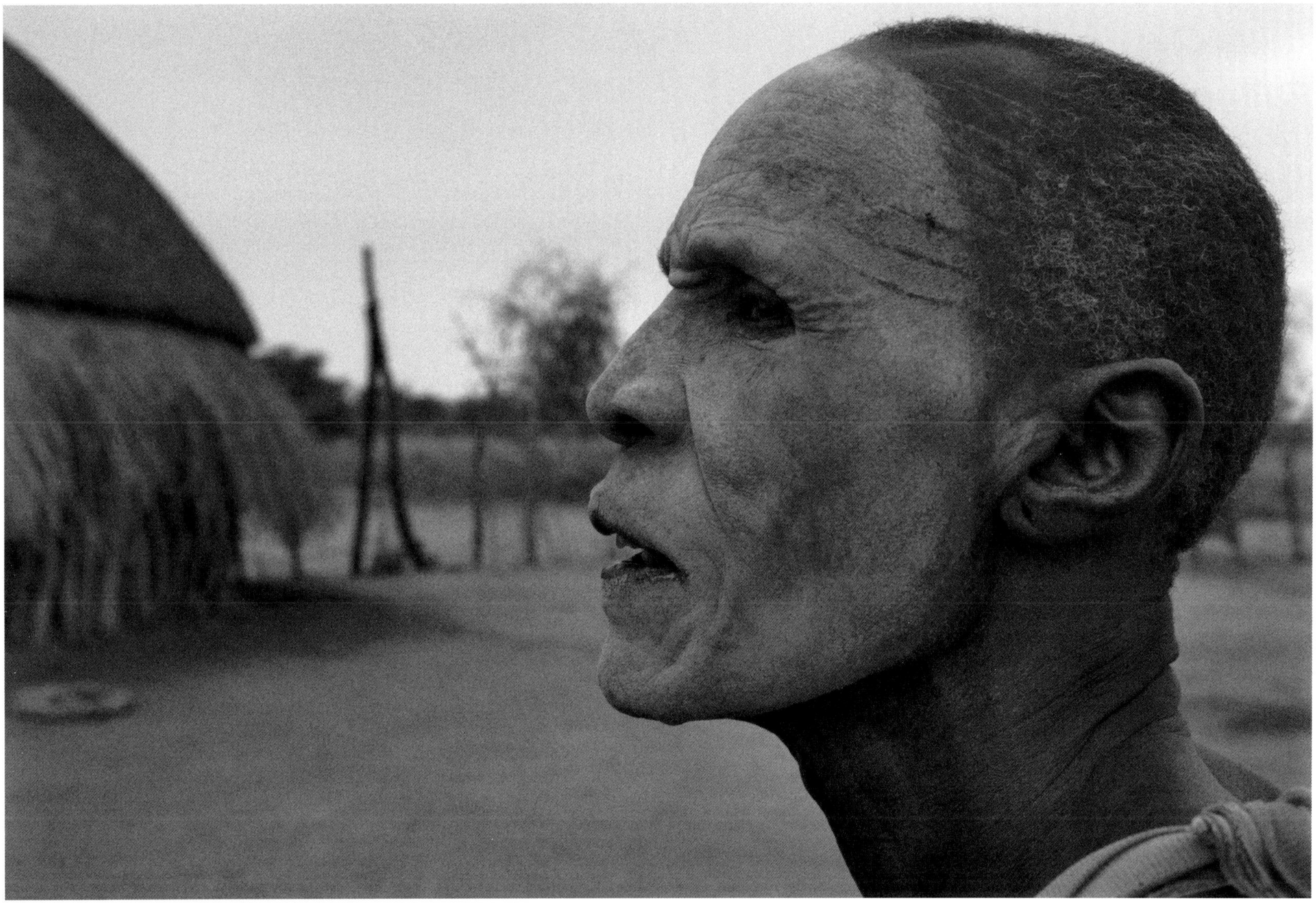

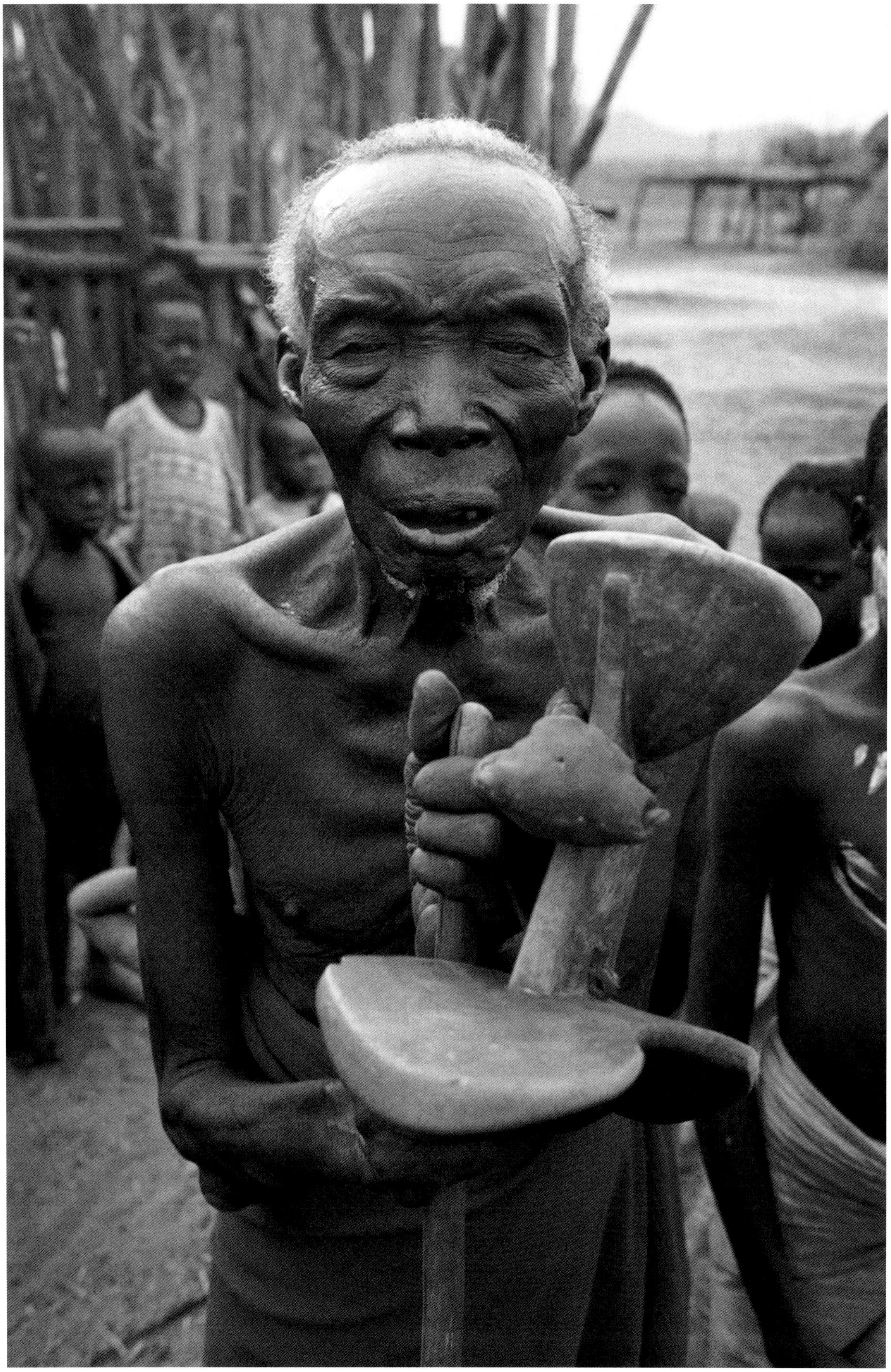

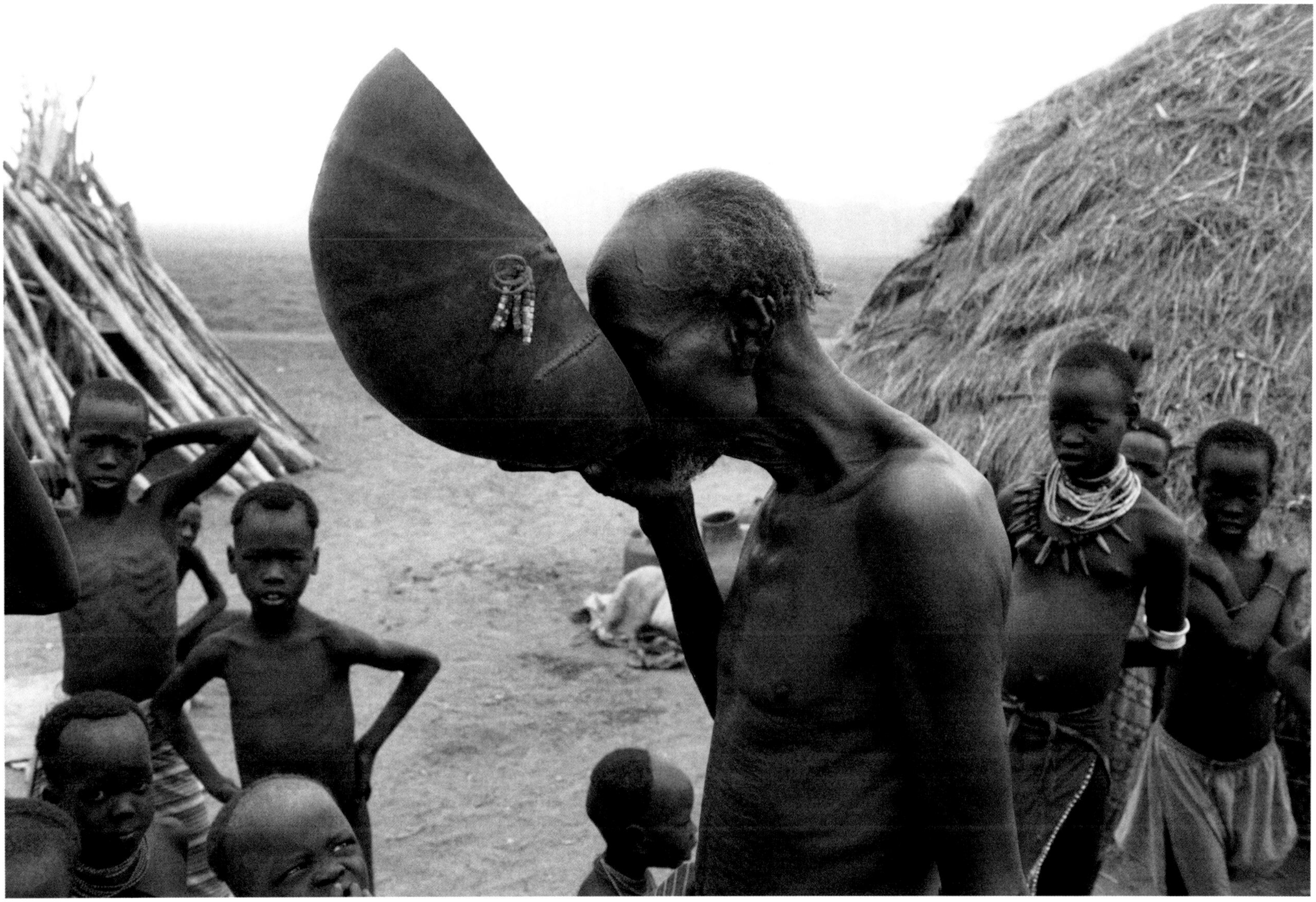

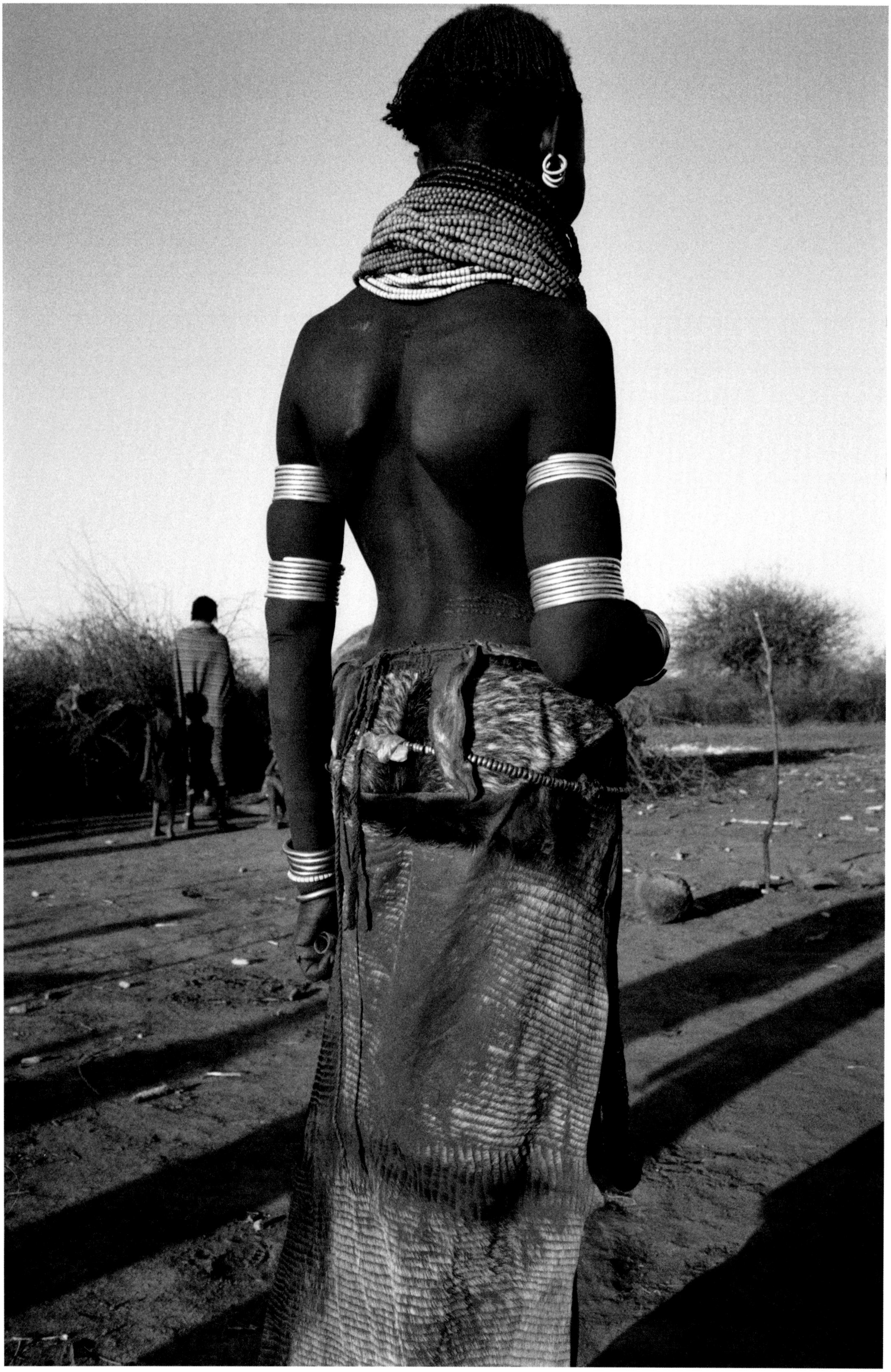

Mankind's true moral test, its fundamental test (which is deeply buried from view), consists of its attitude towards those who are at its mercy: animals. And in this respect humankind has suffered a fundamental debacle, a debacle so fundamental that all others stem from it.

**Milan Kundera, *The Unbearable Lightness of Being* (1984)**

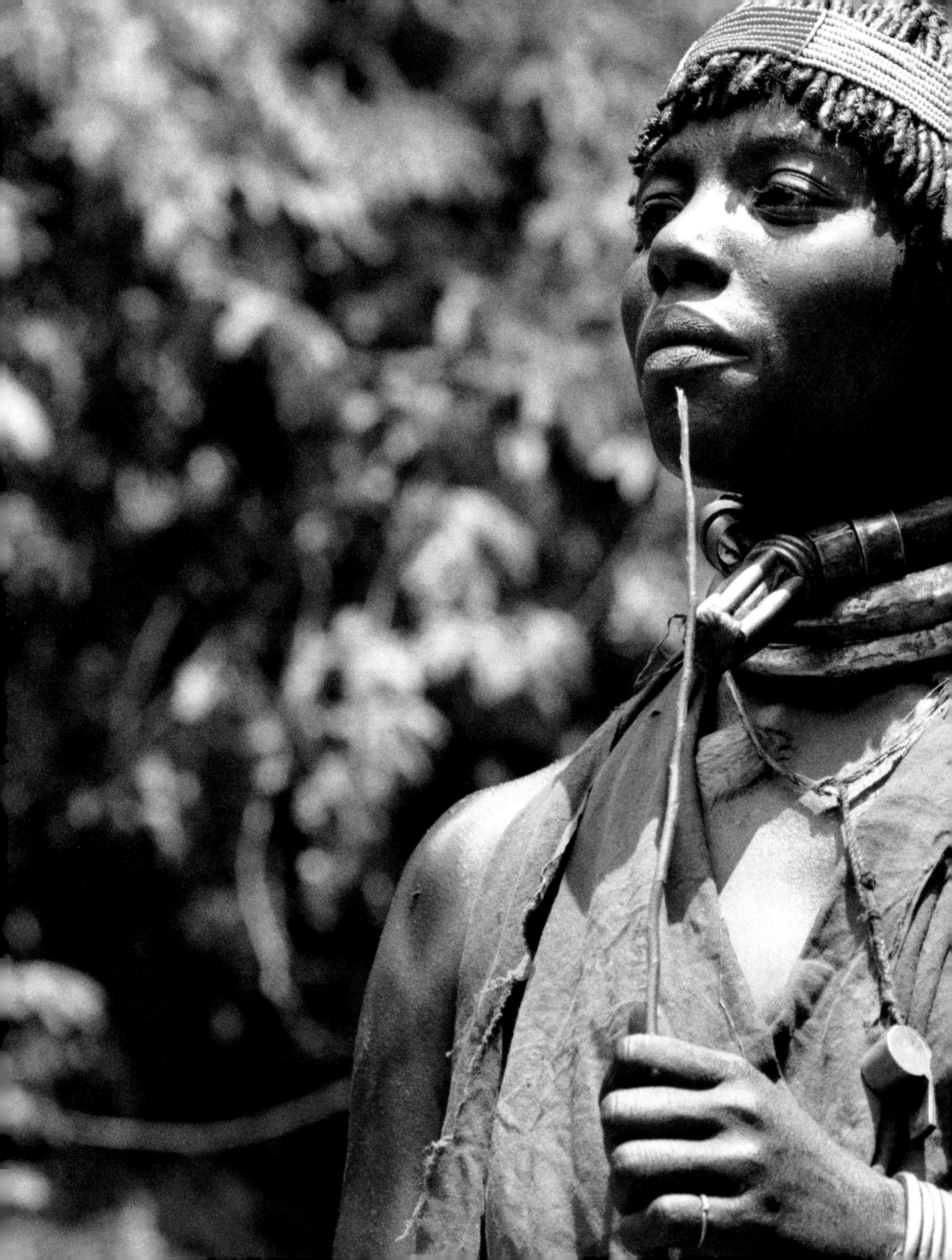

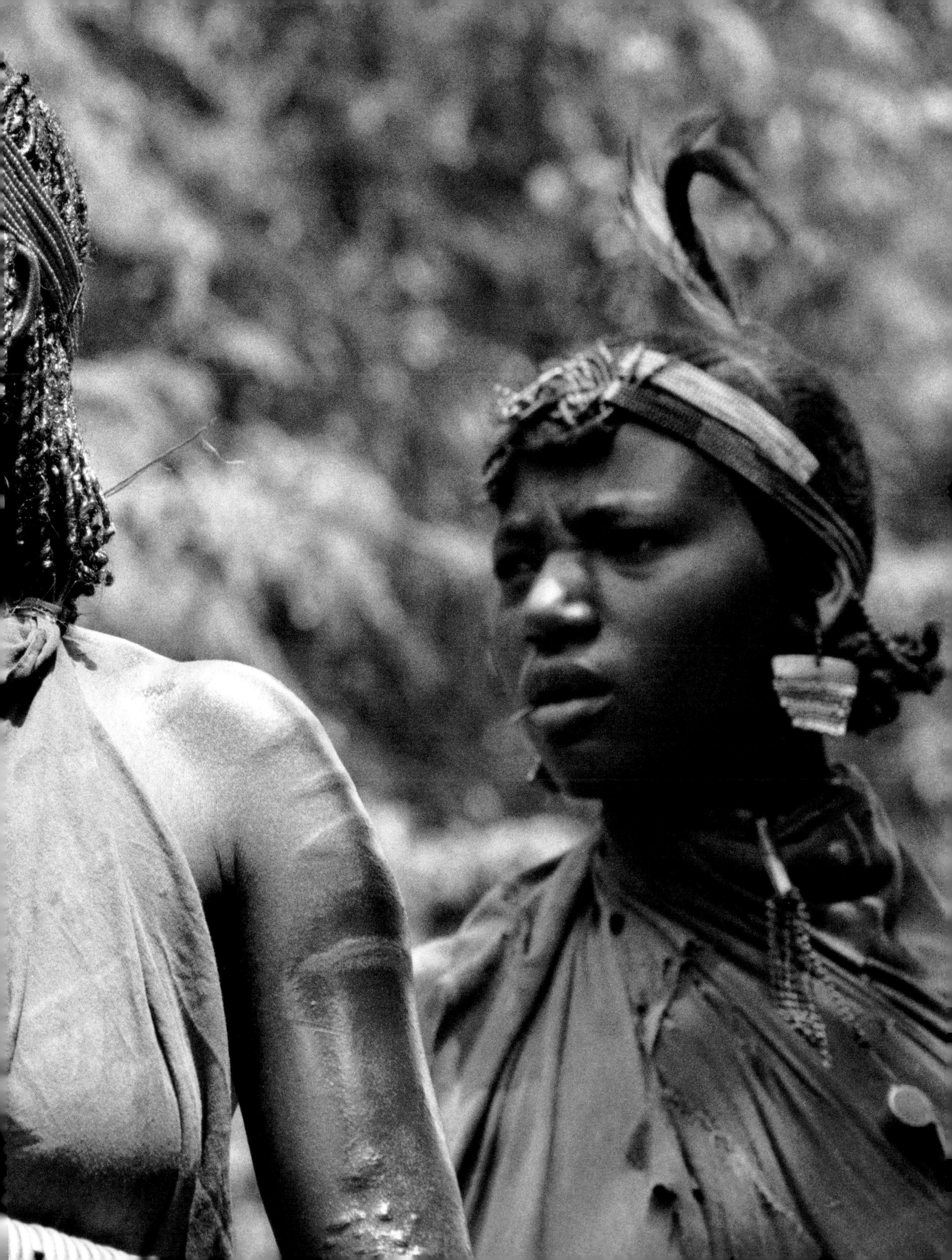

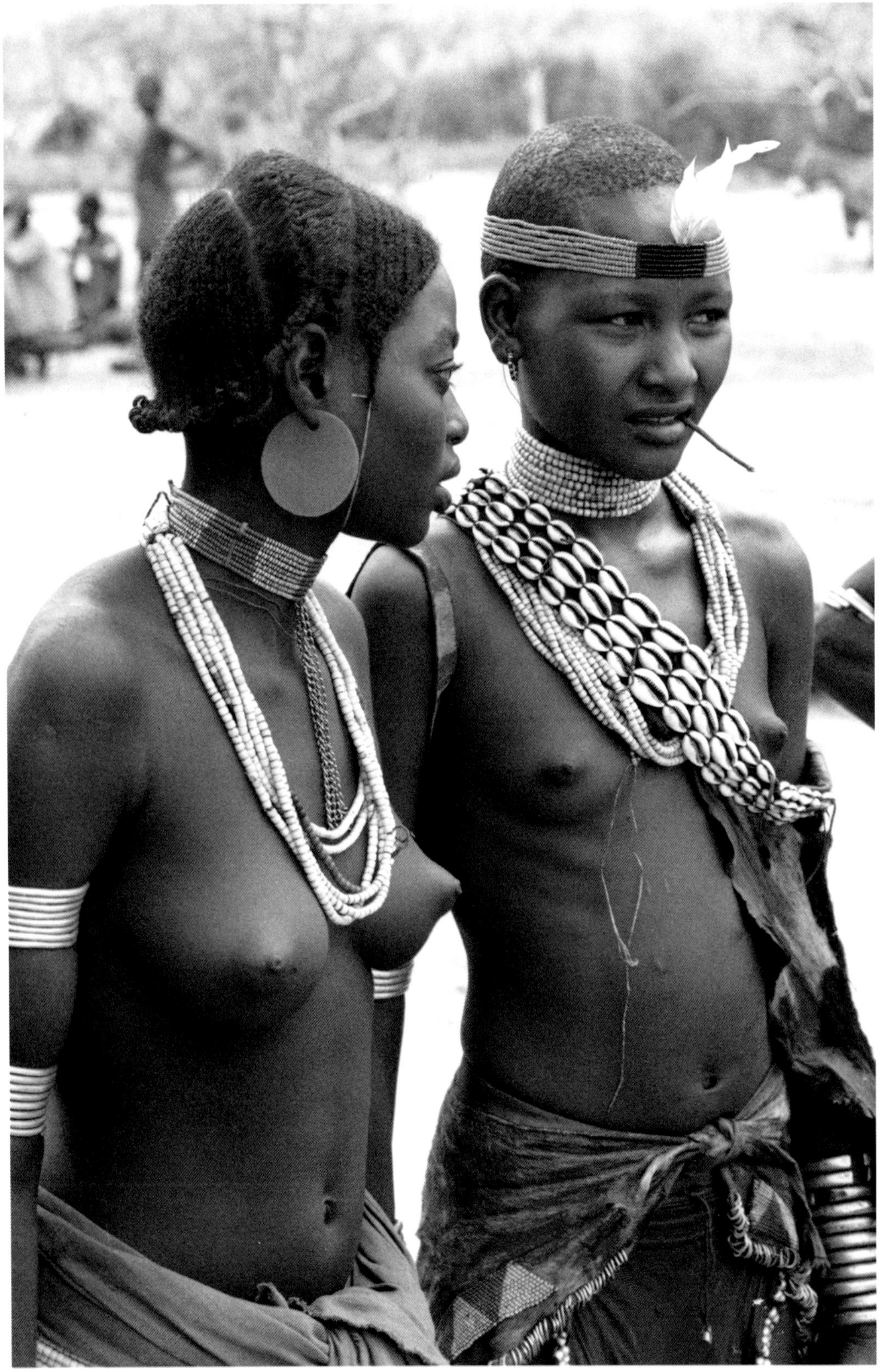

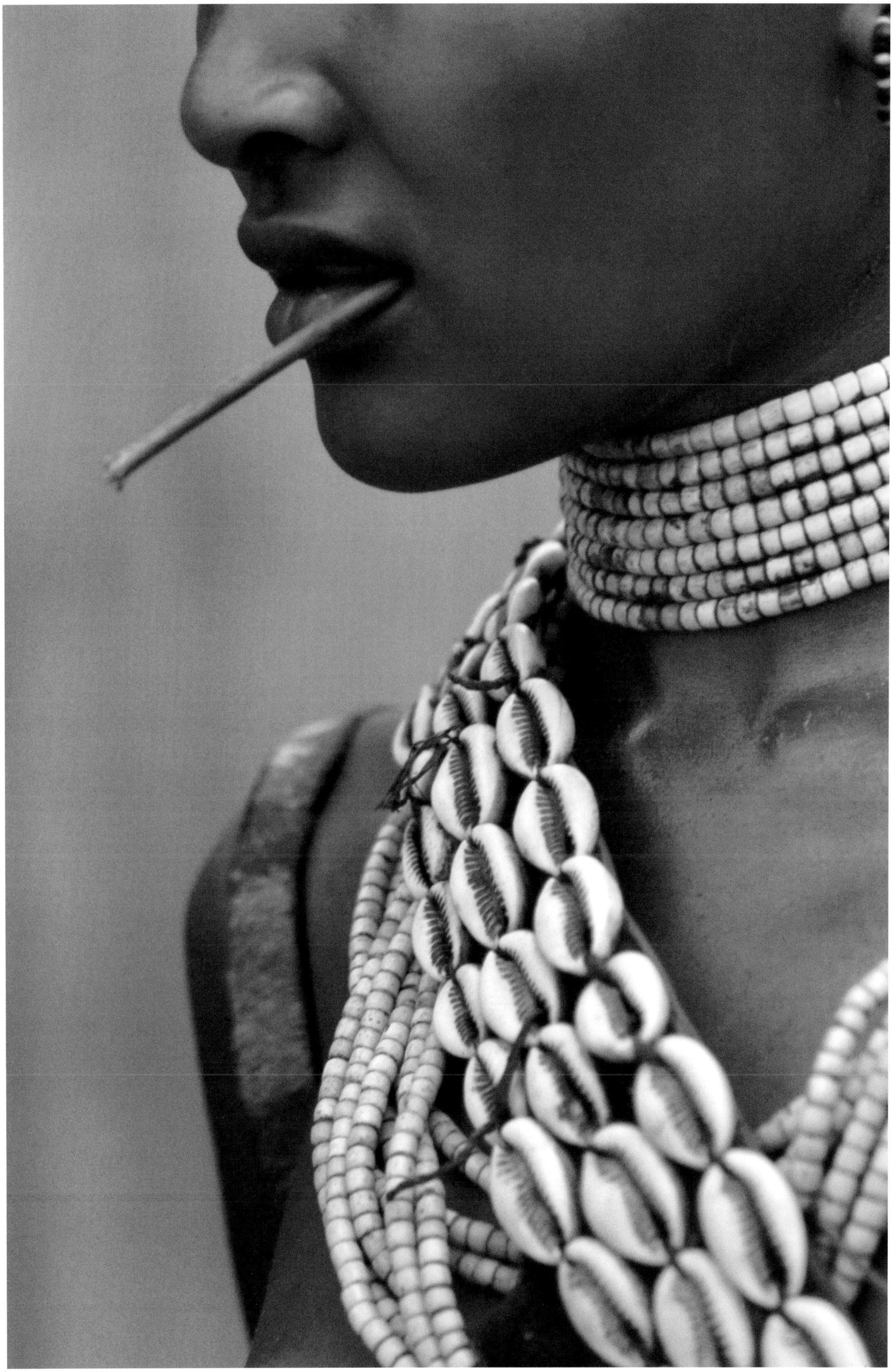

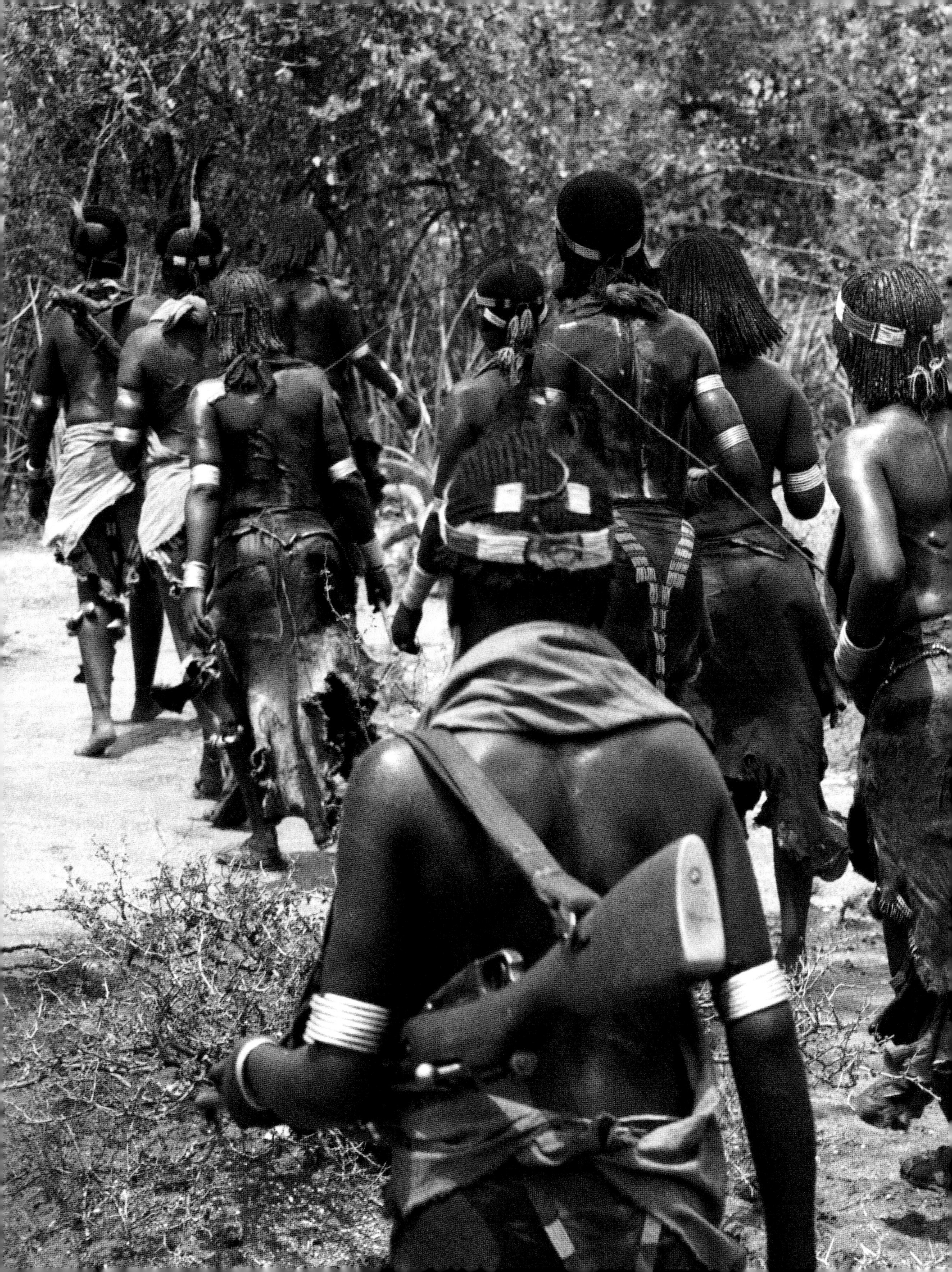

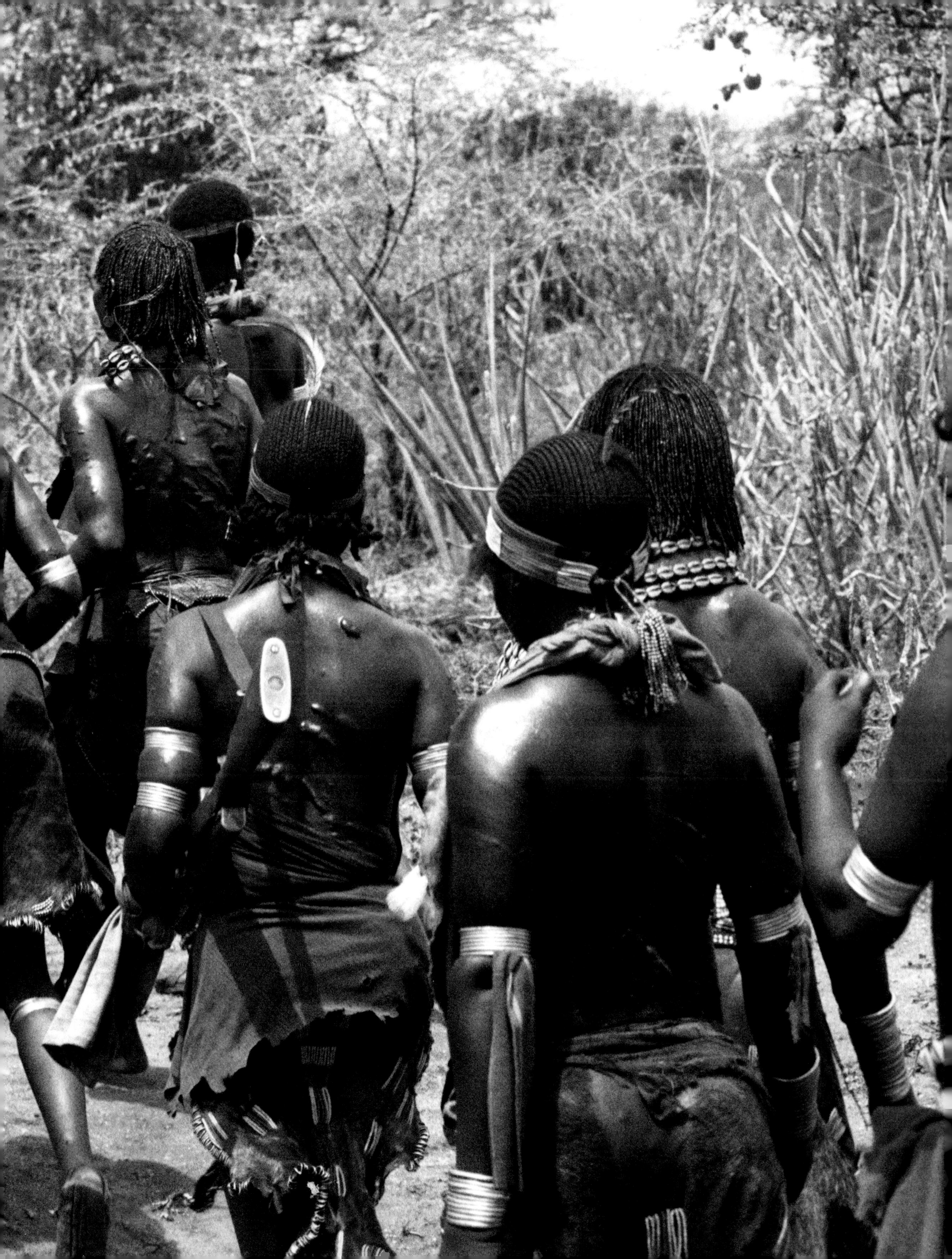

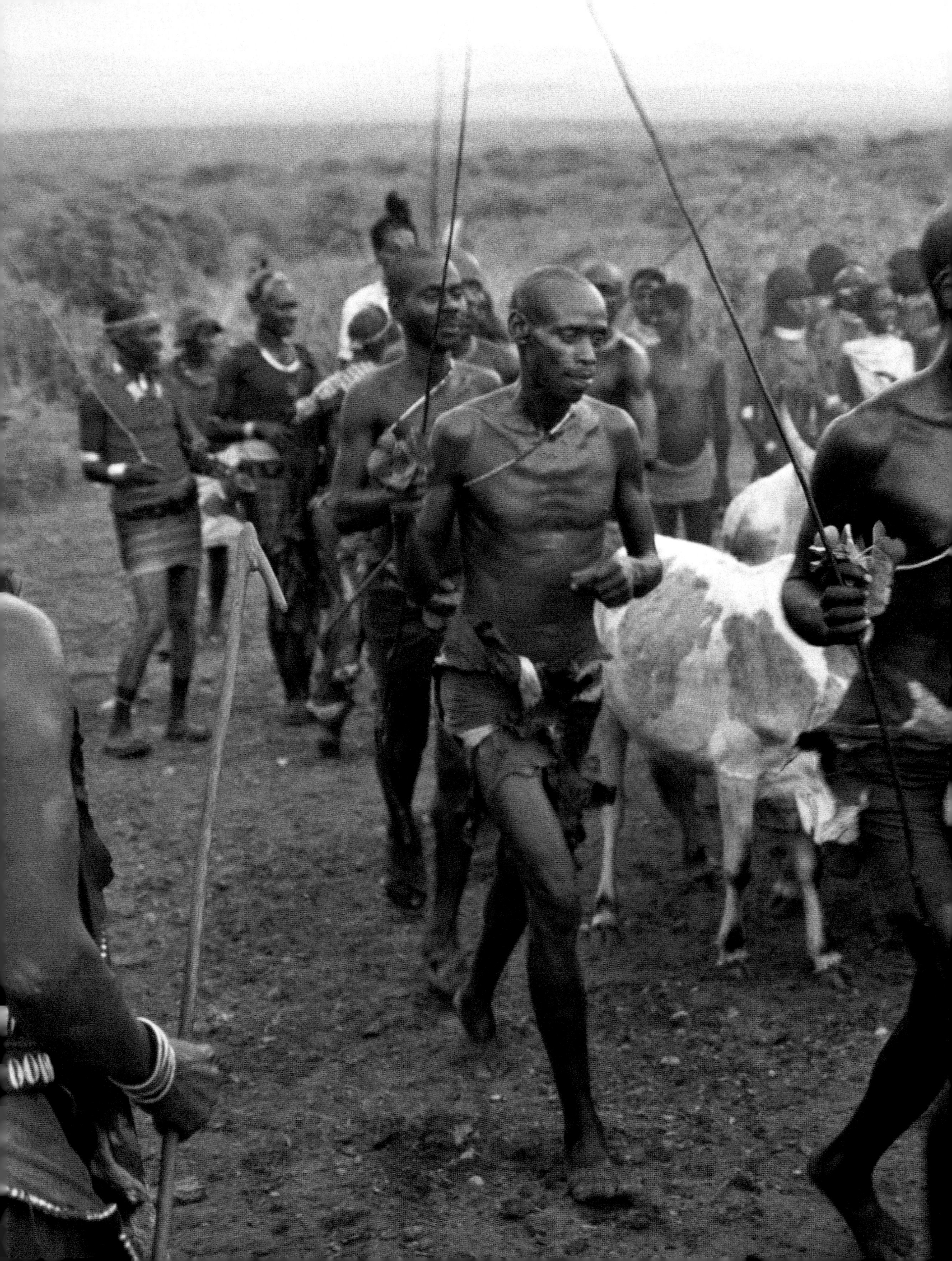

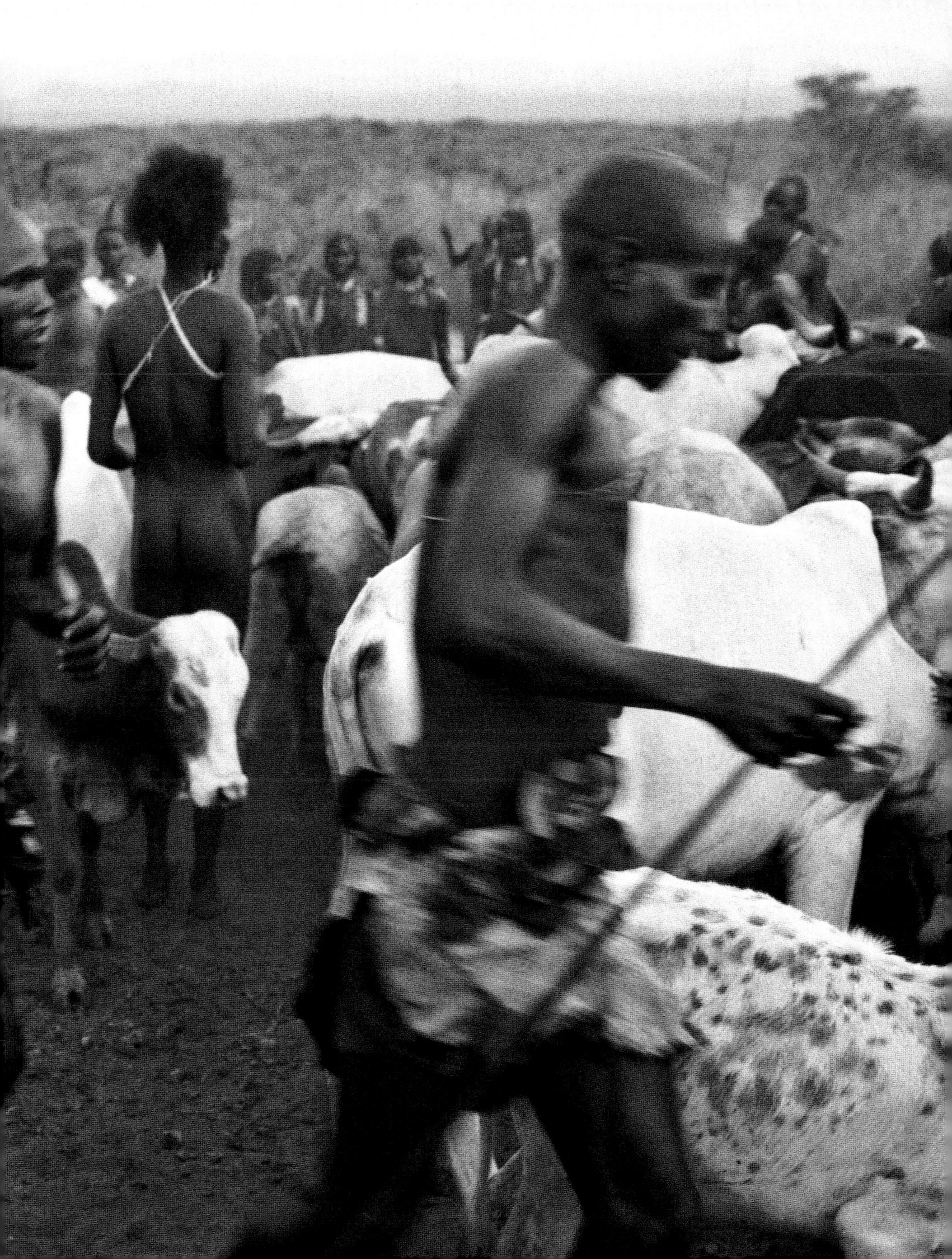

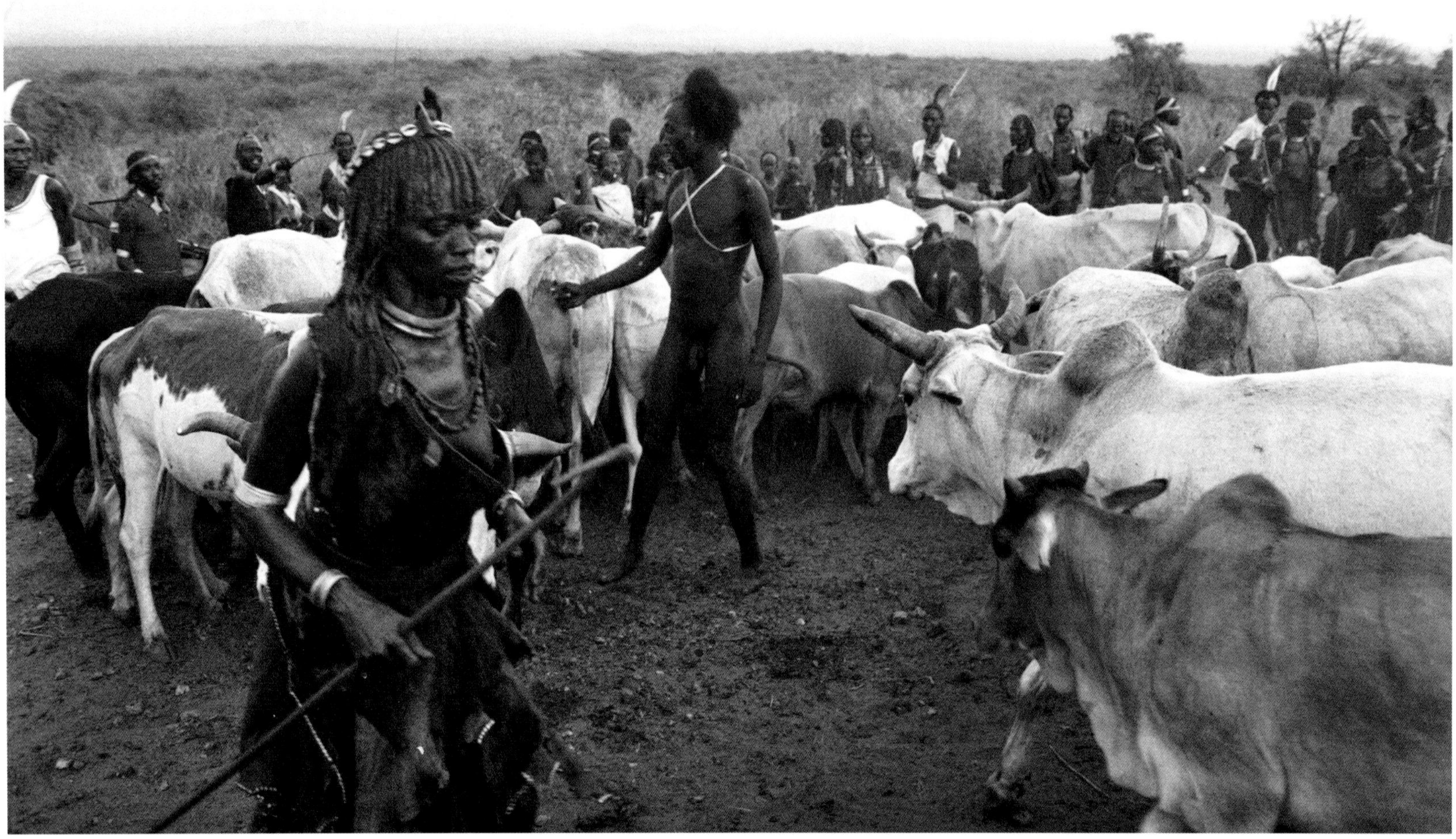

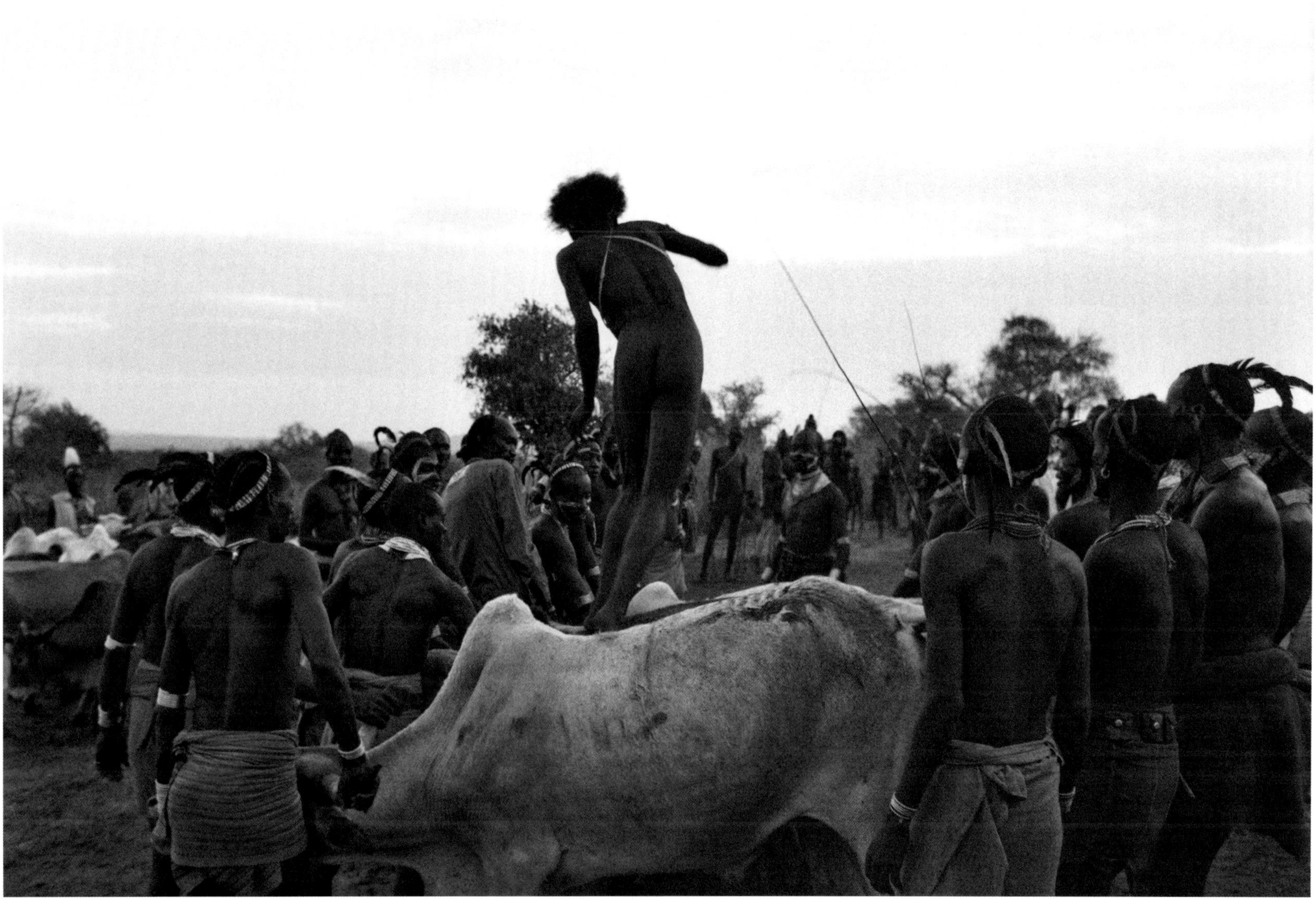

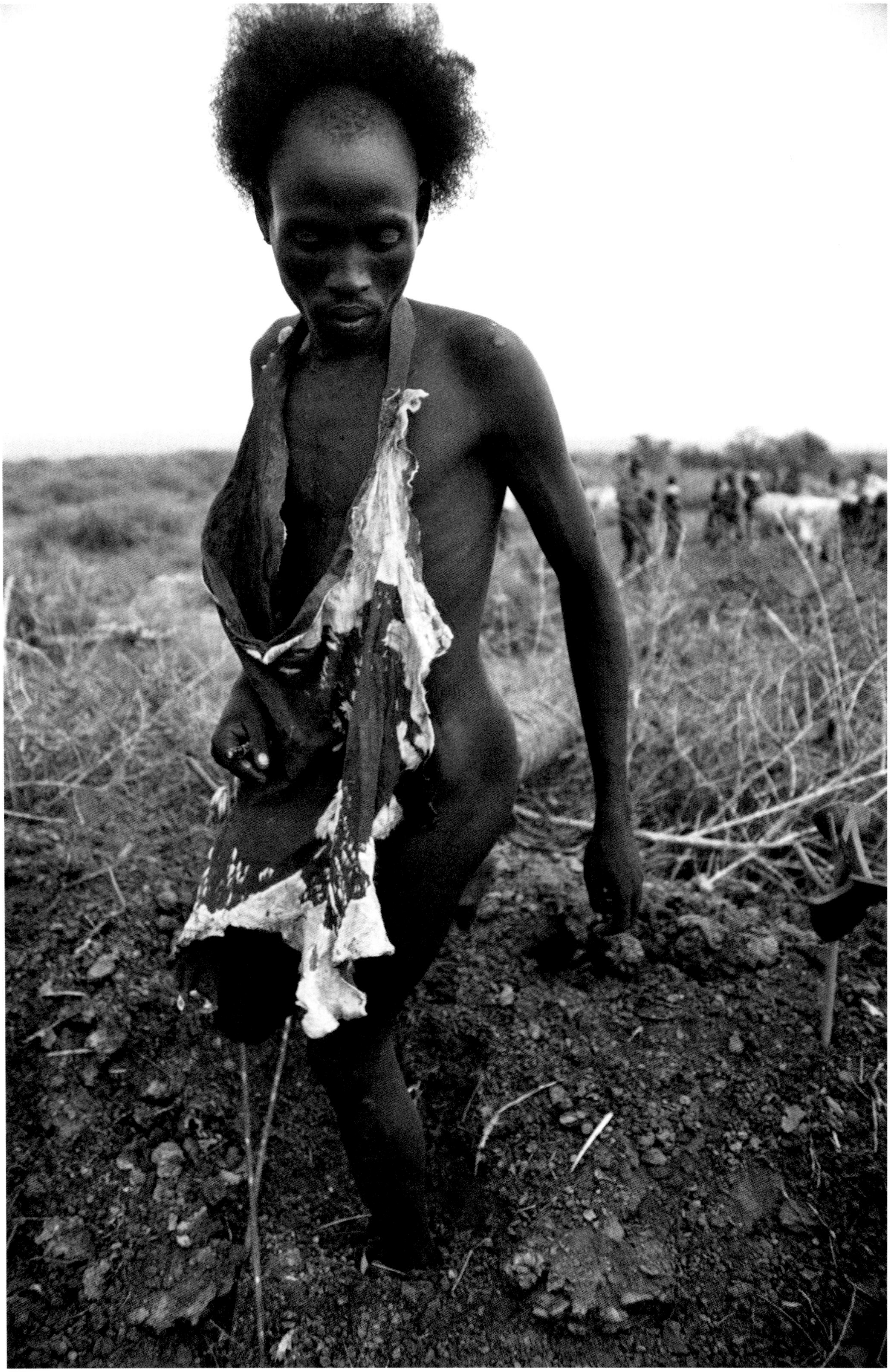

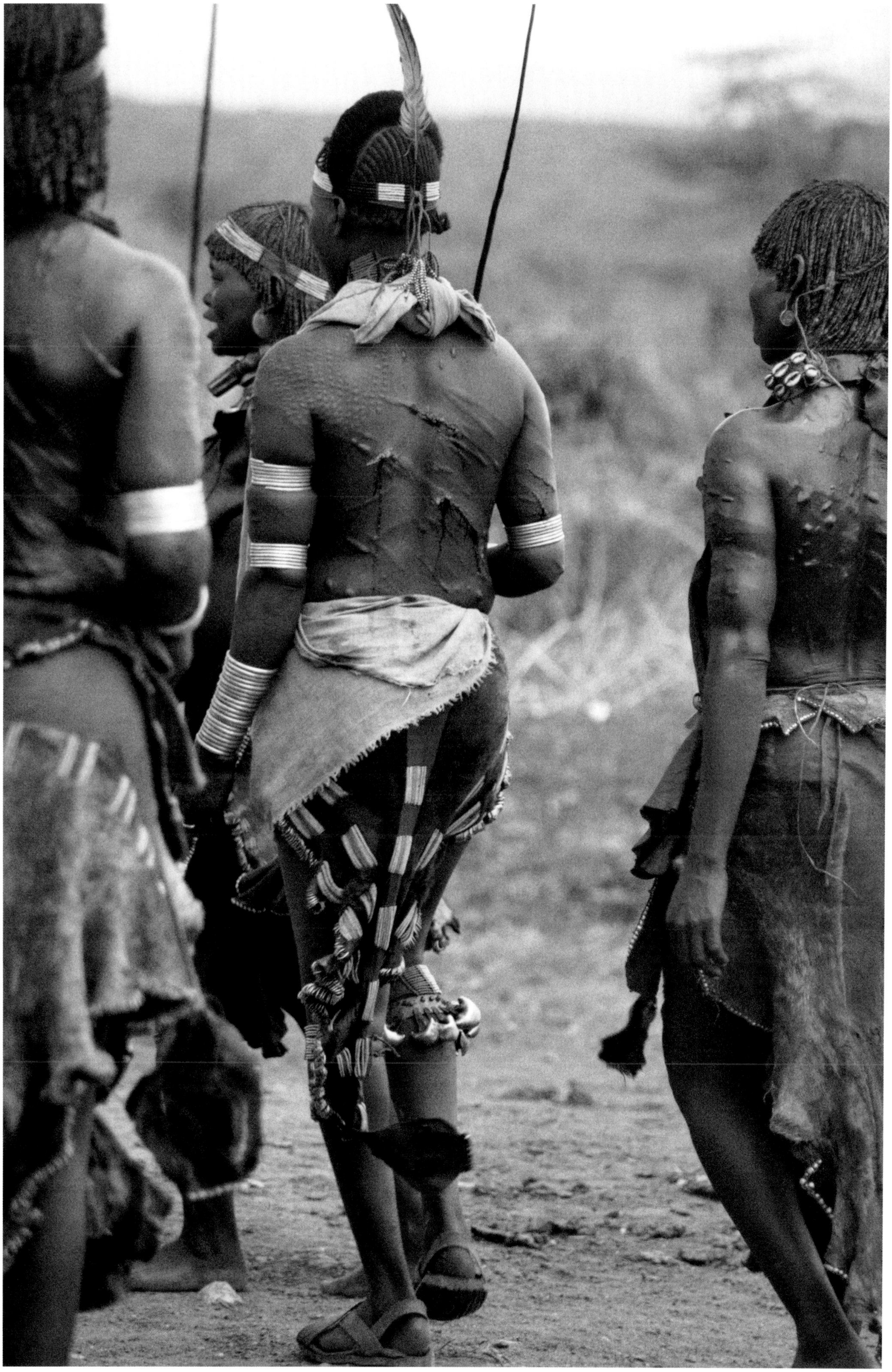

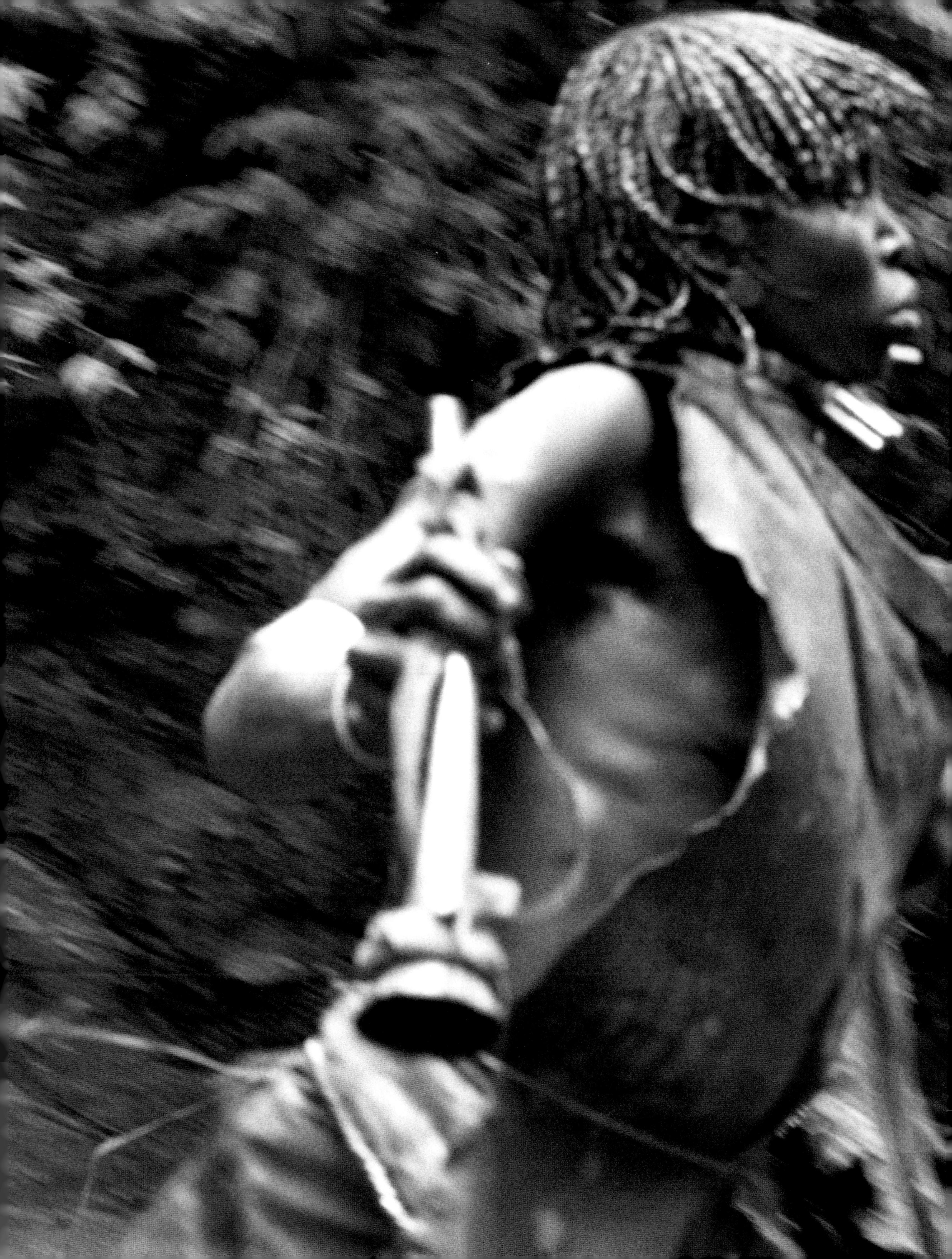

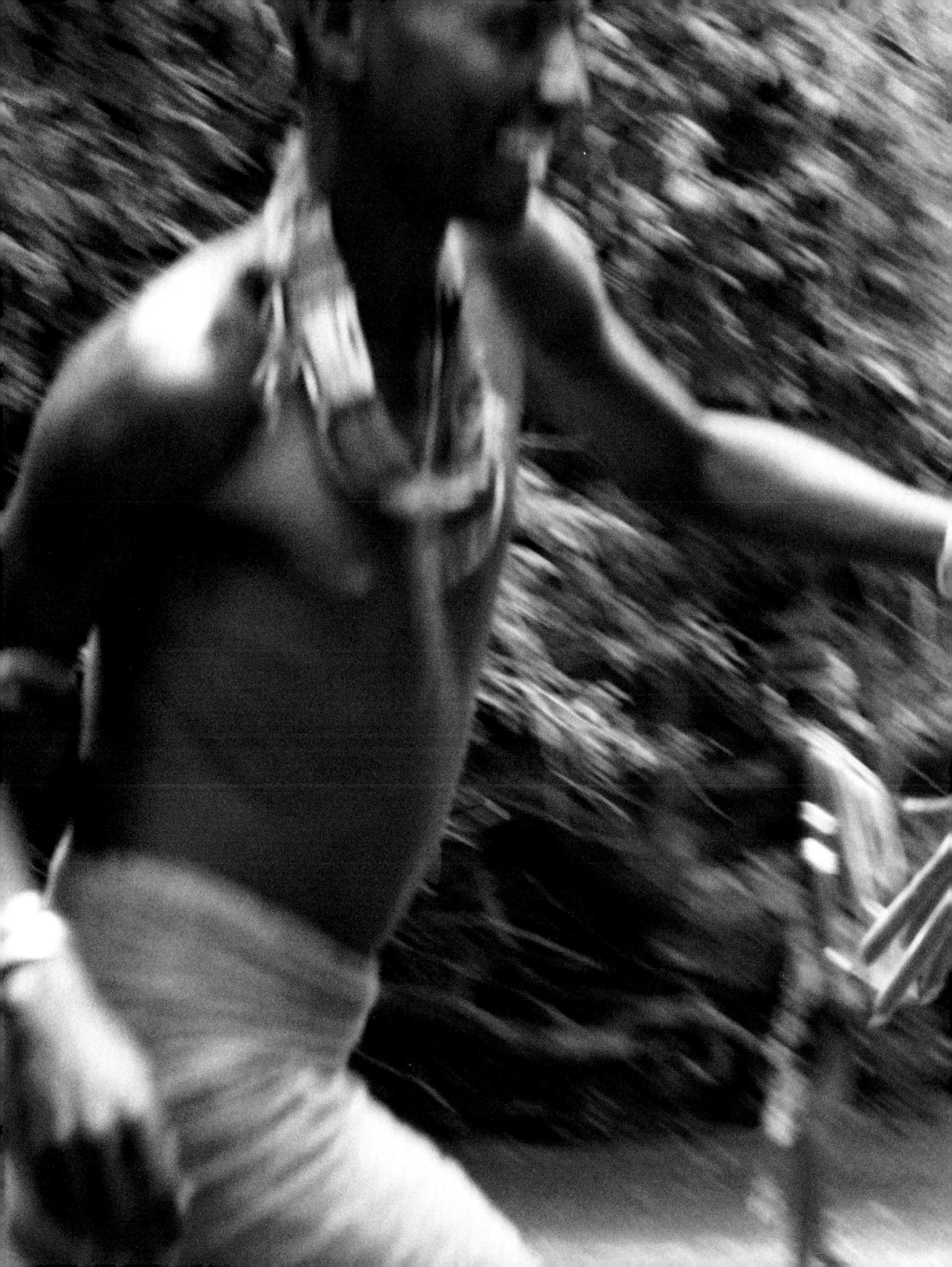

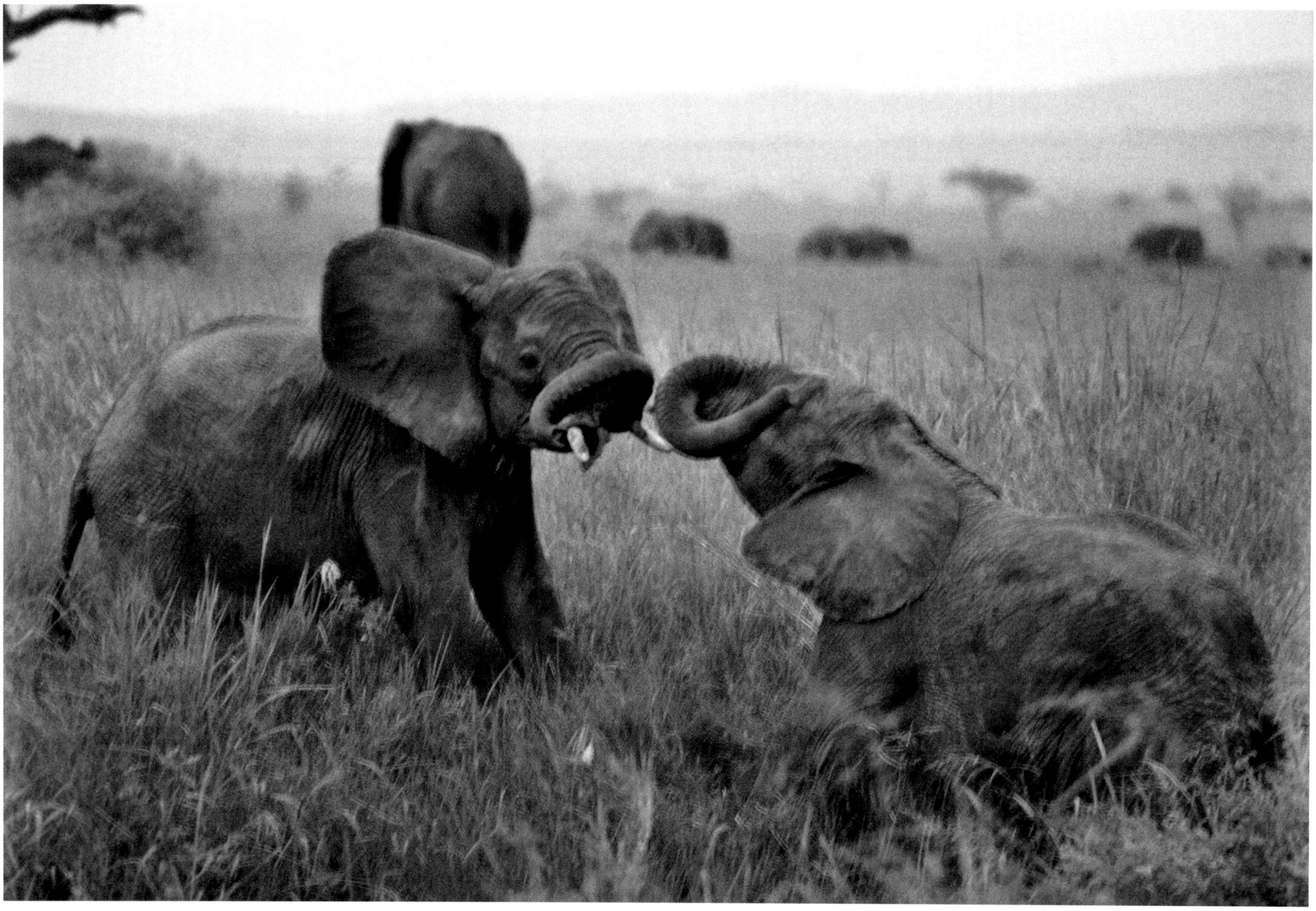

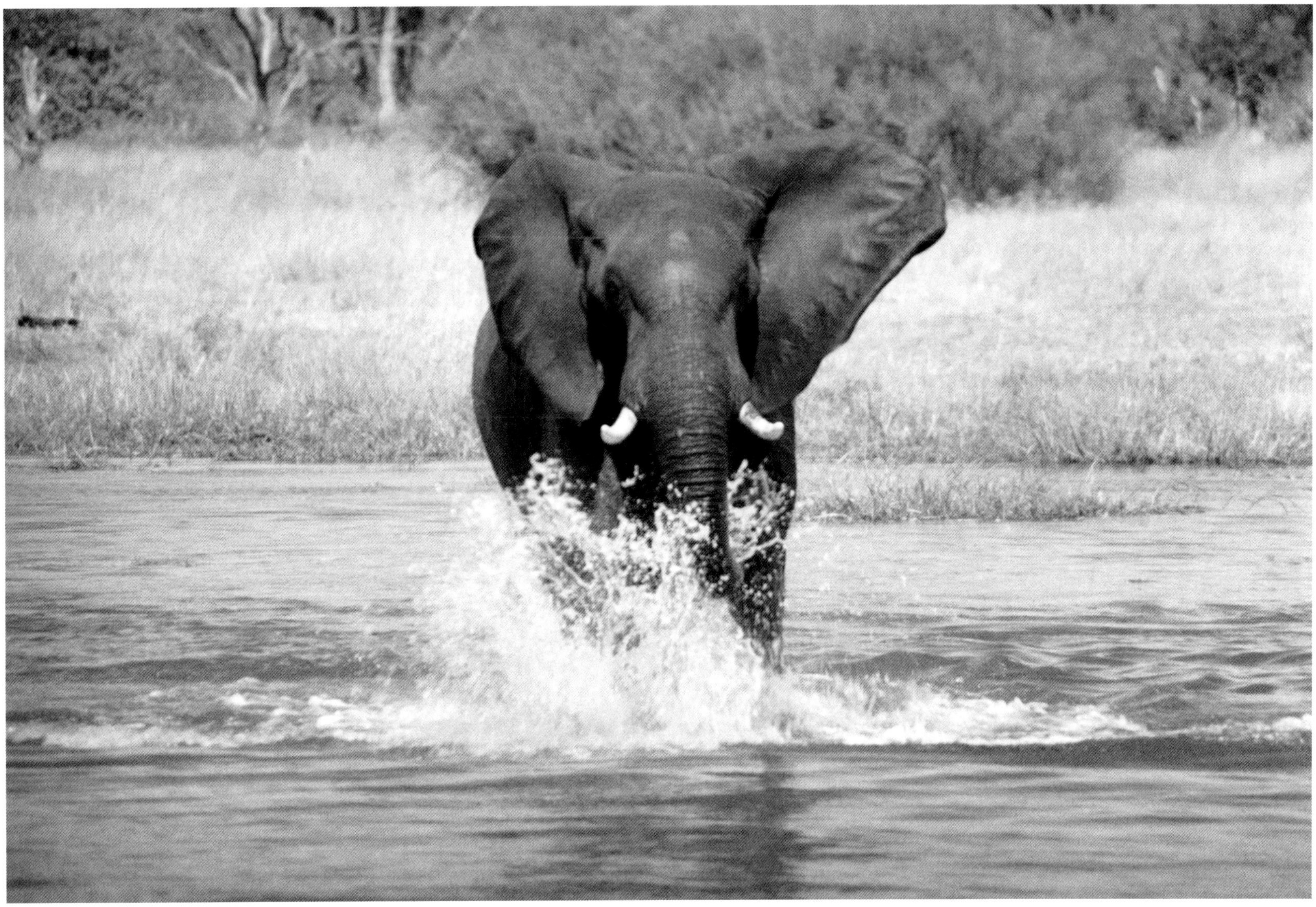

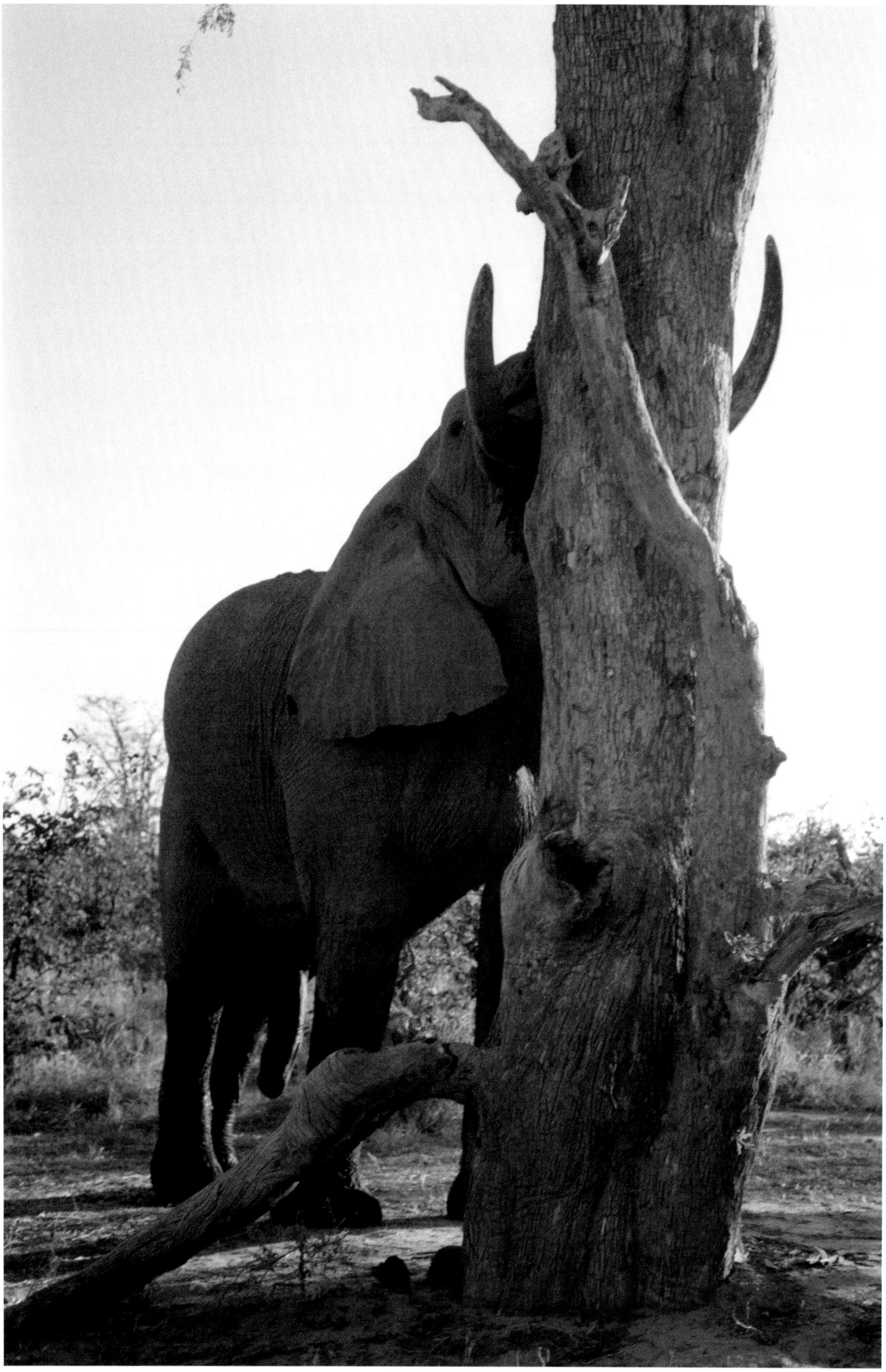

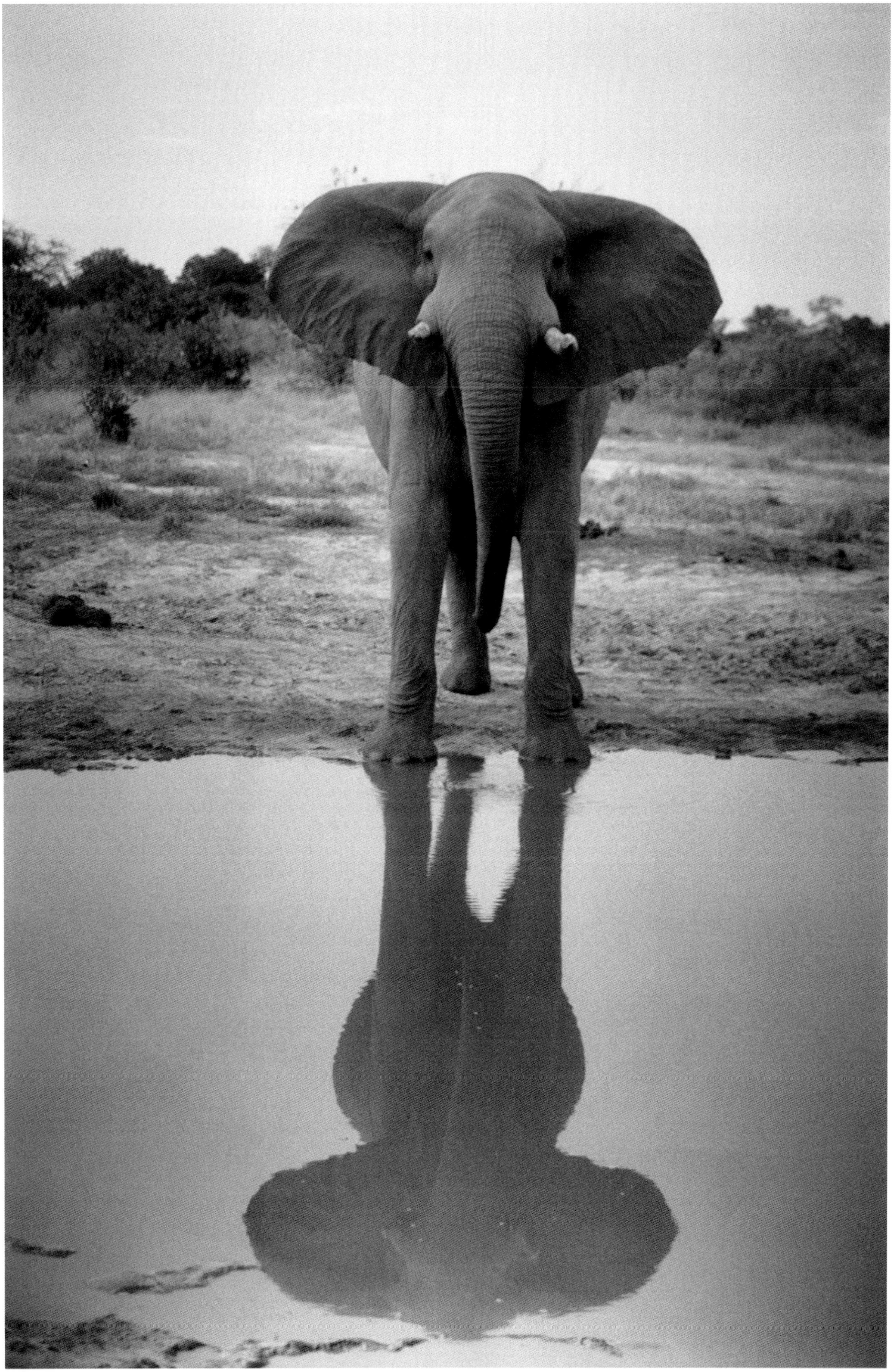

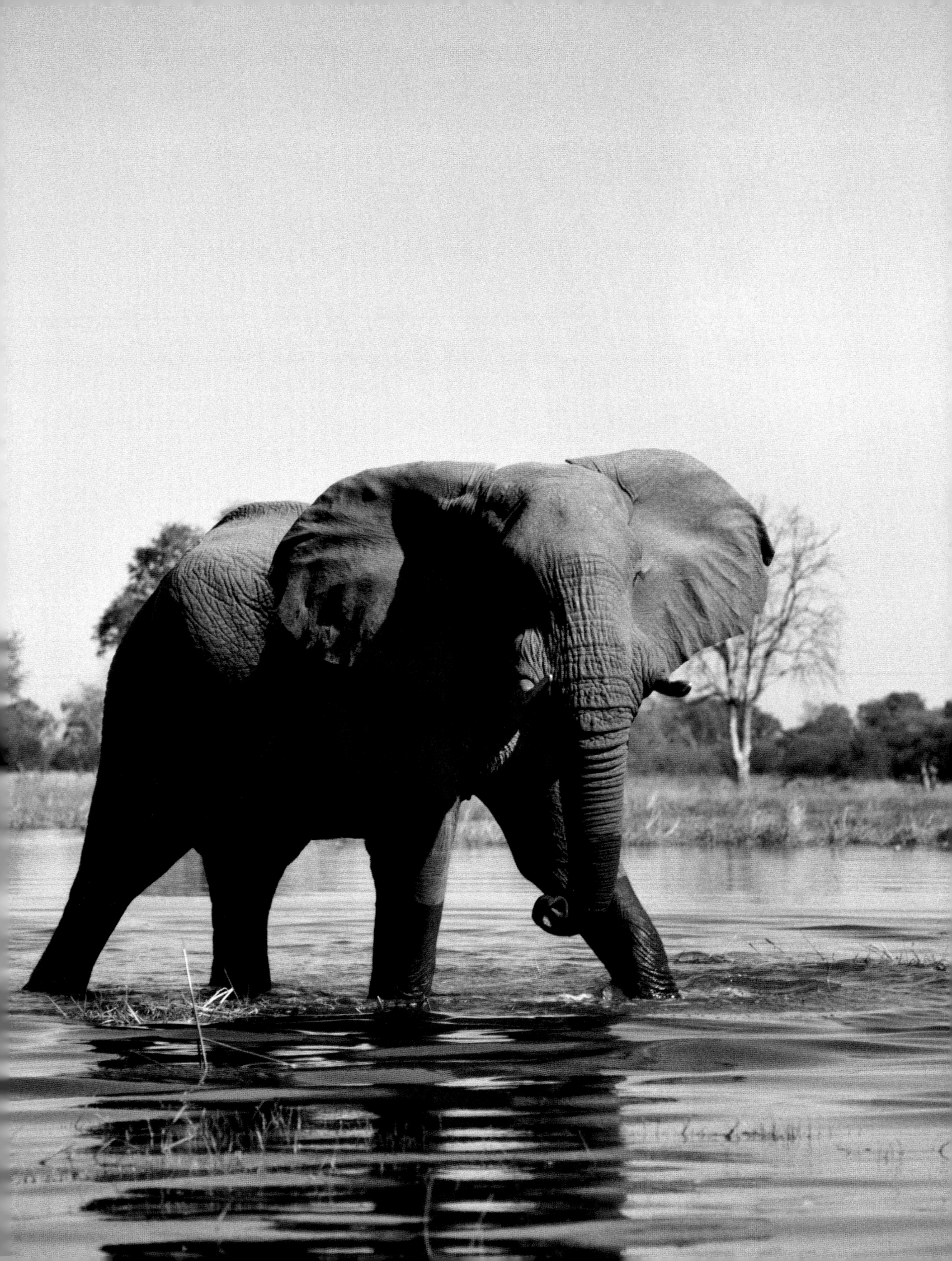

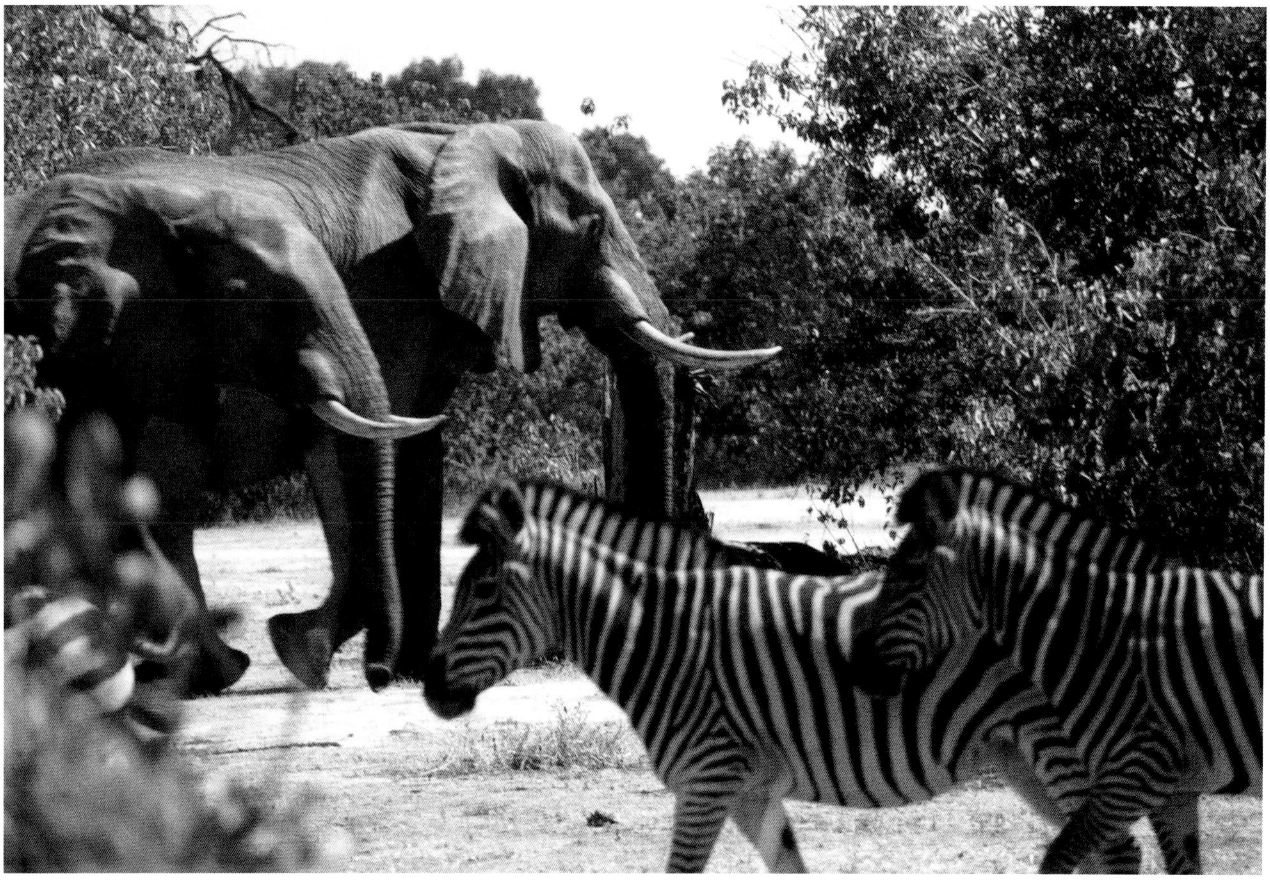

Must there then, even in Africa, be no live creature standing in direct contact with God?

**Isak Dinesen, *Shadows on the Grass* (1960)**

# Epilogue

**Cyril Christo**

Alone amongst the continents, wrote Isak Dinesen, "Africa…will teach it to you: that God and the Devil are one." We are looking for life in our solar system as far away as Pluto, but here on Earth one species, humankind, is challenging not only the megafauna of the second largest continent, Africa, but the entire global immune system of the planet and its countless species. Economic and environmental scourges are straining the social fabric among traditional tribes and pastoralists as never before.

In our first book *Lost Africa: The Eyes of Origin* we listened to elders voice their concerns about climate change and the ravages of globalization, which have never been graver. Foreign investment in Africa, particularly from China, is coming at a great cost. Road implementation, oil exploration, lumber extraction, and the bushmeat trade in the Congo Basin threaten the rainforests across the continent. Many peoples are losing their connection to the earth and its animals, upon which folklore, myth, and their connection to the ancestors depend. Animals which were considered messengers and intermediaries from the world of the spirits are threatened as never before. The bedrock of human origins, the anima and organic tapestry invested in life's myriad forms incarnates a much more integral and coherent relationship to existence than the mesmerizing yet shallow network of the computer-generated reality that so dominates our lives. It was Brian Eno who said something that many would consider quite startling: "There is not enough Africa in the computer."

In Africa, our connection with the larger foundation of who we are in the world is unique on Earth. It is not a more primitive continent. Africa is still a place where humanity's anchor to its past provides an eon-old looking glass into prehistory and the organic template that formed us. It is the place that even Leonardo da Vinci in his ineffable prophecies and his concern for man's relationship to nature wrote about when he said that "All men shall find refuge in Africa."

After the devastating wars of the nineteenth century, Europe saw fit to turn to and carve up the second-largest continent, just as the Industrial Revolution was exploding and the great explorers of the Victorian age were journeying to find the source of the Nile and Africa's deepest secrets. It is no coincidence that Africa provided a haunting refuge, a little-known alien planet in the mind of modern industrializing man. Now China has been added to the mix and continues to carve it up for the "benefits" of the capitalist juggernaut. The search for oil in the Great Lakes region of Africa, specifically in the Virunga Mountains, where the British-based oil company Soco is looking to dig for reserves in fragile mountain gorilla habitat, is indicative of how ruthless modern man's lust for commodities has become. What menace will the Uganda–Tanzania oil pipeline bring its people and the rest of the organic world? Can the rainforests of Africa withstand palm oil plantations? Can the Selous survive the ravages of a dam and Tanzania's need for electricity? Especially after the total desecration of Africa's greatest elephant population in the second decade of this century? The lust for oil playing out between Namibia and Botswana, adjacent to the largest inland delta on Earth, the Okavango, indicates that humanity still does not respect what is at stake. The possible pollution of waters in this Eden of Africa would affect birds, ungulates, and the largest population of elephants, at over 120,000, on the entire continent. The extant Bushmen and Tswana communities would be affected as well, as their drinking water would be spoiled probably forever.

We are sacrificing the "first things of life," as Laurens van der Post warned us, the very soil that makes meaning and life irreplaceable, to obtain things that have no greater value than what the money system can confer. But these things we are so fixated on, such as oil and money and diamonds and coltan, are limited in their supply. By mining them, we undermine the ecological matrix of the world. Ultimately, we have to ask: what is the source of life? For the indigenous peoples of the world, many of whom are found in Africa, it was and still is a relation to Creation. They find the answer not by smashing atoms into each other, but by seeing into the ground of existence with the heart. Subjugation and extraction, the twin evils of modernity, continue to tear at our original home.

Several years ago in South Africa, after seeing the famed white lions of Timbavati, we met an elephant researcher. She had been examining vegetation and elephant diets along their migration paths for years. One night, after the great privilege of watching a white lioness and her cub eating a kudu in the wild, we returned to camp and spoke with Michelle Henley. She told us of her concern for the elephants' future back in 2010, before the world got wind of the elephant crisis. She believed that our ability to save what remains of Earth lies with a poetic understanding of the world, with an emotional connection to life and not just with science. Facts, figures, statistics, and algorithms were but a small part of reality and not the answer to the human dilemma. That some in Africa are willing to sacrifice the very wildlife they are paid to protect, for money, exemplifies the divide in the human heart. That some presidents are willing to sacrifice hundreds of thousands of its indigenous peoples to so-called progress, for modern dams, typifies the perfidy of human rights violations across the globe, where every week indigenous activists are killed for trying to save their environment from money, perfidy, and abject greed.

Mirella Ricciardi wrote a lovely statement for us in *Lost Africa* that should serve as an admonition of what is at stake: "Until Africa finds her 21st century identity, until her new form emerges, her people and her land will first have to pass through the birth pangs of purgatory. The agony will last as long as is needed. In the confusion and disorientation of readjustment, human and wildlife will lose their direction, many will perish, the Earth will be badly damaged and those who survive will be changed forever."

In the recent, second phase of the elephant slaughter that took hold around the time of the global economic recession in 2008, some in China saw fit to make ivory emblematic of their newfound status in society. The Chinese demand for ivory and the Vietnamese demand for rhino horn have ravaged what is left of an imponderable continent. The hunger for lion bones in Laos and Vietnam desecrates the lion across the continent, just like the tiger in Asia. What the economic Moloch of modern industrial society has done in the last decade is to eradicate much of what was once the great miracle of the world: Africa's wildlife.

Every time we have been to East Africa, the cover of *Time* magazine highlighted the advance of robots. One piece on "Singularity" underscored the possibility that human mind and machine would meld by 2040. Mankind's recent venture to Mars to look for life exemplifies the divide in the human condition. Is that the kind of world we want when we know next to nothing of life on Earth? There are so many questions about life on this small planet that would exceed even Darwin's capacity for wonder. Can elephants and whales truly communicate? As we discover radical new questions about the organic world, we are ironically becoming more violent towards it. Everywhere we turn, we are systematically unraveling the organic web of existence. The "magic mirror" which van der Post claimed Africa holds up to the rest of the planet is being shattered. Without Africa's great apes, without the Bushmen cosmology, which is the world's oldest, without the pastoralist ethos that ensures survival on some of the harshest lands on Earth, we face a robotic future of synthetic information without roots, without spirit, without soul.

Charles Lindbergh, of all people, in his *Autobiography of Values*, understood that, in Africa, "The primitive teaches that life itself, unforced life, is progress, a fact that our civilization tends more and more to overlook. In Africa you sense basic qualities of evolution that made life what it is today, made the variety of animals around you, made yourself."

So, too, would he have understood Bernhard Grzmek's exhortation that we must save the Serengeti and not let a permanent road ravage the world's greatest wildlife corridor, or cut down Africa's immense rainforests for lumber syndicates in Europe, or let oil companies desecrate the Virungas, the last refuge for the mountain gorilla, thereby sacrificing all the treasures of an immeasurable continent for short-sighted diplomacy and the wanton mercenaries of global commerce.

The recent assault on Botswana's elephants comes after a decade of severe loss. Can elephants seeking refuges from poachers in Angola, Zambia, or Zimbabwe possibly find a haven in that country? If Botswana were to lose its elephants, the last sanctuary on Earth will have fallen. The future evolution of man will in large measure be tested by the destiny of the elephant, both African and Asian.

Something resides in Africa that makes it more than a player in the global economy; it is an essential strain, the seed of our origin and original homeland, that becomes a lifelong quest for meaning, a fever that drives one to return to one's first ground of being. In his introduction to the book *Vanishing Species*, Romain Gary wrote: "If the relationship between our species and the rest of the earth's inhabitants is to be reduced to the necessities of our own survival, then we are not talking about the same man. It is absurd to cram our museums with art and to spend billions for beauty and then to let beauty be destroyed wantonly in all its living splendor. I may be mistaken, but it's too late in life for me to change my beliefs: I am convinced that we do not have to feel personally threatened by an ecological disaster to feel troubled by the news that there are no more than a hundred swamp deer left in central India. I do not even believe that we need to know exactly what the swamp deer looks like, or even how beautiful it is. I have heard Polish boys in Warsaw discuss the woeful tale of the American bison as if it weighed heavily on their non-American consciences." On an entirely manmade world, all that will be left of us is robots.

The films, books, images we consume about Africa's wildlife, about the idea of safari, life's journey, about those who cherish something deeper in the foundation of their being, resonate with Africa's rhythm, music, and dance more than anything else. The *mal d'Afrique* so well described by the French language is not an affliction, is it on the order of an existential longing, a desire to return to the source of one's self and the wellspring of humanity's primal being. There is no artificial alternative, synthetic semblance, or simulated and animated substitute for the symbolic and cellular memory she harbors. As Lysander said so well, Africa is an introduction to something deeper, "Africa is the introduction to the Alternate Self." The "magic mirror" that Africa holds up to humanity must not be shattered. Only the great tapestry of the organic world, the roar of the lion, the thunderous bellowing of the elephant, and the chanting of the Maasai and Samburu can keep that from happening.

In 2017, I took Lysander to Botswana to return to the greatest wilderness of its kind in the world, the last great sanctuary for elephants on Earth. We witnessed a wonderful male lion eating a buffalo not far from our landing strip and regaled in the waterholes close to camp. The near-mystical lavender light infused the atmosphere, like a shimmer from an otherworldly planet. It is Africa's way of saying welcome, you have arrived. On our way to camp, about four in the afternoon, we got stuck in deep sand with our guide Alistair, who had hosted us two years previously. His father was an old-timer who used to hunt crocodiles to survive and had known all the back roads since he was born. For over four hours we tried digging and using the car jack until our fingers grew numb. We tried the winch, but no trees were available. One tree stood at a ninety-degrees angle to the cable, but naturally could not pull us out of the sand. The angle was totally wrong. We tried the car horn to alert camp a mere kilometer away, but no one heard us. The telephone did not work. By nightfall, Alistair walked up the path with a light and then returned, spooked by the very real possibility of bumping into the lions now converging on the kill. We tried attaching the winch to a small boulder to the right and front of the car, but it was too small. We even toyed with the idea of digging in front of the car with the goal of burying a tire that would then pull us out of the rut, but after a few inches we found the sand was too compacted, so it would have taken an additional several hours of serious digging. Faced with the likely prospect of having to spend the night in the car with predators all around us, Lysander and I walked a few dozen meters from the car and discovered an elephant skeleton. Lysander suggested that maybe the elephant bones could help. I was skeptical at first, seeing only the skull, shoulder blades, and femur bones lying on the ground and wondering whether the elephant had died a natural death or not in these uncertain times. Lysander, in his usual wonderful, excited way, pointed to some ribs and we both decided to carry them back to the car. Alistair was still hard at work digging and trying to put bigger rocks under the tires, but nothing worked because the weight of the car pushed the rocks down even deeper into the sand. He took some of the elephant ribs, about five or six of them, put them under the back tire and the right passenger tire and tried escaping the clutches of the sand, and lo and behold, we were out within a minute and on our way back to camp! Lysander, at the age of eleven, was right, and it is for his generation that we must save those species that have given us so much!

A dead elephant's bones, its ribs, had saved our night, as lions were feeding close by in the darkest night on Earth. This experience introduced us once again to the power and majesty of the African landscape. We were privileged enough to meet a former elephant hunter who knew more about elephants than anyone alive. In this immensely fragile time, the elephant and the people who have grown alongside this incomparable species are making a last stand. I believe civilization will stand or fall on the back of the African elephant. An entire continent was once plundered for its peoples and ivory. Now the world must help the heart of the world. Botswana is showing signs of increased poaching. The very refuge where experts believe poaching could be resisted is now under siege. If Botswana's elephants disappear the continent will have no ballast. Refuge, haven, sanctuary will be no more. We have arrived at the edge of another period in time where the unfathomable possibility of total loss of the greatest land mammal on Earth is fathomable. That several hundred were lost to bacteria poisoning in waterholes impacted by drought and climate change in the pandemic summer of 2020 in Botswana demonstrates that the great titans of the world are vulnerable to more than poaching and hunting at the hands of humanity. Savannah elephants have now been put on the endangered species list. Humanity and the natural world have reached an inflection point. Now geologic, human, and climatic forces are impinging on the life force of the planet, gravely imperiling the fantastic forest elephants, who uphold and fertilize and keep the soul of the second-largest rainforest on Earth alive.

Diplomats, ecologists, the will of the world must stand up for a being who holds up the terrestrial planet as the whales do the seas. Our destiny is written in the gaze the titans throw at us when we walk amongst them and are taken aback by the grandeur of some incomparably larger being than ourselves. Beings who know how to listen to the sun and the moon and who helped mold an entire continent. Their future is truly our fate.

As ecocide will soon become a criminal offense in France and hopefully other countries around the world and the mandate against the continued destruction of the natural world is strengthened, maybe we can change course and urge Africa's leaders to save irreplaceable life forms on the continent for the future of the world. The organic world shaped the matrix of our existence. The other species on Earth, both plant and animal, evolved alongside us and they are our last refuge. Without them we will have no anchor, and our souls will become homeless. This decade, the third of this century, will define where humanity, the indigenous peoples, and Earth's innumerable species are headed. The people of Africa, and those who understand her inimitable place in the destiny of this planet, can work together to salvage and renew what makes Africa, the heart of the world, incomparable—the place where mankind was born.

Until one has loved an animal, a part of one's soul remains unawakened.

**Anatole France**

# Acknowledgments

With immense gratitude to those who have made this work possible over the last generation:

Andrea Hardbattle and the community of the Hardbattle Ranch; Roy Sesana, the Kalahari Peoples Fund, and the community of Xai-Xai; Emma Chen and the Lenges Clan of the Samburu of Desert Rose; Henry Henley and Jacinta at Loyangalani, Turkana; Pacquo Lesorogol and Mike Rainy, whose camp Ol Kanjau in Amboseli initiated us into the wonder and complexities of the Samburu and Maasai world; John Looseyia and translator Said, who introduced us to the Ndorobo people and their indebtedness to everything from bees to elephants; Christian Bethelsson, whose fight against dictatorship in Liberia reminded us that the future of the elephants is indispensable to the future of humanity and peace; Koni Tise, whose spirit of his tribe, the Waliangulu, gave us a rich idea of the extraordinary breadth of his people's spiritual connection to the elephant; Elijah Morintet, whose lion story is a credit to the Maasai culture and their alliance with the animal world; Mohammed Ol Seki has been a guiding spirit for 20 years; Moses Ntuwuasa, whose dedication and love of wildlife brought us a unique perspective of the Maasai and their reaction to the "beauty of God," which is nature; Rodgers Mariki, whose humor and care in the Serengeti was remarkable, especially during times of the tsetse fly invasions; Ithumba Camp and the spirit of the orphaned elephants; and in memory of Dame Daphne Sheldrick, whose devotion to the elephants and rhinos will never be forgotten.

Gee Gaeboelwe Mange and everyone at &BEYOND, whose guiding expertise in the Okavango Delta gave Lysander a serious introduction to the wonder of Africa; Alistair and Lloyd Wilmot, whose attention in the Delta gave us a first-hand understanding of elephant interactions only few have witnessed; Rakita, Fred, and James, who helped care for Lysander when he took his first steps in the Mara years ago; Belinda and Isak and the peoples of the Mokoko, who reminded us of the deep connection between the San and the lion; Soroi Serengeti Lodge in Tanzania, Lake Natron Camp, Divan Singh, and everyone at Satao Elerai Camp in Amboseli, as well as Satao Camp in Tsavo; Justin Kalinga and Vincen Kavaya at Mwagusi Safari Camp in Ruaha for some of the most breathtaking moments in Africa, especially the sunset baobab moments and the baboons drinking from the waterholes in the river; Galdessa Camp in Tsavo, Noncata Laparcho, Peter Litus, Gilbert Salinga, and everyone at Elephant Watch Camp in Samburu; Andersson's Camp; Damaraland Camp; Desert Rhino Camp in Namibia; with great thanks to Dawid, who was first touched on the shoulder by a wild elephant so many years ago.

Special thanks to Cody and Nikkol at Visions for their inestimable care in this fragile time and for making these photos possible; to Elizabeth Marshall Thomas, whose abiding love of the Kalahari has shed inestimable light on the old ways of the first peoples of Africa, the San Bushmen, and their relationship to Africa's great predator, the lion; and to Raza from AfricanMecca Safaris, who understands the spirit of what makes Africa unique, for your devotion over the years. Your understanding of true experience is a testament to what remains authentic in the world.

Lysander, whose eye and heart were opened many years ago when he took his first steps in Africa at 11 months old. May you be able to work for the salvation of the others—for without them we are truly lost.
Marie, whose care, patience, and understanding of what is essential have enabled us to come this far, and whose breathtaking command of detail showed a love that is unmatched.

This book is dedicated to all conservation groups and biologists working tirelessly to save what is left of Africa, its peoples, and its nonhuman beings for the next generation.

Anyone wishing to contribute to the future is encouraged to donate to the many foundations helping indigenous people and conservation groups the world over: Cultural Survival, the Kalahari Peoples Fund, Survival International, International Work Group for Indigenous Affairs, Conservation International, African Wildlife Foundation, Save the Elephants, Space for Giants, the Jane Goodall Institute, Panthera, the Center for Great Apes, International Rhino Foundation, Lion Conservation Fund, Lion Aid, Big Cats Initiative, Painted Dog Conservation, Giraffe Conservation Foundation, and all the others who are dedicated to humanity's greatest allies on Earth: the animals.

Infinite gratitude to Jane Goodall for your words and understanding that humanity is but one of innumerable inestimable species on this fragile and miraculous Earth.

To the Grumeti Fund, where wildlife conservation and community development go hand in hand in the western corridor of the Serengeti ecosystem in Tanzania. Thank you for your vision and commitment to a world in which people and animals can live together sustainably, forever.

To the rangers graduating from the KWS Wildlife Law Enforcement Academy at Manyani, Tsavo West National Park, Kenya. Your dedication and courage constantly shield wild animals from criminal exploitation and abuse throughout Kenya and other countries that send rangers to be trained at Manyani.

The lions had the night. The people had the day, which we think is the preferred time, but in reality, for life in general, the savannah by day is less desirable. The people of the savannah share the daylight mainly with insects and birds, while everything else favors the night and is well equipped to use it. For any species that hunts large animals, night is certainly the best time, which, of course, is why the predators are mostly nocturnal. Thus it was the lions, not ourselves, who roamed the savannah at the preferred time. Humankind had second best.

**Elizabeth Marshall Thomas, *The Old Way* (2006)**

# Captions

| | | | |
|---|---|---|---|
| 6/7 | 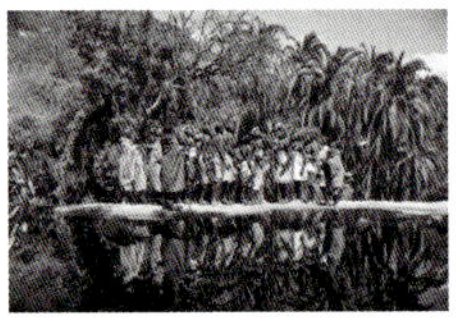 | 2012 | These Samburu dance before a reflecting pool at Mount Ngiro, their sacred mountain, which never dries up even though it is located in some of the harshest land in northern Kenya. |
| 8 | 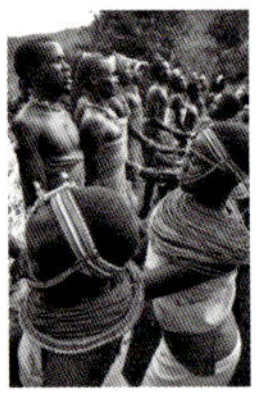 | 2012 | The pride shown when young men court the young women in Samburu is a joy to behold. The Samburu are called the Butterfly People because of the superb colors they wear. |
| 9 | 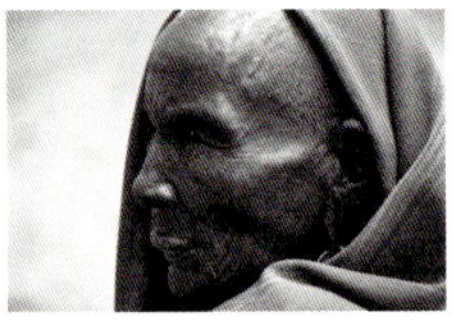 | 2006 | This elder matriarch reminisced about the time when elephants populated the hills on Mount Ngiro. The elephant was considered part of her clan, but the *shifta* (poachers) have long chased the elephants away. |
| 10 | 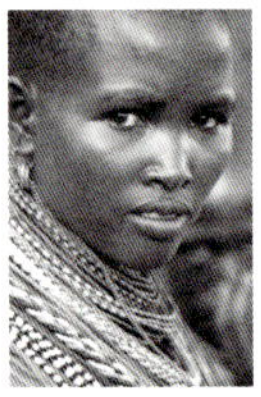 | 2001 | This young bride-to-be turned to face us during the community dance with her young brother behind her. There was tremendous joy during the day, just before 9/11. |
| 11 | 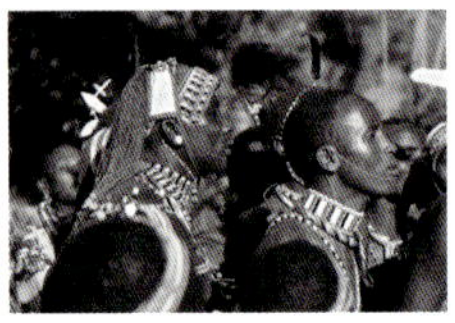 | 2001 | These warriors, a subclan of the Maasai, are among the proudest in East Africa. Their entire way of life is under pressure from the central government to conform to sedentarism. Will they be able to hold on to their seminomadic lifestyle? |
| 12/13 | 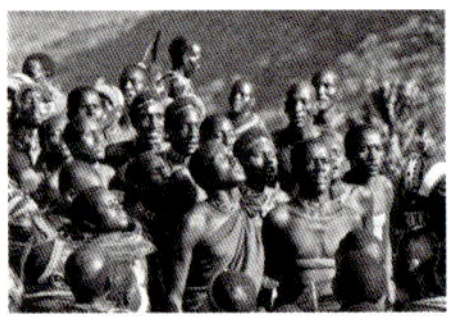 | 2001 | It takes hours for the *morani* warriors and women to go into an altered state or trance. |
| 14 | 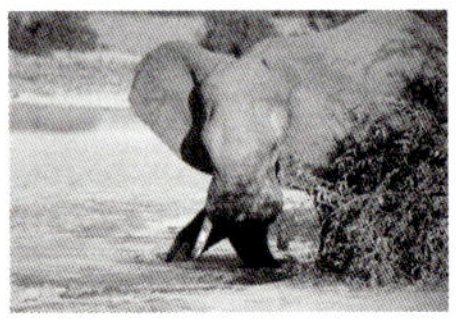 | 2013 | In Ruaha, Tanzania, the largest national park in East Africa, a bull elephant digs for salt in the river with his tusks. |
| 15 | 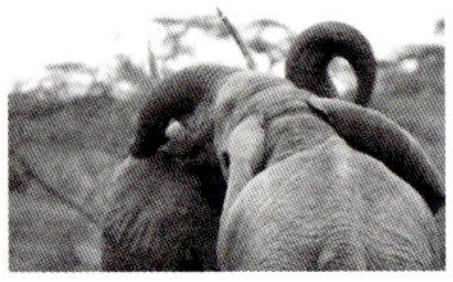 | 2014 | In the Chyulu Hills we had the rare privilege of witnessing bull elephants jousting. More and more migration corridors are being interrupted, creating "biological islands." |

| | | | |
|---|---|---|---|
| 16/17 | 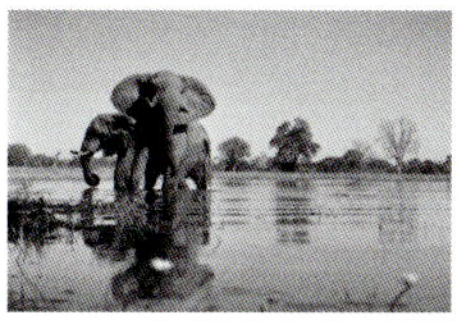 | 2017 | A rare moment on foot. Lysander greeted these bull elephants from 40 feet away in a waterhole in Botswana. |
| 24/25 | 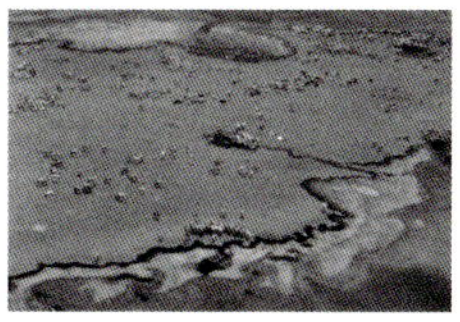 | 2001 | Truly a sight to behold—a large herd of camels drinking from a stream in the Chalbi Desert in northern Kenya together with their owners, the nomadic Rendille. |
| 26 | 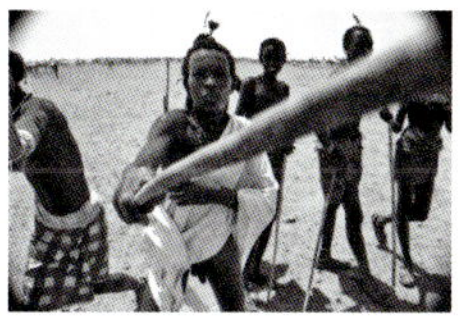 | 2001 | This young Rendille man did not want us to take pictures of his camels, lest their milk turn to water! |
| 27 | 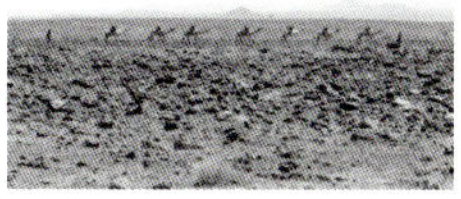 | 2001 | The Rendille lead their camels through some of harshest land in Kenya, not far from the Ethiopian border. Kenya has been undergoing one of the worst droughts in decades. |
| 30/31 | 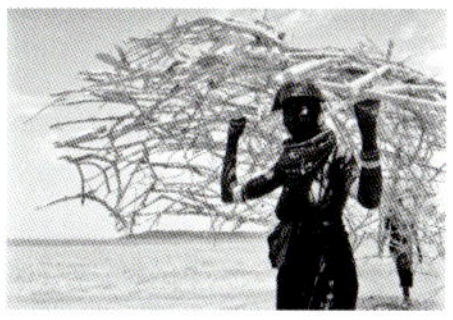 | 2001 | These Turkana women had been looking for firewood for hours and are carrying the dry twigs and branches they found on their heads, which makes the journey much easier. |
| 32/33 | 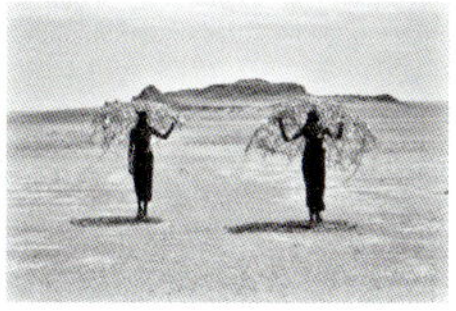 | 2001 | Women with firewood walking in perfect symmetry in the Chalbi Desert, where rhinos, elephants, and even lions once roamed. The Turkana often have to walk over 10 hours to find water. |
| 34 | 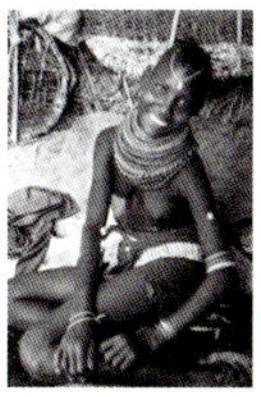 | 2001 | A young bride in her home with her necklaces and shaved head. |
| 40/41 | 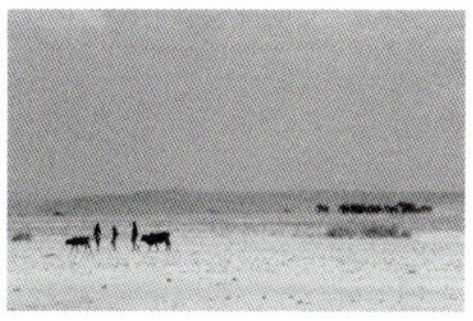 | 2006 | Amboseli, Kenya. A rare moment of Maasai boys herding their cows as they move in harmony with a herd of elephants kicking up dust in the background. |
| 42 | 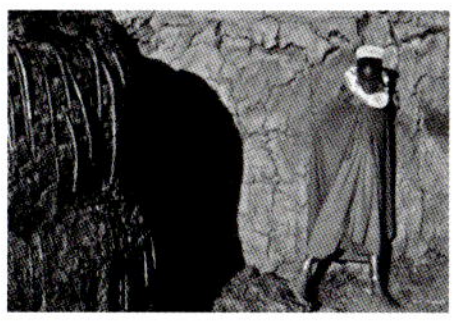 | 1999 | A Maasai woman near her circular *boma* home that is plastered with mud, water, cow dung, and even urine. Only the women build these homes. |

| | | | |
|---|---|---|---|
| 43 | 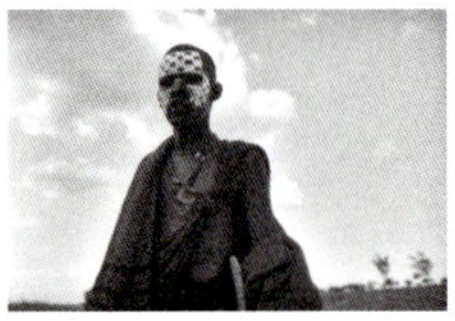 | 2011 | A young Maasai Moran after his initiation near Ngorongoro Crater, Tanzania. |
| 44/45 | 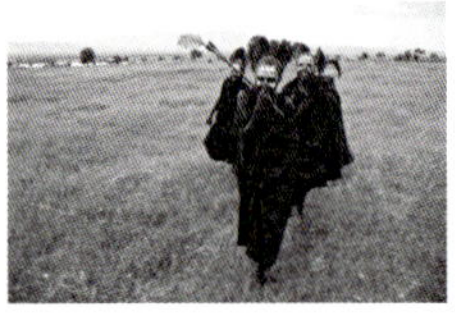 | 2011 | Young initiated boys smile at us with their ritual white paint signifying hope, purity, and light. |
| 52 | 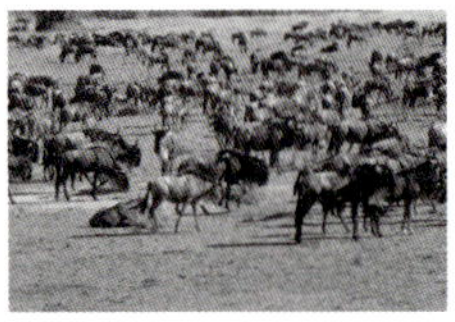 | 2006 | During the migration in Kenya's Maasai Mara, we marveled at a wildebeest unlike any other: the one in the middle of the picture had three horns, with one horn growing out of its shoulder! A very rare mutation indeed. |
| 53 | 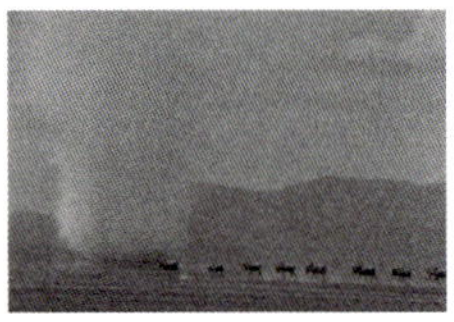 | 2006 | Wildebeest moving alongside a beautiful dust devil in Amboseli, Kenya. |
| 54/55 | 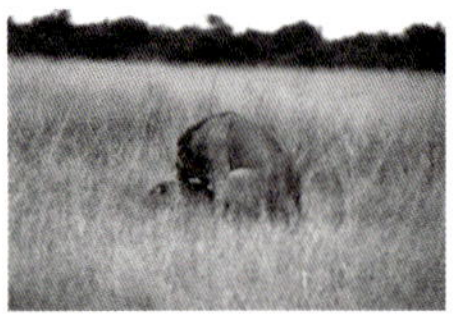 | 2017 | Lysander eagerly photographed this lion couple in Botswana, with the teeth of the male plainly visible. |
| 58/59 | 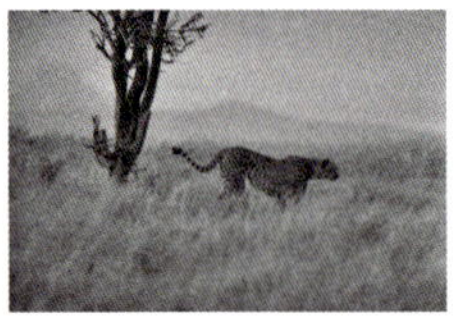 | 2006 | A cheetah's body mirrors the form of the Cherangani Hills in the background, with Mount Kenya looming on the left. |
| 60 | 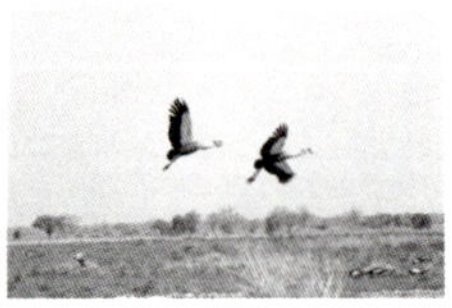 | 2002 | There used to be crowned cranes in Europe and North America, but their population of about 60,000 now reside only in Africa. |
| 66 | 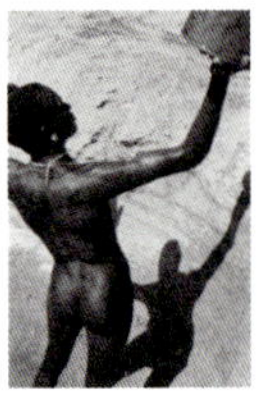 | 2004 | An Ariaal nomadic pastoralist of northern Kenya taking water from his "singing well." There are about 10,000 Ariaal, which form a cultural bridge between the Rendille and the Samburu. |
| 67 | 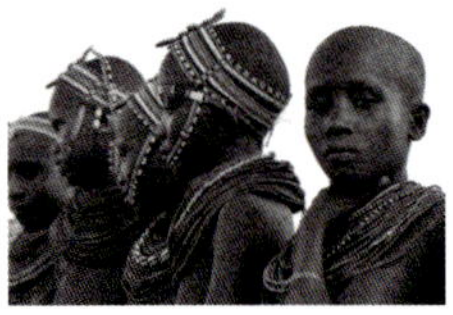 | 2004 | Young Ariaal girls in central Kenya. The one on the right has a fly on her cheek. Pastoralists everywhere are struggling to hold onto their livestock economy. |

| | | | |
|---|---|---|---|
| 74/75 | 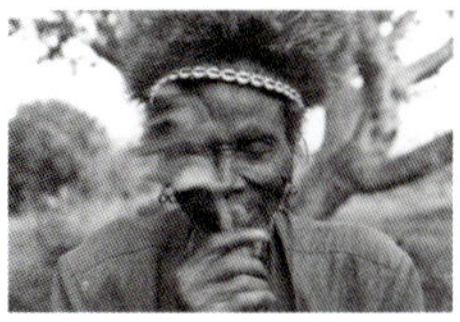 | 2004 | A Pokot elder before the goat-sacrificing ceremony near Mount Elgon in western Kenya. |
| 76 | 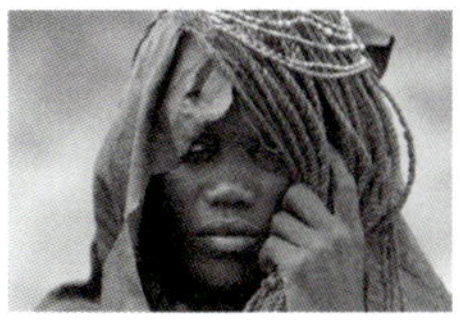 | 2004 | A Pokot boy is initiated into manhood along with a dozen other boys in the wild. |
| 77 | 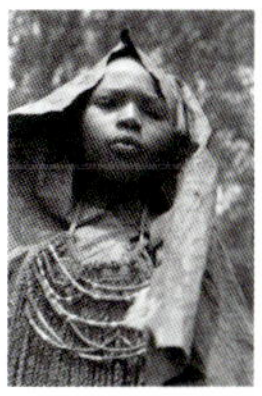 | 2004 | We came upon the Pokot quite by accident, not far from the fabled Kitum caves, where elephants have been looking for mineral salts for countless centuries. |
| 78 | 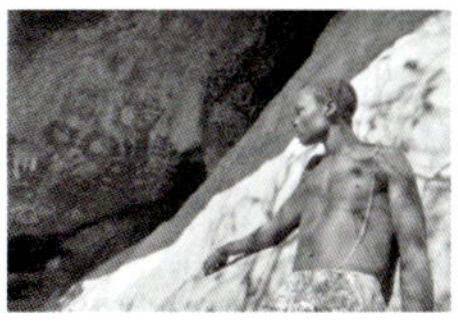 | 1999 | The ancestors depicted on the cave walls still call out to the Hadza, the last of the first, as some call them, the oldest hunter gatherers in all of East Africa. They use click consonants as the Bushmen do. |
| 79 | 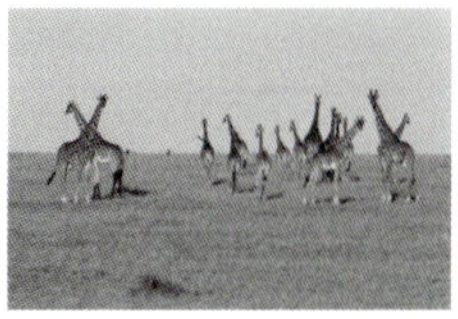 | 2001 | Maasai Mara, Kenya. The total giraffe population stands at less than 100,000. They can make sounds, but they may be too low for humans to hear. |
| 80/81 | 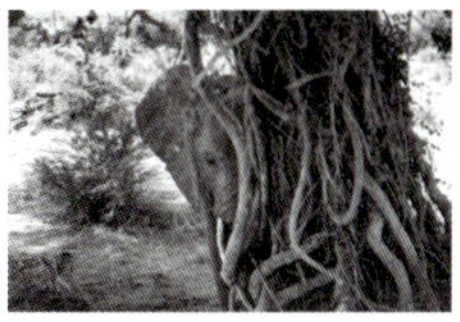 | 2011 | Samburu, Kenya. Lysander took this photo, captivated by the antics of a young elephant calf. |
| 82 | 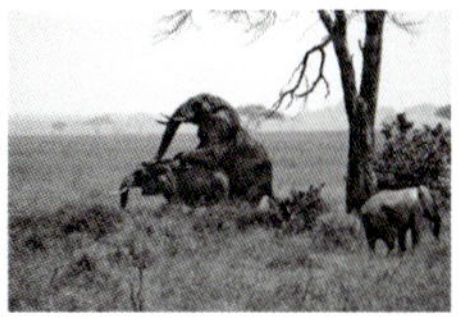 | 2012 | Elephants mating in the Serengeti is not a common sight. The ecosystem is one of the few semi-intact ones on Earth. |
| 83 | 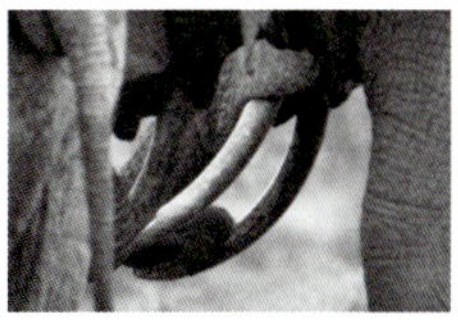 | 2014 | Chyulu Hill elephant bulls greeting each other. The tactility and sensitivity of their trunks, consisting of around 40,000 different muscles, is astounding. |
| 84 | 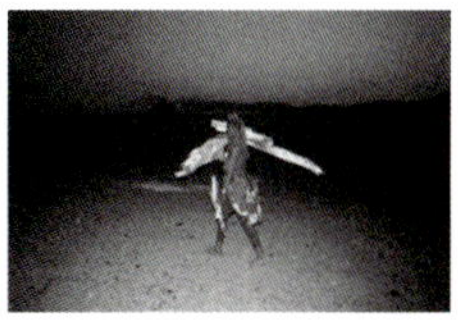 | 2000 | A Himba woman carrying firewood at dusk near the Kunene River on the border with Angola. The Himba still pray to the Holy Fire. A large dam threatens their entire way of life. |

| | | | |
|---|---|---|---|
| 85 | 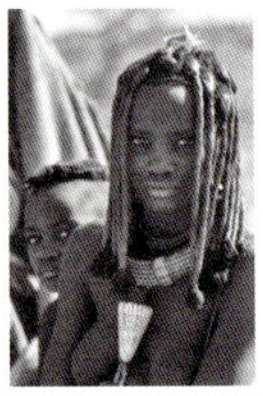 | 2000 | This young Himba girl stared at me for twenty minutes without moving, disbelieving we had come so far just to see her people, one of the most isolated tribes in the world. |
| 86 | 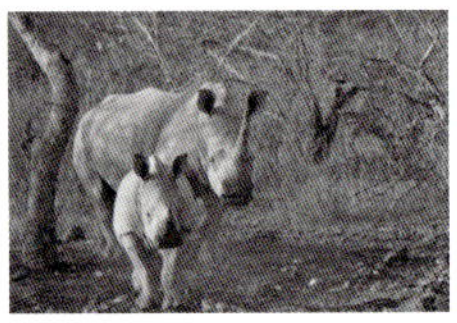 | 2000 | A white rhino mother guards her baby from the back, whereas the black rhino mother always stands in front of her calf. There are no more than 20,000 white rhinos left in the world, and maybe only 6,000 black rhinos. |
| 88/89 | 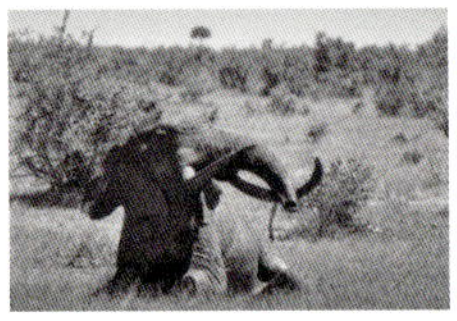 | 2011 | Tsavo, Kenya. It is rare to see a bull elephant lying down. He had taken a mud bath and probably needed to get insects off his back. The mud serves as a sunscreen. |
| 90 | 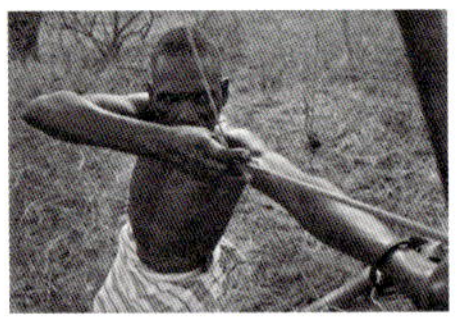 | 2011 | The Waliangulu were the best elephant hunters on Earth, and Koni's knowledge of his people offered us insights into timeless practices of tracking and hunting. |
| 91 | 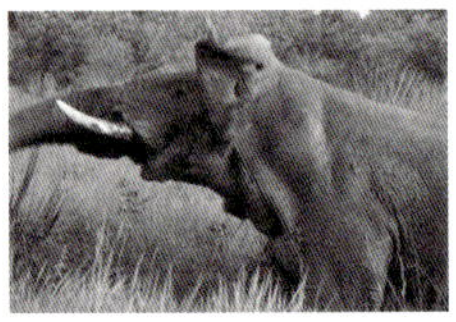 | 2011 | Kenya. This elephant enjoyed his mud bath, but had to struggle to get out of the waterhole. |
| 92/93 | 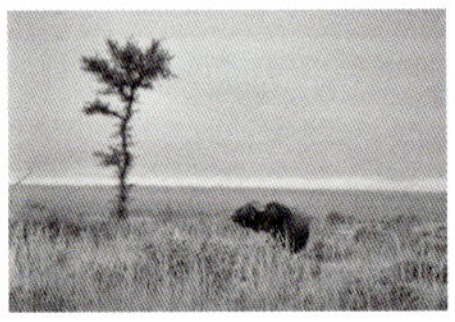 | 2012 | A lone buffalo next to a camel thorn acacia in the Serengeti, Tanzania. |
| 94/95 | 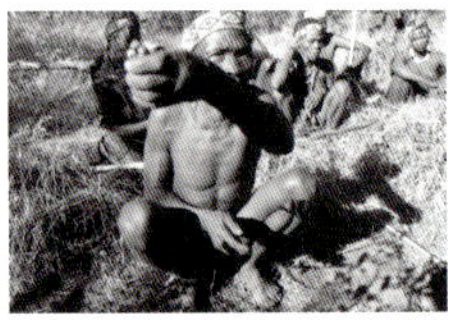 | 1998 | These Bushmen use divining sticks to decide the optimum direction in which to go hunting. It is the oldest divining system on Earth. |
| 96 | 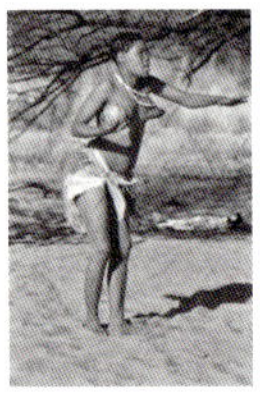 | 1998 | The melon dance using *Mokapane* (wild melons) is practiced by the Basarwa San Bushmen all over the Kalahari. Stories of the animals are kept alive through this tradition, which goes back many millennia. |
| 97 | 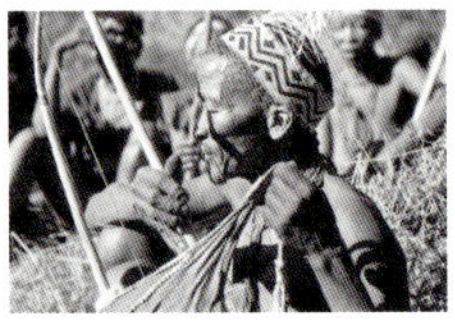 | 1998 | Bom regaled us with stories of lions. Here he holds his bow, which is tipped with poison derived from varieties of the Acokanthera shrub that is used for hunting. |

| | | | |
|---|---|---|---|
| 98/99 | 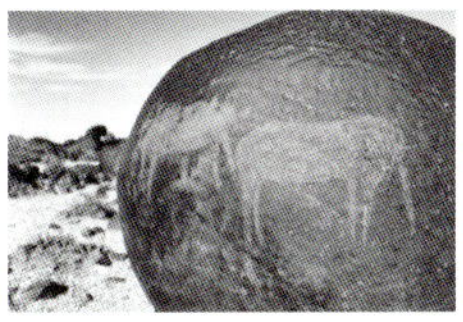 | 2000 | Crossing the Karoo on the way to the Kalahari, one finds petroglyphs of many animals, including elephants drawn on boulders by the San Bushmen. |
| 100/101 | 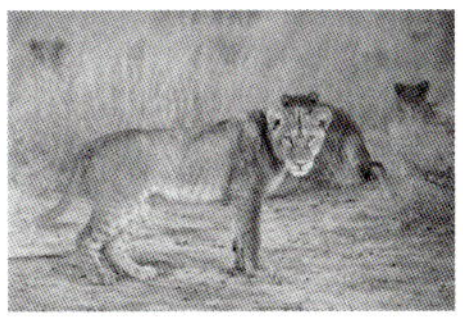 | 2017 | Lysander's lion cub at a distance of twenty feet in Botswana. The mother was away, so Lysander was able to get unusually close. |
| 102 | 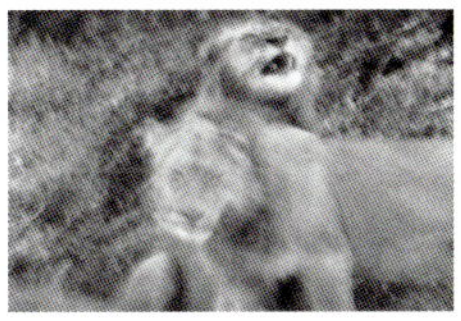 | 2017 | Lysander took this shot of two lion males playing in Botswana. |
| 103 | 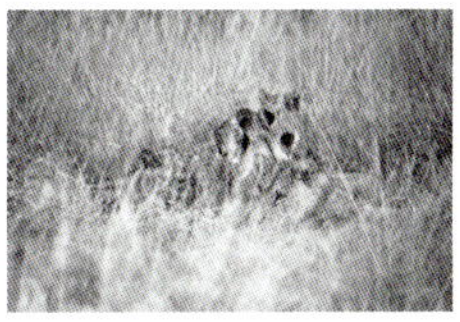 | 2017 | Lysander's moment highlights the fact that the grass may seem safe for travelers and then, all of a sudden, one comes across a pride of lions. |
| 104 | 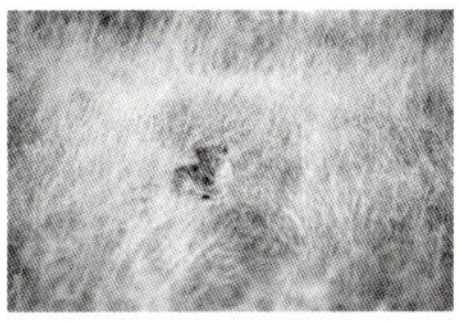 | 2017 | This baby lion in Botswana, photographed by Lysander, is one of the most innocent and fragile cubs we have ever seen. He seems like the last lion cub in the world. |
| 105 | 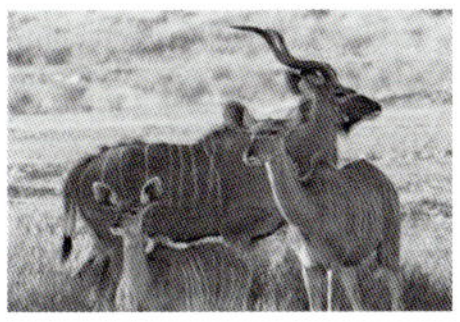 | 2012 | Kenya. The kudu is one of the lion's favorite animals. This male has to be ever alert to protect his harem. We were once very privileged to see a white lioness devouring a Kudu in Timbavati. |
| 106 | 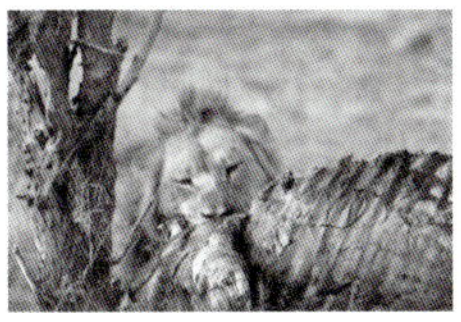 | 2017 | Lysander was greeted by this lion when he returned to Botswana. Lions hunting together have an almost 30% success rate, while lions hunting alone are maybe 20% successful if they are lucky. |
| 108/109 | 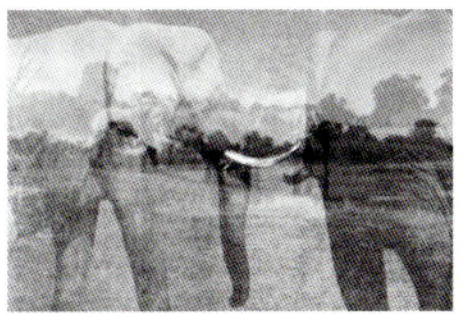 | 2017 | A bull elephant came within eight feet of us while we were seated on the ground next to the car. Lysander could not get the film to go forward, and we had to be very still so as not to excite the elephant as he passed by us, which is why he had multiple exposures on one shot. |
| 110 | 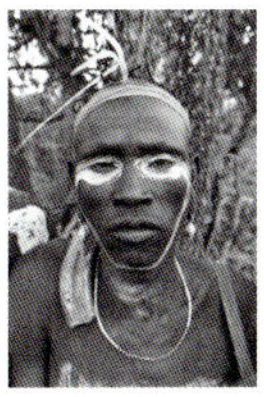 | 2001 | The Mursi have long sought places called *bha lalini* which means a "cool place"—a region with riverside forest appropriate for cultivation and grassland for cattle herding. During the dry season they occupy the banks of the Omo River and during the rains they return to the grasslands. |

| | | | |
|---|---|---|---|
| 111 | 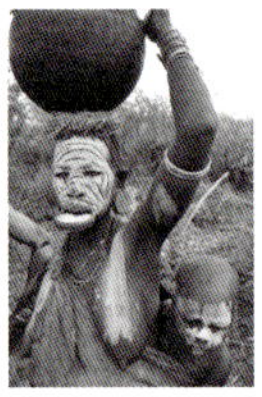 | 2001 | Omo Valley. Some say the lip plates were a sign of beauty, others that they were used to ward off Arab slave traders. One of the challenges the Mursi face is NGOs trying to put an end to the lip plate tradition. |
| 112 | 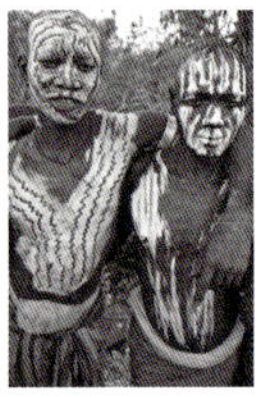 | 2001 | Omo Valley. The Mursi are one of the most isolated tribes on the planet. Their body painting represents social standing, serves ritual purposes, and is used to ward off sickness, to attract the opposite sex, or simply for self-expression. |
| 113 | 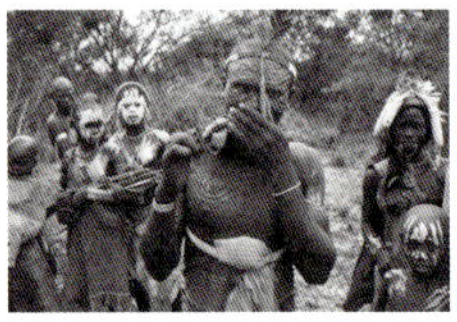 | 2001 | Omo Valley. The Mursi have been using guns since the Ethiopian emperor Menelik II beat the invading Italian army with Russian rifles in 1896. |
| 114/115 | 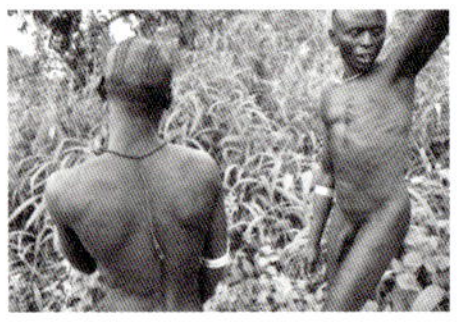 | 2001 | Omo Valley. What lessons can we learn from the first inhabitants of the world? |
| 116 | 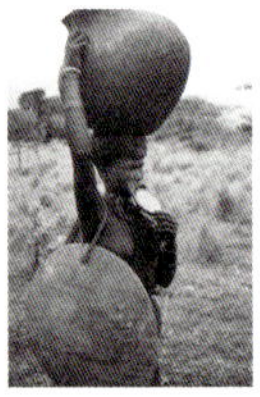 | 2001 | Omo Valley. Girls begin their lip ornamentation at age 15 or 16. This girl is carrying water and also has a pan she uses to look for gold in the river. |
| 117 | 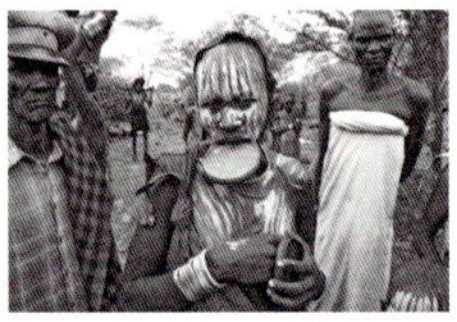 | 2001 | Omo Valley. This woman, accompanied by an elder and another man who would not have covered himself 10 years before, clearly had an interest in the camera. |
| 118/119 | 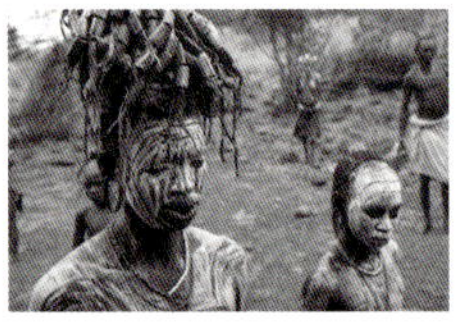 | 2001 | Omo Valley. There is a rawness and a freedom among the Mursi that is unmatched. Foreigners who of late have asked them to paint themselves or dress up for the camera have done them an injustice. |
| 120 | 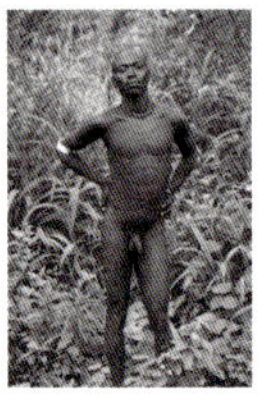 | 2001 | Omo Valley. No inhibitions or sense of shame that would have been thrust upon them by missionaries. |
| 121 | 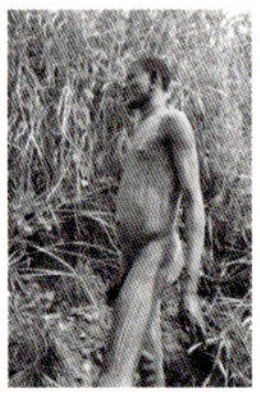 | 2001 | Omo Valley. The Surma, also masterly body painters, are facing the reality of the Gibe III dam. How will their tribe cope? What will be left of their culture? |

122

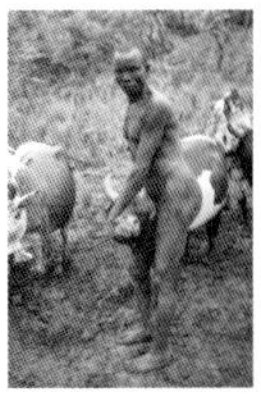

2001 A Surma man about to bleed his cow. The blood is drunk for strength and sustenance, a custom the Maasai have practiced for centuries. Blood is drawn by nicking the jugular vein of the cow, but that does not kill the animal.

124/125

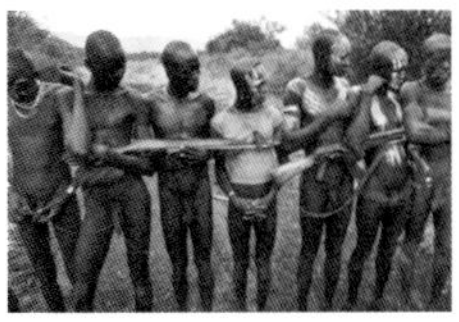

2001 Omo Valley. A remarkable encounter. Young Mursi men initiated this "roadblock" thinking they could perhaps scare any would-be missionaries traveling on the road.

126

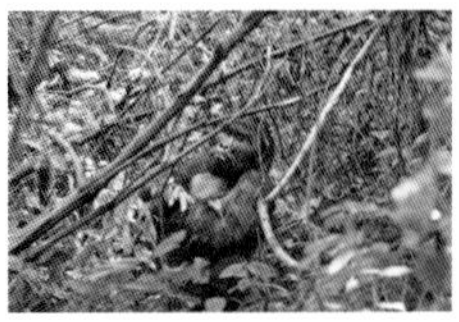

2002 Uganda. A male gorilla feeding in the Bwindi Impenetrable Forest. Although there are more mountain gorillas now (about 1,000) than a generation ago, the fragility of the forest—with rangers regularly being shot by poachers—is ever-present.

127

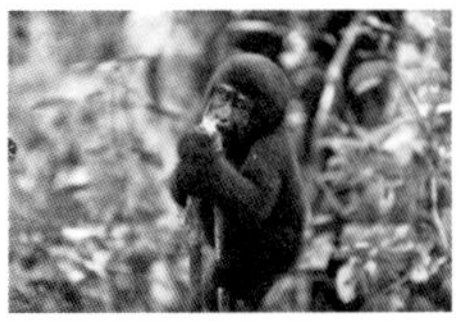

2002 Uganda. A baby gorilla holds on, as the survival of its species and that of the great apes of the world as a whole is threatened. Gorillas are our second-closest relatives on Earth. Most local farmers have never seen their neighbors in the forest.

128

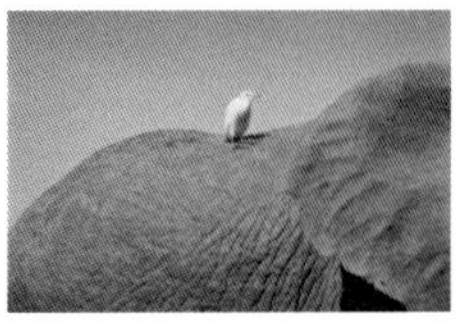

2006 Amboseli, Kenya. Many elephant migration paths are being cut off. An egret looks for ticks on an elephant's back.

129

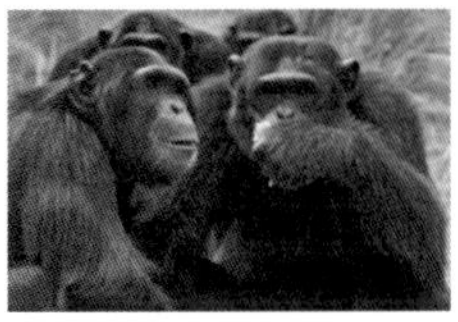

2002 On Ngamba Island chimpanzee sanctuary, 50 orphaned chimps have found refuge. There may be only a few hundred thousand chimps left.

130/131

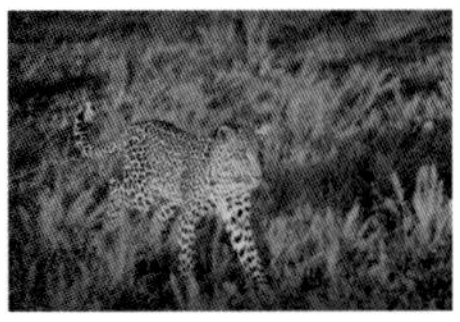

2015 Botswana. This splendid and curious young leopard passed by our car at a distance of 10 feet and inspired Lysander to take a photo before he walked off into the bush.

132

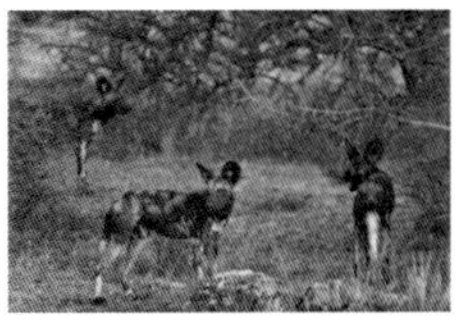

2014 Samburu, Kenya. Lysander took this shot as wild dogs were about to start running after game at full speed. A pack numbers between 15 to 40 individuals, sometimes even 100. There may be no more than 6,000 wild dogs left in Africa.

134/135

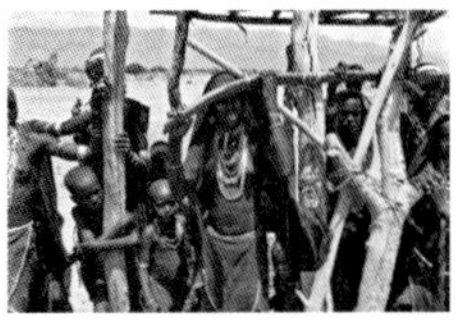

2002 Southern Ethiopia. The Arbore used to be ivory traders. Their supreme being is called Waq.

| | | | |
|---|---|---|---|
| 136 | 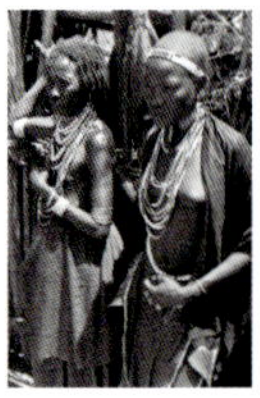 | 2002 | Southern Ethiopia. An Arbore woman stands with her mother near their home. |
| 137 | 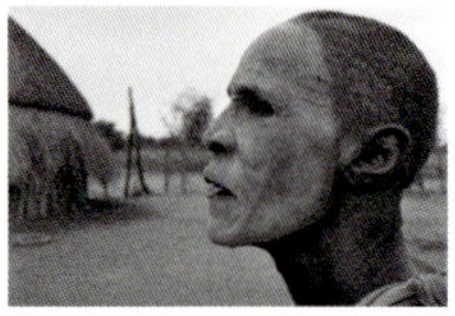 | 2002 | Southern Ethiopia. An elder of the Konso, also know as the Xonsita, a Cushitic tribe. |
| 138 | 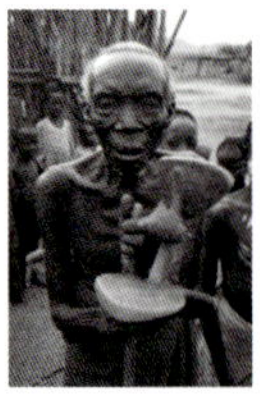 | 2002 | An Arbore elder holds his wooden stool. Old enemies of the Hamer, they often used to raid each other's livestock. The Arbore and Konso are related. |
| 139 | 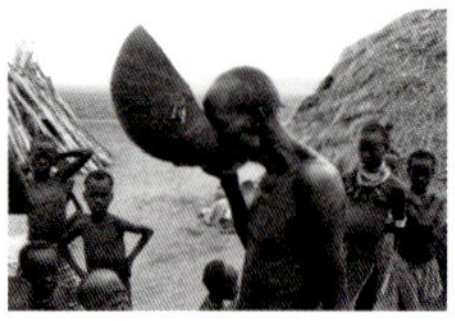 | 2002 | An Arbore elder drinks from his gourd. They grow sorghum and corn and have cattle, sheep, and goats. |
| 140 | 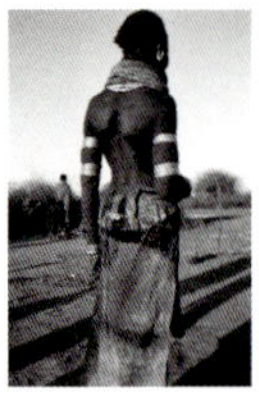 | 2002 | A Konso woman with scars at the bottom of her back, identifying which clan she belongs to. |
| 142/143 | 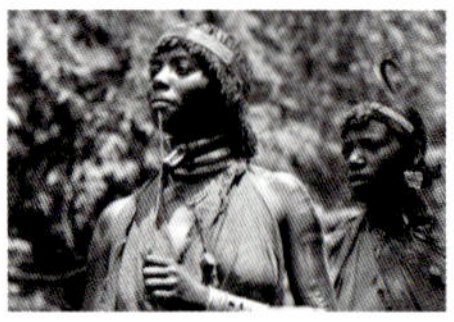 | 2001 | The Hamar people in the Omo Valley number almost 50,000. Their whipping ceremony, where the men whip the women, demonstrates their love and devotion to the initiated bull jumper. The event empowers and emboldens the strength of the women. |
| 144 | 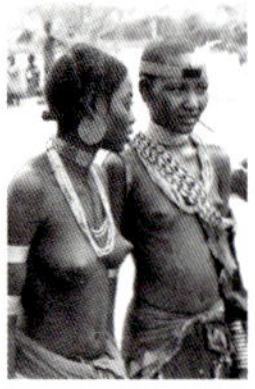 | 2001 | Young Hamar women at the market. Hamar men are allowed more than one wife. |
| 145 | 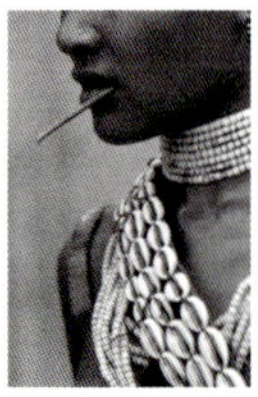 | 2001 | Hamar women at the market. They also look for bush food (grains and tubers). |

| | | | |
|---|---|---|---|
| 146/147 | 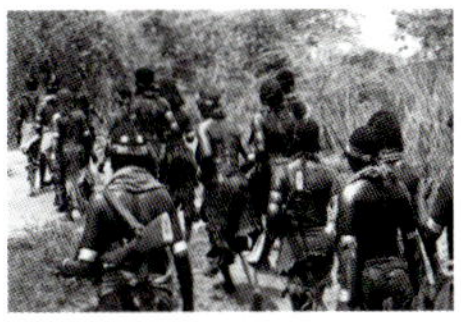 | 2001 | Women proudly wearing their scars after the ceremony with guns from the earlier days of Russian influence on Ethiopia. |
| 148/149 | 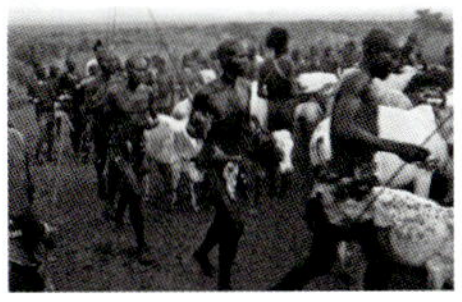 | 2001 | The bull jumping initiate surrounded by his cattle getting ready for the bull jumping ceremony. |
| 150 | 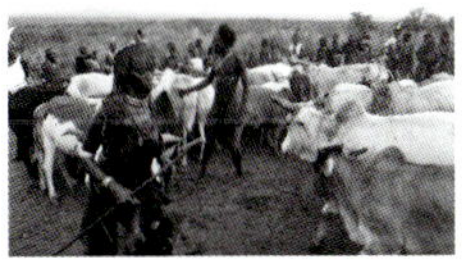 | 2001 | Corralling the cows before the jump. |
| 151 | 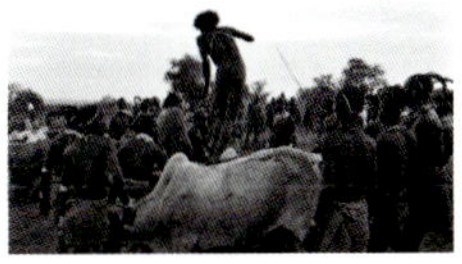 | 2001 | The elders line up about 15 cows and castrated male cattle which represent the women and children of the tribe. To come of age, the initiate must leap across the cattle four times. |
| 152 | 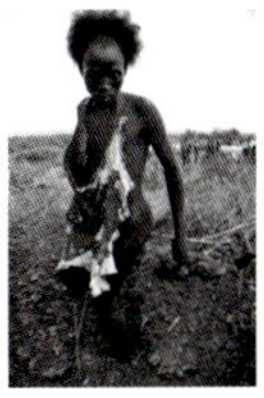 | 2001 | The initiate's head is partly shaved and rubbed with sand to clean away his sins and smeared with cow dung to give him strength. |
| 153 | 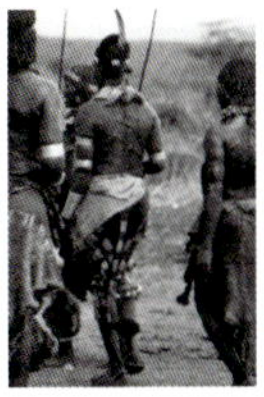 | 2001 | Women taunt men and ask to be struck with whips. Enduring the pain is a sign of loyalty and love towards their male relatives. |
| 154/155 | 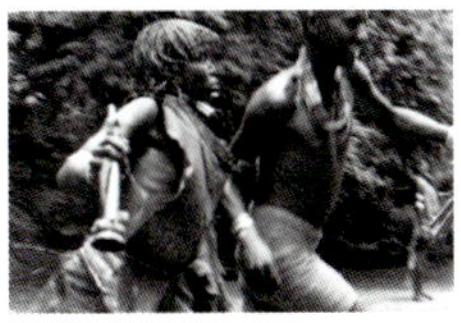 | 2001 | A woman runs in celebration with her escort after the whipping ceremony. |
| 156 | 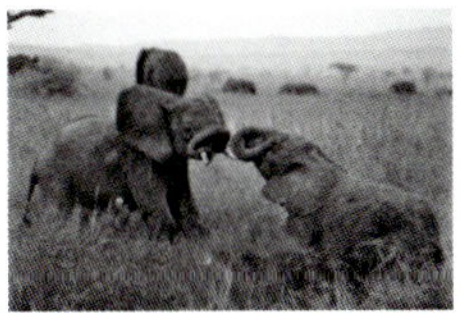 | 2011 | Young elephants greeting each other in the Serengeti, Tanzania. |
| 157 | 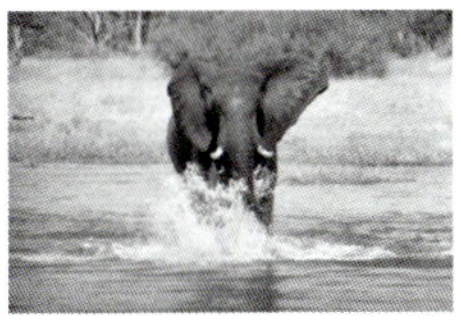 | 2012 | Elephant playing and "surfing" in the Khwai River, Botswana. |

| | | | |
|---|---|---|---|
| 158 | 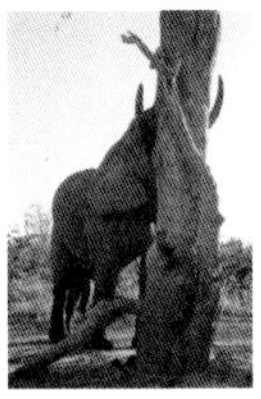 | 2017 | Lysander loved this moment of an elephant reaching for a branch in Botswana. |
| 159 | 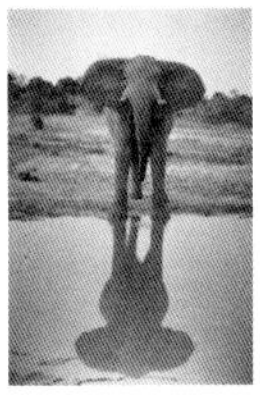 | 2017 | An elephant and his reflection in a perfect moment of equipoise, photographed by Lysander. |
| 160 | 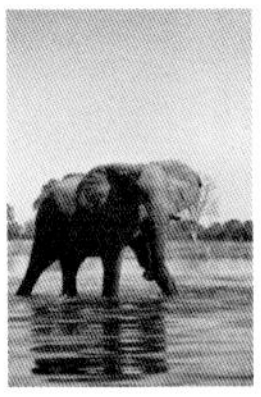 | 2017 | Lysander loved this single bull and the curl at the tip of his trunk. |
| 161 | 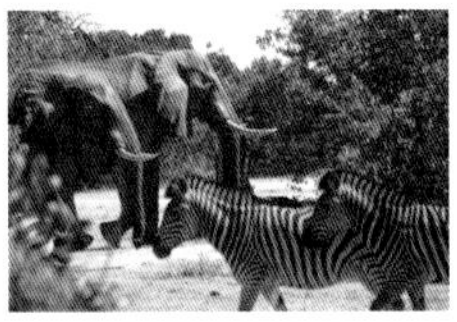 | 2017 | Botswana. Zebras and elephants in symmetry, photographed by Lysander. |
| Last page | 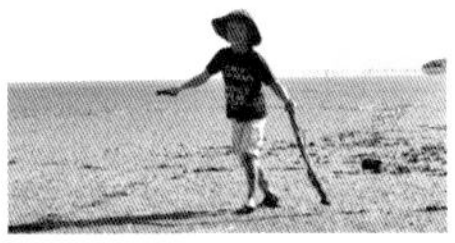 | 2011 | To the future of our children, both human and nonhuman. Lysander on Lake Natron. |

**Photography by**
Cyril Christo, Marie Wilkinson, and Lysander Christo

**Edited with text by**
Cyril Christo, Marie Wilkinson, and Lysander Christo

**Co-edited by**
Matthias Koddenberg

**Foreword**
Jane Goodall

**Proofreading**
Aymone Rassaerts and Stefan Hollstein

**Graphic design**
Kristina Selcho

**Production**
Druckerei Kettler, Bönen, Germany

**Published by**
Verlag Kettler, Dortmund, Germany
www.verlag-kettler.com

ISBN 978-3-86206-944-6



And while I still have much to learn, this much I know: animals are indeed more ancient, more complex and in many ways more sophisticated than us. They are more perfect because they remain within Nature's fearful symmetry just as Nature intended. They should be respected and revered, and perhaps none more so than the elephant, the world's most emotionally human land animal.

**Daphne Sheldrick, *Love, Life and Elephants. An African Love Story* (2012)**

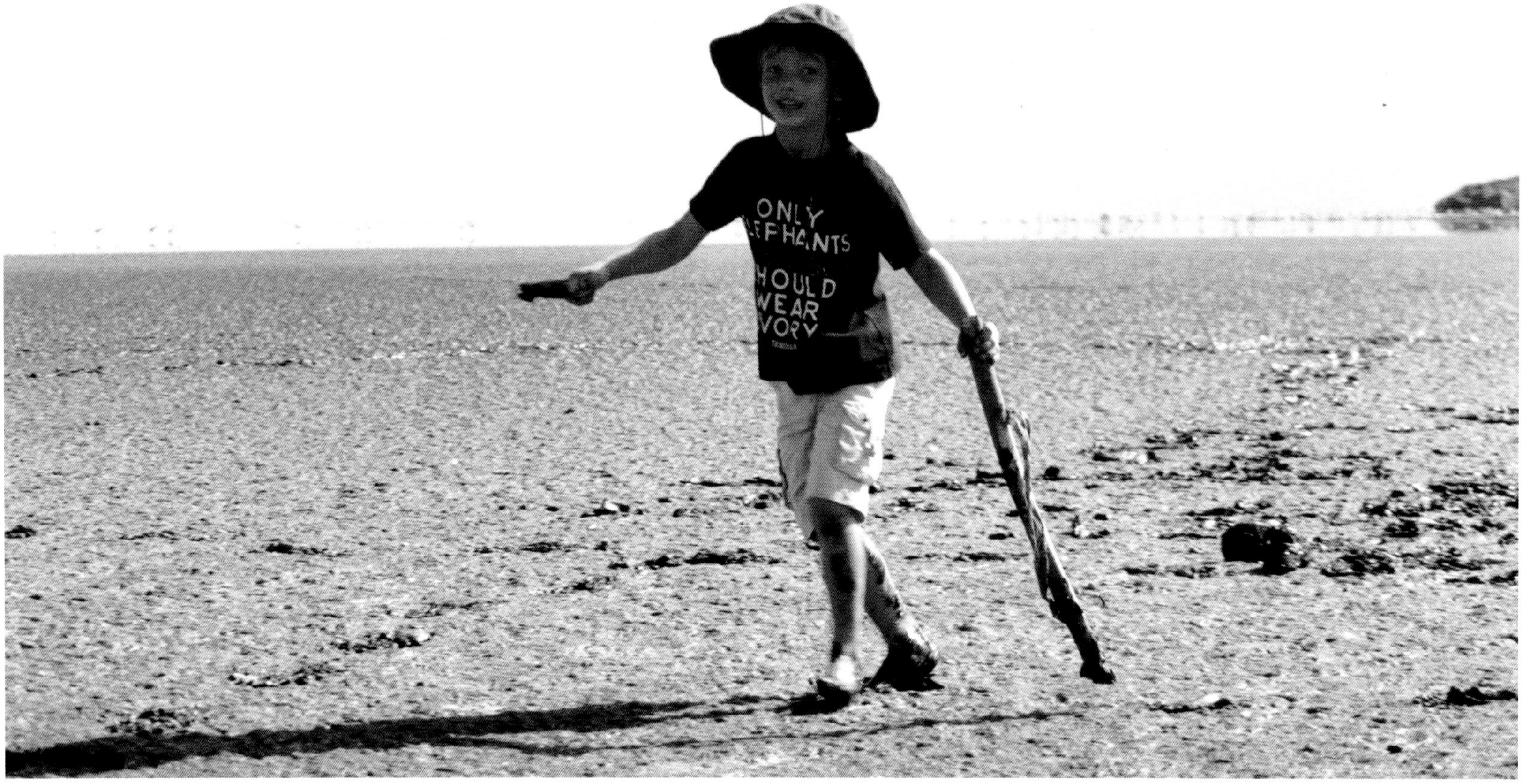
ONLY
WEAR